A Pictorial Record of

SOUTHERN LOCOMOTIVES

A Pictorial Record of

SOUTHERN
LOCOMOTIVES

J. H. Russell

Haynes

Oxford Publishing Co.

A FOULIS-OPC Railway Book

© 1991 J. H. Russell & Haynes Publishing Group

British Library Cataloguing in Publication Data
Russell, J. H. (James Harry) 1915-1991
A pictorial history of Southern locomotives.
1. England. Locomotives, history
I. Title
625.260942

ISBN 0 86093 443 8

Library of Congress catalog card number
91-71114

Published by:
Haynes Publishing Group
Sparkford, Near Yeovil, Somerset. BA22 7JJ

Haynes Publications Inc.
861 Lawrence Drive, Newbury Park, California 91320, USA.

Editor: Peter Nicholson
Page Layout: Tim Rose
Printed by: J. H. Haynes & Co. Ltd
Typeset in Times Roman Medium

Title pages: Class BB No.21C151 *Winston Churchill.*

Publisher's Notes
It is with great regret that we learnt of the death of Jim Russell as this book was being finalised for press. Jim had been associated with OPC from the earliest days, establishing the high quality, illustrated history format for which the imprint has become well known. The present title is the result of many years study and research and is a companion to his *Pictorial Record of Great Western Engines*, the three volumes of which have become the standard reference works on their subject.
Jim Russell will be very much missed by railway enthusiasts, historians and modellers but he has left more than a dozen major railway titles which form an invaluable source of reference and which will stand as a fitting tribute to this outstanding railway author.
We gratefully acknowledge the assistance given by Les Elsey in checking the final page proofs.

Locomotive drawings are reproduced in 4mm to 1ft scale (for 00 gauge), unless stated otherwise. Some have been reproduced from poor quality originals but have been included because of their historical importance and to ensure the work is as comprehensive as possible. (Drawings of components have been reproduced as large as possible, for clarity.)

Bibliography

Locomotive Adventure	H. Holcroft	Ian Allan	1962
Locomotives of the London, Chatham & Dover Railway	D. L. Bradley	RCTS	1960
Locomotives of the South Eastern & Chatham Railway	D. L. Bradley	RCTS	1961
Locomotives of the Southern Railway, Parts 1 & 2	D. L. Bradley	RCTS	1975
Locomotives of the L.B. & S.C.R., Parts 2 & 3	D. L. Bradley	RCTS	1972-74
Locomotives of the L.S.W.R., Parts 1 & 2	D. L. Bradley	RCTS	1965-67
History of S.R. Locomotives 1923-38	C. S. Cocks	RCTS	1948
L.S.W.R. Locomotives 1873-1922	Frank Burtt	Ian Allan	1947
S.E.C.R. Locomotives 1878-1923	Frank Burtt	Ian Allan	1947
L.B.S.C.R. Locomotives 1870-1927	Frank Burtt	Ian Allan	1946
L.S.W.R. Adams Locomotives	D. Bradley	Wild Swan	1987
L.S.W.R. Drummond Locomotives	D. Bradley	Wild Swan	1987
L.S.W.R. Urie Locomotives	D. Bradley	Wild Swan	1987
The London, Brighton & South Coast Railway	Hamilton Ellis	Ian Allan	1960
Bulleid, The Last Giant of Steam	Sean Day-Lewis	Allen & Unwin	1964
Bulleid Pacifics at Work	Col H. C. B. Rogers	Ian Allan	1980
Bulleid Pacifics on the Southern	Cecil J. Allen & S. C. Townroe	Ian Allan	1951
Lynton & Barnstaple Railway	J. D. C. A. Prideaux	David & Charles	1974
World's Locomotives	Chas Lake	P. Marshall	1925
British Steam Locomotive	E. L. Ahrons	Locomotive Publishing Co.	1927
The Locomotives of the Southern Region of British Railways	W. G. Tilling	W. G. Tilling	1948
Locomotives at the Grouping 1 Southern Railway	H. C. Casserley & S. W. Johnston	Ian Allan	1965
The Power of the Bulleid Pacifics	S. Creer & B. Morrison	OPC	1983
The Power of the Arthurs, Nelsons and Schools	J. Whiteley & G. Morrison	OPC	1984
Profile of the Southern Moguls	L. Elsey	OPC	1986

Acknowledgements

Photographs from H. C. Casserley, NRM York, Leslie Elsey, Hugh Ballantyne, Dick Blenkinsop, Peter Nicholson and A. C. Sterndale. All other photographs and diagrams: author's collection. Railway maps by courtesy of John Snell. The author would also like to express his gratitude to Leslie Elsey, ex-Eastleigh Works, and Peter Nicholson, OPC for their checking of the manuscript and data, and resulting corrections.

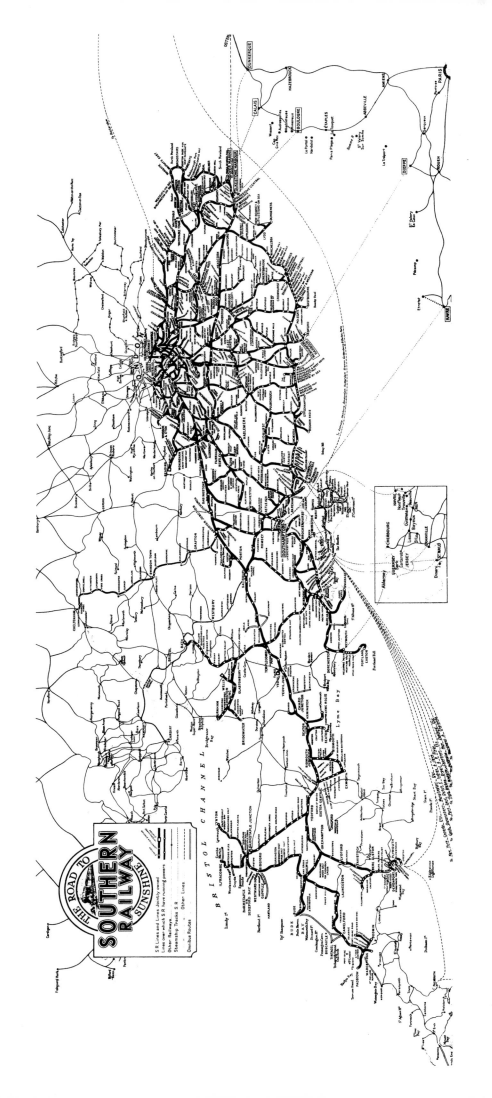

Introduction

The Southern Railway came into being in accordance with an Act of Parliament known as the 'Railways Act 1921' which received Royal assent on 19th August 1921, and so it became one of the four main line railways of the Grouping. The main constituent Companies which comprised the Southern Group were:

1. London & South Western Railway which included the Bridgewater, Isle of Wight, Sidmouth, North Cornwall, Plymouth & Dartmoor and Plymouth, Devonport & South Western Jnc. Railways. The Lynton & Barnstaple narrow gauge was also acquired in 1923.
2. London, Brighton & South Coast Railway, which also included the Hayling Railways Company and the Ryde Pier & Tramway Co. in joint ownership with the LSWR.
3. South Eastern Railway.
4. London, Chatham & Dover Railway.
5. South Eastern & Chatham Railway Company's Managing Committee. (This latter being a committee managing Nos 3 and 4.

The amalgamation took place in 1923 and a glance at the map on page 5 will show the areas covered by the four main constituents. From here on, the SR constituents will be considered as *three*: the LSWR, LBSCR, and the SECR, the latter initials being the combination of the SER and the LCDR.

At the creation of the Southern Railway, there were three Chief Mechanical Engineers, namely Mr R.W. Urie operating for the LSWR at Eastleigh, Mr L.B. Billinton in office at Brighton for the LBSCR and Mr R.E.L. Maunsell working at Ashford for the SECR.

Both Mr Urie and Mr Billinton retired soon after the Grouping which left Mr Maunsell as the Chief Mechanical Engineer of the newly formed Southern Railway. As each one of the three main constituents had its own locomotive stock, workshops, engineers and staff, it was decided to keep the lines of demarcation going pro tem, (especially as each company had its own different loading gauge) until the time came to build new locomotives. Therefore the old SECR was known as the 'Eastern' section with workshops at Ashford, hence the prefix 'A'. The LBSCR, situated at Brighton was known as the 'Central' section which used the prefix 'B' over engine numbers, and the LSWR shops based at Eastleigh were known as the 'Western' section, and used the letter 'E'. The Isle of Wight, being kept separate, placed the letter 'W' in front of its engine numbers.

So there were three main and one subsidiary sections, and although it was originally intended to be of limited duration, in fact the A, B and E divisions lasted right up to the Nationalisation of railways in 1948, although the prefixing of the numbers was phased out after 1931.

It seemed right therefore, to divide this work up into five main categories, as follows:

'A' for the engines of the Eastern section.
'B' for the engines of the Central section.
'E' for the engines of the Western section.
'W' covers the Isle of Wight as well as the Lynton & Barnstaple railways for the sake of convenience.
'SR' for all those engines built by the Southern Railway proper on and from 1923, plus those constructed under the aegis of British Railways.

The operating of trains on the Southern Railway was slightly different to the circumstances pertaining on the other three main lines. First it was mainly a passenger line, freight services being in the minority, and also as an extensive suburban service existed in and around London, quite a large proportion of which was for electric traction, this necessitated that the steam locomotives had to be capable of smart acceleration in order to thread a lively path through the electric services. In the main also, the length of train journeys, especially on the Eastern and Central sections was quite short which enabled tank locomotives to be used which could save time on turn-arounds at termini. Nevertheless, on the other side of the coin, the Western section, which included long journeys to the West Country, had to have large locomotives with huge tenders to supply water for the 100+ mile diagrams. Strangely, water scoops were never fitted to Southern engines, hence the large eight-wheeled tenders.

At the amalgamation in 1923, 2,287 steam locomotives were pooled from the various sources, and the following summary shows how they were made up:-

Eastern Section (A)	Passenger Tender Engines	248
	Goods Tender Engines	216
	Passenger Tank Engines	228
	Shunting Tank Engines	3
	Goods Tank Engines	34
	Total	729
Central Section (B)	Passenger Tender Engines	95
	Goods Tender Engines	83
	Passenger Tank Engines	264
	Shunting Tank Engines	10
	Goods Tank Engines	167
	Total	619
Western Section (E)	Passenger Tender Engines	446
	Goods Tender Engines	96
	Passenger Tank Engines	283
	Goods Tank Engines	5
	Shunting Tank Engines	87
	Total	917
Isle of Wight Section	Passenger Tank Engines	18
Lynton & Barnstaple Railway	Passenger Tank Engines	4
Grand Total at 1923		2,287

This total of 2,287 was divided between approximately 130 different classes of locomotive, and following on from this potpourri, the Southern Railway itself from 1923 onward constructed a further 16 classes of 'modern' engines.

This work endeavours to show in rather brief form, each of these different types of locomotive classes, all in one volume, portraying a drawing of each, an illustrating photograph, and details where possible, of the building dates and withdrawal dates of the majority. Number lists taken from the official records, are included, giving the numbers of engines under the A, B and E prefix, circa 1923-1931, the 1000, 2000, and 3000 prefix, post 1931, and finally the BR 30,000 series of numbering after 1948.

With so much complication and duplication, some minor errors are sure to arise, but it is hoped that readers will accept such lapses after the passing of the years, and at least approve my humble efforts!

Ex-LSWR Class 0380 4-4-0 No.162 at Exmouth Junction in 1924.

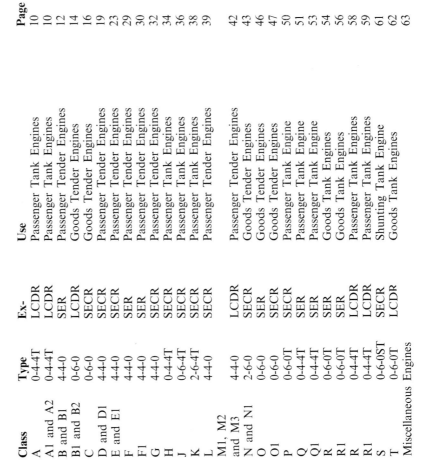

Part One

Eastern Section – Prefix 'A'

A class 0-4-4T

There were 18 in this class of four-coupled tanks which were designed by Kirtley, and built by Messrs Vulcan and Messrs Neilson, all in 1875. Their main work was in the London area, and as they were required to work through the Metropolitan tunnels en route to the GNR with exchange traffic, they were fitted with condensing gear. The driving wheels were 5ft 3in diameter, the boilers were 4ft 3in x 10ft 8in long, and they were pressed for 140lbs, later raised to 150lbs. The side tanks held 970 gallons and the bunker capacity was 2 tons. As this work is only concerned with SECR numbers, although the withdrawal dates are shown with SECR numbers, the building and withdrawal dates were built in LCDR days.

SECR No.	Built	Withdrawn
524	Vulcan	1925
525	Vulcan	1925
526	Vulcan	1923
527	Vulcan	1925
528	Vulcan	1925
529	Vulcan	1925
560	Neilson	1925
561	Neilson	1923
562	Neilson	1926
563	Neilson	1926
564	Neilson	1925
565	Neilson	1926
566	Neilson	1923
567	Neilson	1926
568	Neilson	1926
569	Vulcan	1925
570	Vulcan	1915
571	Vulcan	1926

Class A (ex-LCDR) No.564 at Victoria, 1925.

A1 and A2 class 0-4-4T PAGE 10

Five years after the A class, twelve further, similar engines were built, classified as A1, and in 1884 six more 0-4-4Ts were built, given the A2 coding. These 18 engines were very like their predecessors in the general dimensions, however their driving wheels were originally 1in larger than the A's, being 5ft 7in, but this was later reduced to the standard 5ft 6in. A simple identification was possible by the fact that both A1 and A2 had sandboxes as part of the leading splashers, whereas the 'A' class sandboxes were below the footplate.

Class	SECR No.	Built	Withdrawn
A2	534*	Stephenson 1883	1926
A2	535	Stephenson 1883	1925
A2	536*	Stephenson 1883	1926
A2	537	Stephenson 1883	1925
A2	538*	Stephenson 1884	1925
A2	539*	Stephenson 1884	1925
A1	622	Kitson 1880	1925
A1	623	Kitson 1880	1923
A1	624	Kitson 1880	1925
A1	625*	Kitson 1880	1926
A1	626*	Kitson 1880	1926
A1	627*	Kitson 1880	1926
A1	628	Kitson 1880	1925
A1	629	Kitson 1880	1926
A1	630	Kitson 1880	1925
A1	631	Kitson 1880	1925
A1	632	Kitson 1880	1926
A1	633	Kitson 1880	1926

* Re-painted in SR livery.

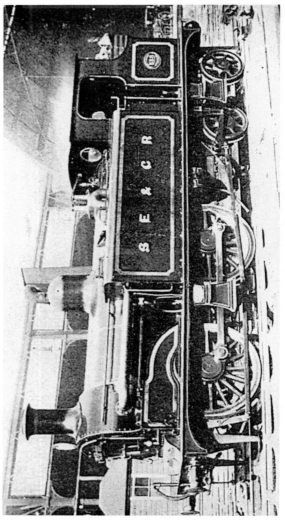

Class A2, SECR No.539.

Class A1, LCDR No.164.

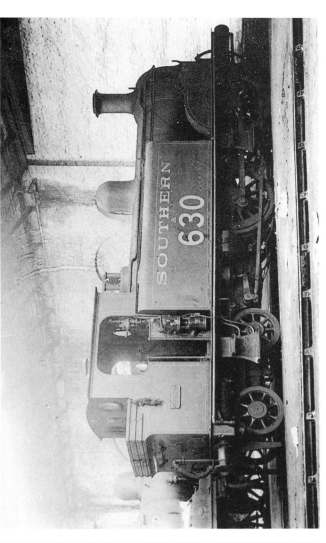

Class A1 No.A630 at Battersea in 1926.

Class A1 No.622 and Class A No.524 at Battersea Park, 1925.

Class A1 No.622 in 1925 (LH side).

Class A1 No.633 at Longhedge, 1924.

Class A1 No.631 at Ashford, 1925.

Class A1 No.A625 at Battersea, 1926.

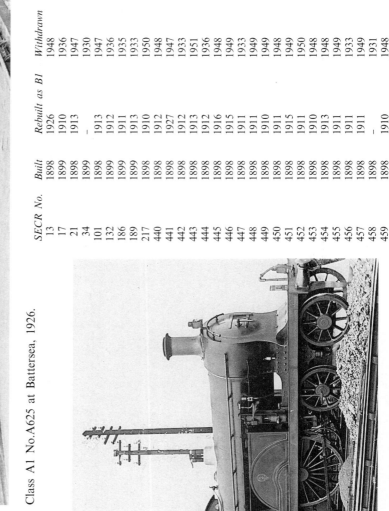

SECR No.	Built	Rebuilt as B1	Withdrawn
13	1898	1926	1948
17	1899	1910	1936
21	1898	1913	1947
34	1899	–	1930
101	1898	1913	1947
132	1899	1912	1936
186	1899	1911	1935
189	1899	1913	1933
217	1898	1910	1950
440	1898	1912	1948
441	1898	1927	1947
442	1898	1912	1933
443	1898	1913	1951
444	1898	1912	1936
445	1898	1916	1948
446	1898	1915	1949
447	1898	1911	1933
448	1898	1911	1949
449	1898	1910	1949
450	1898	1911	1948
451	1898	1915	1949
452	1898	1911	1950
453	1898	1910	1948
454	1898	1913	1948
455	1898	1911	1949
456	1898	1911	1933
457	1898	1911	1949
458	1898	–	1931
459	1898	1910	1948

Nos 440–459 built by Neilson Reid & Co.

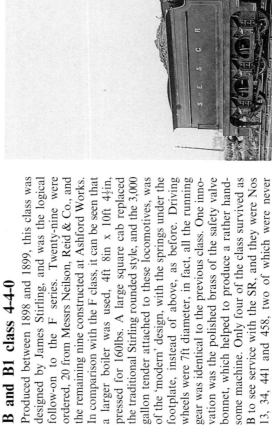

Class B (ex-SER) No.453.

B and B1 class 4-4-0

Produced between 1898 and 1899, this class was designed by James Stirling, and was the logical follow-on to the F series. Twenty-nine were ordered, 20 from Messrs Neilson, Reid & Co., and the remaining nine constructed at Ashford Works. In comparison with the F class, it can be seen that a larger boiler was used, 4ft 8in x 10ft 4½in, pressed for 160lbs. A large square cab replaced the traditional Stirling rounded style, and the 3,000 gallon tender attached to these locomotives, was of the 'modern' design, with the springs under the footplate, instead of above, as before. Driving wheels were 7ft diameter, in fact, all the running gear was identical to the previous class. One innovation was the polished brass of the safety valve bonnet, which helped to produce a rather handsome machine. Only four of the class survived as B to see service with the SR, and they were Nos 13, 34, 441 and 458, two of which were never reboilered, being Nos 34 and 458; all others were rebuilt with Wainwright boilers which made them into B1s, and in the Maunsell era they were fitted with extended smokeboxes as for the F1 class. A detailed list is appended.

Class B1 No.1021.

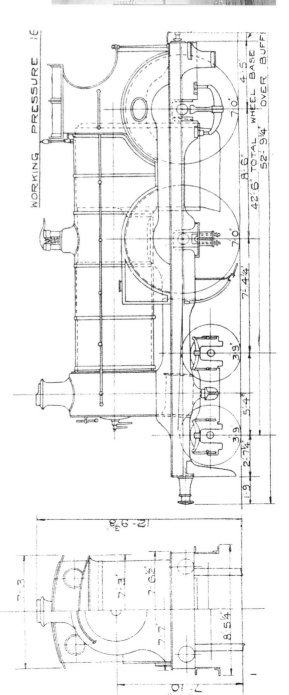

Class B No.458 at Ashford, 1925.

Class B No.34.

WORKING PRESSURE 1[E]

Class B, ex-SER 4-4-0. (Ashford dwg No.A2)

Class B1, ex-SER 4-4-0.
(Ashford dwg No.A3)

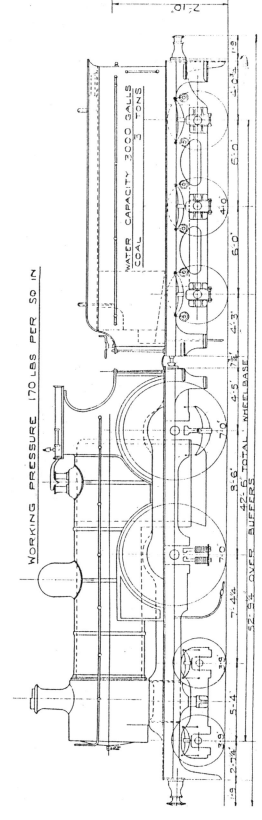

Class B2 No.A653 at Gillingham,
Kent in 1930.

B1 and B2 class 0-6-0

The B class of Kirtley's design for the LCDR was divided into three parts, ie B, B1 and B2. As all six of the B class were withdrawn before the grouping, they do not concern this work. However, two of the B1s did survive until the early 1920s and all of the B2s had nearly ten years of SR service. Six engines were built by Neilson & Co. in 1877 for the LCDR as B1s, having 4ft 10in dia. driving wheels, and a boiler 4ft 3in x 10ft 3½in they becoming Nos 610-615 (SECR numbering) at the union, and only No. 612 and 613 survived, until 1923 and 1924 respectively. Fourteen years after the initial order Kirtley ordered a further six similar locomotives from Vulcan Foundry. These B2 machines only differed from the B1s in having slightly larger driving wheels, 5ft dia. and 18in cylinders. In addition, the tender capacity was increased to hold 4¾ tons and 2,600 gallons. Details are as follows:

SECR No.	Built	Class	Became SR No.	Withdrawn
612	Neilson 1877	B1	A612	1923
613	Neilson 1877	B1	A613	1924
652	Vulcan 1891	B2	A652	1932
653	Vulcan 1891	B2	A653	1932
654	Vulcan 1891	B2	A654	1933
655	Vulcan 1891	B2	A655	1929
656	Vulcan 1891	B2	A656	1930
657	Vulcan 1891	B2	A657	1933

Nos 654, 655 and 656 Reboilered GNR boilers 1914-15
No. 652 Reboilered Std SECR 1927
Nos 612, 613, 653 and 657 Reboilered Wainwright 'C' boilers

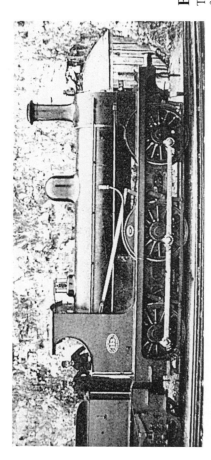

Class B1, LCDR No.153 (RH side).

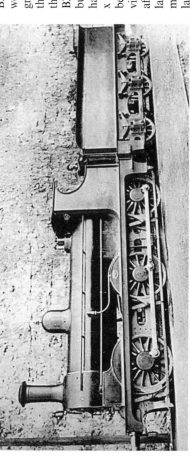

Class B1, LCDR No.153 (LH side).

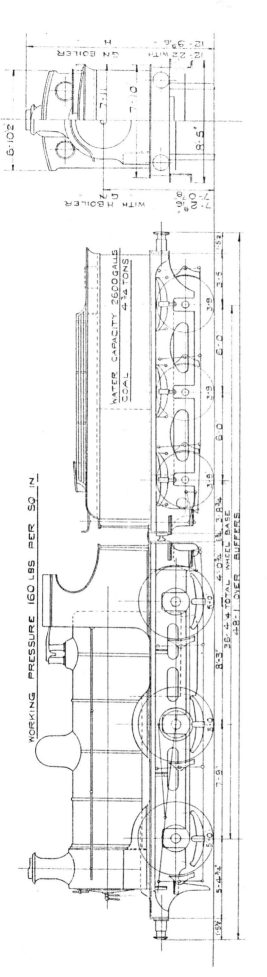

WORKING PRESSURE 160 LBS PER SQ IN

WATER CAPACITY 2600 GALLS
COAL 4¾ TONS

Class B2, ex-LCDR 0-6-0. (Ashford dwg No.A4)

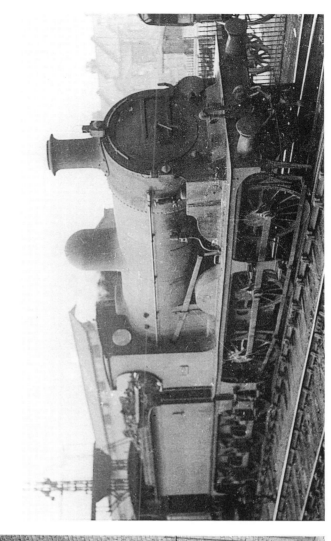

Class B2 No.A656 at Gillingham in 1926.

Class B2 No.A657 at Gillingham, 1930.

C class 0-6-0

The C class standard goods engine was one of the first purely Wainwright *designs for the SECR, and was intended as replacement for the old O class of Stirling locomotive, and in fact, many of the C class took some of the older engine's running numbers. They were stronger machines, having a boiler 4ft 5¾in x 10ft 9in and pressed for 160lbs with cylinders 18½in x 26in. One unusual feature was the small doors between engine and tender. Altogether 109 were built between 1900 and 1908, 15 by Messrs Neilson, Reid in 1900, 15 by Messrs Sharp, Stewart in 1900-1901, and the remainder at the Longhedge and Ashford Works of the SECR. One conspicuous difference between the older O class and the C, was that the driving wheels were fitted with balance weights in the spokes on the Wainwright engines, whereas the Stirling 0-6-0s carried no weights on the wheels. One of the class, No. 685, was taken into Ashford Works in 1917 and converted into a saddle tank shunter, known as the S class; a brief description of which follows the summary of the C class.

*Although ascribed to Wainwright, the power behind the throne was Robert Surtees.

SECR No.	Built	Builder's Nos	Date	Withdrawn
4	Ashford		1901	1962
18	Ashford		1900	1958
33	Ashford		1900	1960
37	Ashford		1901	1962
38	Ashford		1901	1952
54	Ashford		1901	1960

SECR No.	Built	Builder's Nos	Date	Withdrawn
59	Ashford			
61	Ashford			
63	Ashford			
68	Ashford			
71	Ashford			
86	Ashford			
90	Ashford			
102	Ashford			
112	Ashford			
113	Ashford			
150	Ashford			
191	Ashford			
218	Ashford			
219	Ashford			
221	Ashford			
223	Ashford			
225	Ashford			
227	Ashford			
229	Ashford			
234	Ashford			
242	Ashford			
243	Ashford			
244	Ashford			
245	Ashford			
252	Ashford			
253	Ashford			
255	Ashford			
256	Ashford			
257	Ashford			
260	Ashford			
262	Ashford			
267	Ashford			
268	Ashford			
270	Ashford			
271	Ashford			
272	Ashford			

SECR No.	Built	Builder's Nos	Date	Withdrawn
277	Ashford		1902	1958
280	Ashford		1901	1962
287	Ashford		1900	1956
291	Ashford		1903	1959
293	Ashford		1901	1962
294	Ashford		1900	1960
297	Ashford		1903	1953
298	Ashford		1900	1960
317	Ashford		1900	1962
460	Longhedge		1902	1962
461	Longhedge		1902	1958
480	Longhedge		1900	1959
481	Longhedge		1900	1962
486	Longhedge		1900	1959
495	Ashford		1901	1959
498	Ashford		1901	1960
499	Ashford		1900	1955
508	Ashford		1900	1959
510	Ashford		1901	1962
513	Ashford		1901	1953
572	Ashford		1902	1962
573	Ashford		1902	1959
575	Ashford		1902	1962
576	Ashford		1902	1959
578	Ashford		1902	1959
579	Ashford		1903	1959
580	Longhedge		1900	1962
581	Ashford		1900	1962
582	Ashford		1900	1949
583	Ashford		1904	1953
584	Ashford		1904	1947
585	Ashford		1904	1962
588	Ashford		1904	1962
589	Ashford		1904	1959
590	Ashford		1904	1962
592	Longhedge		1904	1959

SECR No.	Built	Builder's Nos	Date	Withdrawn
593	Longhedge		1902	1958
681	Neilson, Reid	5687	1900	1959
682	Neilson, Reid	5688	1900	1962
683	Neilson, Reid	5689	1900	1959
684	Neilson, Reid	5690	1900	1962
685	Neilson, Reid	5691	1900	1951
686	Neilson, Reid	5692	1900	1962
687	Neilson, Reid	5693	1900	1955
688	Neilson, Reid	5694	1900	1960
689	Neilson, Reid	5695	1900	1962
690	Neilson, Reid	5696	1900	1962
691	Neilson, Reid	5697	1900	1962
692	Neilson, Reid	5698	1900	1960
693	Neilson, Reid	5699	1900	1962
694	Neilson, Reid	5700	1900	1962
695	Neilson, Reid	5701	1900	1962
711	Sharp, Stewart	4683	1900	1957
712	Sharp, Stewart	4684	1900	1957
713	Sharp, Stewart	4685	1900	1955
714	Sharp, Stewart	4686	1900	1962
715	Sharp, Stewart	4687	1900	1962
716	Sharp, Stewart	4688	1901	1962
717	Sharp, Stewart	4689	1901	1962
718	Sharp, Stewart	4690	1901	1955
719	Sharp, Stewart	4691	1901	1962
720	Sharp, Stewart	4692	1901	1962
721	Sharp, Stewart	4693	1901	1953
722	Sharp, Stewart	4694	1901	1960
723	Sharp, Stewart	4695	1901	1958
724	Sharp, Stewart	4696	1901	1962
725	Sharp, Stewart	4697	1901	1960

Tenders for C class, capacity 3,300 gallons and 4¾ Tons fuel.

No. 685 was rebuilt to 0-6-0ST Class 'S' in 1917.

No. 592 is now preserved on the Bluebell Railway.

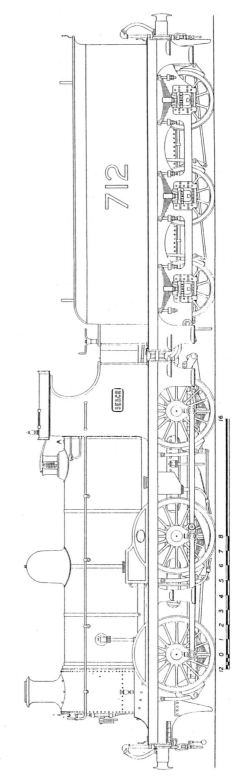

Class C, 0-6-0.

Class C No.A682 (RH side) at Dover Priory, 1927.

Class C No.486.

Class C No.1711 (LH side).

Class C No.A63 at Dover Priory in 1927.

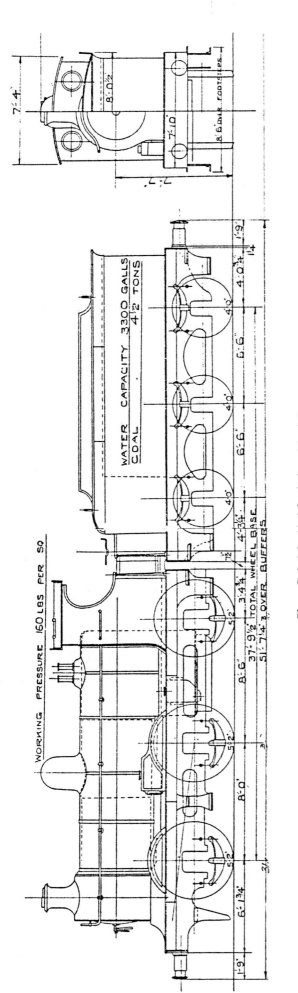

WORKING PRESSURE 160 LBS PER SQ

WATER CAPACITY 3300 GALLS
COAL 4½ TONS

37' 9½" TOTAL WHEEL BASE
51' 7¼" 3 OVER BUFFERS

Class C 0-6-0. (Ashford dwg No.A5)

Class C No.A219 in 1926.

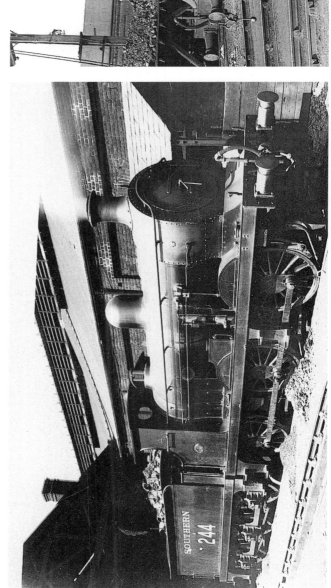

Class C No.A244 in 1926.

D and D1 class 4-4-0

The D class, designed by Wainwright purely for the newly constituted Managing Committee of the SECR were really handsome machines. In their lovely green livery set off by all that lining (seven lines in all!) and surmounted with a shining brass dome, safety valve bonnet and beading, plus a copper-topped chimney, no wonder No. 735 was sent to the Glasgow Exhibition of 1901. A total of 51 'Coppertops', as they were known, were built in the years 1901 to 1907 - 21 at Ashford Works, plus ten by Messrs Dubs & Co., ten by Sharp, Stewart, five by R. Stephenson & Co. and five by Vulcan Foundry. They were big engines for the time, especially for South East England; the boilers were 4ft 8in x 11ft 1in with a 6ft 6in firebox, and pressure was 175lbs. Coupled drivers were 6ft 8in diameter and cylinders were 19in x 26in (a few were 19¼in in diameter!) A large 3,300 gallon tender was attached, which could carry 4½ tons of fuel. Altogether a very fine locomotive, and what a debt we owe to those responsible who have ensured that one of the breed, No. 737, can still be seen in all its glory at the National Railway Museum, York.

Following the usual treatment, 21 of the D class were rebuilt in the Maunsell era as D1 class with a Belpaire firebox which led to a higher boiler centre line, which in turn meant shorter chimneys and domes etc. Those rebuilt at Ashford Works were given new boilers, but those dealt with by Beyer, Peacock, retained their original boilers. A complete summary is appended hereto.

SECR No.	Built	Date	Rebuilt to D1	Withdrawn
57	Ashford	1902		1951
75	Dubs & Co.	1903		1953
92	Dubs & Co.	1903		1951
145	Dubs & Co.	1903	1922	1962
246	Ashford	1902	1921	1962
247	Dubs & Co.	1903	1921	1959
470	Ashford	1906	1926	1951
477	Ashford	1907		1961
487	Ashford	1902	1921	1956
488	Ashford	1902		1961
489	Dubs & Co.	1903	1921	1951
490	Ashford	1902		1960
492	Dubs & Co.	1903	1927	1954
493	Dubs & Co.	1903	1921	1960
494	Dubs & Co.	1903		1955
496	Ashford	1907		1953
501	Dubs & Co.	1903	1921	1951
502	Dubs & Co.	1903	1927	1962
505	Ashford	1907	1927	1962
509	Ashford	1906	1921	1962
545	Ashford	1906		1956
549	Ashford	1907		1956
574	Ashford	1906		1956
577	Ashford	1906		1956
586	Ashford	1907		1955

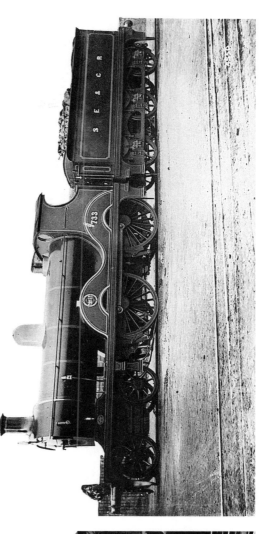

Class D No.733 in SECR livery (LH side).

SECR No.	Built	Date	Rebuilt to D1	Withdrawn
591	Ashford	1907		1955
726	Sharp, Stewart	1901		1947
727	Sharp, Stewart	1901	1922	1962
728	Sharp, Stewart	1901		1953
729	Sharp, Stewart	1901		1954
730	Sharp, Stewart	1901		1951
731	Sharp, Stewart	1901		1951
732	Sharp, Stewart	1901		1951
733	Sharp, Stewart	1901		1953
734	Sharp, Stewart	1901		1955
735	Sharp, Stewart	1902		1961
736	Ashford	1901	1921	1950
737	Ashford	1901	1927	1956
738	Ashford	1902		1950
739	Ashford	1902	1927	1961
740	Ashford	1902		1951
741	R. Stephenson	1903	1927	1959
742	R. Stephenson	1903		1944
743	R. Stephenson	1903	1927	1960
744	R. Stephenson	1903		1953
745	R. Stephenson	1903	1927	1951
746	Vulcan Foundry	1903		1954
747	Vulcan Foundry	1903	1921	1944
748	Vulcan Foundry	1903		1951
749	Vulcan Foundry	1903	1921	1960
750	Vulcan Foundry	1903		1953

No. 737 acquired for the National Collection.
No. 493 carried 'S' prefix from 1948-1954.

Class D No.488 in SECR livery (RH side).

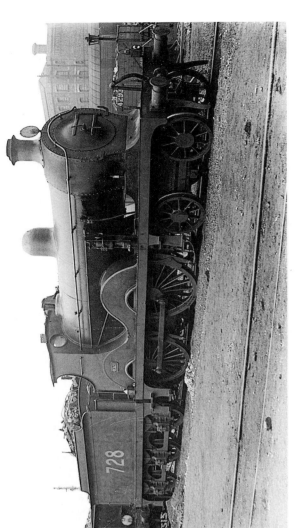

Class D No.728 in 1925.

Class D No.470 at Longhedge, 1924.

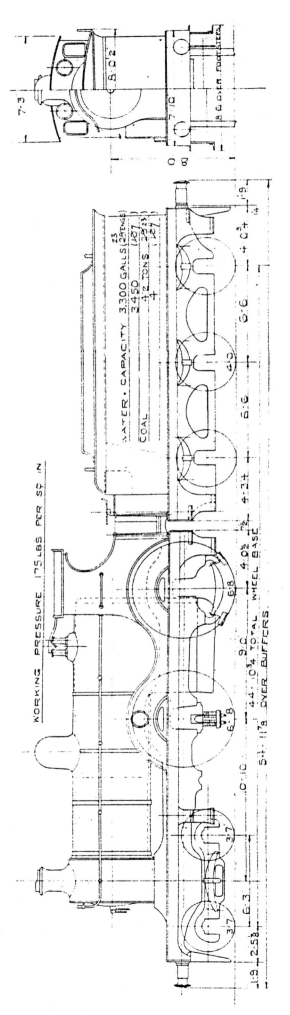

Class D 4-4-0. (Ashford dwg No.A6)

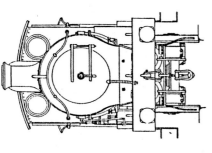

Class D 4-4-0.

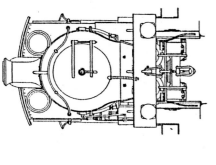

S E & C R

735

Class D No.A591 at Dover Priory in 1927.

Class D as BR No.31734 in 1952.

Class D No.1730 at Tonbridge, 1934.

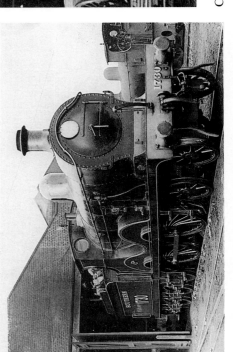

Class D1 No.A739.

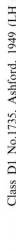

Class D1 No.1735, Ashford, 1949 (LH side).

Class D1 No.502 (RH side).

Class D1, rear view of BR No.31494, Ramsgate in 1949.

SUPERHEATED

WORKING PRESSURE 180 LBS PER SQ IN

WATER CAPACITY 3450 GALLS (1 ENG⁵)
WATER CAPACITY 3,300 GALLS (11 ENG⁵)
COAL 4½ TONS

44'-11³⁄₈" TOTAL WHEELBASE

54'-11⅞" LENGTH OVER BUFFERS

Class D1 4-4-0. (Ashford dwg No.A6A)

E and E1 class 4-4-0

Four years after the appearance of the Wainwright D class, the Superintendent designed his next batch of passenger locomotives, the E class. Although very similar to the Ds, this new series were fitted when new with Belpaire fireboxes. The driving wheels were slightly smaller, being 6ft 6in

in diameter, 2in smaller than the Ds, and the driving wheel splashers did not have the little extra arches for the coupling rods.

Boilers 11ft 1in x 4ft 7in Tender capacity 3,450 gallons and 4 Tons fuel. Twenty-six were built, all at Ashford, between 1905 and 1909, and from

1908 onwards were fitted with extended smokeboxes. Maunsell rebuilt eleven of the class into what became the E1 class, starting in 1919 with No. 179, and in 1920, ten others were so rebuilt by Beyer, Peacock & Co. The old boilers were used, but with a new firebox, and Maunsell superheaters were

installed in Nos 36 and 275. All this changed the exterior appearance of the engines, as can be seen in the diagrams. One other improvement was the replacing of the old slide valves with modern 10in piston valves. The E1s could easily be identified by the raised framing over the driving wheels.

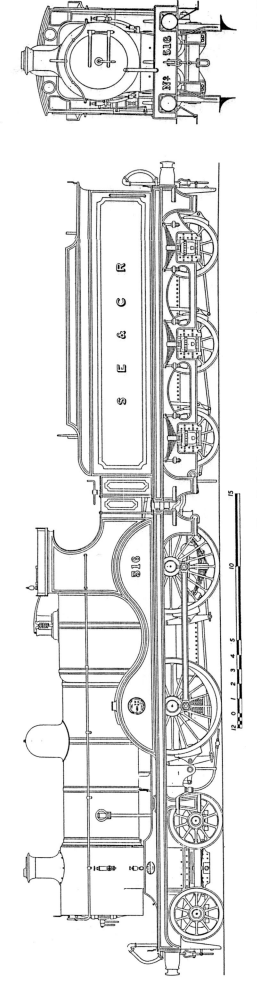

Class E 4-4-0.

Class E No.31516.

SECR No.	Built	Date	Rebuilt to E1	Withdrawn
19	Ashford	1908	1920	1960
36	Ashford	1908		1951
67	Ashford	1908	1920	1960
157	Ashford	1907		1951
159	Ashford	1908		1951
160	Ashford	1907	1920	1960
163	Ashford	1909	1920	1960
165	Ashford	1908	1920	1960
166	Ashford	1907		1955
175	Ashford	1908		1951
176	Ashford	1907		1951
179	Ashford	1908	1919	1960
273	Ashford	1906		1951
275	Ashford	1906		1951
315	Ashford	1909		1954
491*	Ashford	1907		1953
497	Ashford	1907	1920	1960
504	Ashford	1906	1920	1960
506	Ashford	1906	1920	1960
507	Ashford	1908	1920	1960
511	Ashford	1906	1920	1960
514	Ashford	1908		1951
515	Ashford	1907		1951
516	Ashford	1908		1951
547	Ashford	1908		1951
587	Ashford	1907		1951

Nos 36 and 275 superheated in 1912.
No. 1491 carried prefix 'S' 1948-1953.

Class E No.1275 (LH side).

Class E No.1166 at Bricklayers Arms, 1933 (RH side).

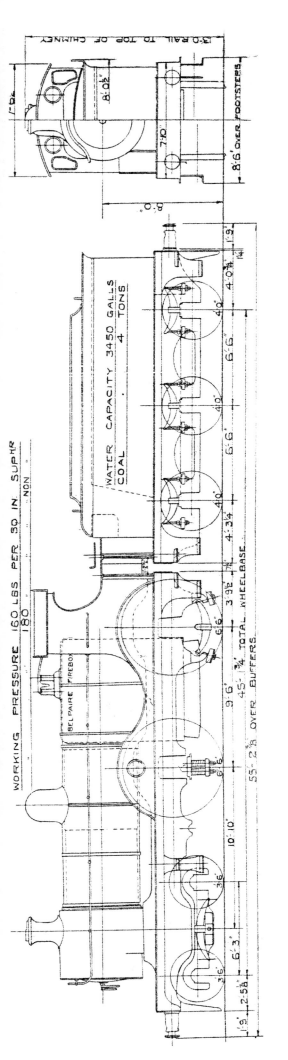

Class E 4-4-0. (Ashford dwg No.A7)

Class E BR No.31273.

Class E No.1176.

Class E No.1516.

Class E No.A491 at Dover Priory in 1927.

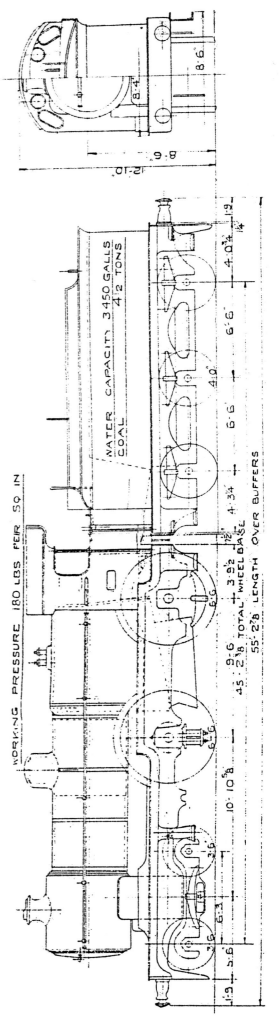

Class E1 4-4-0. (Ashford dwg No.A7A)

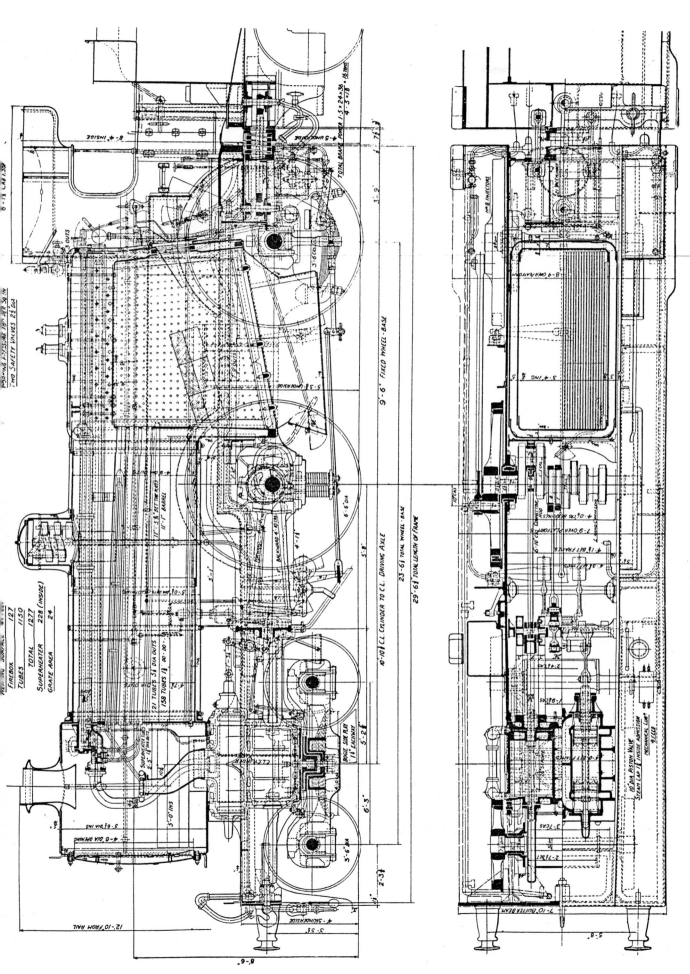

S.E. & C.R. CLASS E¹ LOCOMOTIVE

Class E1 4-4-0. (Ashford dwg No.A7A)

Class E1 No.506 (LH side) at Stewarts Lane.

Class E1 No.165 (RH side) at Stewarts Lane.

Class F No.104 (LH side).

Class E1 as BR No.31160.

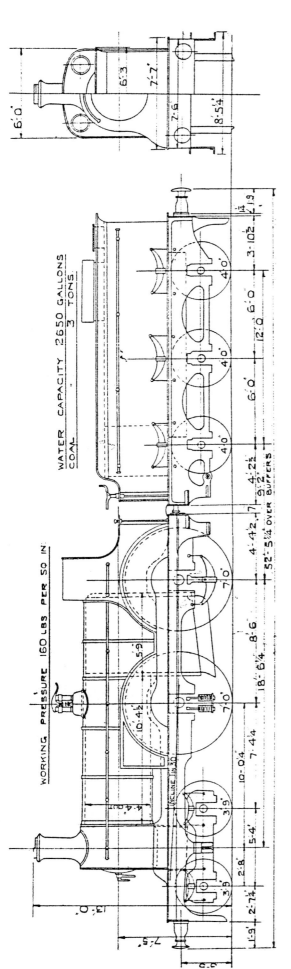

WORKING PRESSURE 160 LBS PER SQ IN.

WATER CAPACITY 2650 GALLONS
COAL 3 TONS

Class F, ex-SER 4-4-0. (Ashford dwg No.A8)

F class 4-4-0

To cope with the competition from the LCDR and the Continental traffic, in 1883 Stirling designed, and had built, the famous 'Mails' class of 4-4-0 Express Passenger engines. There were 88 built between 1883 and 1898 at Ashford Works, and as can be seen, were typical Stirling, with the rounded cab and domeless boiler, 4ft 4in x 10ft 4½in. What was unusual for the time, was the large driving wheels of 7ft diameter. As was the normal practice in those days a century ago, the great majority were eventually reboilered by Wainwright, when they became the F1 class. Those that did not receive this treatment, and lived to see SR days were as follows:

SER No.	Built	Withdrawn
22	1898	1930
45	1896	1925
91	1889	1925
104	1885	1926
139	1891	1930
172	1893	1930
194	1889	1926
198	1884	1926
210	1886	1930
211	1886	1930
222	1897	1930
241	1890	1930

Nos 156 and 172 fitted with Westinghouse brake.
Tenders for F class held 2,650 gallons.

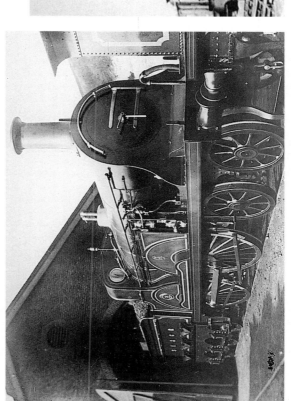

Class F No.198.

Class F No.78 in SECR livery (RH side).

F1 class 4-4-0 (Rebuilt F class)

From 1903 onwards, Wainwright, who had taken over from Stirling on the SER in 1899, started on the massive task of rebuilding the F class, to give the engines the benefit of new boilers, and so extending their useful life. Apart from the running gear and splashers, the whole appearance of the class was changed. The Stirling rounded cab gave way to a more squared version, the boilers had domes, with the Ramsbottom valves sited over the firebox, and the smokebox front wings were dispensed with, showing the smokebox front cylindrical. Seventy-six locomotives were so rebuilt, and all that saw service in the SR are recorded hereunder.

Class F1 No.205 at Bricklayers Arms in 1920 (RH side).

SER No.	Built as F	Rebuilt as F1	Withdrawn
2	1886	1911	1948
9	1893	1904	1932
11	1895	1913	1937
24	1894	1904	1933
25	1894	1909	1936
28	1889	1914	1948
29	1895	1906	1926
30	1898	1914	1935
31	1894	1906	1948
32	1886	1907	1933
35	1896	1905	1934
42	1896	1911	1948
43	1885	1912	1947
53	1897	1912	1933
56	1888	1907	1936
60	1891	1905	1946
62	1897	1909	1947
74	1890	1907	1936
78	1886	1911	1949
79	1892	1904	1946
84	1890	1905	1944
87	1897	1909	1933
88	1897	1912	1933
89	1895	1906	1937
94	1894	1905	1936
97	1893	1913	1926
103	1896	1906	1932
105	1896	1908	1949
110	1895	1907	1946
114	1886	1909	1933
116	1884	1913	1929
117	1895	1911	1936
118	1895	1913	1935
130	1891	1907	1935
133	1892	1907	1933
137	1891	1906	1933
140	1891	1903	1947
143	1890	1906	1935
148	1889	1903	1928
149	1890	1906	1937
151	1889	1913	1949
156	1893	1906	1947
183	1884	1908	1947
185	1884	1919	1933
187	1898	1906	1937
188	1897	1911	1947
190	1888	1912	1935
192	1897	1911	1933
195	1897	1904	1947
196	1894	1908	1933
197	1890	1916	1933
199	1885	1907	1935
201	1885	1909	1933
202	1886	1910	1936
203	1885	1916	1932
204	1885	1911	1937
205	1883	1908	1947
206	1885	1915	1933
208	1884	1905	1936
209	1885	1916	1926
212	1884	1906	1933
213	1886	1909	1925
214	1884	1904	1932
215	1891	1906	1948
216	1895	1909	1935
226	1894	1905	1926
228	1897	1911	1935
230	1897	1905	1933
231	1893	1907	1949
232	1892	1906	1933
233	1898	1913	1937
236	1889	1912	1932
240	1889	1913	1937
249	1897	1906	1944
250	1897	1915	1937

Eventually all the F1 class engines were given extended smokeboxes under the Maunsell regime, which again altered their appearance slightly.

Nine of the class were loaned to the LMSR between 1941 and 1944.

Class F1 No.1043

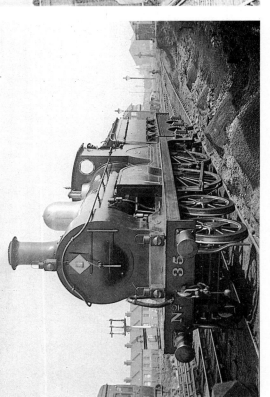

Class F1 No.35.

WATER CAPACITY 2650 GALLONS

COAL 3 TONS

WORKING PRESSURE 170 LBS PER SQ IN

Class F1, ex-SER 4-4-0. (Ashford dwg No.A9)

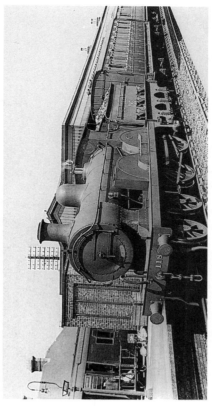

Class F1 No.1183 at Faversham in 1934.

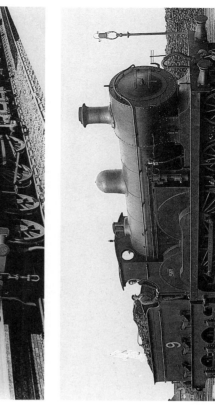

Class F1 No.9.

Class F1 No.88, Reading, 1924.

G class 4-4-0

There were only five of these handsome 4-4-0 engines, and although their ancestry is purely Scottish, they have to be mentioned because all five passed into SR ownership at the Grouping. Built by Neilson, Reid & Co. in 1899, they were a part order from the Great North of Scotland Railway, who originally asked for ten, but reduced the order to five. Designed by Pickersgill, the remaining five were sold to the SECR in 1900. These engines were all left-hand drive, which did not suit the crews in the London area of the SECR who were used to machines driven from the right, and their spacious cabs with the two side windows,

quickly earned them the nickname of "Glasshouses"! The class was never rebuilt, although Nos 676 and 679 did receive secondhand boilers from the GNR in 1914. The summary is as follows:

SECR No.	Built	Date	Withdrawn
676	Neilson, Reid	1899	1926
677	Neilson, Reid	1899	1925
678	Neilson, Reid	1899	1924
679	Neilson, Reid	1899	1925
680	Neilson, Reid	1899	1927

Driving wheels 6ft 1in dia, boiler 10ft 6in x 4ft 6in, Tender 3,000 gallons and 5 Tons fuel. Fitted with vacuum and Westinghouse brakes.

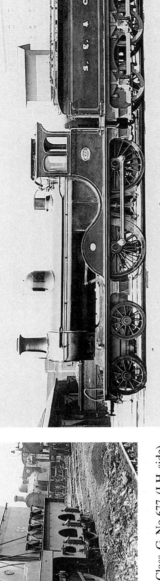

Class G No.A676 at Gillingham, 1926.

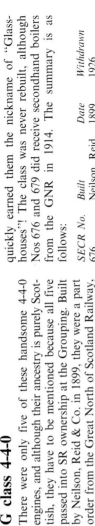

Class F1 No.56.

Class G No.677 (LH side).

Class G No.A680 at Maidstone, 1927.

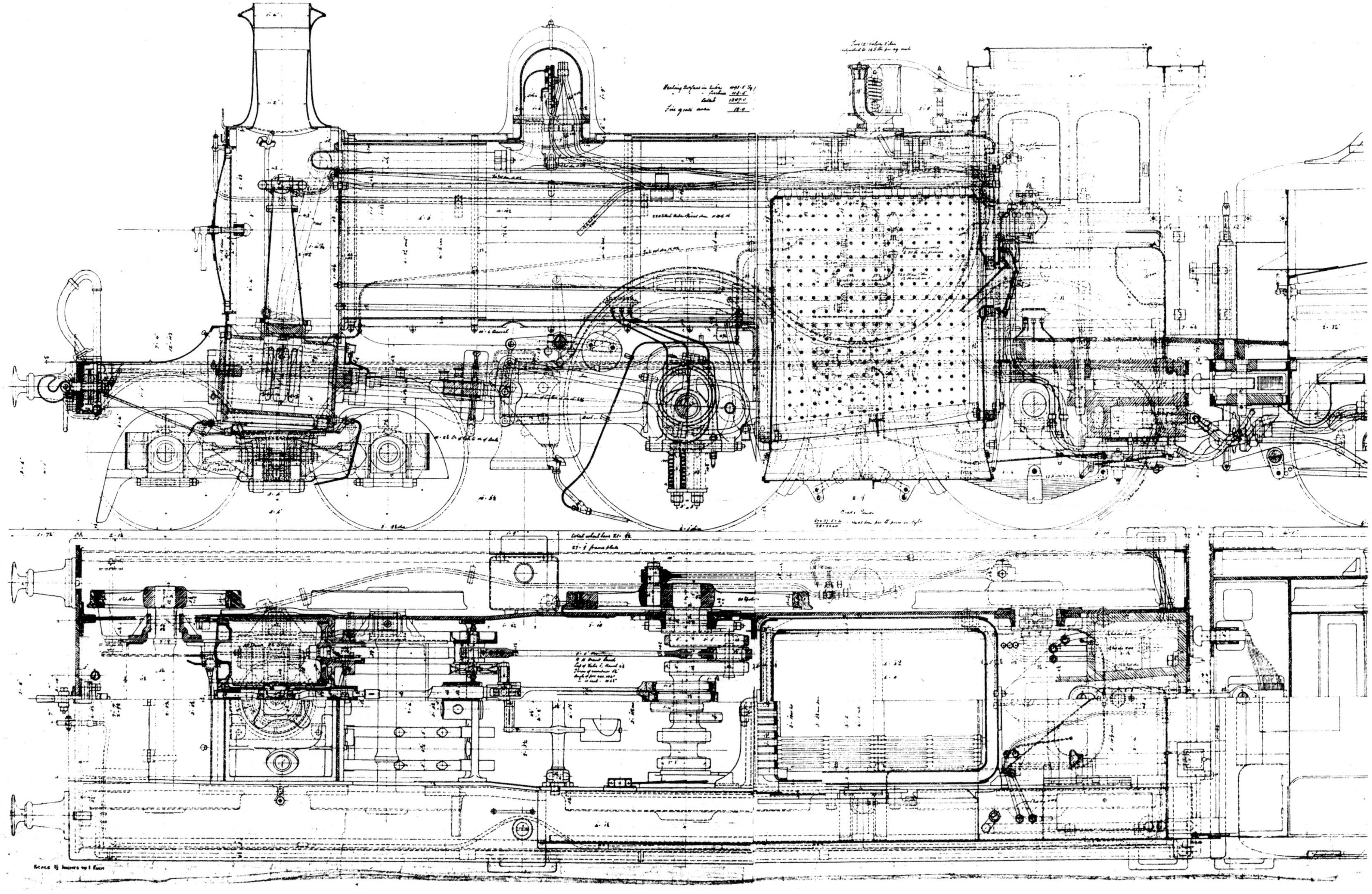

Class G, ex-Great North of Scotland Railway 4-4-0. General Arrangement drawing.

SECR No	Built	Date	P & P. Fitted	Withdrawn
5	Ashford	1907	1960	1962
16	Ashford	1915	1949	1951
158	Ashford	1909	1950	1955
161	Ashford	1909	1950	1962
162	Ashford	1909	1953	1962
164	Ashford	1909	1949	1959
177	Ashford	1909	1953	1962
182	Ashford	1909	1949	1951
184*	Ashford	1915	1952	1958
193	Ashford	1909	1952	1962
239	Ashford	1909	1952	1960
259	Ashford	1905		1959
261	Ashford	1905		1962
263	Ashford	1905	1960	1962
264	Ashford	1905		1944
265	Ashford	1905		1960
266	Ashford	1905	1958	1960
269	Ashford	1905	1953	1959
274*	Ashford	1905	1953	1957
276	Ashford	1905	1953	1962
278	Ashford	1905	1956	1962
279	Ashford	1909	1953	1959
295	Ashford	1909	1952	1959
305	Ashford	1906		1962
306	Ashford	1906	1959	1962
307	Ashford	1906		1962
308	Ashford	1906	1953	1962

SECR No	Built	Date	P & P. Fitted	Withdrawn
309	Ashford	1906	1953	1955
310	Ashford	1906		1960
311	Ashford	1907		1954
312	Ashford	1906		1944
319	Ashford	1909	1950	1960
320	Ashford	1907	1953	1955
321	Ashford	1906		1957
322*	Ashford	1909	1950	1962
324	Ashford	1907	1961	1962
326	Ashford	1906		1962
327	Ashford	1907	1953	1959
328	Ashford	1906		1962
329	Ashford	1906	1956	1959
500	Ashford	1905	1959	1962
503	Ashford	1905		1959
512	Ashford	1909	1951	1962
517	Ashford	1909	1949	1962
518	Ashford	1909	1952	1962
519	Ashford	1909	1952	1957
520	Ashford	1909	1949	1962
521	Ashford	1909	1953	1962
522	Ashford	1909	1949	1959
523	Ashford	1909	1952	1959
530	Ashford	1906	1953	1962
531	Ashford	1905		1962
532	Ashford	1905		1962
533	Ashford	1905		1962

Class G No.A679 at Slades Green, 1925.

H class 0-4-4T

As the London surburban traffic increased on the SECR at the turn of the century, the need for a more modern version of the Q class series of tank engines became imperative. Mr Wainwright actually considered two new classes of 0-4-4T engines, a medium version of passenger tank, which became the H class, and a larger version which was to be a K class. In the event, only the former class was proceeded with, and 66 engines were built to this design between 1904 and 1915, all at Ashford Works.

The new machines were similar to the R and R1 classes, but had 18in cylinders and the boilers were pressed for 160lbs, 10ft 3½in x 4ft 3in. Coupled wheels were 5ft 6in diameter, with the bogie wheels 3ft 7in diameter, the main difference to the viewer was in the provision of a 'Pagoda' cab, with the typical overhung eaves of Wainwright's design. All the class were fitted with complete vacuum brake system, and 15 were given dual braking systems. Much later in the life of these engines, in BR days in fact, many were fitted with 'push-pull' gear to replace the scrapped D3s of the Central section, and the old Eastern section's R and R1 classes.

A complete summary is shown as follows:

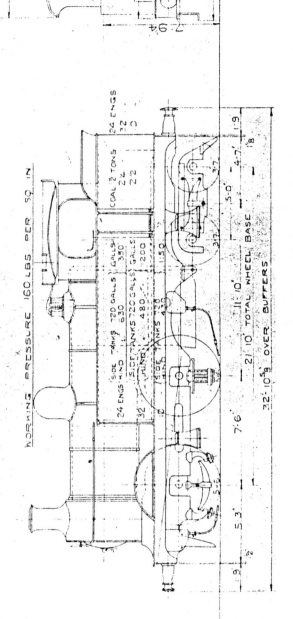

Class H 0-4-4T. (Ashford dwg No. A11)

SECR No	Built	Date	P & P. Fitted	Withdrawn
540	Ashford	1904		1960
541	Ashford	1904		1951
542	Ashford	1904		1962
543	Ashford	1909	1953	1962
544*	Ashford	1904	1954	1962
546	Ashford	1904		1951
548	Ashford	1904	1949	1959
550	Ashford	1904		1962
551	Ashford	1905	1960	1962
552	Ashford	1905		1962
553	Ashford	1905	1960	1962
554	Ashford	1909	1952	1959

***'S' prefix added from 1948-1951
No. 263 now preserved on the Bluebell Railway

Class H No.1521 in 1935.

Class H No.A161 (RH side).

Class H No.5 (LH side).

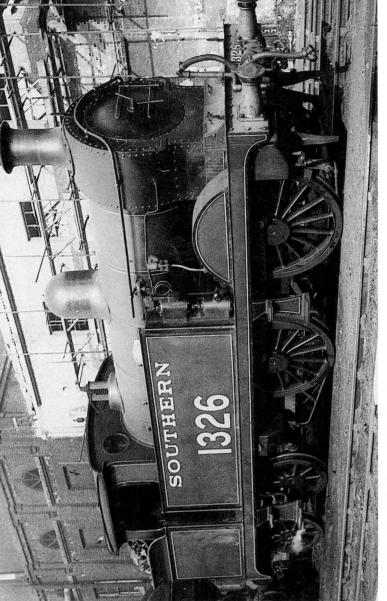

Class H No.1326 in 1936.

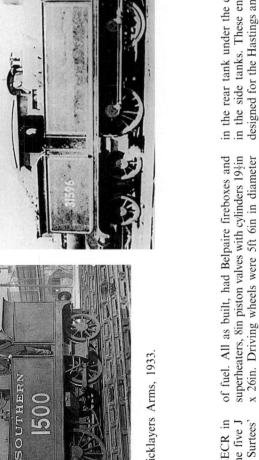

Class J as BR No.31596 (RH side).

Class H No.A532 in 1926.

Class H No.1500 at Bricklayers Arms, 1933.

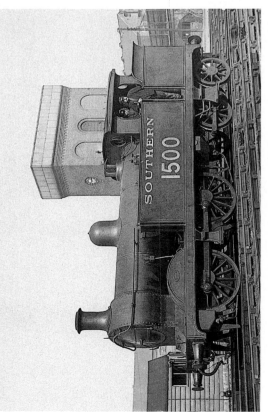

J class 0-6-4T

The largest tank engines built for the SECR in the Wainwright era were undoubtedly the five J class 0-6-4 tanks, another design from Mr Surtees' board. Although originally conceived as a radial tank, a bogie was obviously considered necessary under the large bunker, which could hold 3½ tons of fuel. All as built, had Belpaire fireboxes and superheaters, 8in piston valves with cylinders 19½in x 26in. Driving wheels were 5ft 6in in diameter and the bogie wheels were 3ft 7in. The boiler was 4ft 5¾in x 10ft 7½in, pressed for 160lbs, and the water capacity was a total of 2,000 gallons, 1,400 in the rear tank under the coal, and 600 gallons in the side tanks. These engines were originally designed for the Hastings and Tonbridge business expresses, but the L class 4-4-0s which followed them were found to be more suitable, and the 0-6-4Ts worked on the London–Redhill services.

SECR No.	Built Ashford	Renumbered		Withdrawn
129	1913	A596 in 1927		1951
207	1913	A595 in 1928		1951
597	1913	–		1950
611	1913	A598 in 1927		1950
614	1913	A599 in 1928		1949

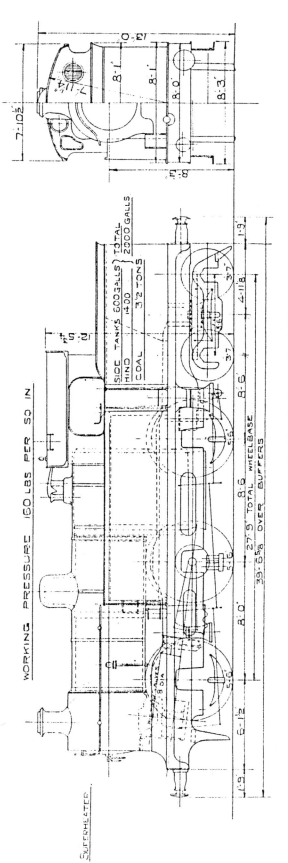

WORKING PRESSURE 160 LBS PER SQ IN

Side tanks 600 galls } Total
Hind 1400 } 2000 galls
Coal 3½ tons

27'-9 total wheelbase
39'-6⅝ over buffers

Class J 0-6-4T. (Ashford dwg No.A12)

Class J No.1596.

Left: Class J No.A207 in 1926 (LH side).

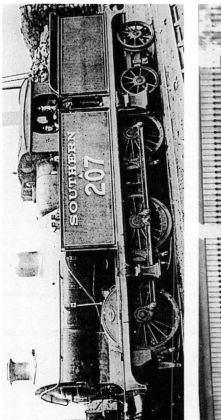

Class J No.1596 in 1936.

Class J, BR No.31599 at Ashford in 1949.

Class K No.A799 *River Test*, as built.

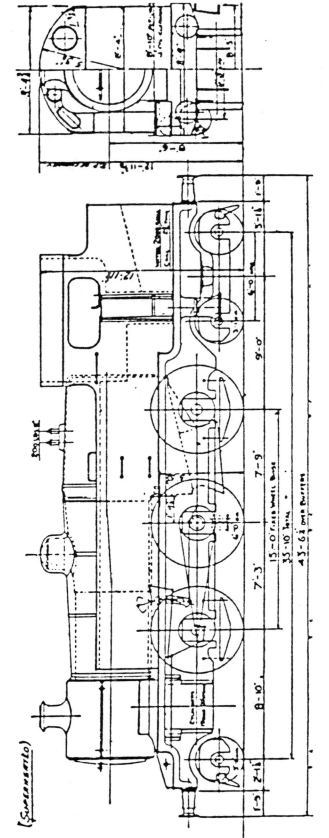

Class K 2-6-4T. (un-numbered SR diagram)

K class 2-6-4T

As mentioned briefly in the synopsis of the N class 2-6-0 engines later, 1917 also saw the introduction of a large passenger tank engine, No. 790. This machine was the prototype of the 'River' class, as under Southern ownership in 1925, all these 2-6-4 tanks were named after rivers which were located in Southern Railway territory.

This first single machine was virtually an N class engine, fitted with 6ft driving wheels instead of the smaller 5ft 6in, and of course with extended frames to provide a coal bunker capable of holding 2½ tons of fuel. The huge side tanks held 2,000 gallons of water and was probably the reason for the "rolling" of the engines at high speed on anything other than top grade permanent way. (For continuity of this class, see Southern Railway section).

No.	Built	Date	Converted to U class	Withdrawn
790	Ashford	1917	1928	1965

Class K No.A790 *River Avon* at Guildford in 1927.

Class K No.A803 *River Itchen*, Redhill, 1925.

L class 4-4-0

Wainwright resigned from the post of Locomotive Superintendent of the SECR in November of 1913, and was followed into that position by R.E.L. Maunsell. At that time Continental traffic was increasing and the Kent coalfields were expanding, all of which meant that more and larger locomotives were needed to cope with the growing rail traffic. Work had been going on for several years to improve the standard, and the weight restrictions on the old LCDR main lines, but even so, the type of machine allowed by the Civil Engineer had to be the 4-coupled express engines. However, the need was very urgent, and the drawings which had been prepared by Mr Wainwright in 1913 for a large 4-4-0, resulted in the L class. The first twelve were ordered from Messrs Beyer, Peacock, and due to the desperate need, a further ten were built by Messrs Borsig of Berlin (with a proviso that they must guarantee delivery by August 1914). All these engines had superheaters, the English ones having the Robinson type, whilst those built in Germany were fitted with the Schmidt pattern. Boilers were 4ft 11in x 11ft 5in with a 7ft 5in firebox and pressed for 160lbs. Cylinders were 20½in x 26in, and driving wheels 6ft 8in in diameter. Some of Maunsell's influence can be seen by the chimney and the extended cab roof, supported on two pillars. The large tenders held 3,450 gallons of water and 4 tons of fuel. Eventually all the class were fitted with Maunsell superheaters. Incidentally, the L class was the final class of locomotive built expressly for the SECR.

SECR No.	Built (1914)	Withdrawn
760	Beyer, Peacock	1961
761	Beyer, Peacock	1956
762	Beyer, Peacock	1960
763	Beyer, Peacock	1960
764	Beyer, Peacock	1961
765	Beyer, Peacock	1961
766	Beyer, Peacock	1961
767	Beyer, Peacock	1958
768	Beyer, Peacock	1961
769	Beyer, Peacock	1956
770	Beyer, Peacock	1959
771	Beyer, Peacock	1961
772	Borsig	1959
773	Borsig	1959
774	Borsig	1958
775	Borsig	1959
776	Borsig	1961
777	Borsig	1959
778	Borsig	1959
779	Borsig	1959
780	Borsig	1961
781	Borsig	1959

No. 1772 carried 'S' prefix from 1948/9   PAGE 39

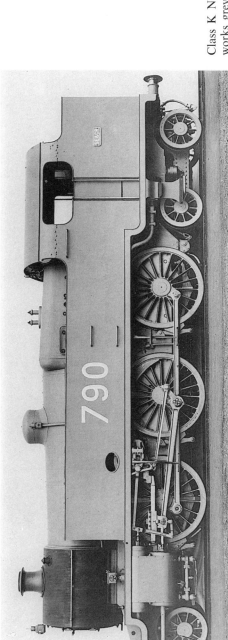

Class K No.790 in works grey livery.

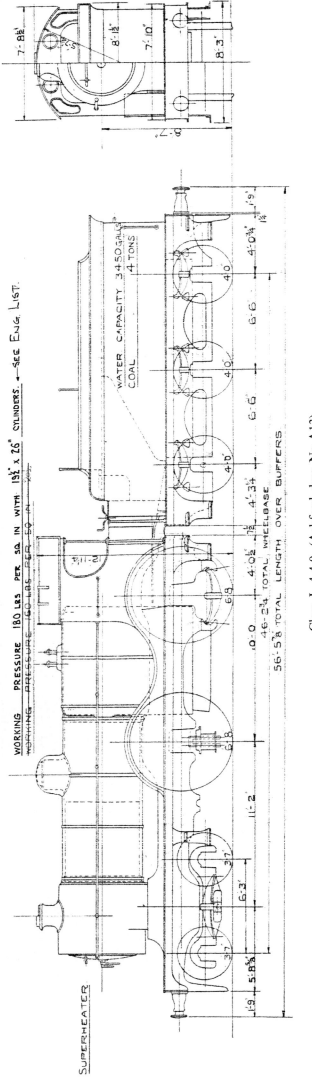

SUPERHEATER.

WORKING PRESSURE 180 LBS PER. SQ. IN. WITH 19½" x 26" CYLINDERS. — SEE ENG. LIST.

WORKING PRESSURE 160 LBS. PER. SQ. IN.

WATER CAPACITY 3450 GALS.
COAL 4 TONS

Class L 4-4-0. (Ashford dwg No.A13)

Class L No.A769 in 1928.

Class L No.1774 at Ashford in 1935.

Class L BR
No.31767.

Class M3
No.464 in
SECR livery.

PAGE 41

Class L No.A763 unofficially named "Betty Baldwin" by its volunteer crew during the 1926 General
Strike. Seen at Hastings in July 1926.

Class L as BR No.31775.

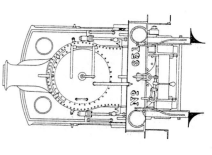

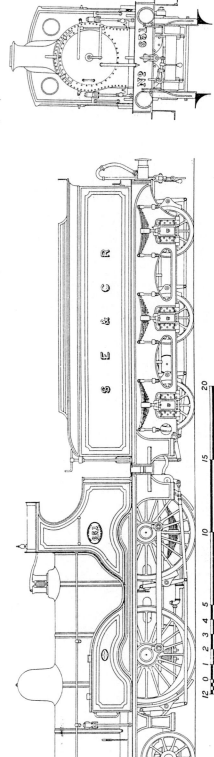

Ramsgate and Margate and were quite lively. The last two, Nos 468 and 469, were eventually rebuilt with larger boilers and fitted with Wainwright chimneys and polished brass domes.

Tenders for M1 and M2 class had capacity of 2,470 gallons
Tenders for M3 class had capacity of 2,600 gallons

SECR No.	Class	Built	Date	Withdrawn
635	M1	Longhedge	1880	1923
641	M2	Dubs	1884	1923
646	M3	Vulcan Foundry	1891	1928
647	M3	Vulcan Foundry	1891	1925
648	M3	Vulcan Foundry	1891	1926
649	M3	Vulcan Foundry	1891	1927
650	M3	Vulcan Foundry	1891	1926
651	M3	Vulcan Foundry	1891	1927
462	M3	Longhedge	1897	1926
463	M3	Longhedge	1899	1928
464	M3	Longhedge	1897	1926
465	M3	Longhedge	1898	1925
466	M3	Longhedge	1898	1927
467	M3	Longhedge	1899	1925
468	M3	Longhedge	1901	1927
469	M3	Longhedge	1901	1926
471	M3	Longhedge	1895	1927
472	M3	Longhedge	1896	1927
473	M3	Longhedge	1892	1926
474	M3	Longhedge	1895	1926
475	M3	Longhedge	1893	1927
476	M3	Longhedge	1894	1927
478	M3	Longhedge	1897	1926
479	M3	Longhedge	1894	1927
482	M3	Longhedge	1896	1927
483	M3	Longhedge	1898	1926
484	M3	Longhedge	1892	1926
485	M3	Longhedge	1900	1927

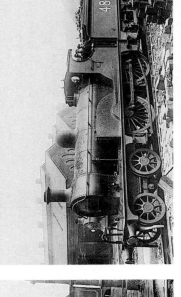

Class M2 No.638 in SECR livery.

Class M3 No.482.

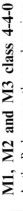

Class M3 No.463, Dover Priory in 1927.

M1, M2 and M3 class 4-4-0

As the B class were the goods engines designed by Kirtley for the LCDR, so the M class were the express passenger engines. There were 44 built in all, in four series, M, M1, M2 and M3. The original Ms had all gone before the formation of the Southern Railway, so must be discounted here. Only one M1, No. 635 of the SECR numbering, lasted until 1923, and likewise one M2, No. 641 (SECR) which was condemned in the same year as No. 635, but all the M3 class just managed to get on to the SR records before honourable retirement. All 44 were very similar, being fitted with 6ft 6in driving wheels and various tenders in their long lives. They were used mainly on the Kent Coast fast trains to

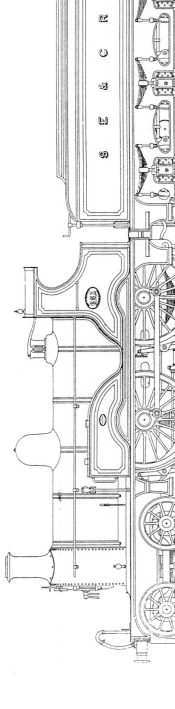

Class M3 4-4-0.

Class N BR No.31854 in 1958.

Class N No.1414 at Salisbury in 1937.

N and N1 class 2-6-0

In 1910, Churchward at Swindon, had asked one of his draughtsmen for the design of a 2-6-0 mixed traffic locomotive, using all the standard parts available and with a No. 4 boiler. As is well known, so the 4300 class of GWR engine was born, and from the designs of Harry Holcroft, many hundreds of these versatile machines were produced at the Swindon workshops over the years.

Harry Holcroft moved to Ashford in 1914, followed by another 'Western' man, one G.H. Pearson, these two then were joined by a 'Midland' man from Derby, James Clayton. Maunsell had more or less at his fingertips lots of up-to-date locomotive thinking of that time. Therefore, upon requiring to improve on the stud of 4-4-0 tender engines of the SECR, the obvious solution was a 2-6-0 which could handle passenger and freight traffic all over the system.

The first N class, No. 810, was built at Ashford in 1917, and as can be seen, was almost pure 'Swindon'. Taper boiler, Belpaire firebox, driving wheels size, etc. all were practically identical. The differences that Maunsell brought about were outside Walschaerts valve gear, instead of Stephenson's, and a different system of top feed etc., whilst Clayton's Midland influence could be seen

in the large smokebox, chimney, roomy cab, and big tender. At the same time, in 1917, a tank version of the N class was produced in the shape of a 2-6-4T engine, No. 790, but these engines will be dealt with later. Only 15 N class engines were authorised by the SECR administration, the further 65 being constructed in SR days, and so are referred to in that section.

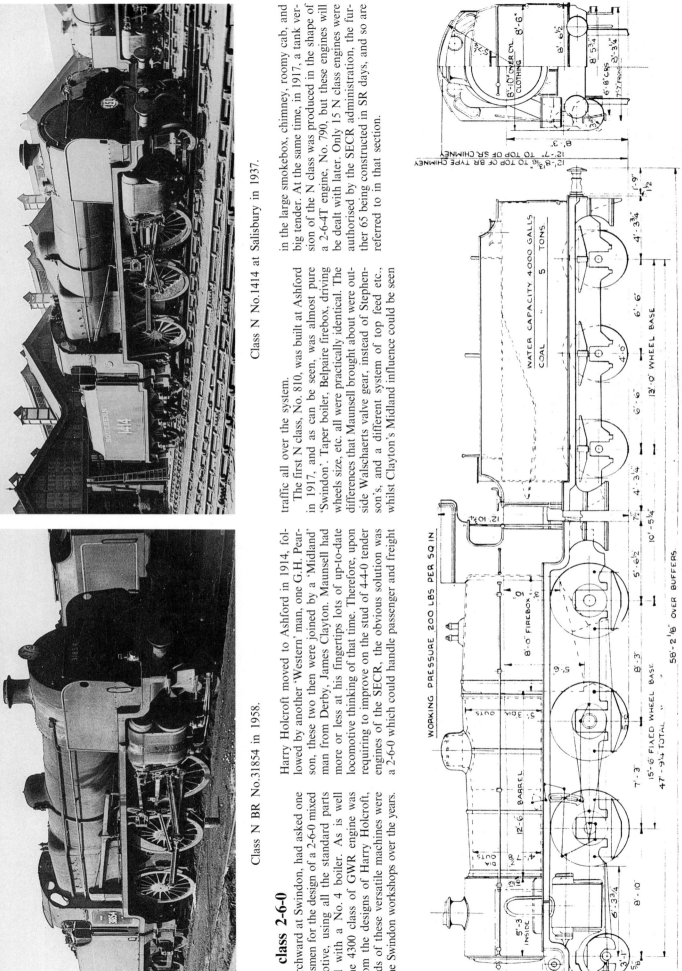

Class N 2-6-0. (Ashford dwg No.N12)

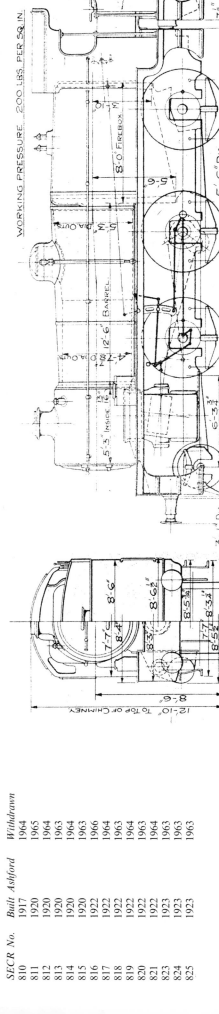

Class N1 2-6-0.
(Ashford dwg No. A14C)

WORKING PRESSURE 200 LBS. PER SQ.IN.

SECR No.	Built Ashford	Withdrawn
810	1917	1964
811	1920	1965
812	1920	1964
813	1920	1963
814	1920	1964
815	1920	1963
816	1922	1966
817	1922	1964
818	1922	1963
819	1922	1964
820	1922	1963
821	1922	1964
823	1923	1963
824	1923	1963
825	1923	1963

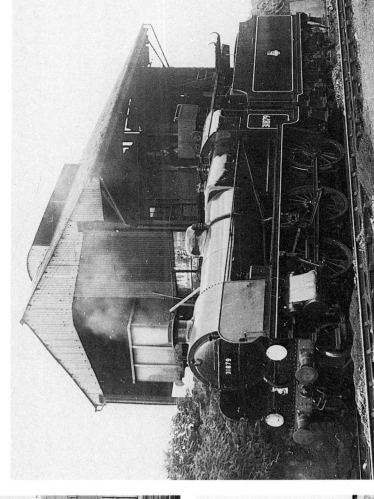

Left: Class N No.1412 (RH side) Ashford, 1935.

Class N1 BR No.31879 at Redhill, 1952.

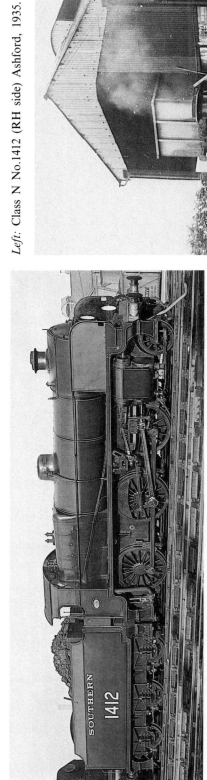

Class N1 No.822 as built (LH side).

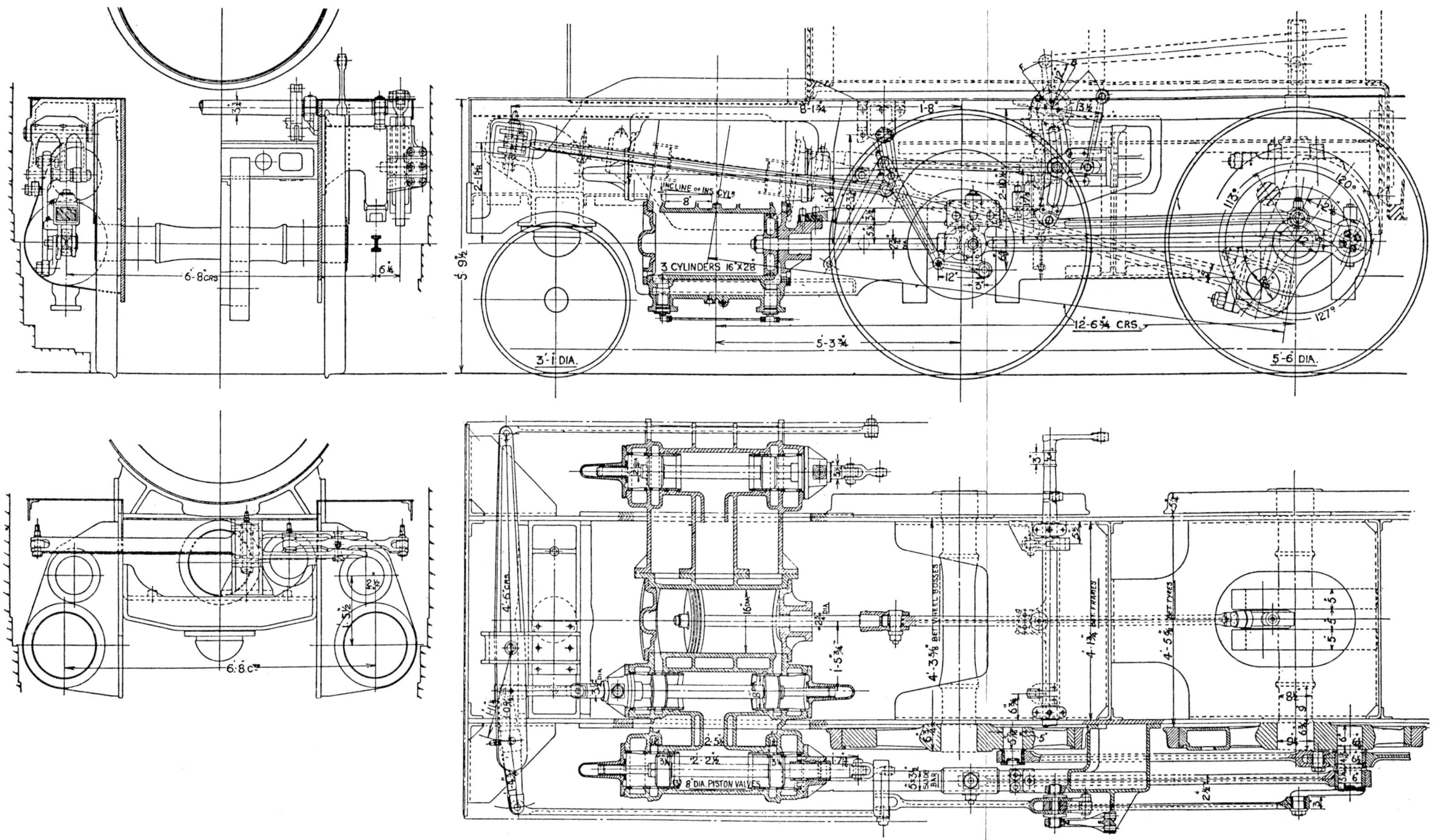

S.E. & C.R. CLASS N¹ LOCOMOTIVE

Class N1 2-6-0. General Arrangement of H. Holcroft's conjugated valve gear for 3-cylinder locomotive.

O class 0-6-0

James Stirling left the Glasgow & South Western Railway to become the Locomotive Superintendent of the SER in 1878. Once down in the South his first design was for 20 0-6-0 goods tender engines, which had a strong family likeness to those he had built for the Scottish railway. As can be seen in the illustrations, the boiler was domeless, with the safety valves on the boiler barrel, the regulator being in the smokebox, operated by a lever in the cab working horizontally. The rounded cab was pure Stirling design and probably accounted for the restricted loading gauge on the SER. Believe it or not, as originally constructed, there were no brakes on the engine wheels, all retarding was accomplished by hand-brake operating on the tender wheels! Later vacuum braking was adopted and some were dual fitted eventually. Driving wheels were 5ft 1in on a wheelbase of 15ft 6in. The boiler was in three rings, 4ft 4in x 10ft 3½in, and tenders carried 3 tons of coal and had a water capacity of 2,000 gallons. These work horses must have proved their

worth because between 1878 and 1899 a total of 122 were built, both at Sharp Stewart's and at the Ashford factory. As this record is only concerned with engines which were carried over into Southern Railway ownership, only those are shown in the data list hereunder:

SER No.	Built	Date	Withdrawn
1	Ashford	1890	1925
8	Ashford	1899	1928
15	Ashford	1890	1925
49	Ashford	1898	1929
52	Ashford	1896	1927
96	Ashford	1896	1926
98	Ashford	1899	1929
99	Ashford	1899	1927
100	Ashford	1899	1926
111	Ashford	1896	1929
142	Ashford	1896	1926
144	Ashford	1890	1925
167	Ashford	1893	1928
170	Ashford	1893	1927
171	Ashford	1884	1923
254	Ashford	1898	1925
332	Ashford	1886	1923

SER No.	Built	Date	Withdrawn
333	Ashford	1887	1926
375	Sharp, Stewart	1891	1924
376	Sharp, Stewart	1891	1928
382	Sharp, Stewart	1893	1924
387	Sharp, Stewart	1893	1926
392	Sharp, Stewart	1893	1925
394	Sharp, Stewart	1893	1926
427	Sharp, Stewart	1897	1926
431	Sharp, Stewart	1897	1926
433	Sharp, Stewart	1897	1928
435	Sharp, Stewart	1897	1927
436	Sharp, Stewart	1897	1932

Nos 372 and 376 sold to East Kent Light Railway. For the remainder of the O class, converted to O1 see next list.

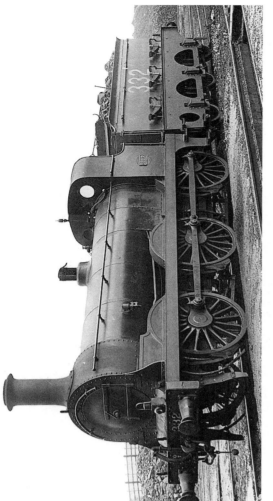

Class O No.332 (LH side).

Class O No.A99 (RH side), Faversham, 1926.

Class N1 No.822 as fitted with three cylinders.

SECR No.	Rebuilt as O1	Withdrawn
64	1914	1958
65	1908	1961
66	1916	1951
80	1916	1949
93	1916	1951
106	1903	1949
108	1915	1951
109	1927	1949
119	1906	1925
123	1915	1950
238	1903	1949
248	1912	1951
251	1918	1946
258	1914	1961
316	1906	1949
369	1914	1951
370	1906	1960
371	1909	1944
372	1932	1949
373	1906	1951
374	1905	1949
377	1906	1950
378	1908	1948
379	1906	1951
380	1908	1949
381	1915	1951
383	1908	1935
384	1910	1949
385	1914	1949
386	1918	1948
388	1914	1948
389	1907	1949
390	1915	1951
391	1907	1951
393	1908	1926
395	1914	1951
396	1913	1948
397	1918	1948
398	1907	1949
425	1914	1959
426	1915	1948
428	1914	1949
429	1914	1949
430	1914	1959
432	1914	1951
434	1918	1959
437	1914	1948
438	1912	1948
439	1914	1949

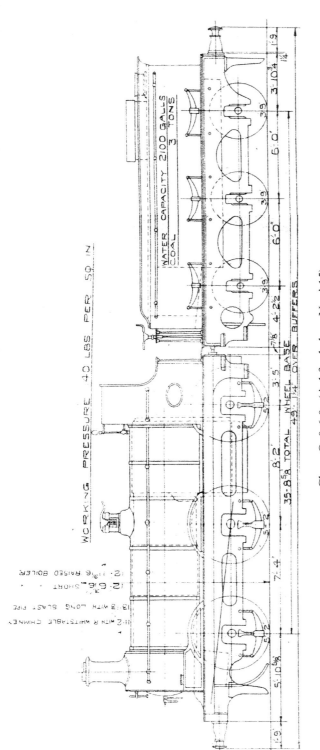

Class O 0-6-0. (Ashford dwg No.A15)

O1 class 0-6-0 (Rebuilt O class)

Fifty-eight of the previous O class were rebuilt by Wainwright from 1903 onward, and all but one, No. 282, saw service on the SR. The rebuilding consisted of fitting the engines with a Wainwright H class boiler in two rings with a dome, and the valves over the firebox. Boiler pressure was increased to 150lbs per sq in. The Stirling cab was replaced by a Wainwright type, similar to that on the C class goods engines, and several were fitted with redundant tenders from the old M series of the LCDR. All of these engines had the vacuum brake. SECR numbers are as follows with rebuilding dates and withdrawals, approximate.

Class O No.1.

Nos 371 and 383 sold to East Kent Light Railway.
No. 372 had been sold to the Kent & East Sussex Railway in 1923.
No. 65 preserved privately.

SECR No.	Rebuilt as O1	Withdrawn
3	1912	1949
7	1913	1949
14	1905	1948
39	1912	1949
41	1908	1951
44	1912	1951
46	1909	1948
48	1908	1960
51	1914	1948

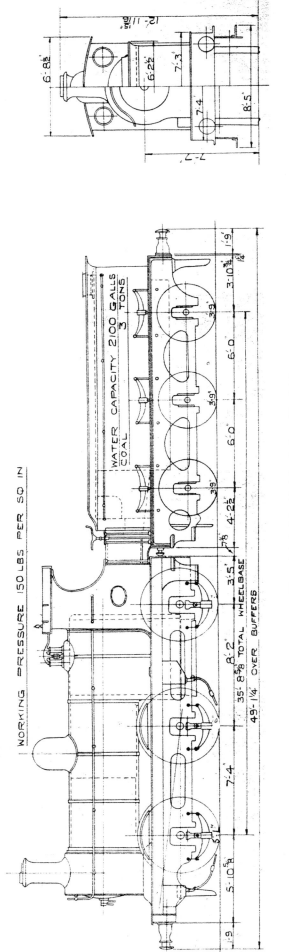

Class O1 0-6-0. (Ashford dwg No.A16)

Class O1 No.1437 at Tonbridge in 1934.

Class O1 No.438 (RH side).

Class O1 No.A7 at Gillingham in 1932.

Class O1 No.373 with M class tender.

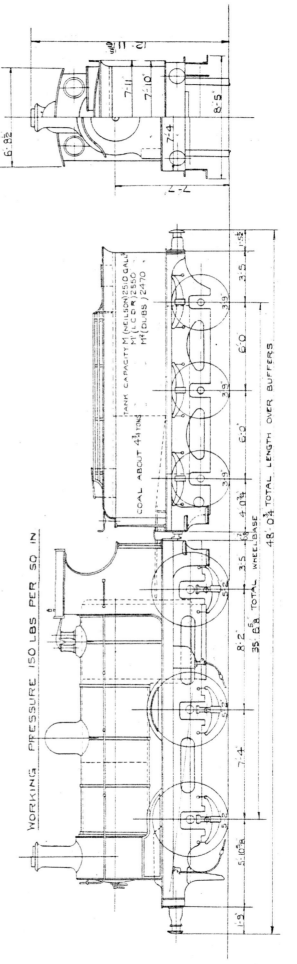

Class O1 0-6-0 with M class tender. (Ashford dwg No.A17)

P class 0-6-0T

These tiny little tanks were built originally to work on light branch services and in rail-motor units. How diminutive they really were one can still judge, as no less than four have been preserved. Some of the measurements are as follows. Cylinders 12in x 18in. driving wheels 3ft 9in diameter on a wheel base of 11ft. Boiler 3ft 3in x 7ft 7½in and firebox 3ft 10in. Pressure 160lb, water tanks 550 gallons and bunker space 18cwt. Only eight were built, all at Ashford, and had complete vacuum brake; all had the Wainwright 'Pagoda' cab roof, but the first two engines had higher cabs than the rest. It was soon found that the rail-motor duties assigned to the little machines, taxed them to the limit and they eventually found their way all over the SR system on carriage shunting and shed pilot duties.

To make, and paint one of these little engines in the full glory of the SECR livery, in 4mm scale, is a task for an expert in fine art work! I know, I used to have a model, hand painted by Frederick Berry – it was a joy to behold.

SECR No.	Built (Ashford)	Withdrawn
27	1910	1961
178	1910	1958
323	1910	1960
325	1910	1960
555	1910	1955
558	1910	1960

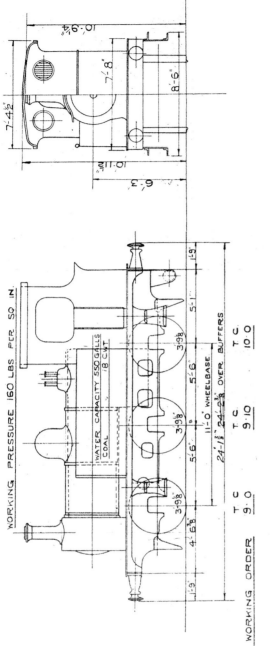

Class P 0-6-0T. (Ashford dwg No.A20)

SECR No.	Built (Ashford)	Withdrawn
753	1909	1961
754	1909	1957

No. 1178 carried 'S' prefix 1948-51. Sold to Bowaters, then Bluebell Railway.
No. 753 Taller cab roof. Renumbered 556 in 1925. Sold to industry, then KESR.
No. 754 Taller cab roof. Renumbered 557 in 1925.
Nos 27 and 323 sold to Bluebell Railway.

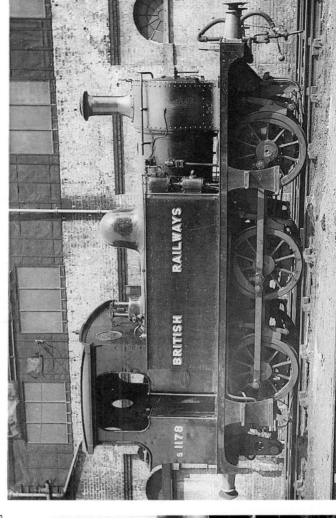

Class P as BR No S1178 later 31178

Class P No.A558 (LH side).

Class Q No.135 (LH side) — locomotive No.135

Class Q, ex-SER 0-4-4T

SECR No.	Built	Date	Withdrawn
136	Ashford	1892	1927
169	Ashford	1893	1927
173	Ashford	1888	1928
220	Ashford	1889	1926
235	Ashford	1887	1927
237	Ashford	1887	1926
345	Neilson	1889	1925
346	Neilson	1889	1929
349	Neilson	1889	1926
352	Neilson	1889	1926
356	Neilson	1891	1927
358	Neilson	1891	1926
360	Neilson	1891	1926
368	Neilson	1891	1929
399	Sharp, Stewart	1893	1927
401	Sharp, Stewart	1893	1928
405	Sharp, Stewart	1893	1926
410	Neilson	1893	1927
414	Neilson	1897	1927
417	Neilson	1897	1926
418	Neilson	1897	1926
421	Neilson	1897	1927
422	Neilson	1897	1926
424	Neilson	1897	1927

As built the Q class had one peculiarity, the exhaust steam vented into the L/H tank only, this warm water being the supply for the pump, whereas the R/H tank (kept separate) supplied cold water for the injector.

Boiler size 4ft 5in x 10ft 3½in, tanks 1,000 gallons, fuel 25cwt.

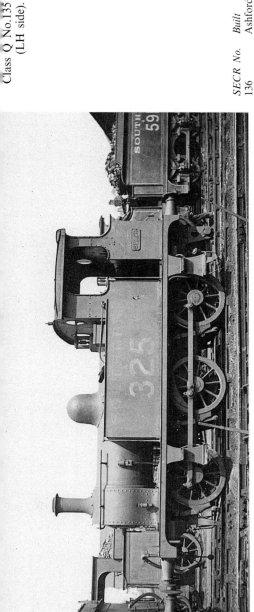

Class P No.A325 at Dover Priory, 1927.

SECR No.	Built	Date	Withdrawn
6	Ashford	1894	1927
23	Ashford	1889	1928
26	Ashford	1889	1927
40	Ashford	1887	1926
72	Ashford	1891	1926
73	Ashford	1889	1926
82	Ashford	1892	1926
135			

Q class 0-4-4T

Stirling designed and had built for the SER 118 0-4-4T engines for passenger services. Their construction was divided between Ashford Works, Messrs Sharp, Stewart & Co. and Neilson & Co. of Glasgow. All were built between 1881 and 1897, but only those which survived into SR days need to be recorded here, and their numbers are as follows:

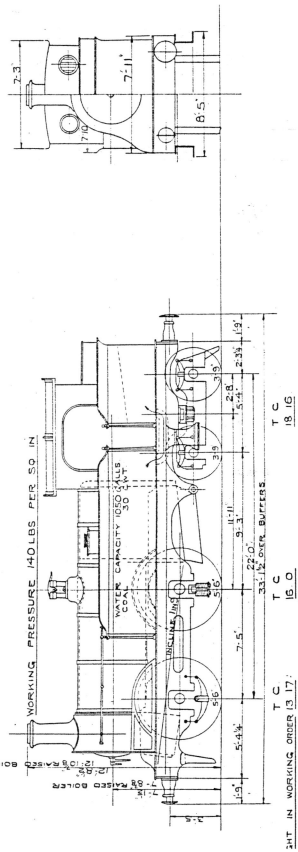

WORKING PRESSURE 140 LBS PER SQ IN
WATER CAPACITY 1050 GALLS
COAL 30 CWT
WEIGHT IN WORKING ORDER 13 17

Class Q, ex-SER 0-4-4T.
(Ashford dwg No.A20)

Class Q No.A26.

Class Q No.A422 (LH side).

Class Q No.23 at Bricklayers Arms in 1920.

Class Q No.410 (RH side).

Q1 class 0-4-4T

Mr Wainwright rebuilt 55 of the Q tanks into a Q1 version, these engines being fitted with H class boilers, which increased the height of the boiler centre and the pressure was raised from 140lbs to 150lbs per sq in. In the majority of the rebuilds, the sandboxes which were combined with the front splasher, were removed, and placed under the running plate. Of the 55 which formed the Q1 class, only 47 were taken into SR stock and were as follows:

SECR No.	Rebuilt	Withdrawn
12	1912	1927
50	1914	1926
58	1914	1926
76	1914	1927
81	1905	1928
83	1907	1928
85	1914	1927
95	1912	1926
115	1914	1928
134	1905	1926
138	1906	1927
141	1912	1926
146	1906	1928
168	1914	1926
200	1914	1928
224	1914	1925
343	1914	1926
344	1916	1926
347	1914	1927
348	1914	1925
350	1907	1927
351	1910	1925
354	1915	1925
355	1914	1927
357	1912	1926
359	1909	1926
361	1908	1929
362	1903	1929
363	1914	1926
364	1914	1930
365	1914	1928
366	1906	1926
367	1912	1930
400	1915	1929
402	1914	1926
403	1914	1926
404	1910	1927
406	1912	1928
408	1914	1929
411	1916	1928

SECR No.	Rebuilt	Withdrawn
412	1912	1929
413	1912	1926
415	1919	1926
416	1914	1926
419	1915	1926
420	1914	1927
423	1915	1926

Class Q1, ex-SER 0-4-4T. (Ashford dwg No.A21)

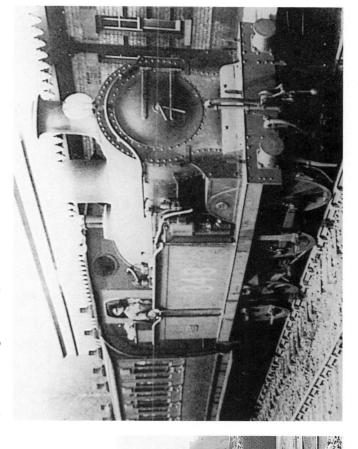

Class Q1 No.348.

Class Q1 No.184 (LH side).

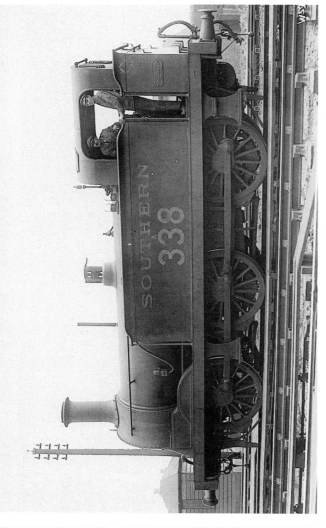

Class R (ex-SER) No.338 (LH side).

Class Q1 No.403 (LH side).

R class 0-6-0T

Not to be confused with the Kirtley R class of 0-4-4T engines, this R series was designed by Stirling mainly for shunting duties in Kent, and to some passenger work on the Eltham Valley and Whitstable branches. They were of 0-6-0T configuration, and were the first class of side tank, six coupled engines, to work on the SER, (apart from three earlier on the Folkestone Harbour branch). There were 25 in the order – all built at Ashford Works between 1888 and 1898, and used many standard parts such as the Q class boiler and the same frames as the O class goods engines. Originally they carried the rounded Stirling cab and so were the only Stirling engines on the SER of the tank variety to do so. Coupled wheels were 5ft 2in diameter, water tanks carried 750 gallons, and bunkers held just 35cwt of fuel. Six of the class were fitted later with a short N class chimney for working over the restricted gauge of the Whitstable branch.

Class R ex-SER 0-6-0T (Ashford dwg No A25)

Class **R** No.A155 at Folkestone Junction in 1927.

Class **R** No.A336 at Folkestone Harbour in 1927.

Class **R** No.A70 at Folkestone Junction, 1927.

Class **R** No.1070 (RH side), 1935.

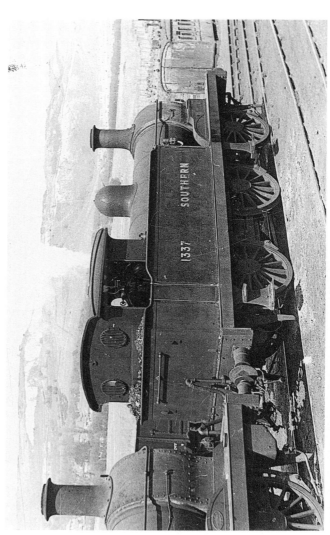

Class R1 (and Class P No.A555) at Dover Priory, 1927.

SER No.	Built	Rebuilt R1	Withdrawn
340	1889	1913	1959
342	1889		1931

*Short chimney fitted.
Final external condition of 31047, 31107, 31337: Tall chimney and dome, Wainwright cab.
Final external condition of 31128, 31340: Tall chimney low dome, Wainwright cab.
Final external condition of 31174: Tall chimney low dome and 'pop' safety valves.
Final external condition of 31010, 31147, 31339: Stove pipe chimney, 'pop' safety valves and Stirling cab.
Final external condition of 31069: Tall chimney and dome, Stirling cab.

SER No.	Built	Rebuilt R1	Withdrawn
126*	1895		1934
127	1895	1914	1949
128	1892	1913	1959
147*	1890	1912	1958
152	1892		1934
153	1892		1935
154	1892	1912	1955
155	1898		1939
174	1892	1914	1959
335	1888	1915	1955
336	1888		1941
337	1888	1922	1960
338	1888		1934
339	1889	1911	1959

Class R1 No.1337, Folkestone Junction, 1947.

Class R1 as BR No.31107, Folkestone Junction, 1954.

R1 class 0-6-0T

When Wainwright succeeded Stirling, many of the R class 0-6-0Ts were rebuilt with new boilers carrying domes, and the 'Pagoda' type cab. (Although one engine, No. 69 (1069), had the Stirling chimney and cab reinstated in 1943). Thirteen engines were so rebuilt and become the R1 class 0-6-0Ts.

Numbers were as follows (No. 341 has been omitted as this machine did not enter the SR records):

SER No.	Built	Rebuilt R1	Withdrawn
10*	1890	1913	1959
47	1895	1913	1960
69*	1898	1910	1958
70	1898		1942
77	1890		1932
107*	1898	1914	1959
124*	1892		1943
125	1895		1937

Class R1, BR No.31047, Folkestone Harbour, 1958.

Class R1, ex-SER 0-6-0T.
(Ashford dwg No.A26)

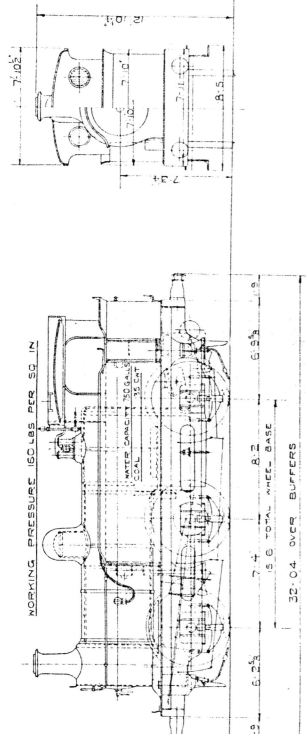

WORKING PRESSURE 160 LBS PER SQ IN

WATER CAPACITY 750 GALS

COAL 35 CWT

15.6 TOTAL WHEEL BASE

32.04 OVER BUFFERS

Class R1, ex-SER 0-6-0T.

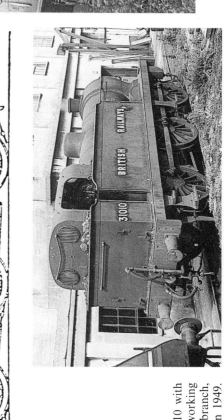

Class R1 BR No.31010.

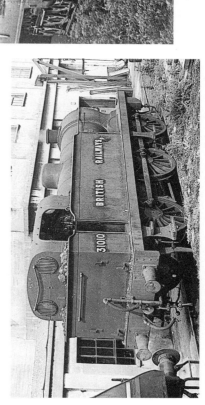

Class R1 No.31010 with cut-down cab for working the Whitstable branch, seen at Ashford in 1949.

Class R1, ex-SER 0-6-0T.
(Ashford dwg No.A26A)

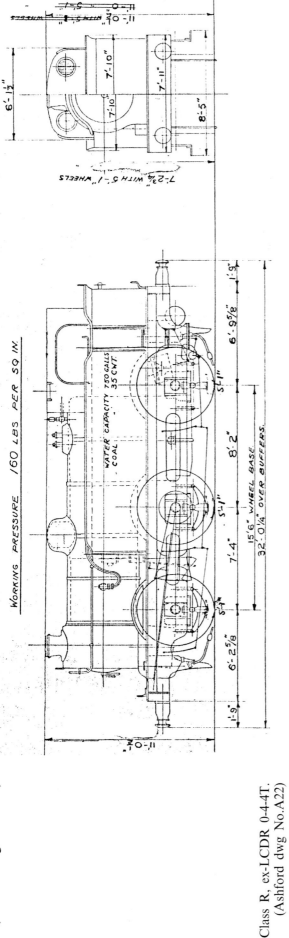

Class R, ex-LCDR 0-4-4T.
(Ashford dwg No.A22)

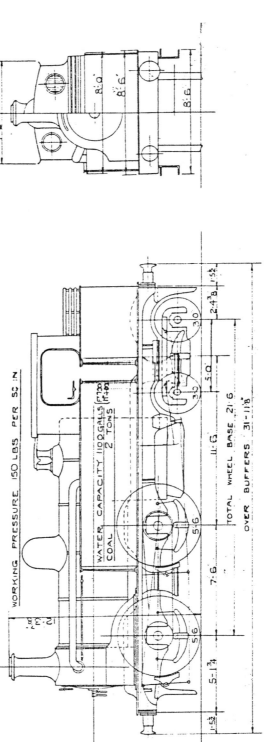

700 gallons. Fuel 2 tons. The whole class (including their sisters, the R1s), were built by Messrs Sharp, Stewart & Co.

SECR No.	Withdrawn
658*	1952
659*	1951
660*	1953
661	1955
662*	1953
663*	1953
664*	1940
665*	1952
666	1955
667*	1951
668*	1940
669*	1940
670*	1951
671*	1954
672*	1949
673	1952
674	1952
675*	1952

* Push-pull gear fitted 1947.

R class 0-4-4T

The R class of 0-4-4Ts was the last to be introduced by Kirtley in 1891. Eighteen were built in fact, and were very similar to the old A class, the minor differences were that the exhaust pipes from the smokebox led into the side tanks from the top, whereas the A class fed the exhaust steam into the tanks by the front of same. These same tanks had square tops, whereas the As were rounded, and the bunker tops were straight instead of the curve down from the cab side. Originally fitted with boilers 4ft 3in x 10ft, all except four eventually received the H class Wainwright type, 4ft 4in x 10ft 3½in. Coupled wheels were 5ft 6in, with bogie wheels 3ft diameter. Water tanks held

Class R (ex-LCDR) No.1661 (RH side), 1935.

R1 class 0-4-4T

This further batch of 0-4-4Ts, designed by Kirtley which were the last of his design constructed, were almost identical to the original Rs, except that the bogie wheels were larger by 6in. The bunker was also bigger, able to hold an extra

30cwts, and all 15 were dual fitted with Westinghouse and vacuum brakes when built. As with the Rs all in time received the Wainwright H boilers. All were built by Sharp, Stewart in 1900.

Class R No.A671 in 1928.

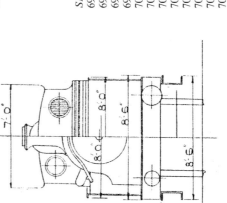

SECR No.	Withdrawn
696	1951
697*	1953
698	1955
699	1950
700*	1952
701	1929
702	1929
703*	1954
704*	1956
705	1951
706*	1952
707*	1949
708	1952
709	1949
710*	1951

*Fitted with push-pull gear.

Class R1 ex-LCDR 0-4-4T. (Ashford dwg No.A23)

Class R1 BR No.31703 with H class boiler.

Class R1 No.709 (RH side).

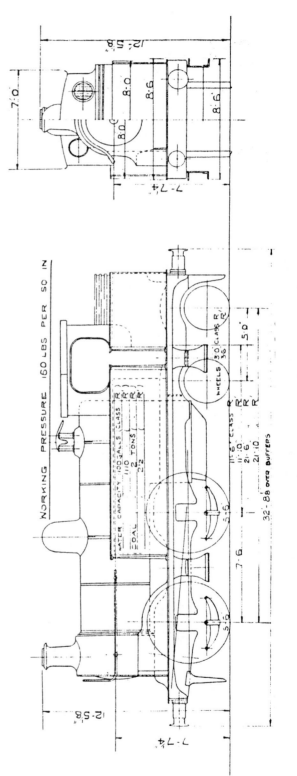

Class R1 ex-LCDR 0-4-4T. (Ashford dwg No.A24)

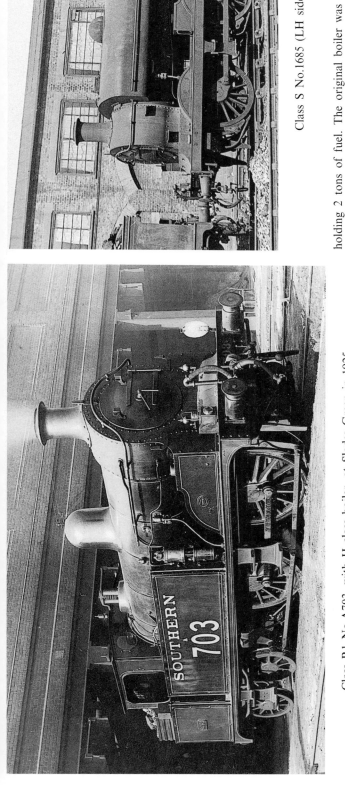

Class R1 No.A703, with H class boiler, at Slades Green in 1925.

S class 0-6-0ST

As mentioned in the C class detail, one engine, No. 685, was taken into shops under the instructions of Maunsell and converted into a saddle tank engine for shunting work. This was achieved by a complete strip down, the tender removed, and the main frames lengthened to accommodate a large enclosed cab and a coal bunker capable of

Class S No.1685 (LH side), Bricklayers Arms, 1946.

weight of 53 tons, and although quite successful and spending most of its working life at Bricklayers Arms, it was the one and only conversion from the C class goods.

SECR No.	Rebuilt	Withdrawn
685	1917	1951

holding 2 tons of fuel. The original boiler was replaced by one off No. 581, which had a new firebox and more up-to-date boiler fittings. A large saddle tank, extending from the cab front to the smokebox, and with a capacity of 1,200 gallons, was attached over the boiler. This rebuilding produced a locomotive with an increased adhesive

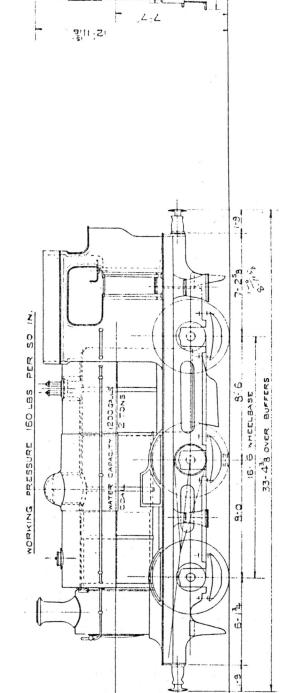

Class S 0-6-0ST. (Ashford dwg No.A27A)

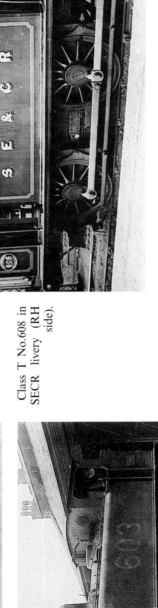

Class S No.685, as built (RH side).

Class T No.608 in SECR livery (RH side).

Class T No.603 (LH side).

work. These engines were fitted with 4ft 6in dia. wheels and had a boiler 4ft 0½in x 10ft in length, with a pressure of 150lbs. All were eventually reboilered and the pressure raised to 160lbs, and the whole class saw service on the SR. Some of the later engines had larger frames to accommodate a bigger bunker, and those fitted with Westinghouse brakes as an extra had the pump attached to an extended cab side sheet on the right-hand side. Water tanks held 830 gallons.

SECR No.	Built	Withdrawn
600	1879	1936 (Sold)
601	1879	1933
602	1893	1951
603	1893	1936
604	1891	1950
605	1890	1932
606	1891	1936
607	1890	1936
608	1889	1936 (Sold)
609	1891	1936

Nos 600 and 601 fitted with steam brakes only. No. A607 became 500S in Service Stock in 1938 at Meldon Quarry.

T class 0-6-0T

The ten T class engines, designed by Kirtley, and built at Longhedge Works between 1879 and 1893, were expressly for shunting duties and local goods

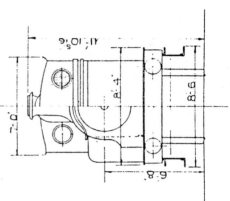
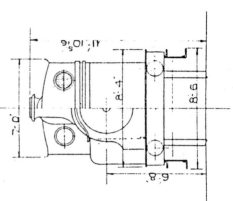

WORKING PRESSURE 160 LBS PER SQ IN

WATER CAPACITY 830 GALLS.

COAL 1½ TONS.

TOTAL WHEEL BASE 15'.0

OVER BUFFERS 28.11⅝

Class T, ex-LCDR 0-6-0T. (Ashford dwg No.A28)

Crane Tank No.1302 (LH side) at Longhedge, 1946.

Crane Tank No.A234S (RH side).

Miscellaneous Engines.
0-4-0 Crane Tank No. 302

This small crane engine was built by Messrs Neilson & Co. in 1881 and was used at Ashford Works. Of limited capacity (it could only lift 2½ tons), nevertheless, the engine had a long life. The driving wheels were 3ft 3in diameter and cylinders were 11in x 20in. The original number was 302, renumbered into the Service Stock List as A234S, and in 1938, became No. 1302, its old number plus 1000. It was active at Folkestone Harbour, Stewarts Lane and Lancing Carriage Works, and was finally condemned in 1949. Another similar engine, No. 409 (later A235S) was scrapped in 1935.

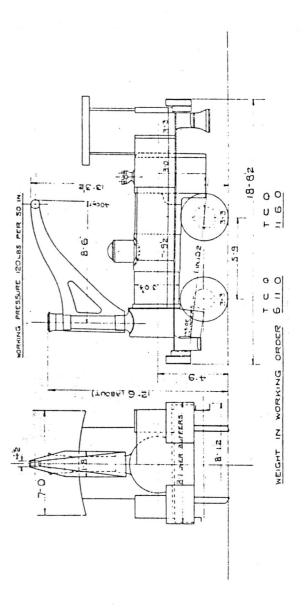

Ex-SER 0-4-0 crane tank. (Ashford dwg No.A33)

"Terrier" No.751 (ex-LBSCR No.54 Waddon) at Ashford, 1925.

Ex-LBSCR A1 class 0-6-0T No. 751

The SECR's "Terrier" was LBSCR No. 54 *Waddon* changing hands in 1904, and reboilered in 1910. Into SR stock at 1923, a major refit in 1932 and given service number 680S. Ended service at Lancing Works. Repainted LBSCR colours at Eastleigh and now preserved in Canada.

0-6-0 Saddle Tank No. 353

Used for shunting at Ashford Works. Built 1890. Renumbered A236S in Service Stock. (Never carried the Service number.) Withdrawn 1929 and scrapped 1932.

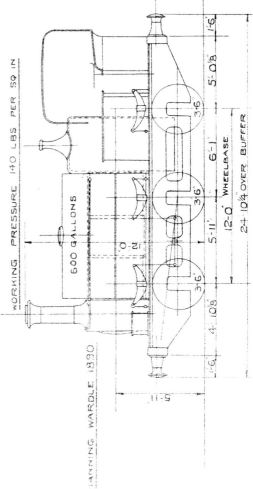

Manning Wardle 0-6-0ST ex-SER, No.353. (Ashford dwg No.A30)

Manning, Wardle 0-6-0 saddle tank No.353 (LH side).

Ex-LBSCR A1 class "Terrier" No.751 at Eastbourne, 1932 (LH side).

SOUTHERN RAILWAY (EASTERN SECTION)

0·6·0 TANK ENGINE

SCALE ¼" = 1 FT.

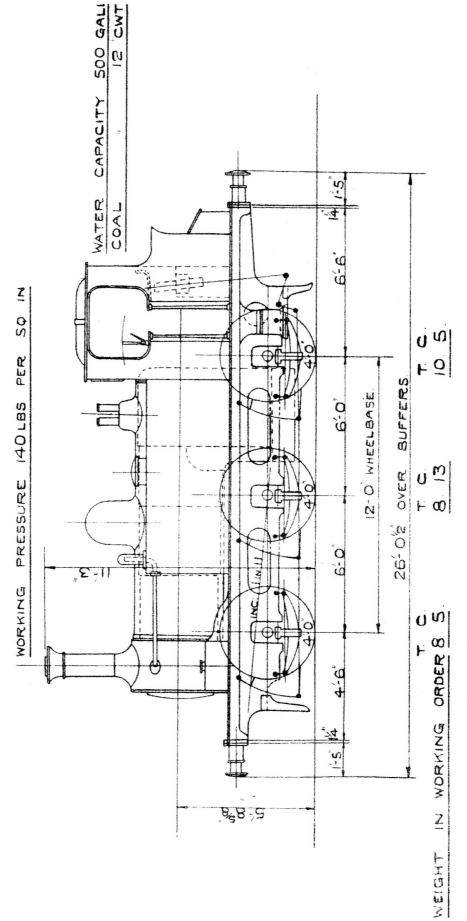

WORKING PRESSURE 140 LBS PER SQ IN

WATER CAPACITY 500 GALL
COAL 12 CWT

	T.C.	T.C.	T.C.	T.C.
WEIGHT IN WORKING ORDER	8 5	8 13	10 5	

TOTAL WEIGHT OF ENGINE IN WORKING ORDER 27 TONS 3 CWT.

Ex-LBSCR A1 class 0-6-0T, No.751. (Ashford dwg No.A31)

Departmental Locomotive No.225S at Okehampton in 1928.

0-4-0 Saddle Tank Dock Shunting Engine No. 313

One other small engine should be mentioned here although no drawing is to hand. Purchased by James Stirling in 1881 from Messrs Manning Wardle & Co. for service as a docks shunter at Folkestone Harbour, this little locomotive was an 0-4-0ST with outside cylinders size 10in x 16in, coupled wheels were 2ft 10in diameter, and the boiler 2ft 8in pressed for 120lbs. Water capacity was 450 gallons and fuel 8cwt. Originally fitted with a tall copper-topped chimney, it was reboilered in 1905.

In 1925, the locomotive was given new cylinders and smokebox, plus a plain chimney and re-numbered A225S. It was sent to the Engineering Dept. at Meldon Quarries, and finally scrapped at Eastleigh in 1938.

0-6-0 Saddle Tank No. 752

Purchased in 1905 for shunting services at Folkestone Harbour, this little engine was a product of the Manning Wardle factory who built it in 1879. Originally open cab, the roof was fitted in 1905. It was reboilered in 1911, and only just saw service on the Southern Railway being sold in 1925 to Northfleet Deep Water Wharf Ltd.
Cylinders 12in x 17in, wheels 3ft 2in, Boiler 2ft 10in diameter. Pressure 120lbs. Water 430 gallons. Coal 12½cwt.

Departmental Locomotive No.225S at Meldon Quarry in 1928. (Formerly at Folkestone Harbour, No.313).

Departmental Locomotive No.752 at Ashford in 1925.

Part Two

Central Section – Prefix 'B'

A1/A1x class 0-6-0T

The Stroudley 0-6-0T "Terriers". When Wm Stroudley first designed these diminutive tank engines it was with the need to produce a small, lightweight, versatile little machine, which could tackle the traffic on the far from robust tracks of the East and South London suburban lines. The original version was the A class, but as only two of these (re-classified as A1) came into the SR from the LBSCR, compared with 17 of the rebuilt A1x class, the former only need a brief description.

They were tiny engines as can be seen by the drawing. The six coupled wheels were 4ft diameter, the boiler 3ft 6in x 7ft 10in pressed for 140lbs, the side tanks held 500 galls and the coal space held only 1 ton of fuel. Fifty engines were built between 1872 and 1880.

Some of the A class were reboilered by Marsh in 1911 and so became A1x class. These engines so dealt with between the years 1911 and 1922, outwardly differed only slightly from the originals in that the new boilers were constructed in one ring and the tube plate was of the drum head type, the position of the steam dome was the indication of reboilering, as it was further ahead than previously. The smokebox, being circular, rested on a saddle, and the Stroudley type sandboxes were removed, the new ones being under the running plate. The particular engines so dealt with and which were taken into the Southern Railway are as under.

Original LBSCR No.	LBSCR Name	Renumbered	Disposal from LBSCR	BR No.	Withdrawn
68	Clapham	668	To L.S.W.R. No 735. later S.R. E735		1936
69*	Peckham	669	To IWCR No. 10		1936
72*	Fenchurch	636	To Newhaven Hbr Co. To SR 1927	32636	1963
75	Blackwall		To IWR No. 9		1926
77*	Wonersh	677	To IWR No.3; later No.13	32677	1959
78*	Knowle	678	To IWR No. 4, later No. 14	32678	1963
80*	Bookham	680	SR		1926
82	Boxhill	682	SR No. 380S		1946
84*	Crowborough	-	To IWCR No. 12		1936

*Reboilered to become A1x class.
No. 54 is preserved in Canada.
No. 55 preserved on the Bluebell Railway.
No. 61 preserved on the KESR.
No. 62 is preserved at Bressingham Steam Museum, Norfolk.
No. 72 sold in 1898, returned to SR in 1927. Now preserved on the Bluebell Railway.
No. 78 now preserved on the KESR.
No. 82 is preserved in the National Collection.
(See also Part Five for Isle of Wight locomotives.)
Also, No. 70 was withdrawn by the LBSCR prior to Grouping and was sold to the Kent & East Sussex Railway, passing to BR at Nationalisation as No. 32670, so this locomotive was never in fact owned by the Southern Railway and therefore has not been included in the lists.

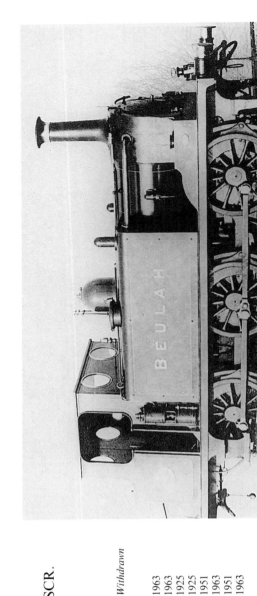

Class A1 No.81 *Beulah* in original LBSCR livery.

Brighton "Terriers" – Classes A1 and A1x List of disposals from LBSCR. (Eventually to Southern Railway and elsewhere).

Original LBSCR No.	LBSCR Name	Renumbered	Disposal from LBSCR	BR No.	Withdrawn
35*	Morden	635	SR	DS377/32635	1963
40*	Brighton	-	To IWCR No.11	32640	1963
42	Tulsehill	642	SR		1925
43*	Gipsyhill	643	To WCPR later GWR No.5		1925
44*	Fulham	644	SR	32644	1951
46	Newington	646	To LSWR No 734; FYNR No.2	32646	1963
47*	Cheapside	647	SR		1951
50*	Whitechapel	650	To IWR No. W9; returned to Lancing	515S/32650	1963
53*	Ashstead	653	To WCPR later GWR No. 6		1937
54	Waddon	654	To SECR No. 751 SR No. 680S	DS680	1962
55*	Stepney	655	SR	32655	1960
59*	Cheam	659	SR	32659/DS681	1963
61*	Sutton	661	SR	32661	1963
62*	Martello	662	SR	32662	1963
63	Preston	663	SR		1925

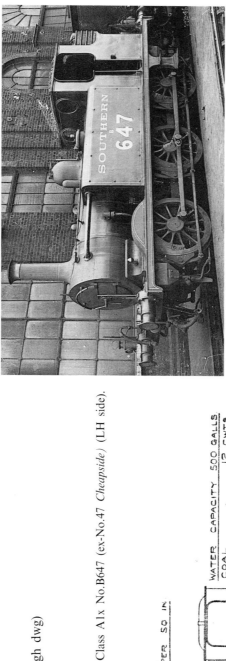

Class A1 No.659, formerly No.59 *Cheam* (RH side).

Class A1x No.B647 (ex-No.47 *Cheapside*) (LH side).

Class A1 0-6-0T. (Eastleigh dwg)

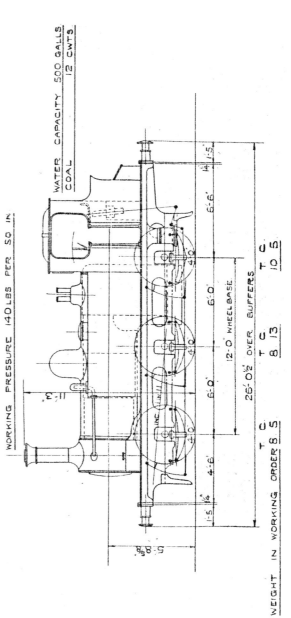

Class A1x No.2636, originally No.72 *Fenchurch*. PAGE 69

WORKING PRESSURE 150 LBS PER SQ IN.

1 TON COAL

113 TUBES 1¾ DIA

7'-10" BARREL

4'-7 FIREBOX

6'-0"

6'-0"

12'-0"

26'-0½"

T.C. 8-10.

T.C. 9-0.

T.C. 8-10.

WATER CAPACITY 500 GALLS
COAL 12 CWTS

WORKING PRESSURE 140 LBS PER SQ IN.

WEIGHT IN WORKING ORDER 8 5

12'-0 WHEELBASE

26'-0½" OVER BUFFERS

4'-6'

6'-0"

6'-0"

6'.6"

14'-5"

T.C. 8 5

T.C. 8 13

T.C. 10 5

Class A1 0-6-0T

Original LBSCR No.	Name	Built	Renumbered	Withdrawn
223	Balcombe	1885		1925
224	Crowhurst	1885		1940
225	Ashburne	1885		1925
226	Westham	1885		1940
227	Heathfield	1885		1939
228	Seaford	1884		1933
229	Dorking	1884	700S 10/47	1947
230	Brookhouse	1884		1926
231	Horsham	1884		1933
232	Lewes	1884		1944
233	Handcross	1883		1944
234	Rottingdean	1881		1950
235	Broadwater	1881		1949
236	Ardingly	1881		1926
237	Cuckfield	1881		1940
238	Lindfield	1881		1925
239	Patcham	1881		1948
240	Ditchling	1881		1946
241	Stanmer	1881		1933
242	Ringmer	1881		1925
243	Ovingdean	1881		1925
244	Hassocks	1881		1949
245	Withdean	1881		1926
246	Bramber	1881		1926
247	Arlington	1881		1938
248	Ashurst	1881		1933
249	Hilsea	1881		1938
250	Hoathly	1881		1925
251	Singleton	1881		1926
252	Buckhurst	1882		1950
253	Pelham	1882		1949
254	Hambledon	1882		1940
255	Willingdon	1882		1947
256	Standford	1882		1933
257	Brading	1882		1926
258	Cosham	1882		1926
259	Telford (Barnham from 1898)	1882		1948
260	Lavington	1882		1946
261	Wigmore	1882		1938
262	Oxted	1882		1933
264	Langston	1882		1926
265	Chipstead	1882		1926
266	Charlwood	1882		1934
267	Maresfield	1882		1935
268	Baynards	1880		1926
269	Crawley	1880		1948
270	Warnham	1880		1940
271	Eridge	1880		1928
272	Nevill (Goring from 1897)	1880		1925
273	Dornden	1880		1936
274	Guildford	1879		1950
275	Cranleigh	1879		1940
276	Rudgwick	1879		1935
277	Slinfold	1879		1926
278	Groombridge	1879		1926
279	Tunbridge Wells	1879		1936

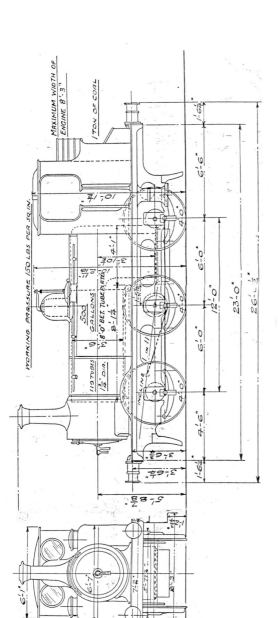

Class A1x 0-6-0T. (Brighton dwg No.B1)

D1 class 0-4-2T

There were 125 engines of this class built between 1873 and 1887, 112 of which survived into SR ownership. They were built mainly for handling the London suburban traffic, being more powerful than the A class tanks. Upon reboilering the position of the dome was on the back ring and the manhole over the firebox was dispensed with. During Marsh's period, many engines were fitted with 'push-pull' gear for working 'Auto trains' and known as class D1/M. Nine of the class were fitted with a steam pump for fire-fighting in the Second World War. The pump was erected over the rear buffer beam, and three suction hoses, 20ft long, were carried on the front buffer beams. The particular engines were: Nos 2215, 2239, 2244, 2252, 2253, 2357, 2220 and 2260 (1931 renumbering). It might be of interest to note that during the war period, one engine, No. 2699, was reported working at Wick in the far north of Scotland. Four others, Nos. 276, 359, 612 and 633, were altered by reducing the water tanks to 580 gallons, and the coal bunker to 1 ton, intended for the Lyme Regis branch, but to no avail.

Original LBSCR No.	Name	Built	Renumbered	Withdrawn
1	Sydenham	1873	684 2/07	1926
2	Wandsworth	1873	75 3/07, 298 4/09	1933
5	Streatham	1874	605 2/07	1948
6	Wimbledon	1874	76 3/07, 299 4/09	1949
12	Wallington	1874	612 2/07	1934
13	Pimlico	1874	77 3/07, 77A 10/09, 347 9/13, 214 8/20	1933
14	Chelsea	1874	614 3/07	1936
15	Brompton	1875	615 2/07	1937
16	Silverdale	1875	616 2/07	1938
17	Dulwich	1875	617 2/07	1926
18	Stockwell	1875	78 2/07, 78A 11/09, 348 3/13, 215 8/20	1950
20	Carshalton	1875	79 2/07, 79A 11/09, 349 6/13, 216 12/20	1933
23	Mayfield	1875	623 8/08	1934
24	Brambletye	1875	624 8/08	1925
25	Rotherfield	1876	625 8/08	1940
26	Hartfield	1876	626 8/08	1940
27	Uckfield	1876	627 8/08	1943
29	Lambeth	1876	628 4/09	1936
31	Borough	1876	629 4/09	1940
32	Walworth	1876	80 6/08, 80A 11/09, 350 9/13, 217 9/20	1933
33	Mitcham	1876	633 12/08	1944
34	Balham	1876	634 12/08	1926
35	Southwark	1876	298 5/78, 698 4/09	1923
36	New Cross	1876	299 5/78, 699 3/09	1948
221	Warbleton	1885		1940
222	Cuckmere	1885		1923

Original LBSCR No.	Name	Built	Renumbered	Withdrawn
280	Grinstead	1879		1926
281	Withyham	1879		1926
282	Rowfant	1879		1936
283	Aldgate	1879		1948
284	Ashburnham	1879	701S 10/47	1951
285	Holmwood	1879		1926
286	Ranmore	1879		1948
287	Buryhill	1879		1925
288	Effingham	1879		1937
289	Holmbury	1879		1948
290	Denbies	1879		1936
291	Deepdene	1879		1926
292	Leigham	1877		1926
293	Norbury	1877		1925
294	Rosebery (Falmer from 1897)	1877		1936
295	Whippingham	1877		1937
296	Osborne (Peckham from 1901)	1877		1933
297	Bonchurch	1877		1937
351	Chailey	1886		1927
352	Lavant	1886	218 9/20	1933
353	Keymer	1886	219 12/20	1946
354	Lancing	1886	220 12/20	1925
355	Worthing	1886		1946
356	Coulsdon	1886		1940
357	Riddlesdown	1886		1947
358	Henfield	1886		1948
359	Egmont	1886		1951
360	Leconfield	1887		1927
361	Upperton	1887		1948
362	Kidbrooke	1887		1927

Nos 233 to 267 built by Neilson, all others at Brighton.
Nos 700S and 701S modified to pump oil for oil burning locomotives.
Dimensions of D1 class
Couple wheels 5ft 6in. dia. Trailing wheels 4ft 6in.
Boiler 4ft x 10ft 2in
Water 860 gallons
Fuel 1½ Tons

Class D1 No.239 *Patcham* in original LBSCR livery (RH side).

Class D1 No.255 *Willingdon* in original livery (LH side).

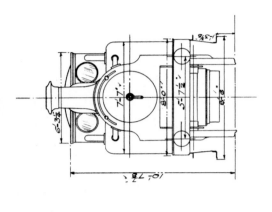

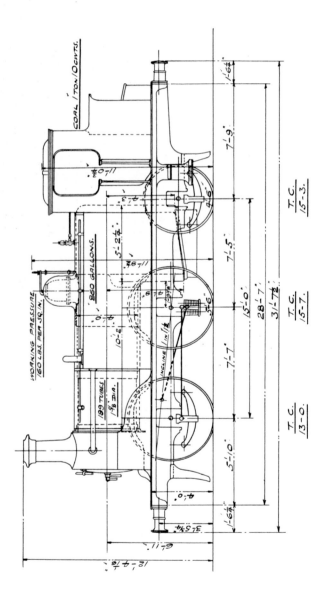

Class D1 0-4-2T. (Brighton dwg No.B19)

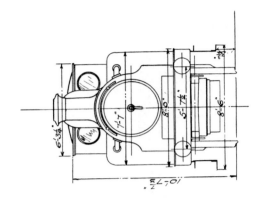

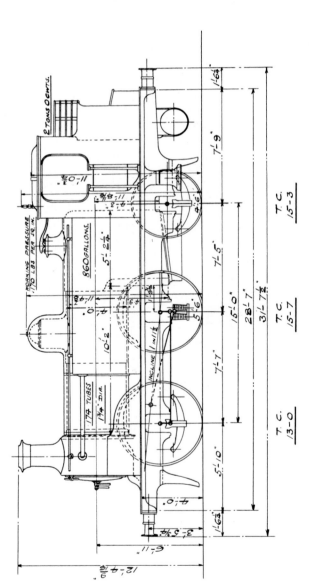

Class D1 0-4-2T. (Brighton dwg No.B20)

Class D1 No.245, formerly *Withdean* at Brighton, 1925.

Class D1 No.249, formerly *Hilsea.*

Class D1 No.B234 at Eastleigh in 1931.

Class D1 No.2623 (ex-No.23 *Mayfield*) at Fratton, 1931.

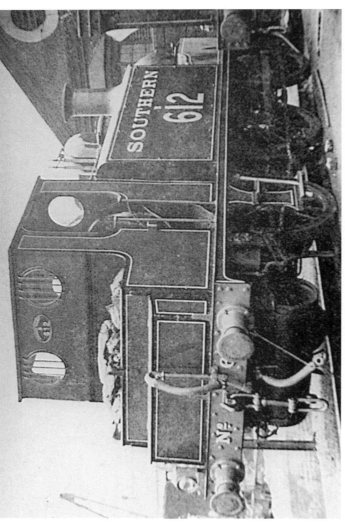

Class D1 No.B612, minus coal rails.

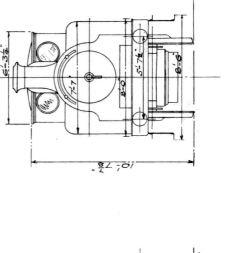

Class D1 No.626, Clapham Junction, 1921.

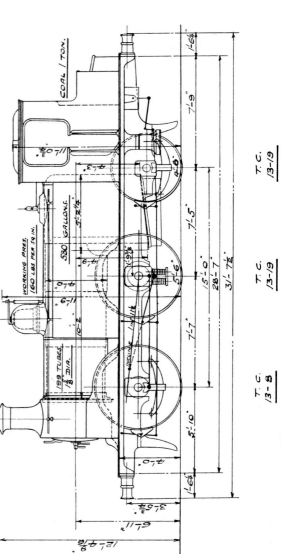

Class D1 0-4-2T. (Brighton dwg No.B21)

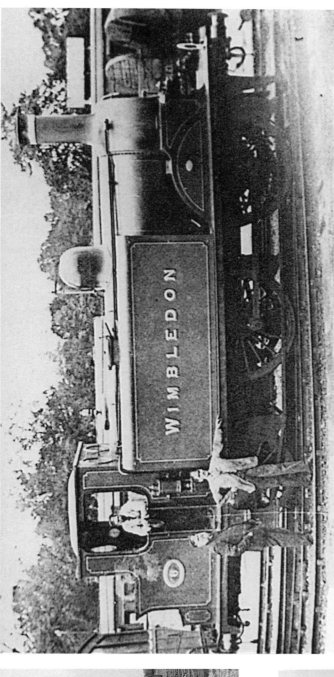

Class D1 LBSCR No.6 *Wimbledon* (RH side).

Class D1x LBSCR No.A79, originally D1 class No.20 *Carshalton*, later Nos 349 and 216.

Class D1 No.2282 at Eastleigh in 1933.

Class D1 SR No.2235 (LH side).

D1x class 0-4-2T

Only one engine of the D1 class was fitted with an enlarged Marsh type boiler, which gave it the x suffix. This boiler was 10ft 7in long, and of 4ft 6in diameter, and resulted in increased height measurements, even the cab roof was 8½in higher. No. 20 'Carsharlton', was renumbered to 79, then 79A, followed by 349, and finally became 216, and was withdrawn in 1933.

B1 class 0-4-2

The D2 class, from the Stroudley stable, was really a tender-ised version of the D1. They had the same coupled wheels, cylinders and motion, but as none of the 14 built lasted into the SR era, they do not concern this summary, only in that they led to the evolution of the D3 class in 1878-1880. These in their turn brought about the slightly more powerful 'Gladstone' class, designated eventually B1.

As the D3 class tender engines were all withdrawn by 1905, we can move onto the 'Gladstones'. Much more powerful than the D3s by virtue of 18¼in diameter cylinders and larger boiler, they were created originally for handling the Brighton expresses which were getting heavier and faster. There were 36 built between the years of 1882 and 1891. In 1906 a start was made by Marsh to reboiler these engines, and although the dimensions were the same, they could be identified by the Ramsbottom safety valves and larger dome. All these engines originally carried names on the trailing driver-splasher, locomotives that carried over into Southern ownership were as follows:

LBSCR No.	Name	Built	Withdrawn
172	Littlehampton	1891	1933
173	Cottesloe	1891	1927
174	Fratton	1890	1930
175	Hayling	1890	1926
176	Pevensey	1890	1929
177	Southsea	1890	1927
179	Sandown	1890	1929
180	Arundel	1890	1925
181	Croydon	1890	1929
183	Eastbourne	1889	1929
184	Carew D. Gilbert	1889	1932
185	George A. Wallis	1889	1923
187	Philip Rose	1889	1931
188	Allen Sarle	1889	1925
190	Arthur Otway	1888	1930
191	Gordon-Lenox	1888	1930
192	Jacomb-Hood	1888	1927
193	Fremantle	1888	1930
194	Bickersteth	1888	1931
197	Jonas Levy	1888	1931
198	Sheffield	1887	1931
199	Samuel Laing	1887	1925
200	Beresford	1887	1929
214	Gladstone	1882	1927
217	Northcote	1883	1927
219	Cleveland	1885	1928

No. 214 is now preserved in the National Collection.

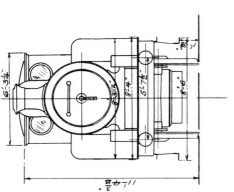

Class D1x 0-4-2T. (Brighton dwg No.B22)

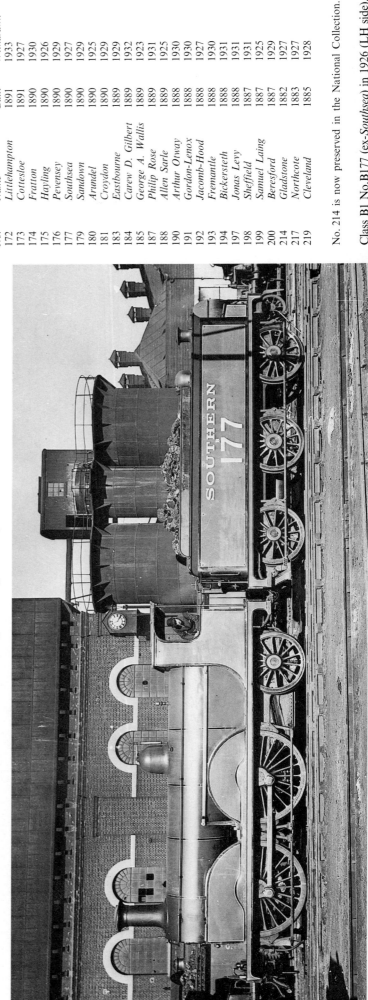

Class B1 No.B177 (ex-*Southsea*) in 1926 (LH side).

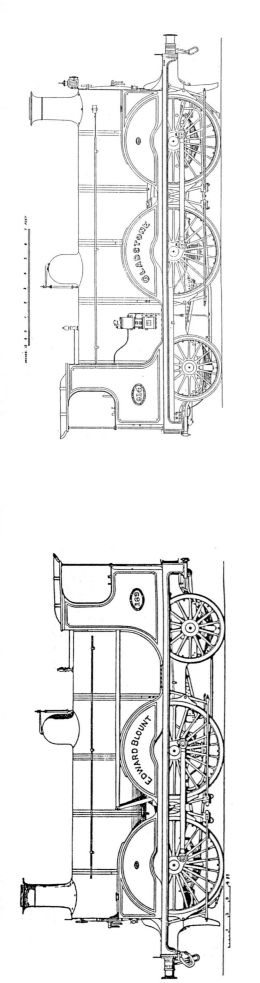

Class B1 0-4-2 (RH side).

Class B1 0-4-2.

Class B1 No.B172 (ex-*Littlehampton*) in 1929.   PAGE 77

Class B1 0-4-2 (LH side).

C1 class 0-6-0

In this same period Stroudley designed and introduced a six-wheeled coupled freight engine with wheels of 5ft diameter, and cylinders the same size as the 'Gladstones'. There were twelve built between 1882 and 1887, but only one survived into the SR at the Grouping, being No. 430, which was scrapped in 1925. This engine's claim to fame was that in 1914 it hauled a troop train from Brighton right through to the Great Northern Railway at Doncaster. A sister engine, No. 428, went to the Stratford-on-Avon & Midland Junction Railway in 1920 and was taken into L.M.S. stock in 1923 and withdrawn in 1925.

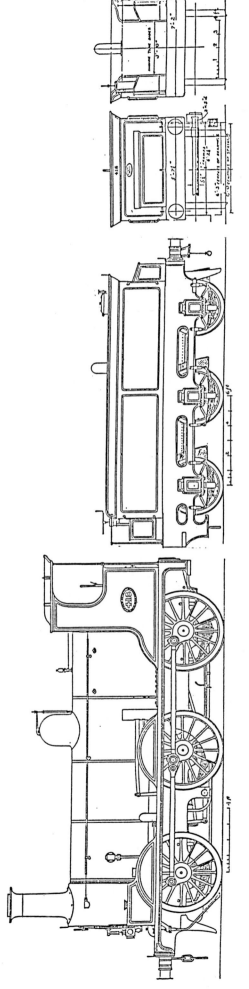

Class C1 0-6-0.

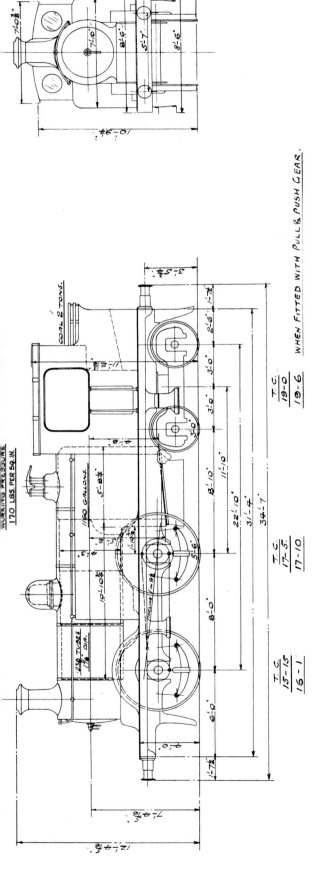

Class D3 0-4-4T. (Brighton dwg No.B23)

LBSCR No.	LBSCR Name	Built	Withdrawn
367	Norwood	1892	1949
368	Newport	1892	1953
369	Burgess Hill	1892	1933
370	Haywards Heath	1892	1948
371	Angmering	1892	1948
372	Amberley	1892	1953
373	Billingshurst	1893	1948
374	Pulborough	1893	1949
375	Glynde	1893	1935
376	Folkington	1893	1953
377	Hurstpierpoint	1893	1948
378	Horsted Keynes	1893	1952
379	Sanderstead	1893	1952
380	Thornton Heath	1893	1953
381	Fittleworth	1893	1933
382	Farlington	1893	1934
383	Three Bridges	1893	1948
384	Cooksbridge	1893	1953
385	Portsmouth	1894	1953
386	Chichester	1894	1952
387	Steyning	1894	1949
388	Emsworth	1894	1951
389	Shoreham	1894	1949
390	St. Leonards	1894	1955
391	Drayton	1894	1952
392	Polegate	1894	1933
393	Woodside	1896	1951
394	Cowfold	1896	1951
395	Gatwick	1896	1949
396	Clayton	1896	1937
397	Bexhill	1896	1948
398	Haslemere	1896	1949

D3 class 0-4-4T

Not to be confused with the Stroudley D3 passenger tender engines, this class of 36 passenger tank engines, was designed by R. J. Billinton for the longer distance trains from London to Tunbridge Wells and the south coast. Built between 1892 and 1896, they had coupled wheels of 5ft 6in diameter, a 4ft 3in diameter boiler by 10ft 11in in length, with the usual Stroudley type fittings. Later, Marsh reboilered many with his own type of boiler, with the Marsh chimney and Ramsbottom safety valves. The whole class saw service with the Southern Railway and a complete name and number list is appended. One small anecdote concerning No. 365 *Victoria*, is that on 28th November 1942 a German aircraft dived down low, whilst the train was proceeding along the coast, and machine-gunned the engine. However, whilst so doing the aeroplane actually touched the steam dome of No. 2365, and it was the aircraft that crashed, while the locomotive and its crew survived! Two of the class, Nos. 396 and 397, were altered to D3x in 1909.

LBSCR No.	LBSCR Name	Built	Withdrawn
363	Goldsmid	1892	1947
364	Truscott	1892	1952
365	Victoria	1892	1952
366	Crystal Palace	1892	1949

Class D3 BR No.32372, originally No.372 *Amberley*.

Class D3 No.2367 (LH side) in 1934.

Class D3 No.B381 at Redhill in 1932.

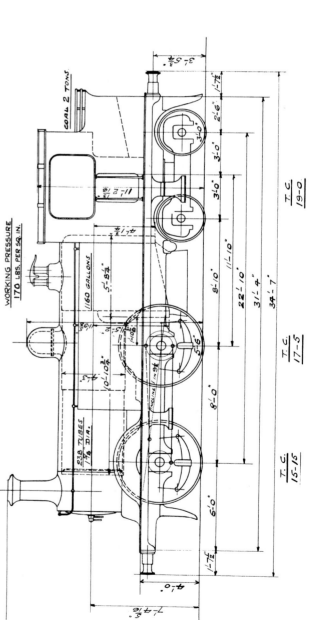

Class D3 0-4-4T. (Brighton dwg No B26)

Class D3 No.B375 in 1928.

Class D3 No.B393 in 1927 (RH side).

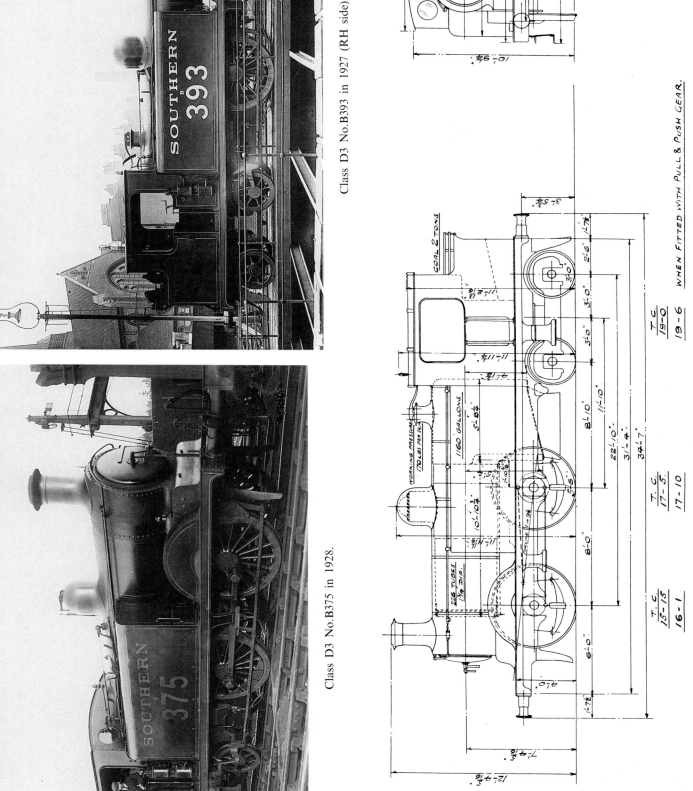

Class D3 0-4-4T. (Brighton dwg No.B24)

D3x class 0-4-4T

Nos 396 and 397, *Clayton* and *Bexhill* respectively, were the two engines chosen from the D3 class to be fitted with new boilers in 1909. They entered into Southern ownership therefore as a class of two, classified D3x. They were given boilers which were the same dimensions as the 12 class, made in two rings, and of 4ft 6in over the largest diameter. The working pressure was raised from 160 to 170lbs and the cylinders, which were originally 18in were replaced by two of 17½in diameter. Being a much larger boiler, the height of the engine was raised by 3½in which included the driving cab. Although the rebuilds were more powerful than the original design, only the two machines were so altered. No. B396 which became 2396 after 1931 was withdrawn in 1937 and B397, renumbered 2397 after 1931 was withdrawn in 1948.

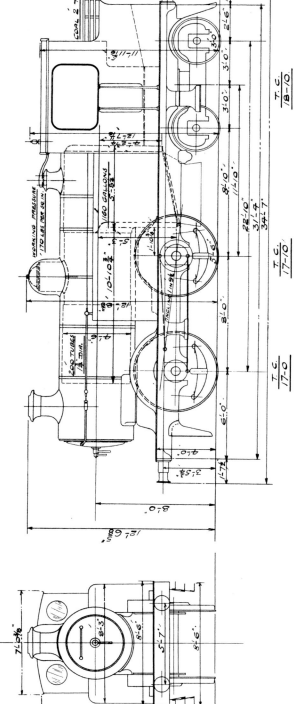

Class D3x 0-4-4T. (Brighton dwg No.B25)

Class D3x No 397 (RH side)

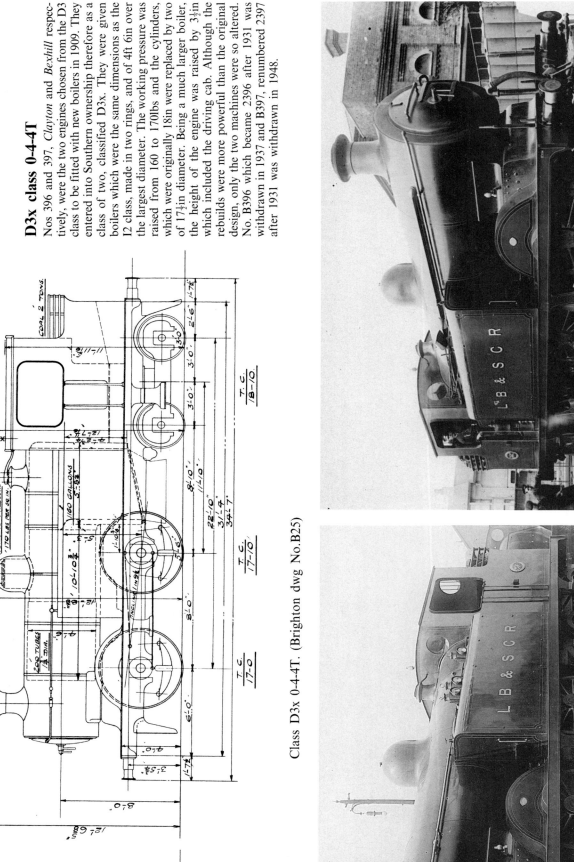

Class D3x No.396 (LH side).

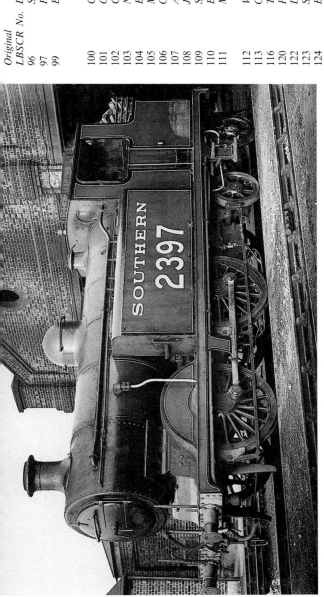

Class D3x SR No.2397, 1935.

E1 class 0-6-0T

Stroudley introduced this design for use with goods trains, either local, or short distance freights. The boilers, cylinders and motion were interchangeable with the D class engines, but the main difference, apart from the Ds being 0-4-2Ts and these being 0-6-0Ts, was in the driving wheel diameter. That of the E1 being 4ft 6in compared with the 5ft 3in of the D class tanks. Also the water capacity of the E1 was 50 gallons more than the D1 and more coal could be carried (1¾ Tons). Seventy-nine of the class were built at Brighton and 63 were taken over into Southern ownership, notwithstanding that one had been rebuilt as an E1x in 1911. (This was No. 89, later 689, B689 and finally 2689.) Ten engines were later converted to 0-6-2T E1R class. Four of these E1 locomotives were transferred to the Isle of Wight section and were No. 136 Brindisi, renumbered in 1932 W1 and renamed Medina; No. 152 Hungary became W2 Yarmouth; No. 154 Madrid became W3 Ryde, and No. 131 Epernay became W4 Wroxall. When shipped to the Island, all four were carrying Drummond type chimneys.

Original LBSCR No.	LBSCR Name	Built Brighton	Renumbered	Rebuilt as E1R	Withdrawn
85	Cannes	1883	685 4/12		1926
86	Geneva	1883	686 6/12		1925
87	Bologna	1883	687 6/12		1925
89	Brest	1883	89A 10/11, 689 12/12 To E1X 1911	1930	1960
90	Berne	1883	690 12/12		1950
91	Fishbourne	1883	691 11/11		1951
92	Polesden	1883			1936
94	Shorwell	1883		1927	1955
95	Luccombe	1883		1927	1956

Original LBSCR No.	LBSCR Name	Built Brighton	Renumbered	Rebuilt as E1R	Withdrawn
96	Salzberg	1883		1928	1956
97	Honfleur	1874			1949
99	Bordeaux	1874	610 6/22 Loco Dept. Brighton 3/09 to 6/22	1929	1956
100	Calvados	1875			1926
101	Orleans	1875			1924
102	Cherbourg	1875	692 5/13		1961
103	Normandy	1876	693 5/13		1957
104	Brittany	1876	694 10/13	1928	1956
105	Morlaix	1876	695 10/13	1928	1959
106	Guernsey	1876	696 10/13	1929	1956
107	Alderney	1876	697 4/15		1934
108	Jersey	1876	606 4/15	1928	1957
109	Strasbourg	1877	607 1/16		1948
110	Burgundy	1877	608 1/16		1927
111	Montpelier	1877	609 9/16		1932
112	Versailles	1877	611 6/22 Loco Dept. New Cross 6/08 to 6/22		1949
113	Granville	1877	Renamed Durdans 12/83		1958
116	Touraine	1877			1926
120	Provence	1877			1925
122	Leghorn	1878			1948
123	Seine	1878			1925
124	Bayonne	1878		1928	1959
125	Navarre	1878			1926
126	Gascony	1878			1925
127	Potiers	1878			1949
128	Avignon	1878			1952
129	Alencon	1878			1957
131	Gournay	1878	W4 Wroxall		1960
132	Epernay	1878			1926
133	Picardy	1878			1952
135	Foligno	1879			1959
136	Brindisi	1879	W1 Medina	1928	1957
137	Dijon	1879			1933
138	Macon	1879			1956
139	Lombardy	1879			1959
140	Toulouse	1879			1925
141	Mentone	1879			1949
142	Toulon	1879			1950
143	Nuremberg	1879			1936
144	Chambery	1879			1936
145	France	1880			1951
147	Danube	1880			1951
150	Adriatic	1880			1925
151	Helvetia	1880			1960
152	Hungary	1880	W2 Yarmouth		1956
153	Austria	1881			1949
154	Madrid	1881	W3 Ryde		1959
156	Munich	1881			1951
159	Edenbridge	1891			1930
160	Portslade	1891			1951
161	Aldrington	1891			1925
162	Southwater	1891			1949
163	Southwick	1891			1932
164	Spithead	1891			1948

No. 110 sold to industry and now preserved on the East Somerset Railway.

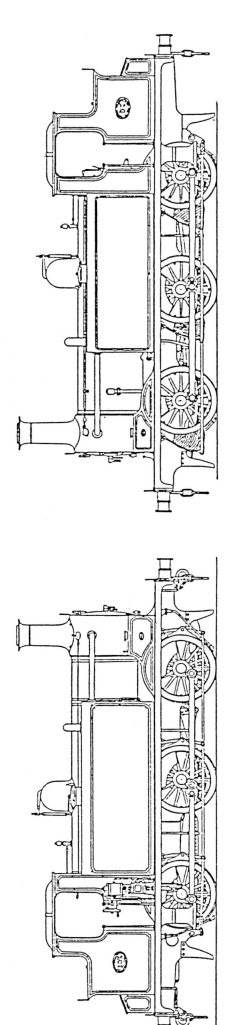

Class E1 0-6-0T

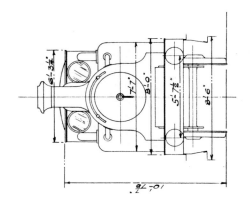

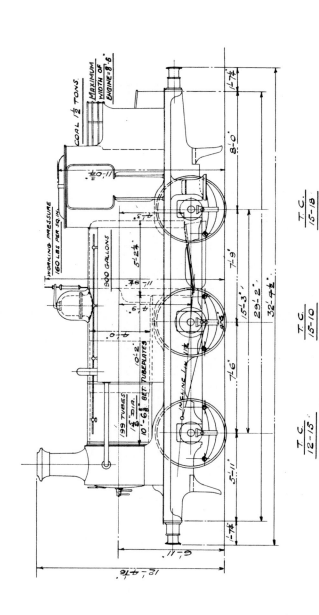

Class E1 0-6-0T (Brighton dwg No B28)

Class E1 LBSCR No.143 *Nuremberg.*

Class E1 LBSCR No.122 *Leghorn.*

E1/R class 0-6-2T

In 1927-28, Maunsell then CME of the SR, took ten of the E1 class, and to relieve the weight on the coupled wheels, fitted a radial pony truck under an extended bunker. The water capacity was increased from 900 gallons to 1,260 gallons and a larger cab was fitted. The driving wheels were re-balanced, as these engines were required to work over the severe gradients which pertained on the West Country branches. For many years these engines handled the passenger trains between Calstock, Torrington and Halwill. They were Nos 94, 95, 96, 124, 135, 608, 610, 695, 696 and 697, withdrawn in 1955, 1956, 1956, 1959, 1959, 1957, 1956, 1957, 1956, 1959 respectively.

Class E1/R No.2697 (LH side), in 1937.

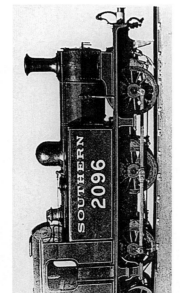

Class E1/R SR
No.2096 in 1936
(LH side).

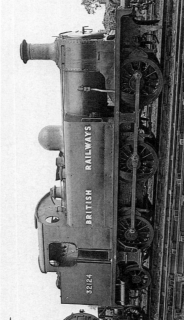

Class E1/R No.32124
in early BR livery.

Class E1/R BR No.32608.

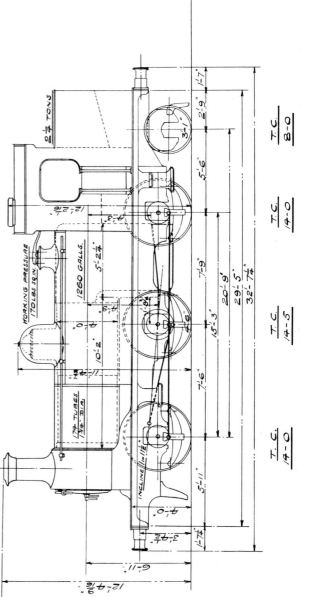

Class E1/R 0-6-2T. (Brighton dwg No.B31)

Class E1x LBSCR No.89.

E1x class 0-6-0T

This one single example of the E1 series, was fitted with a 4ft 6in boiler with an extended smokebox. New cab, bunker and side tanks of greater

capacity were exchanged for the originals, and No. 89 was the guinea pig to test the idea of extending the life of the class. The rebuilding took place in 1911 but by 1930 the replacement boiler

was just about life-expired, so the frames of the old engine received a secondhand Marsh boiler, new cylinders, bunker and cab, so that it was a renovated machine from cannibalised parts and

reverted to an E1. It still carried the number 89, later amended to 689, which became B689, then 2689 and finally 32689, being withdrawn in 1960.

Class E1x SR No.2689 in 1929.

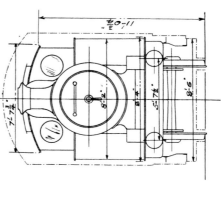

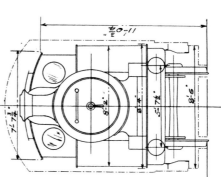

No.689

REVERTED TO E1. MARCH 1930.

Class E1x 0-6-0T. (Brighton dwg No.B30)

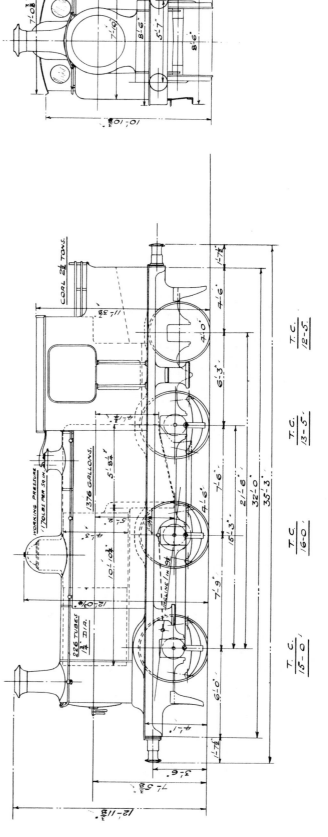

Class E3 0-6-2T.
(Brighton dwg
No.B36)

Class E3 0-6-2T. (Brighton dwg No.B37)

E3 class 0-6-2T

Although designed and ordered by Stroudley, these six-coupled radial tanks were produced in the reign of Billinton. There were 17 in this class, with 4ft 6in driving wheels and trailing radials of 4ft diameter. The overall design could be seen to be that of Stroudley in the first engine, No. 158 built in 1891, but when the further 16 were ordered between 1894 and 1895, Billinton introduced some innovations in the shape of Duplex injectors to replace the crosshead feed pumps, a cast-iron chimney, removal of the exhaust steam pipes to the tanks, and changing the sandboxes from above the running plate to below. All the class were eventually fitted with Mr Marsh's boiler, with a set of Ramsbottom safety valves and a plain dome, which allowed the pressure to be raised from 160 to 170lbs. A list of names and numbers is shown, but a note should be made that *Broadbridge*, No. 453, briefly carried the name *Charles C. Macrae* for reasons of photographic publicity.

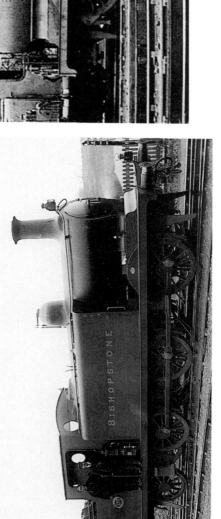

LBSCR No.	LBSCR Name	Built	Withdrawn
158	West Brighton	1891	1934
165	Blatchington	1894	1959
166	Cliftonville	1894	1959
167	Saddlescombe	1894	1955
168	Southborough	1894	1956
169	Bedhampton	1894	1955
170	Bishopstone	1894	1957
453	Broadbridge	1895	1955
454	Storrington	1895	1958
455	Brockhurst	1895	1958

LBSCR No.	LBSCR Name	Built	Withdrawn
456	Aldingbourne	1895	1959
457	Watersfield	1895	1949
458	Chalvington	1895	1957
459	Warlingham	1895	1957
460	Warminghurst	1895	1956
461	Staplefield	1895	1957
462	Washington	1895	1957

No. 158 Boiler replaced with Marsh I1 class in 1921.

Class E3
LBSCR No.170
Bishopstone.

Class E3 No.2455 in 1933.

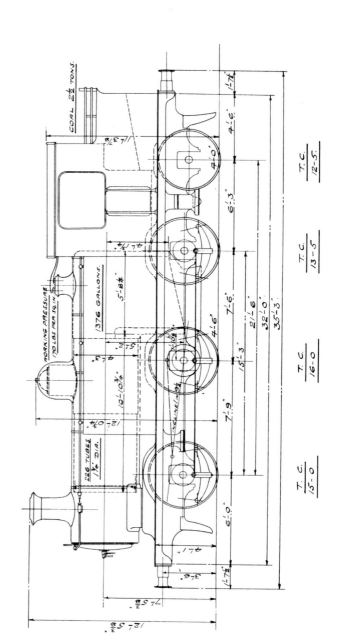

Class E3 0-6-2T. (Brighton dwg No.B38) (Engine Nos 2166, 2455, 2458 and 2459 only.)

Class E3 No.2453 in 1935.

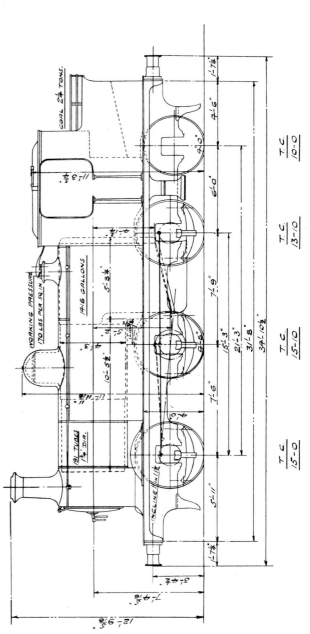

Class E3 No.2453 in 1935.

Class E3 LBSCR No.158 at Littlehampton in 1927. (Built in 1891 as Stroudley F class *West Brighton*).

Class E3 0-6-2T. (Brighton dwg No.B39)

C2 class 0-6-0

These six-coupled goods engines were the logical sequence to Stroudley's C1s. The main differences being that the C2s had boilers of 4ft 3in diameter x 10ft 8½in long, and the C1's largest ring was 4ft 8in with the length of the boiler being 10ft 2in. The whole class of 55 engines designed and ordered by Mr Billinton, were built by Vulcan Foundry between 1893 and 1902. In later years a few engines received new boilers made in two rings, which had safety valves on the firebox and

the dome on the first ring. Running numbers and building dates were as follows, dates of scrapping shown after C2x lists:

Nos	Built	Withdrawn
433-444	1893	433/439 1936 & 1937
		respectively
445-452	1894	452/530 1935
521-540	1900	531 1936
541-545	1901	542/555 1937
546-555	1902	

Class C2 No.B535 in 1927.

Class C2 No.B535 in 1929.

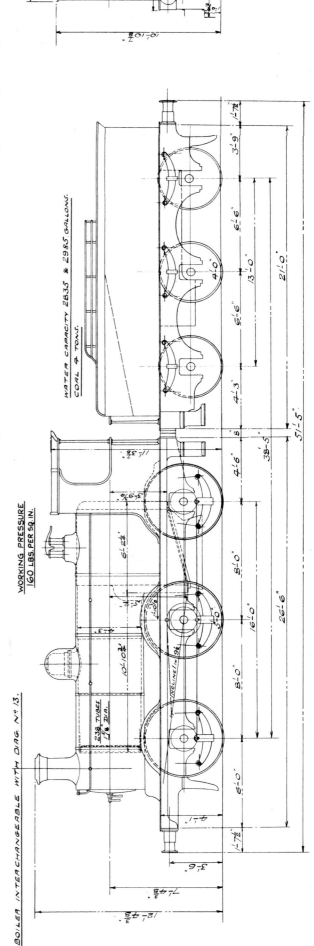

Class C2 0-6-0. (Brighton dwg No.B12)

C2x class 0-6-0

During Marsh's years as CME it was decided to increase the power and boiler capacity of the C2 class. With this in mind, 45 were eventually rebuilt with a C3 boiler with extended smokebox and saddle, new cylinders and cab, plus an addition of extra water space in the tender, making the capacity 2,985 galls. The rebuilding started with No. 545 in 1908, and the process continued right through until 1940. In 1921 six of the class were given boilers with an extra dome for Billinton's top feed, but this system had been abandoned by 1930, although the second dome remained in place. There were 15 of these boilers, with others used on C3, B2x, E5x and E6x classes and they were moved around as locomotives were overhauled. All were used on C2xs at one time or another. Details of the rebuilding from C2 to C2x were:

Nos	Date rebuilt
545, 547, 553	1908
551	1909
434, 444, 450, 522, 525, 538, 541, 550	1910
437, 440, 445, 447, 450, 528, 532, 534, 544, 554	1911
441, 446, 448, 449, 524, 546, 549	1912
543	1915
540	1922
442	1922
438, 443, 451, 523, 529, 536, 537, 539	1924
521, 548	1925
527, 535	1939
526, 552	1940

No. 2545 carried 'S' prefix 1948/50.

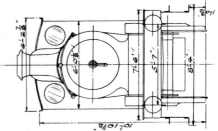

Class C2 0-6-0.

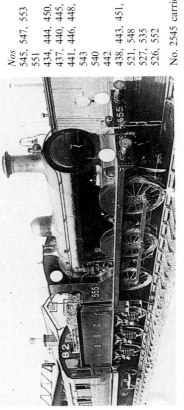

Class C2 No.555 at Clapham Junction, 1921.

Class C2 0-6-0. (Brighton dwg No.B13)

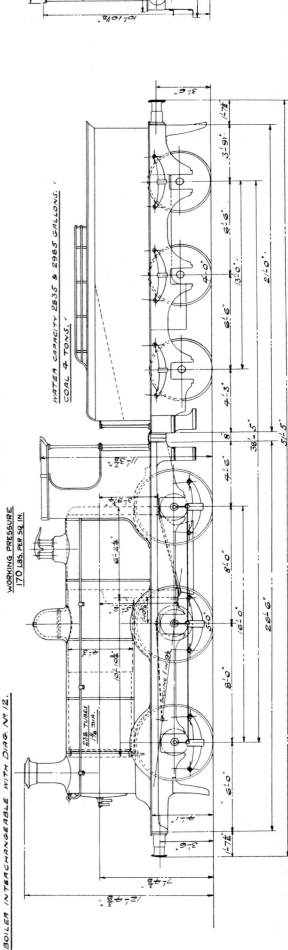

WATER CAPACITY 2835 & 2985 GALLONS. COAL 4 TONS.

WORKING PRESSURE 170 LBS. PER SQ. IN.

238 TUBES 1¾ DIA.

BOILER INTERCHANGEABLE WITH DIAG. N° 12.

Dates of scrapping of C2 and C2x class:

Year	Nos							
	440, 524, 540							
1935	452, 530							
1936	433, 531							
	437, 529							
1937	439, 542, 555							
1948	435							
1950	533, 436							
1957	537, 434							
1960	442, 443, 444, 446, 447, 526, 527, 532,							
	543, 551, 554							
1961	438, 441, 445, 448, 449, 450, 521, 451,							
	522, 528, 534, 536, 538, 539, 541, 544,							
	545, 546, 547, 548, 549, 550, 552, 553							
1962	523, 525, 535							

Class C2x No.2448 (RH side), SR livery.

Class C2x No.534 (LH side), LBSCR days.

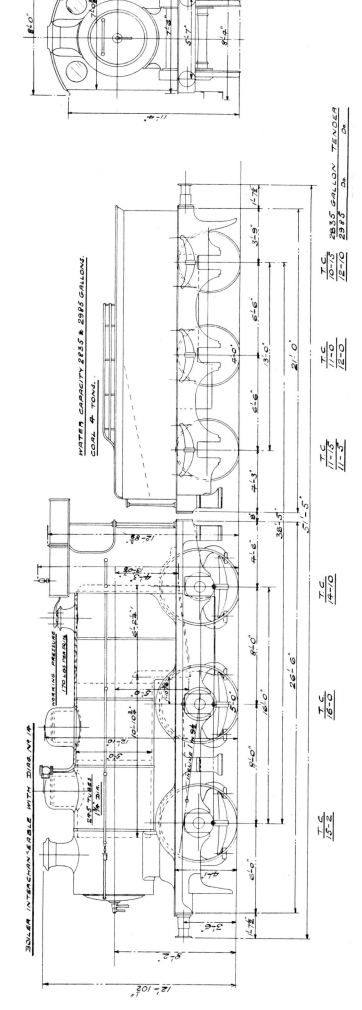

Class C2x 0-6-0. (Brighton dwg No.B15)

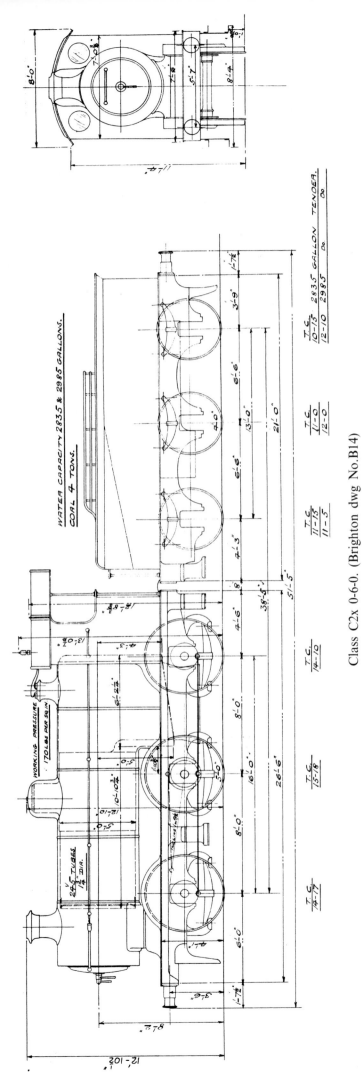

WATER CAPACITY 2835 & 2985 GALLONS.
COAL 4 TONS.

WORKING PRESSURE 170 LBS PER SQ IN

Class C2x 0-6-0. (Brighton dwg No.B14)

Class C2x LBSCR No.448 (LH side).

Class C2x LBSCR No.541 (RH side).

E2 class 0-6-0T

L. B. Billinton, after deputising for Mr Marsh during the latter's illness, as Locomotive Engineer of the LBSCR, finally took over the position upon the retirement of Marsh in December of 1911. The first of Billinton's designs was for ten compact tank engines, designed expressly for handling short distance goods traffic, and for use in the shunting yards. The six-coupled wheels were of 4ft 6in diameter on a total wheelbase of 16ft. The first five engines carried tanks with a water capacity of 1,090 galls, but the second batch of five had larger tanks, capable of holding 1,256 galls. All ten were fitted with a Weir feed water pump, carried on the front end of the tanks and also had hot water injectors. Details of building and withdrawal are:

LBSCR No.	Built	Withdrawn
100	1913	1961
101	1913	1962
102	1913	1961
103	1913	1962
104	1914	1963
105	1915	1962
106	1915	1962
107	1916	1961
108	1916	1961
109	1916	1963

The following E2 class lost their feed pumps which were replaced with injectors:

32100	1951	2105	1944
32101	1951	32106	1950
32102	1948	32107	1949
32103	1950	2108	1947
2104	1947	32109	1948

In BR days some locomotives had their running numbers on the bunker sides, others had them sited on the tank sides ahead of the cab entrance.

Class E2 0-6-0T. (Brighton dwg No.B33A)

Class E2 LBSCR No.100 when new (RH side).

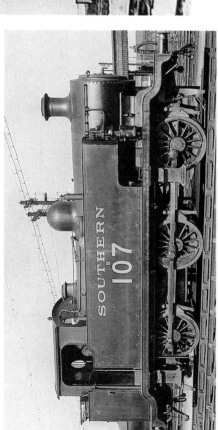

Class E2 SR No.B107 with extended tanks, 1927.

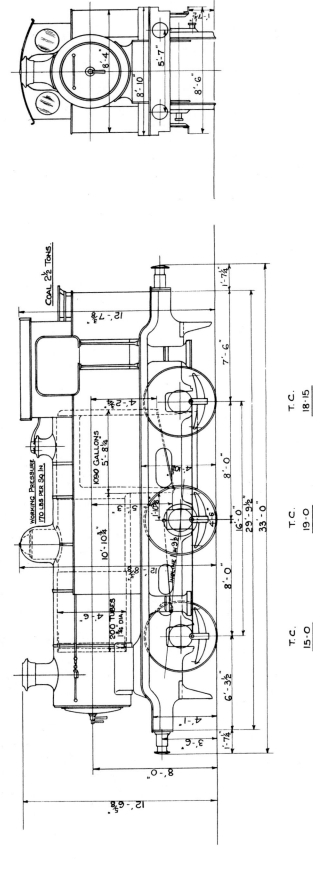

COAL 2½ TONS.

WORKING PRESSURE 170 LBS PER SQ IN.

1090 GALLONS

200 TUBES 1¾ DIA

T.C. 15-0   T.C. 19-0   T.C. 18-15

Class E2 0-6-0T. (Brighton dwg No.B33B)

E4 class 0-6-2T

This class of mixed traffic tank engine, built between 1897 and 1903, was very similar to the E3 class, except that the driving wheels were larger, being 5ft 6in of diameter against the 4ft 6in of the earlier engines. Over their long life, the chimneys were replaced, first by the Marsh type, and later by the short style as fitted to the E5 class. This all came about as the boilers were changed, which meant various safety valves and dome positions. A list of the numbers, dates of building, and withdrawals is appended, together with all their names. Four were eventually fitted with larger boilers and formed the E4x class.

LBSCR No.	LBSCR Name	Built (Brighton)	Rebuilt as E4x	Withdrawn
463	Wivelsfield	1897		1959
464	Woodmancote	1897		1956
465	Hurst Green	1898		1955
466	Honor Oak	1898	1909	1958
467	Berwick	1898		1958
468	Midhurst	1898		1963
469	Beachy Head	1898		1961
470	East Hoathly	1898		1962
471	Forest Hill	1898		1959
472	Fay Gate	1898		1962
473	Birch Grove	1898		1962
474	Bletchingly	1898		1963
475	Partridge Green	1898		1961
476	Beeding	1898		1957
477	Poynings	1898	1911	1959
478	Newick	1898	1909	1956
479	Bevendean	1898		1963
480	Fletching	1898		1959
481	Itchingfield	1898		1958
482	Newtimber	1898		1955
483	Hellingly	1899		1944
484	Hackbridge	1899		1960
485	Ashington	1899		1957
486	Godalming	1899		1959
487	Fishergate	1899		1962
488	Oakwood	1899		1957
489	Boxgrove	1899	1909	1955
490	Bohemia	1899		1955
491	Hangleton	1899		1961

LBSCR No.	LBSCR Name	Built (Brighton)	Rebuilt as E4x	Withdrawn
492	Jevington	1899		1957
493	Telscombe	1899		1958
494	Woodgate	1899		1959
495	Chessington	1899		1960
496	Chiddingfold	1899		1955
497	Dennington	1900		1959
498	Strettington	1900		1961
499	Woodendean	1900		1957
500	Puttenham	1900		1962
501	Stoats Nest	1900		1955
502	Ridgewood	1900		1958
503	Buckland	1900		1963
504	Chilworth	1900		1961
505	Annington	1900		1961
506	Catherington	1900		1961
507	Horley	1900		1959
508	Bognor	1900		1960
509	Southover	1900		1962
510	Twineham	1900		1962
511	Lingfield	1901		1956
512	Kingswood	1901		1961
513	Densworth	1901		1956
514	Barcombe	1901		1956
515	Swanmore	1901		1961
516	Rustington	1901		1955
517	Limpsfield	1901		1959
518	Porchester	1901		1955
519	Portfield	1901		1959
520	Westbourne	1901		1957

LBSCR No.	LBSCR Name	Built (Brighton)	Rebuilt as E4x	Withdrawn
556	Tadworth	1901		1961
557	Northlands	1901		1962
558	Chiltington	1901		1956
559	Framfield	1901		1960
560	Penbury	1901		1958
561	Walberton	1901		1956
562	Laughton	1901		1960
563	Wineham	1901		1961
564	Nettlestone	1901		1961
565	Littleton	1902		1961

LBSCR No.	LBSCR Name	Built (Brighton)	Rebuilt as E4x	Withdrawn
566	Durrington	1902		1959
577	Blackstone	1903		1959
578	Horsebridge	1903		1961
579	Roehampton	1903		1959
580	Shermanbury	1903		1962
581	Warningcamp	1903		1962
582	Horndean	1903		1956

No. 473 is preserved on the Bluebell Railway
No. 497 was renamed *Donnington* in 1905.

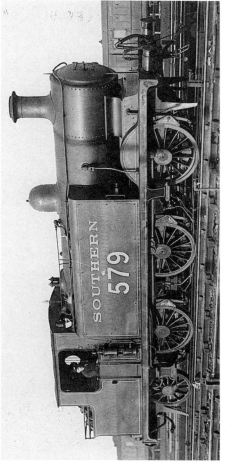

Class E4 No.579 at Reading in 1948.

Class E4 No.2487 at Reading in 1948.

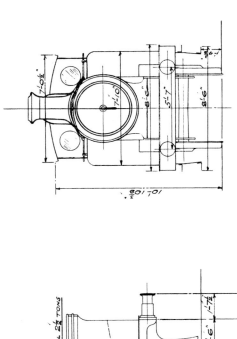

Class E4 No.B579 at New Cross, 1933 (RH side).

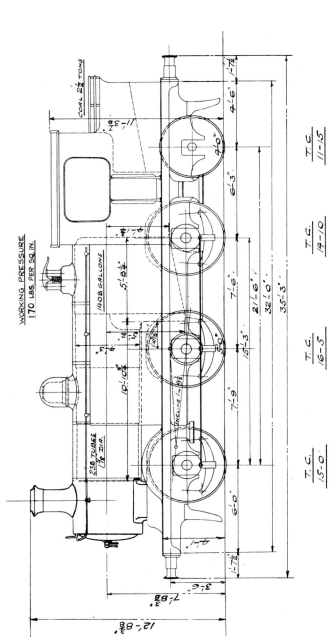

Class E4 0-6-2T.
(Brighton dwg No.B40)

WORKING PRESSURE 170 LBS. PER SQ. IN.

COAL 2½ TONS

1408 GALLONS

235 TUBES 1¾″ DIA.

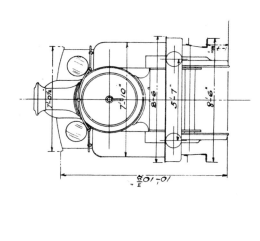

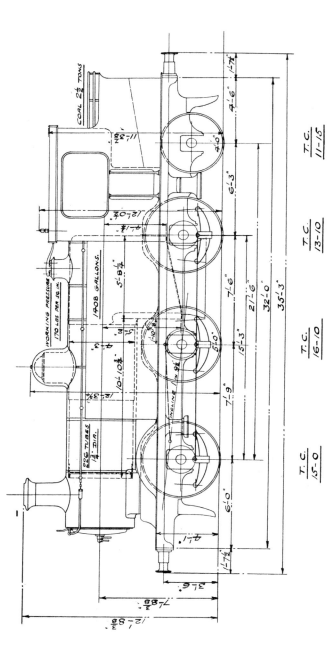

Class E4 0-6-2T. (Brighton dwg No.B41)

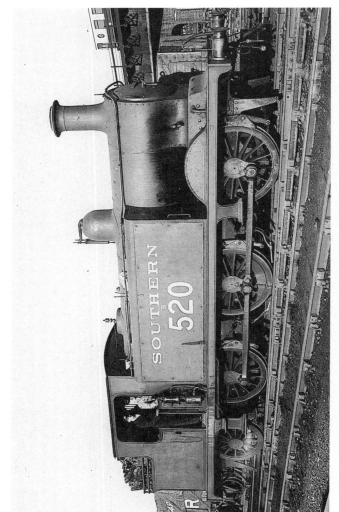

Class E4 No.B520

Class E4 No.B463 (LH side)

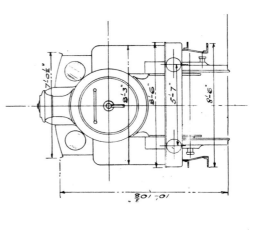

Class E4x No.2478 in 1934.

Class E4x LBSCR No.478.

E4x class 0-6-2T

As previously mentioned, four of the E4 class were rebuilered by Marsh, between 1909 and 1911, with a much larger boiler, 4ft 6in in diameter, with a greater heating surface and a higher pressure of 170lbs per sq in. Being a bigger boiler, the side tanks had to be pushed outward for 2½in on each side and the centre line of the boiler was raised 1in.

LBSCR No.	LBSCR Name	Built	Rebuilt	Withdrawn
466	*Honour Oak*	1898	1909	1958
477	*Poynings*	1898	1911	1959
478	*Newick*	1898	1909	1956
489	*Boxgrove*	1899	1909	1955

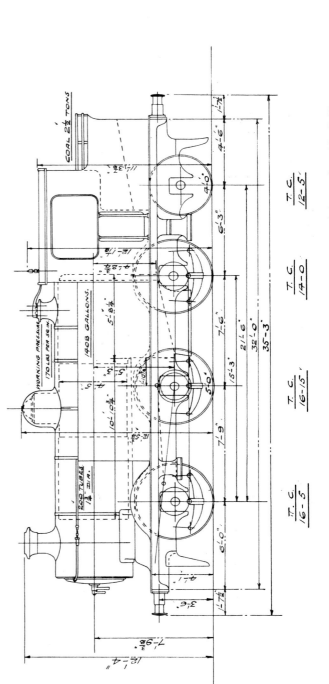

Class E4x 0-6-2T. (Brighton dwg No.B42)

Class E4x SR No.2564.

Class B2x No.205 (ex-B2 class *Hackworth*).

Class B2x No.B207 (ex-B2 class *Brunel*) (LH side).

B2, B3 and B2x class 4-4-0s

Breaking new ground in 1893, Billinton designed a new type of passenger tender engine for the express services. The first engines were built in 1895 and were equipped with 2,420 gallon tenders. These were Nos 314 *Charles C. Macrae*, 315 *Duncannon*, and 316 *Goldsmid*. Later on No. 315 was renamed *J. Gay*, but before entering SR service this name was removed. The whole class of 25 were used on the London–Portsmouth route, and later on the Hastings and Eastbourne service. The boilers on 24 of these machines were 4ft 5in x 10ft 7½in, with 18in x 26in cylinders. The one exception was No. 213 *Bessemer* which was the last to be erected and was fitted with a larger boiler of 4ft 8in x 10ft 8½in with a firebox 6in longer than the rest. This variant was classed as a B3.

All 25 had driving wheels of 6ft 9in diameter, with bogie wheels 3ft 6in. Eventually, all of these engines were rebuilt between 1907 and 1916 and became the B2x series. The details here show the complete history.

As can be seen by the data aforementioned, all 24 B2s and the one B3, were rebuilt to B2x between 1907 and 1916. The slender outline of the early design had to give way, to a larger boiler and more commodious cab, which gave the engines a stronger more sturdier look, especially as the boiler mountings were of the shorter style. Also the boiler being longer, it extended forward of the smokebox saddle almost to the curve of the framing. Note that Nos 206 and 319 were fitted with Billinton top feed in 1921.

LBSCR No.	Name	Built	Rebuilt as B2x	Withdrawn
171	Nevill	1897	1910	1931
201	Rosebery	1897	1909	1930
202	Trevithick	1897	1909	1931
203	Henry Fletcher	1897	1909	1930
204	Telford	1897	1911	1929
205	Hackworth	1897	1910	1931
206	Smeaton	1897	1909	1931
207*	Brunel	1897	1909	1931
208*	Abercorn	1897	1911	1929
209*	Wolfe Barry	1897	1913	1930
210*	Fairbairn	1897	1909	1931
211*	Whitworth	1897	1910	1930
212*	Armstrong	1898	1910	1930
213	Bessemer	1898	1908	1932
314*	Charles C. Macrae	1895	1911	1930
315	Duncannon	1895	1909	1933
316*	Goldsmid	1895	1916	1930
317	Gerald Loder	1896	1908	1929
318	Rothschild	1896	1910	1930
319	John Fowler	1896	1914	1930
320	Rastrick	1896	1910	1932
321	John Rennie	1896	1907	1930
322	G. P. Bidder	1896	1908	1931
323*	William Cubitt	1896	1908	1932
324*	John Hawkshaw	1896	1913	1932

* Fitted with larger tenders 3,112 gallons ex-C3 class.
Nos 202/206 and 208 were used for oil firing trials in 1903-4 but were unsuccessful
... with Billinton top feed in 1921.

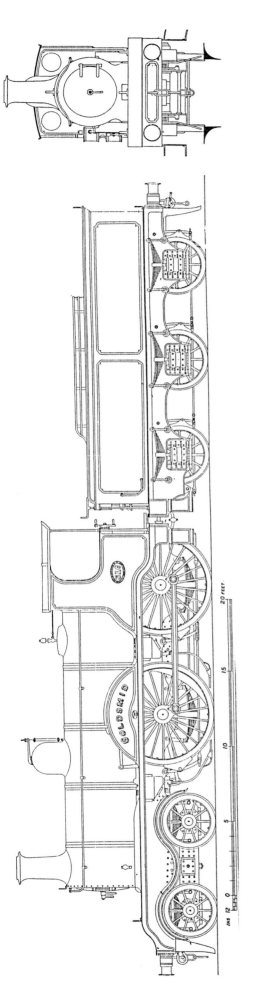

Class B2 4-4-0.

Class B4 LBSCR No.61 (formerly *Ladysmith*) (LH side).

B4 class 4-4-0

The experiment with No. 213 *Bessemer* as a B3, proved the point that as trains were getting heavier, more power was going to be required to move them. This need, brought about in 1899, was fulfilled by a new class which was to all effects an enlarged *Bessemer*. The boiler diameter was increased to 4ft 10in and the cylinders were 19in diameter x 26in stroke. Thirty-three were built between 1899 and 1902, six were rebuilt to B4x, and these, together with all the remainder saw service on the Southern Railway. Note that eight of the class were built at Brighton, these being Nos 42–46 and 52–54, with the remaining 25 being constructed by Sharp, Stewart & Co. who were also responsible for the boilers fitted to Nos 42, 43 and 45. As this was the time of the Boer War, this is reflected in many of the names in the summary which follows hereunder.

LBSCR No.	Name	Built	Rebuilt as B4x	Withdrawn
42	His Majesty	1902		1947
43	Duchess of Fife	1902	1923	1951
44	Cecil Rhodes	1902		1948
45	Bessborough	1902	1923	1951
46	Prince of Wales	1902		1936
47	Canada	1901		1937
48	Australia	1901		1936
49	Queensland	1901		1936
50	Tasmania	1901	1923	1951
51	Wolferton	1901		1949
52	Siemens	1901	1923	1951
53	Sirdar	1900		1935
54	Empress	1900		1951
55	Emperor	1901	1922	1951
56	Roberts	1901	1923	1951
57	Buller	1901		1936
58	Kitchener	1901		1936
59	Baden-Powell	1901		1935
60	Kimberley	1901	1922	1951
61	Ladysmith	1901		1935
62	Mafeking	1901		1951
63	Pretoria	1901		1951
64	Windsor	1901		1951
65	Sandringham	1901		1934
66	Balmoral	1901		1935
67	Osborne	1901	1923	1951
68	Marlborough	1901		1935
69	Bagshot	1901		1934
70	Holyrood	1901	1923	1951
71	Goodwood	1901	1923	1951
72	Sussex	1901	1924	1951
73	Westminster	1901	1923	1951
74	Cornwall	1901		1950

Notes on renaming:
49 became *Duchess of Norfolk* in 1904
52 became *Sussex* in 1908
53 became *Richmond* in 1906
54 became *Princess Royal* in 1906
64 became *Norfolk* in 1908
66 became *Billinton* in 1906
70 became *Devonshire* in 1907

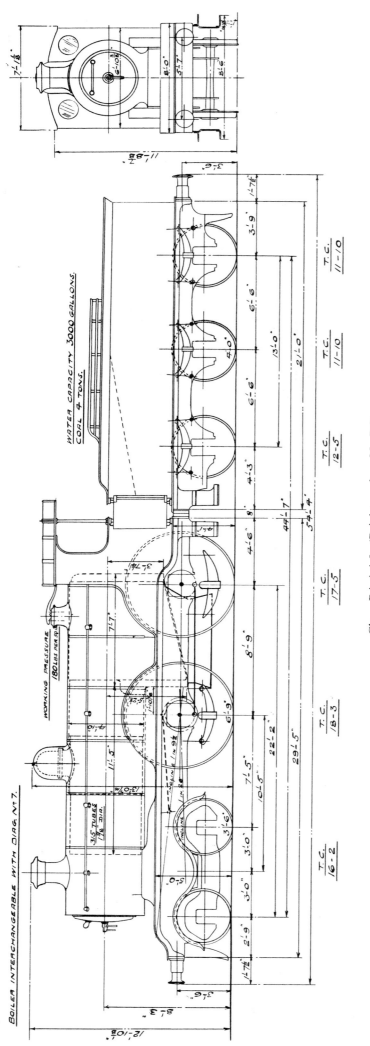

Class B4 4-4-0. (Brighton dwg No.B6)

Class B4 LBSCR No 67 (formerly Osborne)

Class B4 LBSCR No 63 (formerly Pretoria) (RH side)

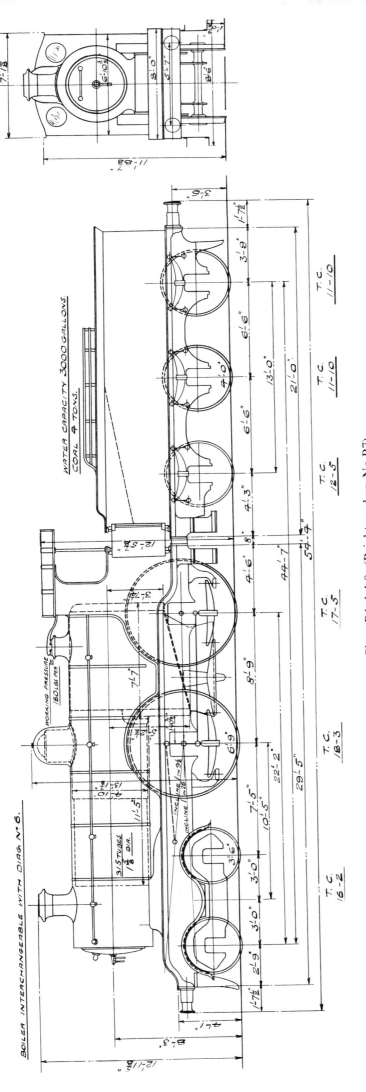

Class B4 4-4-0. (Brighton dwg No.B7)

E5 class 0-6-2T

Getting bigger and better all the time, the next progression of the passenger radial tank engines was the E5 class. In general they followed the same pattern as the previous radial tanks, but were different in that they had a larger firebox, the length being increased to 6ft 2¼in, and the driving wheels were 5ft 6in in diameter. They were quite fast engines, being used in the main on passenger duties. When built they had 18in cylinders,

but later these were reduced to 17½in but with an increase in the pressure to 175lbs per sq in. The boilers were of the two ring type with the dome on the second ring. Coal bunkers held 3½ tons of coal, and the water tanks were increased to carry 1,665 gallons.

Thirty engines were constructed between 1902 and 1904 and all carried names of southern county towns and villages, as under.

LBSCR No.	LBSCR Name	Built	Rebuilt as E5x	Withdrawn
399	Middleton	1904		1953
400	Winchelsea	1904		1951
401	Woldingham	1904	1911	1954
402	Wanborough	1904		1951
403	Fordcombe	1904		1944
404	Hardham	1904		1951
405	Fernhurst	1904		1951
406	Colworth	1904		1951
567	Freshwater	1902		1949
568	Carisbrooke	1902		1955
569	Kensington	1902		1936
570	Armington	1902	1911	1956
571	Hickstead	1903		1956

Class B4x No.52 (LH side).

LBSCR No.	LBSCR Name	Built	Rebuilt as E5x	Withdrawn
572	Farncombe	1903		1949
573	Nutbourne	1903		1953
574	Copthorne	1903		1951
575	Westergate	1903		1951
576	Brenchley	1903	1911	1955
583	Handcombe	1903		1956
584	Lordington	1903		1951
585	Crowborough	1903		1954
586	Maplehurst	1903	1911	1955

LBSCR No.	LBSCR Name	Built	Rebuilt as E5x	Withdrawn
587	Brighton	1903		1954
588	Hawkenbury	1903		1953
589	Ambersham	1904		1949
590	Lodsworth	1904		1951
591	Tillington	1904		1954
592	Eastergate	1904		1953
593	Hollington	1904		1956
594	Shortbridge	1904		1951

Class E5 No.B575 in 1928.

Class E5 No.2571 in 1933 (RH side).

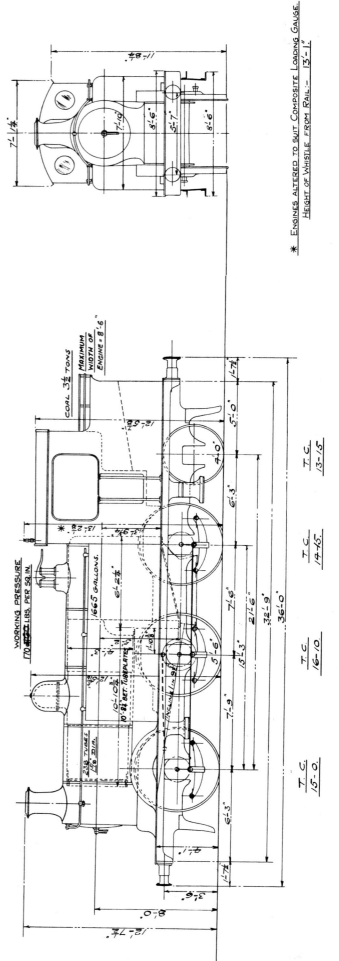

Class E5 0-6-2T. (Brighton dwg B45)

* ENGINES ALTERED TO SUIT COMPOSITE LOADING GAUGE. HEIGHT OF WHISTLE FROM RAIL:- 13'-1"

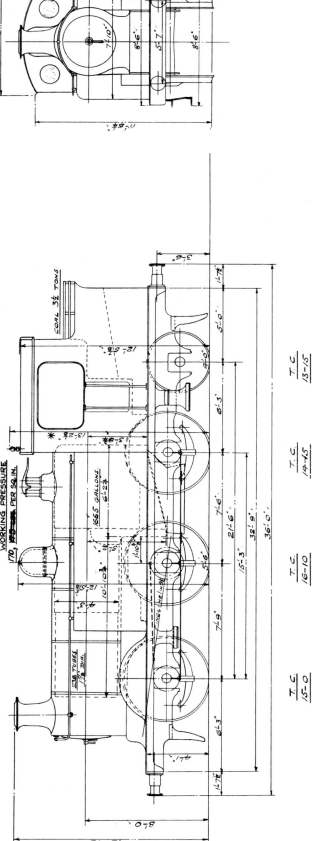

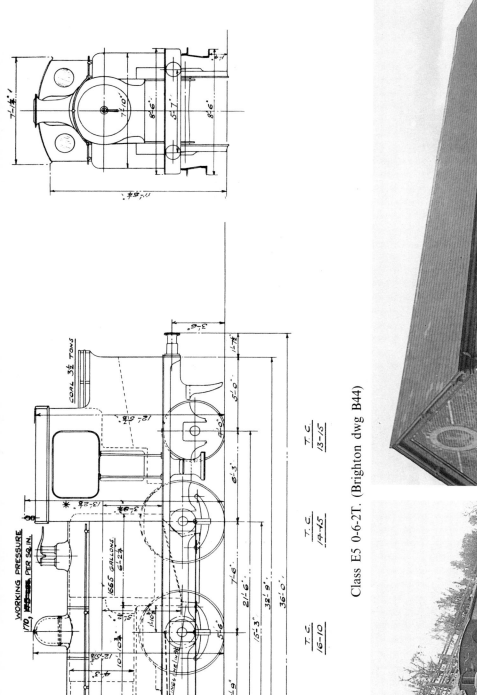

Class E5 0-6-2T. (Brighton dwg B44)

Class E5 No.B584 at Dorking in 1928.

Class E5 BR No.32404 at St. Leonards in 1950.

Class E5 BR No.32588 (LH side).

Class E5x No.2576 in 1946.

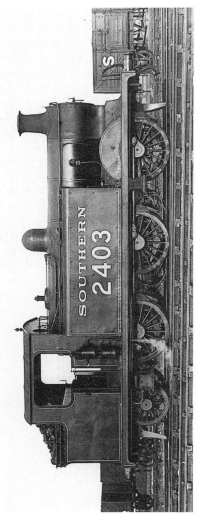

Class E5 No.2403 at Eastbourne, 1933 (RH side).

E5x class 0-6-2T

As was the normal practice of the LBSCR a few of the E5 class locomotives were fitted with larger boilers which gave them the 'x' suffix. The engines so dealt with were Nos 401, 570, 576 and 586, and in 1911 Marsh fitted these four with new boilers of the C3 class type, which increased the boiler diameter up to 5ft and so raised the boiler centre line to 8ft 5in from rail head.

Class E5x No.2576 in 1936. (LH side).

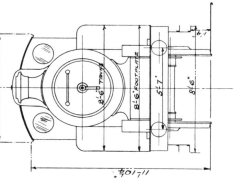

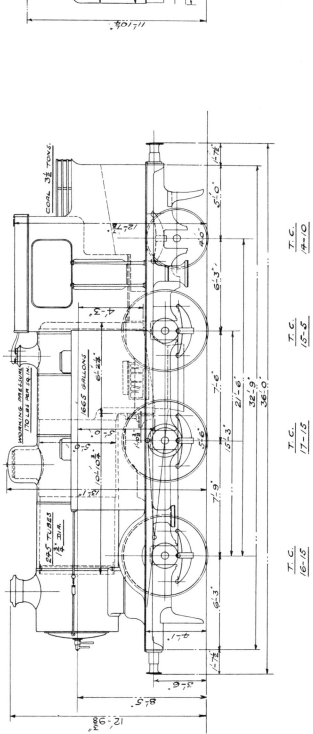

Class E5x 0-6-2T. (Brighton dwg No.B46)

E6 class 0-6-2T

Built expressly for goods work, the twelve engines which comprised this class were the last of Mr R. Billinton's reign, and indeed were not built until after his death in 1904. Although their designer had planned for the last two of this order to be 0-8-0 tanks, this order was cancelled by Marsh and all were constructed between 1904 and 1905 as 0-6-2Ts. These engines had 4ft 6in driving wheels and differed from the previous 'E' classes in having the valves under the cylinders, similar to those on the B4 class. The boilers were in two rings and 4ft 3in diameter. Only eight received names, the last four having numbers only:

LBSCR No.	LBSCR Name	Built	Rebuilt as E6x	Withdrawn
407	Worplesdon	1904	1911	1957
408	Binderton	1904		1962
409	Graffham	1904		1958
410	Chilgrove	1905		1961
411	Blackheath	1905	1911	1959
412	Tandridge	1905		1957
413	Fenchurch	1905		1958
414	Piccadilly	1905		1958
415	—	1905		1961
416	—	1905		1962
417	—	1905		1962
418	—	1905		1962

Class E5x BR No.32586.

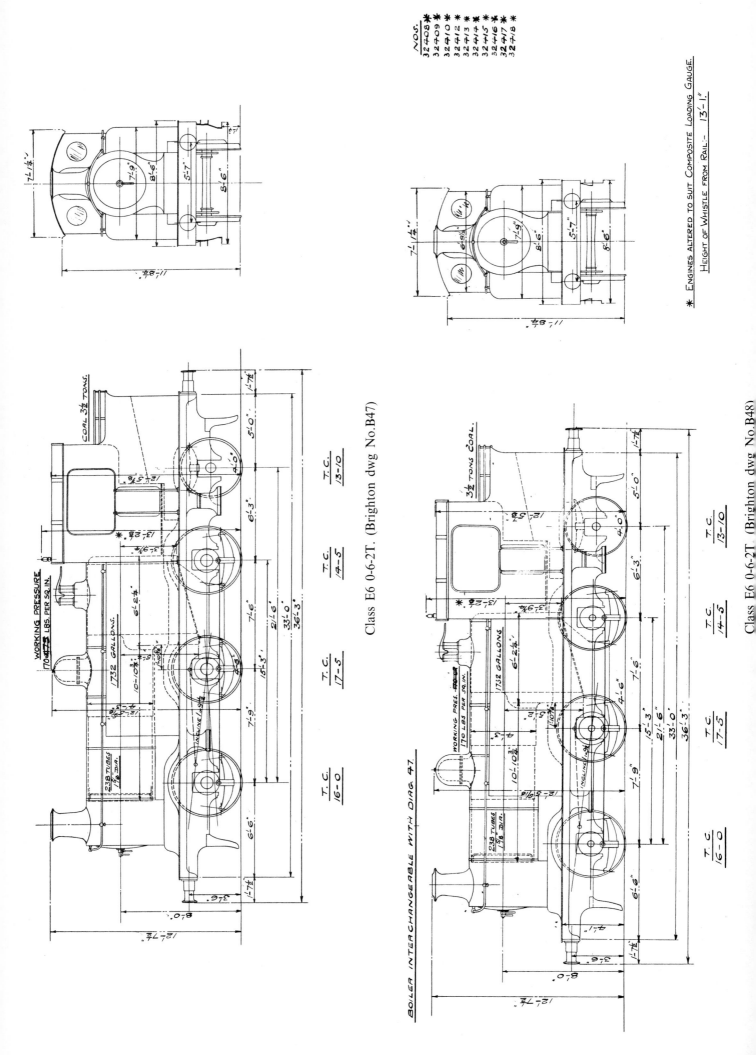

Class E6 0-6-2T. (Brighton dwg No.B47)

Class E6 0-6-2T. (Brighton dwg No.B48)

Class E6 LBSCR No.418.

Class E6 No.2415 in 1938 (RH side).

E6x class 0-6-2T

As shown above, two engines of the E6 class were fitted with the larger C3 class boilers in 1911 and were re-classed with the 'x'. This raised the total weight up by 2 tons, to make 63 tons in working order.

Class E6x No.2411 in 1936 (RH side).

Class E6x LBSCR No.411.

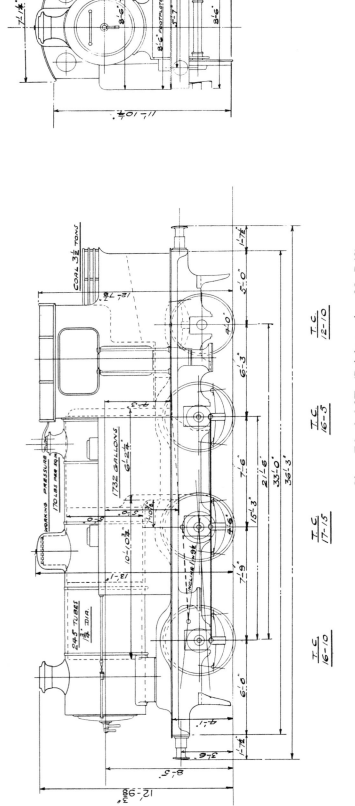

Class E6x 0-6-2T. (Brighton dwg No.B49)

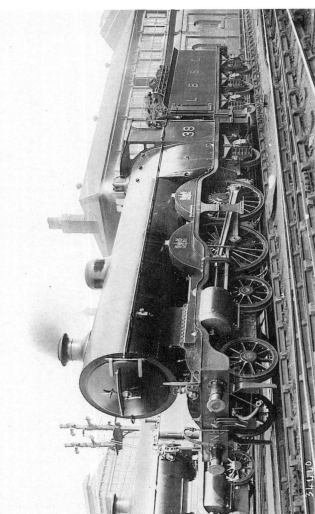

Class H1 No.38 in LBSCR livery.

H1 class 4-4-2

At this period in time, Marsh, who had succeeded R. J. Billinton, started to change the locomotive design for the LBSCR, and one of the first really 'big' engines to appear, was the outside cylinder Atlantic type built at Messrs Kitson's works at Leeds. Having been instrumental in the detail work of the GNR Atlantics at Doncaster, designed by Mr Ivatt, previous to joining the LBSCR, it follows that his 'magnum opus' for express passenger services, should be very similar to those working to such good effect on the Great Northern Railway.

There were five in the class, No. 37 built in 1905, and Nos 38-41 in 1906. The main differences between the Marsh engines and those of Ivatt were that the former had deeper fireboxes, the LBSCR cab, and also the framing was different over the wheels and cylinders. The driving wheels were 6ft 7½in in diameter on a wheelbase of 6ft 10in. The boiler had a diameter of 5ft 6in by 16ft 3⅞in long. It was pressed at 200lbs per sq in. It was only after entering into Southern Railway service that these engines received names, which were as follows:

LBSCR No.	SR Name	Built	Superheated	Withdrawn
37	Selsey Bill	1905	1926	1951
38	Portland Bill	1906	1925	1951
39	Hartland Point	1906	1926	1951
40	St Catherine's Point	1906	1926	1944
41	Peveril Point	1906	1927	1944

Note No. 39 was named La France in 1913 when used for the train conveying the President of France, but was renamed Hartland Point in 1926. As No. 2039 this engine was used as a mobile test bed for the 'Leader' class in 1947. As can be seen, these engines were saturated when built, but were all superheated between 1925 and 1927.

Class H1 No.39 *La France* in 1922.

Class H1 No.2038 in 1935.

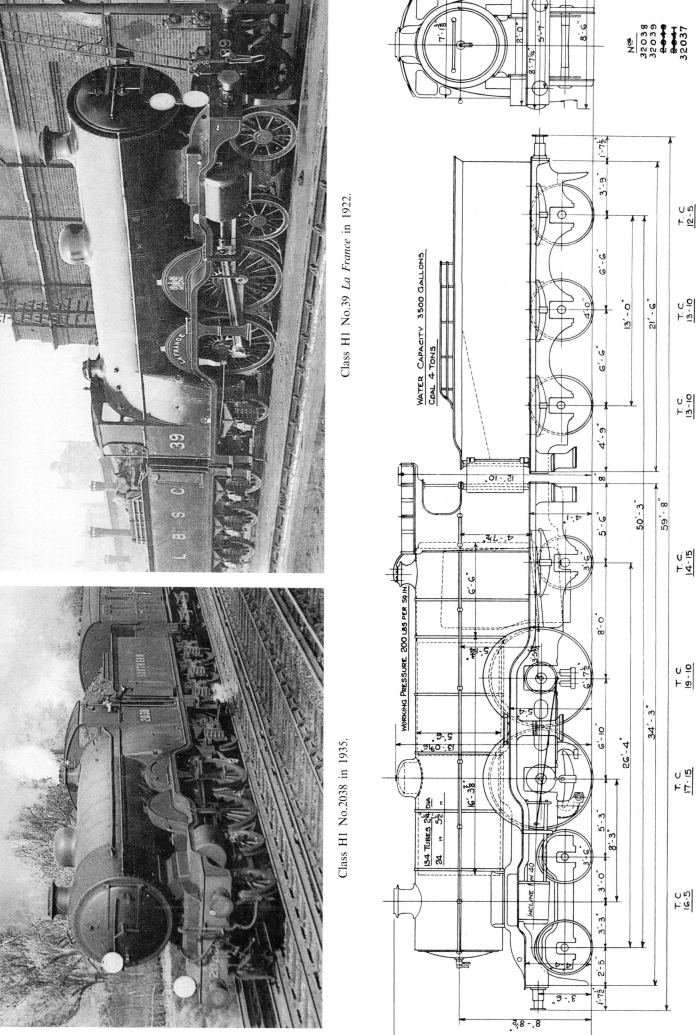

WATER CAPACITY 3500 GALLONS
COAL 4 TONS

WORKING PRESSURE 200 LBS PER SQ IN.

134 TUBES 2¼ DIA
24 " 5¼ "

Class H1 4-4-2. (Brighton dwg No.B51A)

Nos
32038
32039
32037

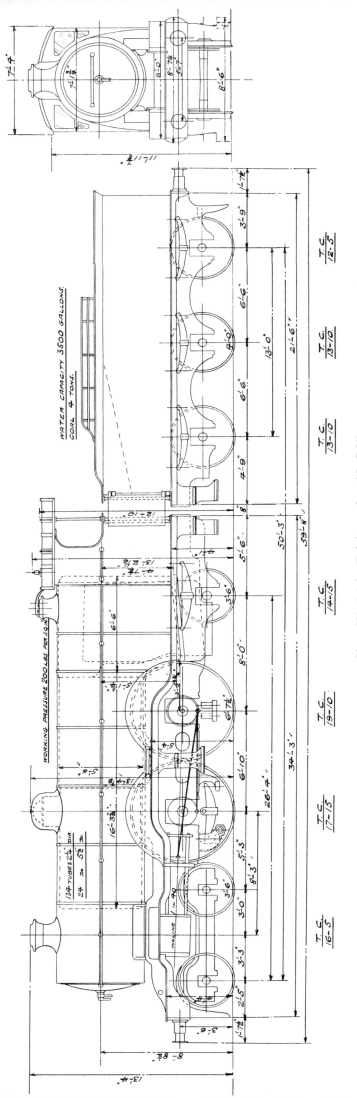

Class H1 4-4-2. (Brighton dwg No.B51)

Details of building are:

LBSCR No.	Built	Reboilered with double dome	Withdrawn
300	1906	1920	1951
301	1906		1951
302	1906		1952
303	1906		1951
304	1906	1920–In 1933 extended smokebox	1936
305	1906	1920	1937
306	1906		1951
307	1906		1949
308	1906		1948
309	1906	c1920	1949

C3 class 0-6-0

Following on from his first Atlantic design on the LBSCR, Marsh turned to the needs of the freight traffic, and in 1906, had built at Brighton Works, ten six-coupled goods engines. Although classed as C3, they were generally known as the "Horsham goods", simply because most of them were based at this shed. Fitted with a large boiler in two rings, the diameter being 5ft over the largest ring, with an overall length of 10ft 10¾in, and pressed for 170lbs per sq in. It was this boiler which was used when reboilering classes B2, C2, E5 and E6, and so giving them their 'x' suffix. The driving wheels on the C3 were 5ft in diameter, and a large tender with 3,112 gallons capacity and carrying 4 tons of fuel was attached to the class originally. But in later years, redundant tenders of 2,985 gallons from the withdrawn B2xs were used. Originally fitted with crosshead feed pumps, these were removed in the early 1930s and the 'Eastern' section type of injector was substituted. Later in Southern days the cab roofs were extended backward to give greater protection, and although they originally had the Billinton chimney, after ten years these were changed for the Marsh style.

Class H1 No B37 at Eastbourne in 1925.

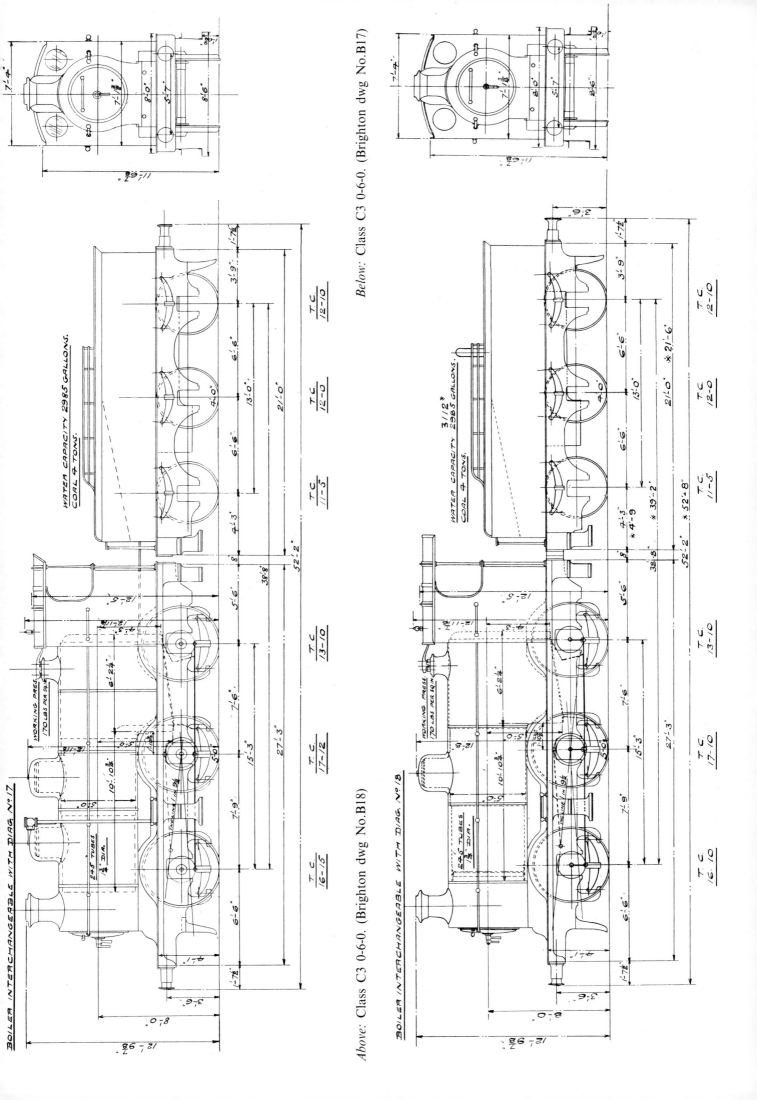

Above: Class C3 0-6-0. (Brighton dwg No.B17)

Below: Class C3 0-6-0. (Brighton dwg No.B18)

Class C3 SR No.2304, New Cross 1932.

Class I1 No.2 in 1932 (LH side)

Class C3 LBSCR No.302, New Cross 1925 (RH side).

I1 class 4-4-2T

It would seem that the year of 1906 was one of progress and innovation on the LBSCR. Marsh not only designed his six-coupled goods engines, but with the aid of the GNR and Messrs Kitsons, produced the big Atlantics, and then went on to design what one could perhaps call, a series of inside-cylindered 4-4-2 Atlantic tanks. Following the alphabet classification, this series of four different types within the class were given the prefix 'I'. For some reason it was said that I1s and I2s were bad steamers and engine crews gave them a bad name. However, they gave the appearance of being large engines, but perhaps this was because of the big side tanks.

The I1 series were built in two lots of ten during 1906-1907. The first batch were given the numbers 595 to 604, and a further ten were numbered 1-10

Although both series had 5ft 6in driving wheels, 4ft radial and 3ft 6in bogie wheels, nevertheless there was a difference between the lots, and this was in the coupled wheelbase. The first batch were spaced at 8ft 9in and the second at 7ft 7in, the reason being that use was made of some of the running gear from withdrawn D1 and D2 class engines at this time. All of the class, except No. 595, had a clerestory roof in the cab, and although originally fitted with the Billinton type chimney, when working on the SR they received the tall Marsh type. Although passenger engines, none of the I1 class ever received names. With the exception of the H2s and the J and L class tanks, this practice ceased on the LBSCR. Perhaps it should be noted that latterly, engines Nos 1 to 10 had water tanks of 1,839 gallons, engines 595-599 1,983 gallons, and Nos 600-604 had reduced capacity tanks holding a total of 1,924 gallons

I1x class 4-4-2T

When passing into the Southern Railway aegis, still with their 'shy steamer' record, Maunsell in 1925, with a view of improving the class, followed the old LBSCR tradition and reboilered them. A case of "waste not, want not"; the boilers used were from the old B4 class and some from the I3 class. The boiler pressure was increased from 170 to 180lbs, all of which increased the performance to a marked degree. The larger boiler raised the centre line, and the length meant the smokebox extending in front of the saddle. The other alteration was in rounding off the cab corners, so that the engines would conform to the new composite loading gauge.

LBSCR No.	Built	Reboilered to I1x	Withdrawn
1	1907	1931	1948
2	1907	1931	1951
3	1907	1931	1948
4	1907	1932	1948
5	1907	1931	1951
6	1907	1932	1948
7	1907	1931	1948
8	1907	1931	1951
9	1907	1929	1951
10	1907	1929	1948
595	1906	1927	1951
596	1906	1925	1951
597	1906	1928	1946
598	1907	1925	1948
599	1907	1928	1948
600	1907	1927	1944
601	1907	1928	1948
602	1907	1926	1951
603	1907	1928	1951
604	1907	1927	1948

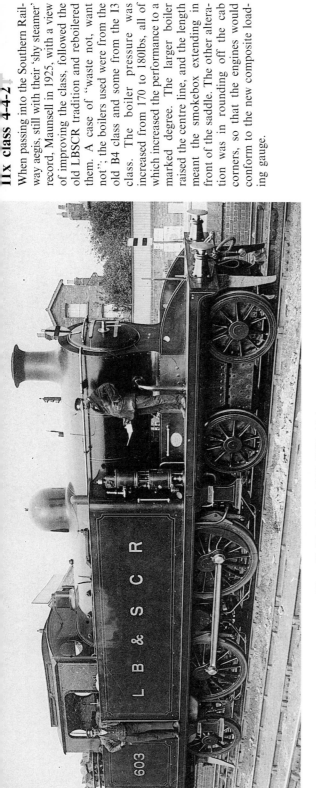

Class I1 No.603 in 1918 (RH side).

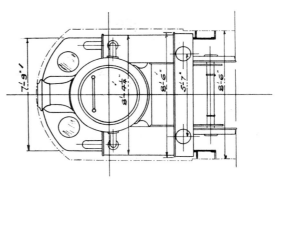

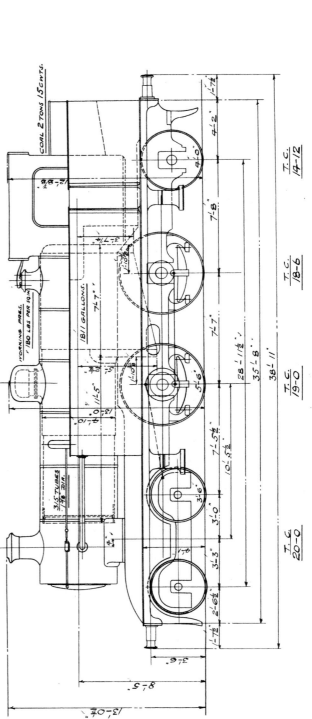

Class I1 4-4-2. (Brighton dwg No.B54)

Class IIx No.B595 in 1927.

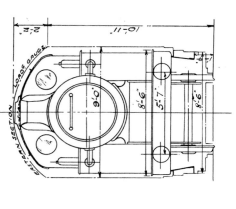

Class IIx No.B600.

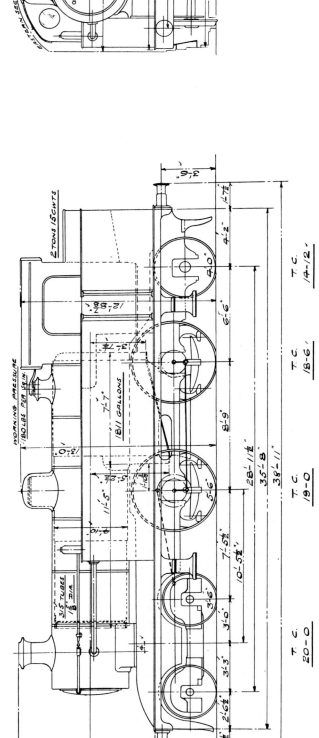

Class IIx 4-4-2 (Brighton dwg No.B55)

Class I1 No.B1 at Coulsdon, 1928 (LH side).

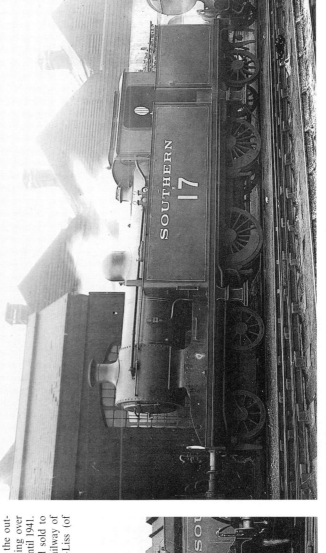

Class I1 No.B8 at Fratton, 1928.

I2 class 4-4-2T

The I2 class of ten engines, built for suburban traffic were very similar to the I1 series, and with two exceptions, they had larger boilers, 4ft 6in x 10ft 4¼in in length, and larger capacity side tanks, the latter holding 2,238 gallons and a bunker of 3 tons capacity. Unfortunately, they were no more successful than their sisters in the I1 class, and despite their large boilers and heating surfaces, enginemen complained about their poor steaming. There were only ten in this class, and they had a comparatively short life (with the exception of two, as noted).

LBSCR No.	Built	Withdrawn
13	1908	1939
14	1908	1933
15	1908	1936
16	1908	1933
17	1908	1938
18	1908	1936
19	1908	1937
20	1908	1936

Nos 13 and 19 were sent to Bournemouth at the outbreak of war, and covered in sandbags standing over engine pits, formed temporary air raid shelters until 1941.
The two engines were then reconditioned and sold to H.M. Government for use on the Military Railway of the Royal Engineers at Bordon–Longmoor–Liss (of happy memories!).

LBSCR No.	Built	Withdrawn
11	1907	1933
12	1908	1935

Class I2 No.B17 (LH side), 1924.

Class I1x No.2009 at Eastleigh, 1931 (RH side).

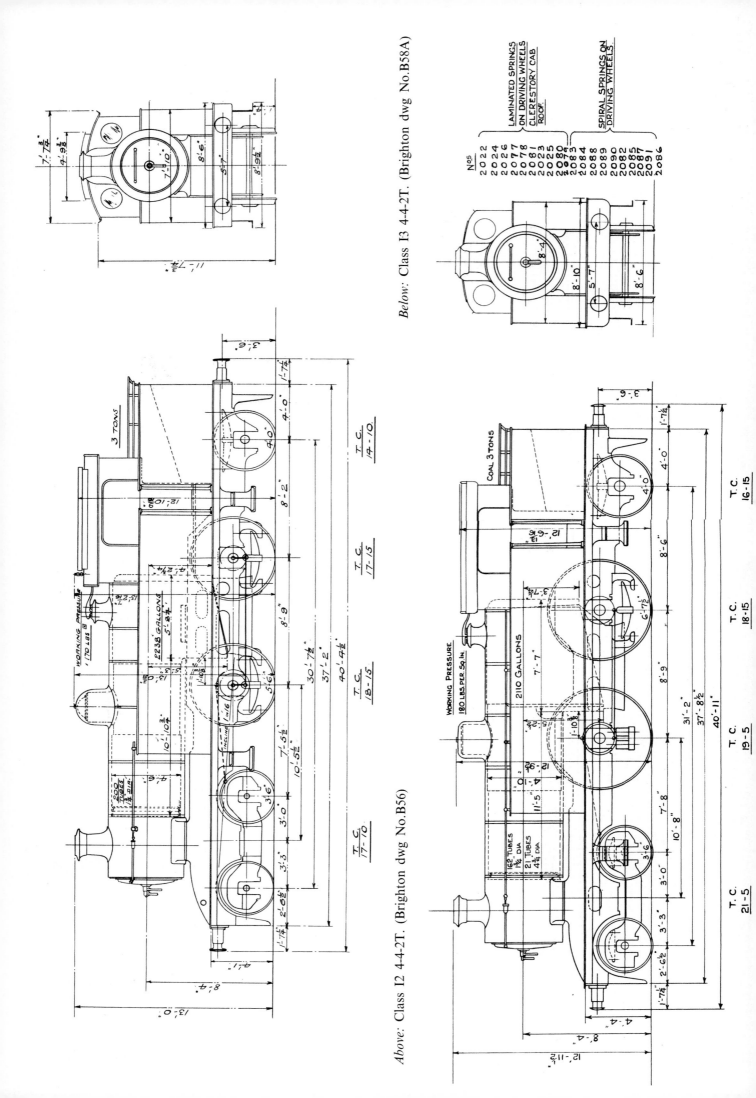

Above: Class I2 4-4-2T. (Brighton dwg No.B56)

Below: Class I3 4-4-2T. (Brighton dwg No.B58A)

Class 13 BR No.32082.

I3 class 4-4-2T

Probably the most successful of the I series, were the 27 engines designed and built at Brighton between 1907 and 1913. It would appear to be Marsh's version of a tank locomotive, based on the B4 tender engines. This series carried the same boiler and motion as the B4s and were fitted with large 6ft 7½in driving wheels. The first to be built, No. 21, was slightly different to the following 26, in that this machine had 6ft 9in drivers, and although having an extended smokebox, there was no saddle. (See diagrams B59 and B59A). The class was no doubt experimental, as Marsh built some with superheaters and some saturated, so that comparative performance could be studied. All were eventually superheated after the 1909 trials with the LNWR when the Brighton engines proved more economical on water for the journey between Rugby and Brighton.

Building details are as follows:

LBSCR No.	Built	Cylinders	Superheated	Withdrawn
21	1907	19 x 26in	1919	1951
22-25	1908	21 x 26in	As built	1950-51 (No. 24 1944)
26	1909	21 x 26in	As built	1950-51
27-29	1909	19 x 26in	1925/23/27	1950-51
30	1910	19 x 26in	1926	1950-51
75-76	1910	19 x 26in	1925/27	1950-51
77-81	1910	21 x 26in	As built	1950-51
82-89	1912	21 x 26in	As built	1950-51
90-91	1913	21 x 26in	As built	1950-52 (No. 91 1952)

Nos 30 and 75 had 21in stroke cylinders.

Class 13 No.2082 in 1934.

Class 13 LBSCR No.21.

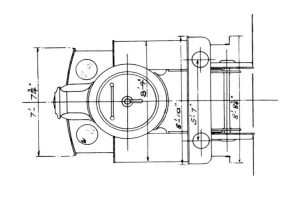

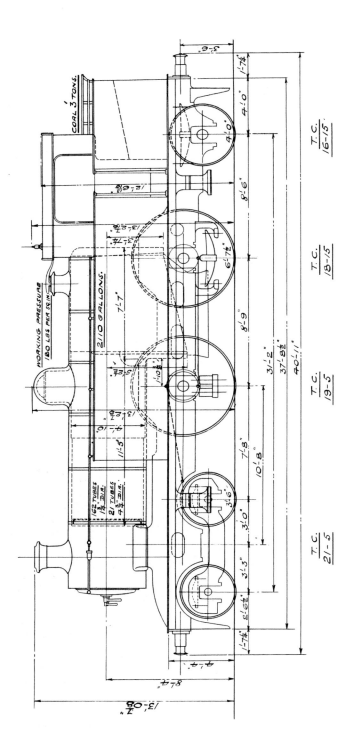

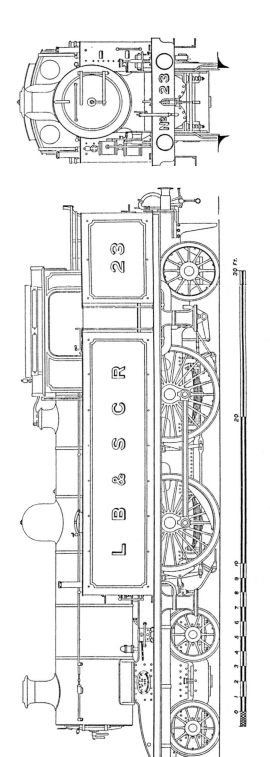

Class I3 4-4-2T. (Brighton dwg No.B58)

Class I3 4-4-2T.

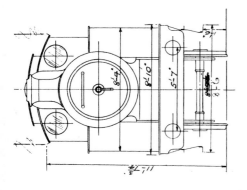

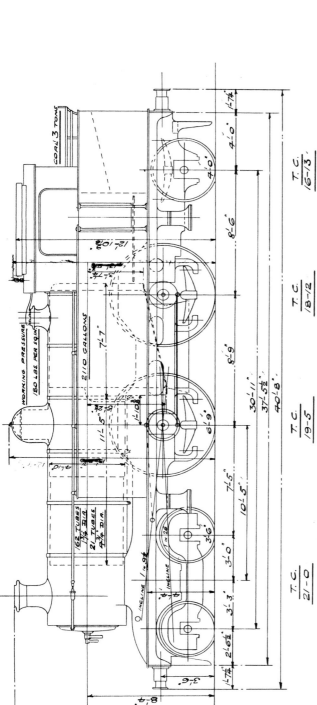

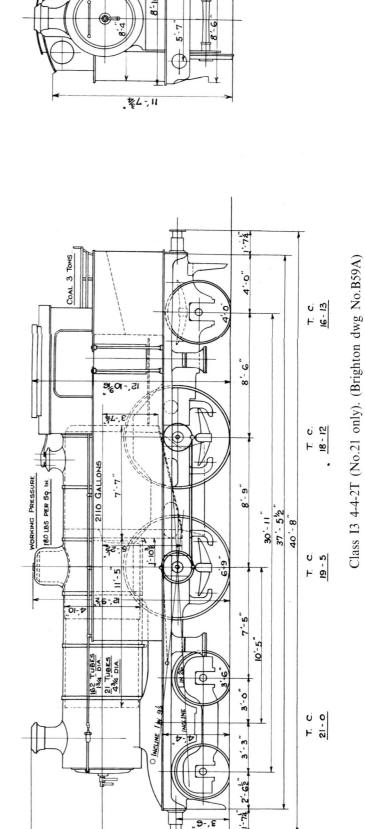

Class I3 4-4-2T (No.21 only). (Brighton dwg No.B59)

Class I3 4-4-2T (No.21 only). (Brighton dwg No.B59A)

Class 13 No.2079 at Eastleigh, 1938.

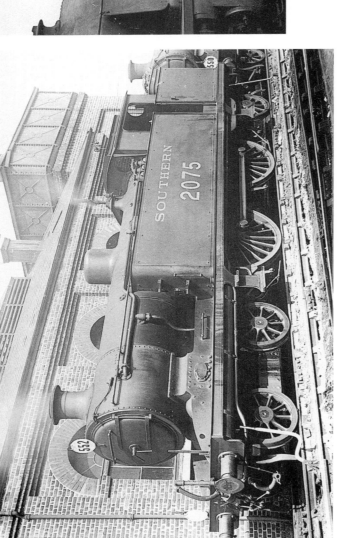

Class 13 No.2075 in 1937 (LH side).

I4 class 4-4-2T

The final batch of I class engines was built at Brighton in 1908, and consisted of five locomotives only, Nos 31-35. The class was identical to the 12 series, with the exceptions that the I4s were superheated as built, and were $2\frac{1}{2}$in longer over the total wheelbase. Details are as follows:

LBSCR No.	Built	Withdrawn
31	1908	1936
32	1908	1937
33	1908	1937
34	1908	1940
35	1908	1937

Class I4 SR No.2035, Eastleigh in 1937.

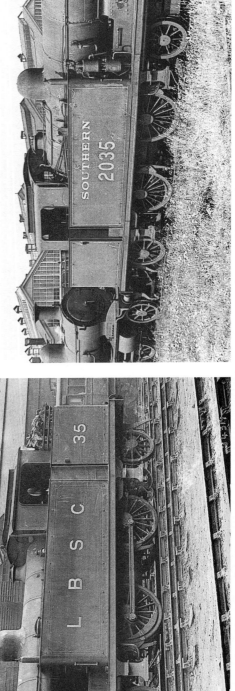

Class I4 LBSCR No.35 in 1921.

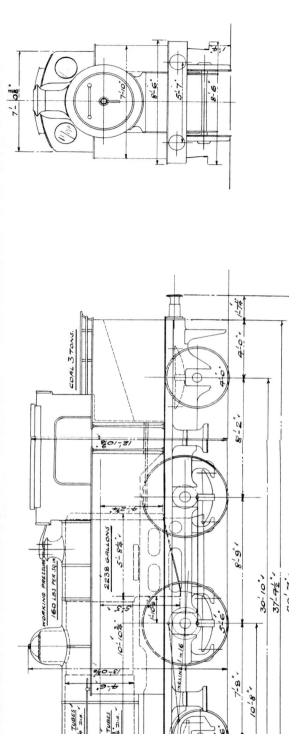

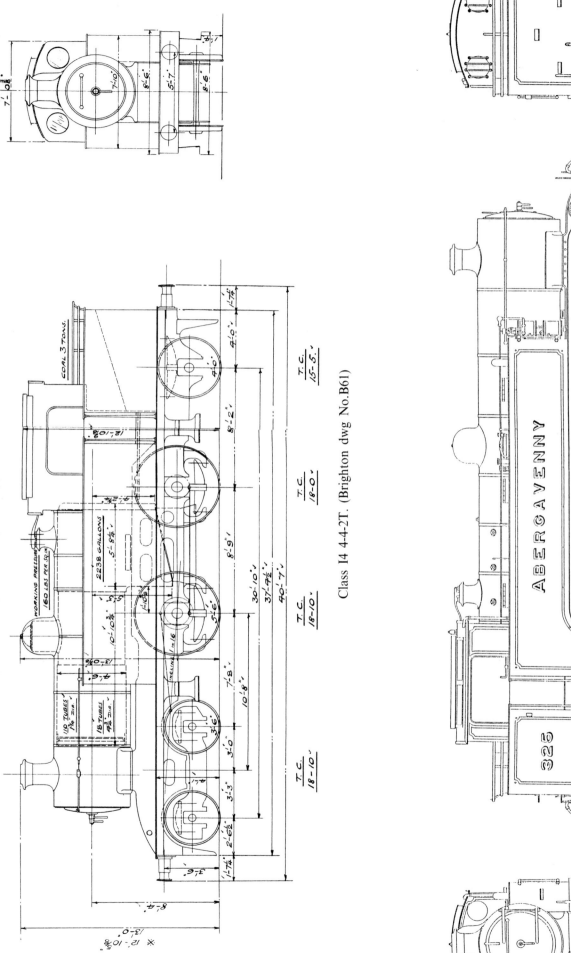

Class I4 4-4-2T. (Brighton dwg No.B61)

Class J1 4-6-2T.

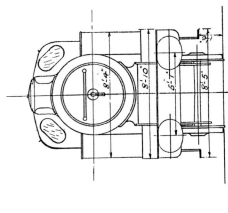

Class J1 No.B325 in 1928.

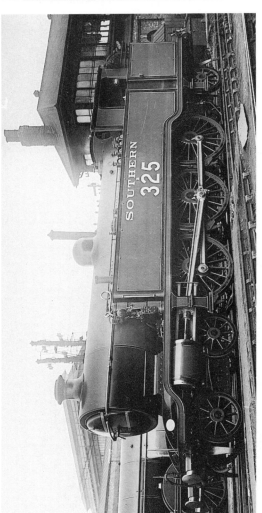

Class J1 BR No.32325 in 1950 (LH side).

J1 and J2 class 4-6-2T

Now we come to the really big engines of the LBSCR and these two engines, and the six H2s of 1911, were really the swan song of the Marsh era. Nos 325 and 326 were very handsome locomotives and were given the names *Abergavenny* for No. 325 and *Bessborough* for the sister, No. 326. Although both were classed as 'J', there were a number of differences between the two. *Abergavenny*, which was built in 1910, had

LBSCR No.	Name	Built	Withdrawn
325	*Abergavenny*	1910	1951
326	*Bessborough*	1912	1951

No. 325 had 2,230 gallons water capacity and No. 326 had 2,019 gallons.

Stephenson inside valve gear, whilst *Bessborough*, built in 1912 had outside Walschaerts valve gear. Both engines originally had clerestory roofs to their cabs, but these were later altered to suit the composite gauge of the SR.

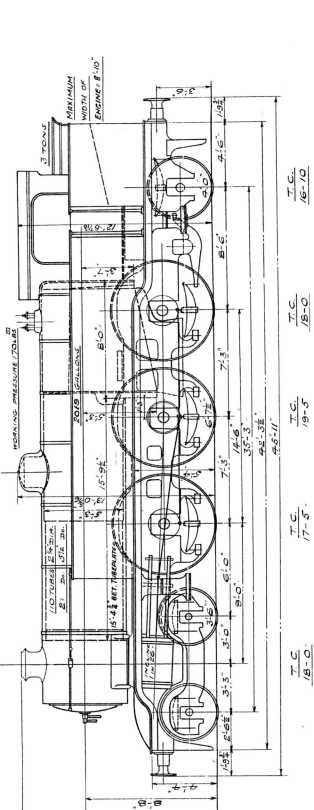

Class J1 4-6-2T (Brighton dwg No.B63).

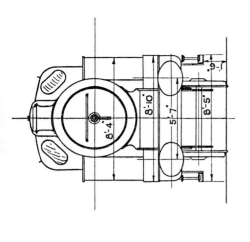

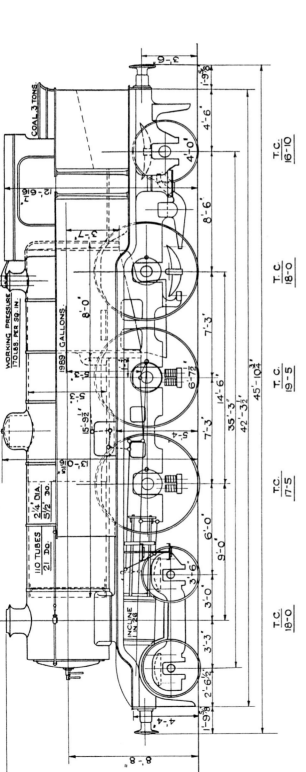

Class J2 4-6-2T. (Brighton dwg No.B64)

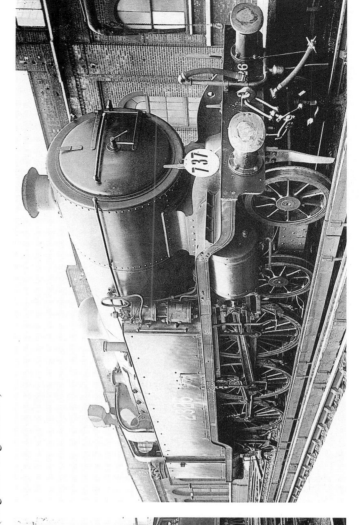

Class J2 SR No.2326 in 1934 (RH side).

Class J2 LBSCR No.326 *Bessborough* in 1920.

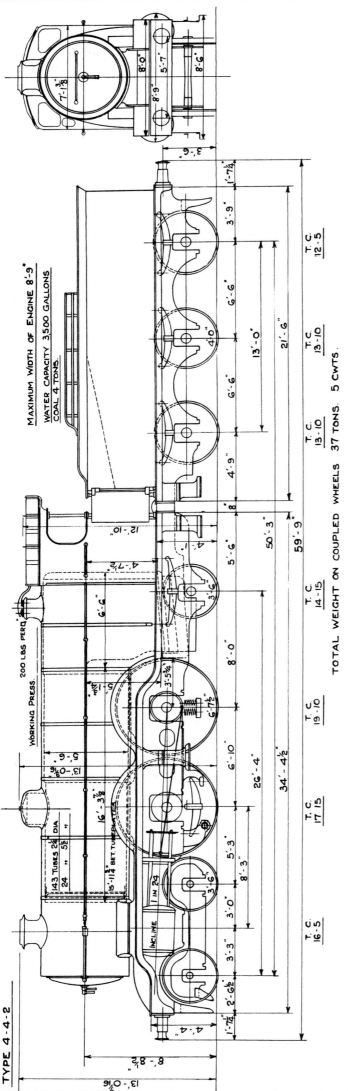

TYPE 4-4-2

MAXIMUM WIDTH OF ENGINE 8'-9"

WATER CAPACITY 3,500 GALLONS
COAL 4 TONS.

200 LBS PER □"
WORKING PRESS.

TOTAL WEIGHT ON COUPLED WHEELS 37 TONS. 5 CWTS.

Above: Class H2 4-4-2. (Brighton dwg No.B52A)

Below: Class H2 4-4-2.

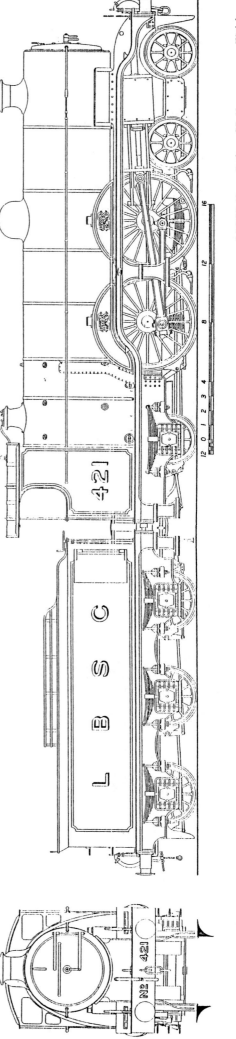

LBSC

421

H2 class 4-4-2

The last engines to be built to Marsh's designs were the six Atlantics. Nos 421-426. Very similar to the H1 series, except that as built, these machines were superheated and the main difference to the lineside observer was that the framing was straightened out at the leading end, and did not have the double curvature of the H1 class. Originally, both series were fitted with brakes on the leading bogie, but these were eventually dispensed with. Also, both classes had their cab profiles rounded off to suit the SR gauge, and received Maunsell type chimneys. Names were also bestowed in Southern Railway days, following the example of the H1s

LBSCR No.	Built	SR Name	Withdrawn
421	1911	South Foreland	1956
422	1911	North Foreland	1956
423	1911	The Needles	1949
424	1911	Beachy Head	1958
425	1911	Trevose Head	1956
426	1912	St Alban's Head	1956

Class H2 BR No.32421 *South Foreland.*

Class H2 No.B421 in 1926 before being named *South Foreland.*

Class H2 No.B422 *North Foreland* in 1928.

Class H2 LBSCR No.422 (RH side), 1920.

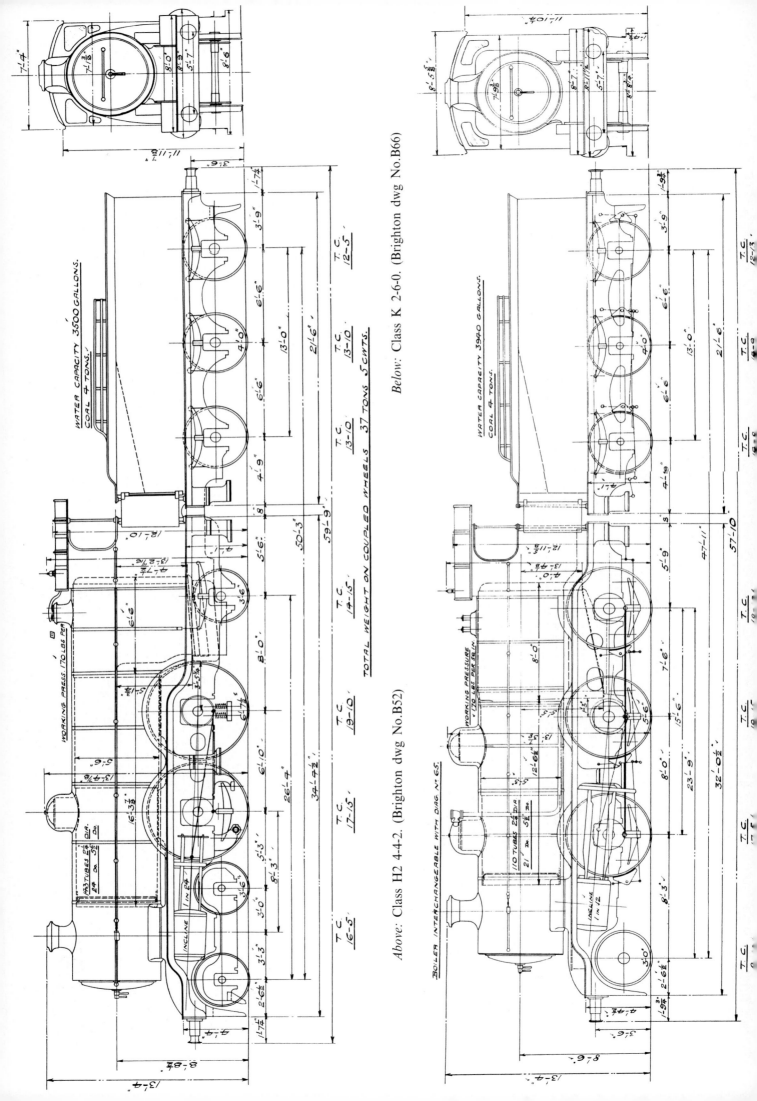

Above: Class H2 4-4-2. (Brighton dwg No.B52)

Below: Class K 2-6-0. (Brighton dwg No.B66)

K class 2-6-0

This Billinton design of 2-6-0 was another move forward to obtain more power. Most of the other British railways at this time were constructing the ubiquitous Moguls, as it was soon found that this form of locomotive, with its 5ft 6in driving wheels, could handle practically any kind of traffic from express passenger to the lowliest of freights. The LBSCR version was the first on that railway to make use of the Belpaire firebox, and together with a boiler 5ft 3in in diameter by 12ft 6½in long, pressed at 170lb per sq in, and superheated, they were very free steamers.

Two were built in 1913, three more in 1914, another five in the war years of 1916, and a final seven between 1920 and 1921, making a total of 17 engines in this class. As built, they carried the Brighton cab, but all were altered later to suit the composite gauge, and flat-topped domes were fitted. Mr Billinton also experimented with extra domes on some engines, with a top feed clack box on each side, but all were eventually removed.

LBSCR No.	Built	Withdrawn
337	1913	1962
338	1913	1962
339	1914	1962
340	1914	1962
341	1914	1962
342	1916	1962
343	1916	1962
344	1916	1962
345	1916	1962
346	1916	1962
347	1920	1962
348	1920	1962
349	1920	1962
350	1920	1962
351	1921	1962
352	1921	1962
353	1921	1962

All adapted for the composite gauge between 1935 and 1939, and the Weir pumps were replaced by injectors between 1949 and 1953.

Class K LBSCR No.352 (LH side) with top feed apparatus.

Class K SR No.2338, Fratton, 1937.

Class K LBSCR No.339 at New Cross in 1920.

Class K BR No.32344 in 1950.

Class K No.2343
at Eastleigh in
1938.

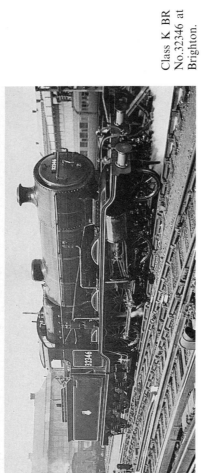

Class K BR
No.32346 at
Brighton.

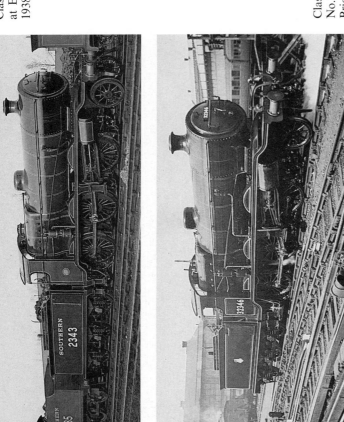

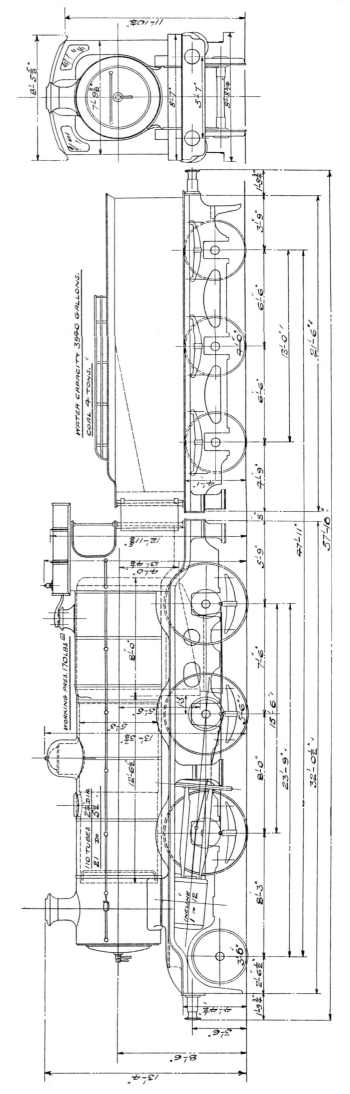

Class K 2-6-0. (Brighton dwg No B65)

L Class 4-6-4T

These seven express passenger tank engines were the largest locomotives to be built at Brighton, and were unique in having the 4-6-4T configuration.

With huge side tanks carrying 2,700 gallons, these machines had a tendency to roll at speed, and later, in order to bring down the centre of gravity, the tank capacity was reduced, to 2,686 galls with an extra tank fitted lower between the leading and centre driving axles. The first engine, No. 327, was named *Charles C. Macrae*, when built, and in 1921, No. 329, after being in service

for a while,, was given the name *Stephenson*. In 1922, No. 333, in memory of the staff of the railway who gave their lives in the First World War, was named *Remembrance* with a bronze plaque suitably inscribed and fixed to each of the side tanks.

Perhaps this is the right place to record that Mr Maunsell, in due concern about the stability of the big tanks after trouble with the 'Rivers' on the Eastern section, converted all these Brighton 4-6-4Ts to 4-6-0 express tender engines, classed N15, and all seven were then given names.

LBSCR No.	Built	LBSCR Name	Rebuilt to 4-6-0	SR Name	Withdrawn
327	1914	Charles C. Macrae	1935	Trevithick	1956
328	1914		1936	Hackworth	1955
329	1921	Stephenson	1934	Stephenson	1956
330	1921		1935	Cudworth	1955
331	1921		1936	Beattie	1957
332	1922		1935	Stroudley	1956
333	1922	Remembrance	1935	Remembrance	1956

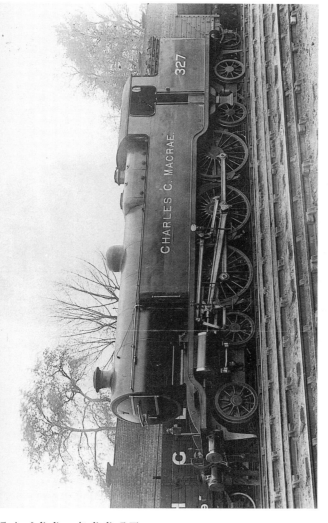

Class L LBSCR No.327 *Charles C. Macrae* at Battersea, 1921 (LH side).

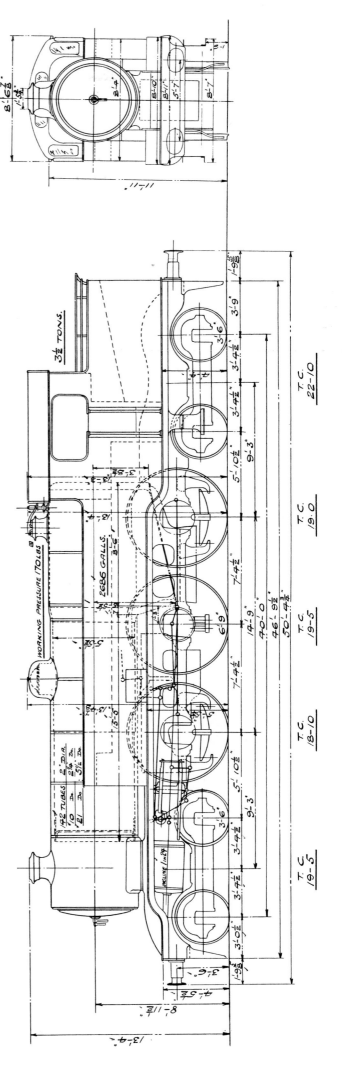

Class L 4-6-4T. (Brighton dwg No.B69B)

Class L LBSCR No.328 in 1920.

Class L No.B328 in 1927.

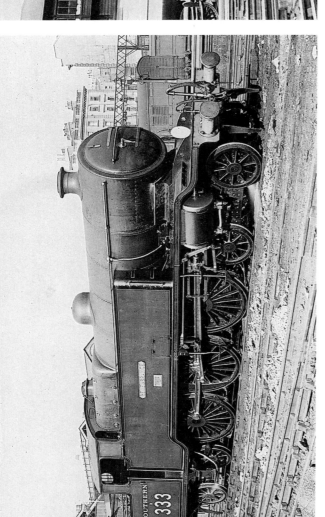

Class L SR No.B333 *Remembrance* in 1927 (RH side).

Class L No.B331 in 1925.

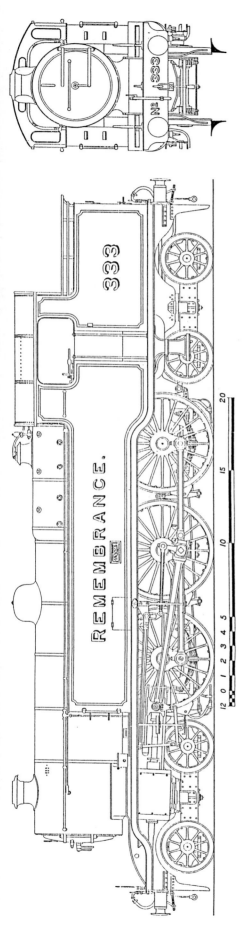

Class L 4-6-4T.

B4x class 4-4-0

The last class of locomotive to be built for the LBSCR at Brighton Works, was the 4-4-0 B4x. Although the classification records them as 'rebuilds', they were in essence a 4-4-0 version of the so successful K class Moguls. The only item which was carried over from earlier engines was the bogie. The old tenders from the B4 class were attached to these engines, but were enlarged to carry 3,600 gallons of water, against the original 3,000 capacity.

When first outshopped, these engines were painted grey with white lettering, which earned them the pseudonym of "greybacks". The reason for this was that the Southern Railway as such had just come into being and no decisions as to painting and colour had been decided.

Only one was ever named, No. 72 the last to be built, was called *Sussex* and renumbered 52! All twelve had the cab roof profile altered later and fitted with Maunsell chimneys to suit the SR loading gauge.

LBSCR No.	Rebuilt	Withdrawn
43	1923	1951
45	1923	1951
50	1923	1951
52	1923	1951
55	1922	1951
56	1923	1951
60	1922	1951
67	1923	1951
70	1923	1951
71	1923	1951
72	1924	1951
73	1923	1951

(For names see list of B4 engines.)

Class B4x No.55 in 1921 (LH side).

Class B4x LBSCR No.55 in 1920 (RH side).

Class B4x No.2067 in 1939.

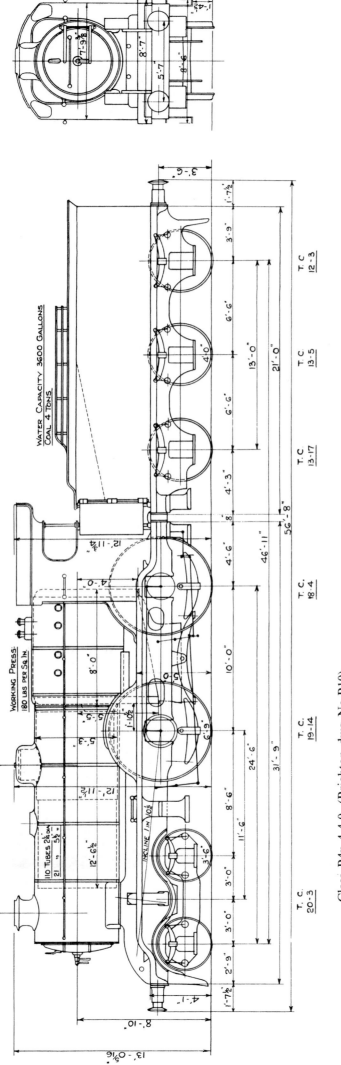

Water Capacity 3600 Gallons
Coal 4 Tons

Working Press:
180 lbs per Sq. In.

110 Tubes 2⅛ Dia

Incline 1 in 10½

Class B4x 4-4-0. (Brighton dwg No.B10)

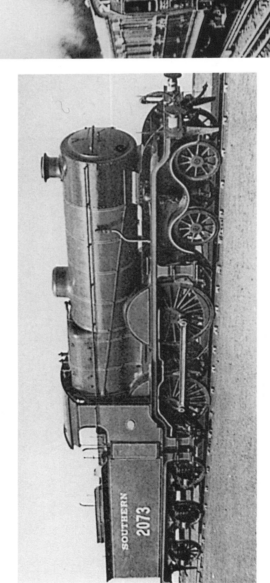

Class B4x No.2073 in 1937.

Part Three

Western Section – Prefix 'E'

Class	Type	Built	Use	Page
0278 (273)	0-6-0	1872-73	Goods Tender Engines	136
0298 (329)	2-4-0T	1874-78	Passenger Tank Engines	137
0302 (302)	0-6-0	1874-78	Goods Tender Engines	139
0330 (330)	0-6-0ST	1876-82	Shunting Tank Engines	141
046 (46)	4-2-2T	1879	Passenger Tank Engines	143
0380 (380)	4-4-0	1879	Passenger Tender Engines	145
0307 (135)	4-4-0	1880	Passenger Tender Engines	146
0395 (395)	0-6-0	1881-83	Goods Tender Engines	147
0415 (415)	4-4-2T	1882-85	Passenger Tank Engines	150
0445 (445)	4-4-0	1884-87	Passenger Tender Engines	154
0460 (460)	4-4-0	1887-95	Passenger Tender Engines	156
A12 (and O4)	0-4-2	1889-96	Passenger Tender Engines	159
T1 (and F6)	0-4-4T	1889-95	Passenger Tank Engines	164
O2	0-4-4T	1890-92	Passenger Tank Engines	169
X2	4-4-0	1890-92	Passenger Tender Engines	172
T3	4-4-0	1892-93	Passenger Tender Engines	175
B4 (and K14)	0-4-0T	1891-93	Shunting Tank Engines	178
G6 (and M9)	0-6-0T	1894-00	Shunting Tank Engines	182
T6	4-4-0	1895-96	Passenger Tender Engines	185
X6	4-4-0	1895	Passenger Tender Engines	187
M7 (and X14)	0-4-4T	1897	Passenger Tank Engines	188
T7	4-2-2-0	1897	Passenger Tender Engine	196
700	0-6-0	1897	Goods Tender Engines	197
C8	4-4-0	1898	Passenger Tender Engines	200
T9	4-4-0	1899-01	Passenger Tender Engines	204
F9	4-2-4T	1899	Inspection Saloon	214
E10	4-2-2-0	1901	Passenger Tender Engines	216
K10	4-4-0	1901	Passenger Tender Engines	217
L11	4-4-0	1903-07	Passenger Tender Engines	221
S11	4-4-0	1903	Passenger Tender Engines	227
L12	4-4-0	1904	Passenger Tender Engines	230
C14/S14	0-4-0T/2-2-0T	1910	Passenger Tank Engines	233
F13 (H15)	4-6-0	Rbt 1905	Goods Tender Engines	236
E14	4-6-0	1907	Passenger Tender Engine	236
G14	4-6-0	1908-11	Passenger Tender Engines	236
P14	4-6-0	1908-11	Passenger Tender Engines	236
T14	4-6-0	1911	Passenger Tender Engines	236
T14 Rbt	4-6-0	1930-31	Passenger Tender Engines	236
D15	4-4-0	1912-13	Passenger Tender Engines	249
H15	4-6-0	1913-25	Passenger Tender Engines	252
N15 (Urie)	4-6-0	1918	Passenger Tender Engines	253
S15 (Urie)	4-6-0	1921-21	Goods Tender Engines	257
G16	4-8-0T	1921	Shunting Tank Engines	261
H16	4-6-2T	1921	Goods Tank Engines	262
0111/0458	0-4-0T	1878-90	Dock Tank Engines	264
735	0-6-0T	1874-76	Passenger Tank Engines	266

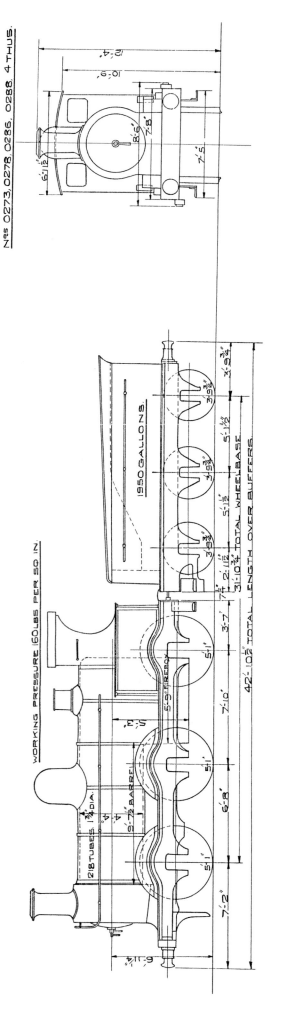

Nºs 0273, 0278, 0286, 0288, 4 THUS.

WORKING PRESSURE 160LBS PER SQ IN.

1950 GALLONS.

218 TUBES 1¾" DIA.

5'-7½" BARREL

5'-3" FIREBOX

31'-0¾" TOTAL WHEELBASE

42'-10½" TOTAL LENGTH OVER BUFFERS

Class 0278 0-6-0. (Eastleigh dwg No.E2)

0278 class 0-6-0

Six old outside framed engines, ordered by Beattie Snr in 1871 as the 273 class and built by Beyer, Peacock & Co. of Gorton in 1872-3, lived on to enter the Southern Railway stock list in 1923. All were withdrawn in 1924, but to be as complete as possible, this work must record them. Adams reboilered them, the sizes being 4ft 4in x 9ft 7½in, and the pressure was 160lbs. Cylinders were 17in x 24in, and coupled wheels 5ft1in diameter. The tenders which had the raked coping, held 1,950 gallons, and originally had the footboard and handrails of the Beattie engines. Summary is as follows:-

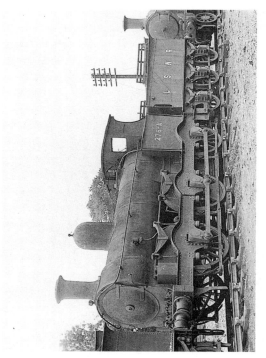

Class 0278 No.278A at Eastleigh in 1924 (LH side).

LSWR No.	Built	Rebuilt	Renumbered (date)	Withdrawn
273	1872	1893	0273 (1898) 273A (1914)	1924
274	1872	1893	0274 (1898) 0229 (1914)	1924
277	1872	1896	0277 (1900) 277A (1914)	1924
278	1872	1886	0278 (1900) 278A (1914)	1924
286	1873	1886	0286 (1900) 286A (1914)	1924
288	1873	1894	0288 (1900) 288A (1914)	1924

Class 0278 No.229 at Eastleigh in 1922 (RH side).

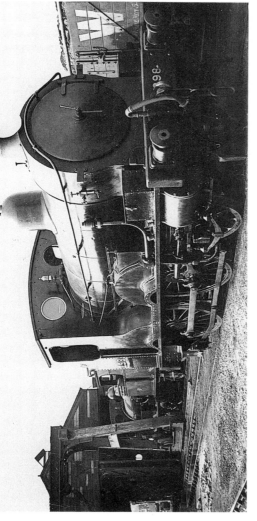

Class 0298 No.298 at Wadebridge in 1922.

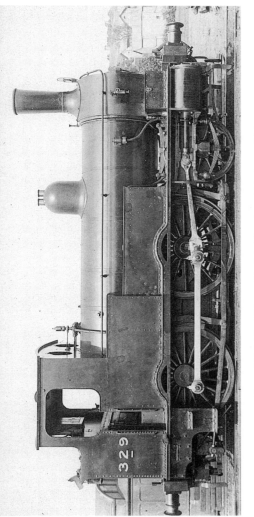

Class 0298 No.329 at Wadebridge in 1922 (RH side).

0298 class 2-4-0WT

A couple of years after the delivery of the previous 273 class of 0-6-0 goods engines, Messrs Beyer, Peacock & Co. built the celebrated suburban well tanks for the London & South Western Railway. They were delivered in two lots, six in 1874 and six in 1875, as the 329 class and there were slight differences between the two orders, the main being

that the later six had rectangular splashers and were six inches longer in the frames. Astonishing as it may seem, three of the class not only survived into Southern Railway days, but worked on into British Rail ownership, probably because they were tucked away in Cornwall, working the China clay traffic on the Wenford Bridge mineral line. Over the decades, they were rebuilt many times,

first with an Adams boiler, then in the 1920s with a Drummond boiler, but throughout they retained their old vintage appearance. It is pleasant to report that BR Nos 30585 and 30587 have been preserved.

Class 0298 No.298 at Wadebridge in 1922.

LSWR No	Built	Duplicate list (1898-1901)	BR No.
298	1874	0298	30587
314	1874	0314	30585
329	1875	0329	30586

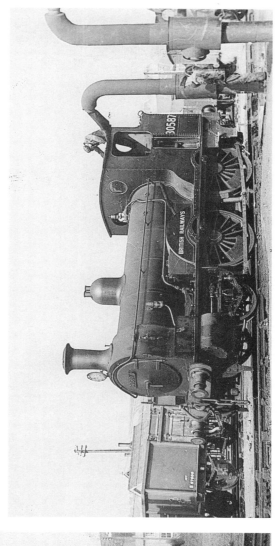

Class 0298 BR No.30587, Wadebridge, 1949.

Class 0298 No.E0329 at Wadebridge in 1926.

Class 0298 No.0298 at Eastleigh, 1931.

Class 0298 BR No.30586, Wadebridge, 1954.

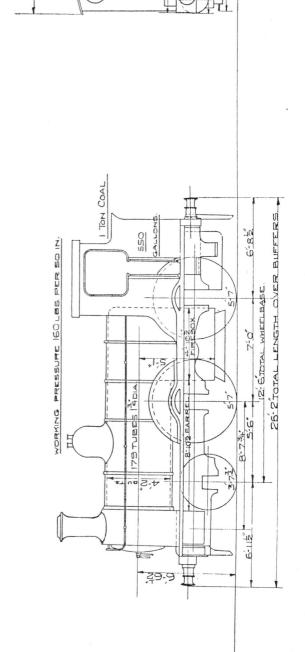

Class 0298 2-4-0WT (Eastleigh, dwg. No.E4)

WORKING PRESSURE 160 LBS PER SQ IN.

1 TON COAL

550 GALLONS.

179 TUBES 1¾ DIA

8'-02 BARREL

12'-6 TOTAL WHEELBASE.

26'-2 TOTAL LENGTH OVER BUFFERS.

0302 class 0-6-0

1874 also saw the introduction of Beattie Jnr's own design of 0-6-0 goods engines, the 302 class. Different from the 0278 class in that these newer engines were inside framed, and the footplating was straight, except for the small coupling rod arches. The boilers were replaced in Adams' time, with those of his design, and Drummond boiler fittings were substituted in the era prior to Southern Railway ownership. 36 engines were constructed by Beyer, Peacock between 1874 and 1878, but only 15 of the class managed to be passed on to the Southern Railway; they are as follows with duplication dates.

LSWR No.	Built	Rebuilt	Duplicate list	Renumbered	Withdrawn
151	1878	1890	0151 (1902)	–	1924
152	1878	1891	0152 (1902)	–	1924
160	1878	1890	0160 (1900)	160A (1916)	1924
162	1878	1886	0162 (1900)	162A (1916)	1924
229	1878	1886	0229 (1894)	229A (1916)	1925
311	1874	1886	0311 (1901)	–	1925
337	1876	1893	0337 (1901)	337A (1917)	1924
338	1876	1892	0338 (1901)	–	1924
341	1876	1893	0341 (1901)	–	1924
342	1876	1894	0342 (1901)	–	1924
343	1876	1891	0343 (1902)	–	1924
345	1876	1891	0345 (1901)	–	1925
347	1876	1893	0347 (1901)	347A (1916)	1925
369	1878	1888	0369 (1901)	–	1925
370	1878	1890	0370 (1901)	370A (1916)	1924

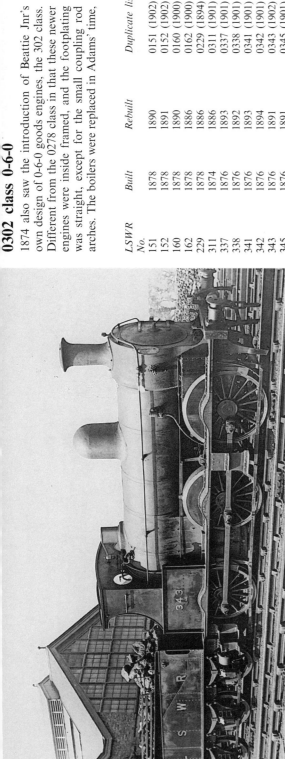

Class 0302 No.343 in LSWR livery at Strawberry Hill, 1920.

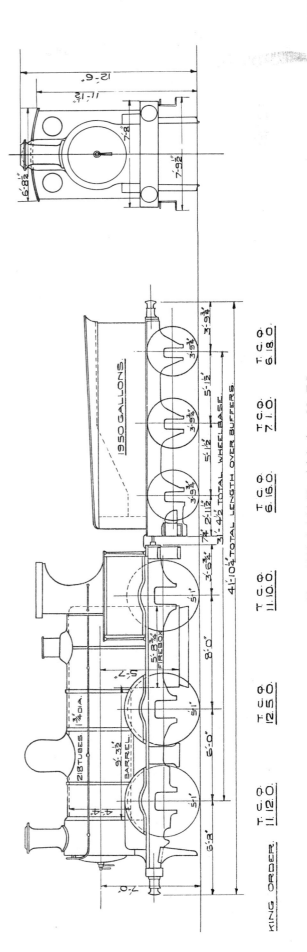

Class 0302 0-6-0. (Eastleigh dwg No.E6)

Class 0302 No.151, Guildford, 1921.

Class 0302 No.347A, Strawberry Hill, 1922.

Class 0302 No.342 at Eastleigh in 1922 (RH side).

Class 0302 No.162A, Strawberry Hill, 1923 (LH side).

Class 0302 No.338 at Eastleigh in 1922.

Class 0302 No.152 at Strawberry Hill, 1921.

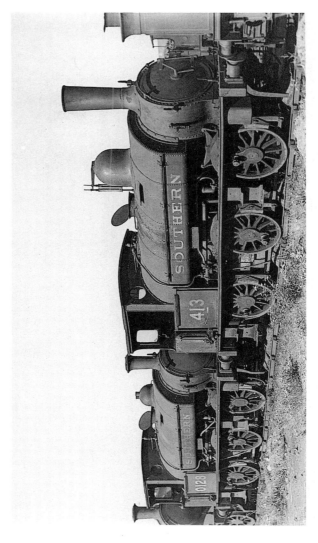

Class 0330 Nos 0128 and 413 at Eastleigh in 1931.

PAGE 141

0330 class 0-6-0ST

Known as the "Saddlebacks", the LSWR 330 class of 20 engines, were Beyer, Peacock's own design of 1875, and were ordered by Beattie in 1876 for shunting duties. Until this time, marshalling yards had been used to old redundant engines which, relegated to shunting from traffic duties, caused much delay and lost time by their unsuitability for yard work. The 0-6-0 saddle tank engines with all their weight, plus the water in their tanks available for adhesion, made light work of heavy shunting. As built, they had Salter safety valves mounted on the dome, and were only pressed for 150lbs. As delivered they sported Beyer, Peacock's copper-topped chimneys, but later, twelve engines were refitted with Adams' 'stove-pipe' type, and later still Drummond chimneys were installed. The coupled wheels were 4ft 3in on a 13ft 9in total wheelbase, and the boiler was 4ft x 9ft 4in. It is surprising that none of these machines ever had power brakes, the retarding was via a hand brake in the cab. I would imagine a full day's duty shunting on one of these engines was a nightmare of winding the brake handle on and off! (or did they use the reversing lever?).

Out of the 20 built between 1876 and 1882, all went into the Southern Railway, but seven were scrapped before the end of 1926.

A summary with renumbering is as follows:

LSWR No.	Built	Duplicate list	Withdrawn
127	1882	0127 (1911)	1925
128	1882	0128 (1911)	1931
131	1882	0131 (1911)	1924
149	1882	0149 (1902)	1930
150	1882	0150 (1902)	1929
161	1882	0161 (1903)	1926
227	1877	0227 (1894)	
		316 (1899)	
		0316 (1912)	1930
228	1877	0228 (1894)	
		328 (1899)	
		0328 (1911)	1929
330	1876	0330 (1905)	1924
331	1876	0331 (1905)	1930
332	1876	0332 (1905)	1933
333	1876	0333 (1905)	1929
334	1876	0334 (1905)	1933
335	1876	0335 (1907)	1932
409	1882	0409 (1906)	1924
410	1882	0410 (1906)	1930
411	1882	0411 (1906)	1927
412	1882	0412 (1906)	1925
413	1882	0413 (1906)	1931
414	1882	0414 (1906)	1924

No. 0335 Sold to East Kent Railway.

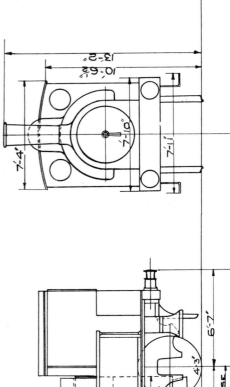

Class 0330 No.0412 partly dismantled at Eastleigh in 1925.

Class 0330 No.316, Fratton, 1921.

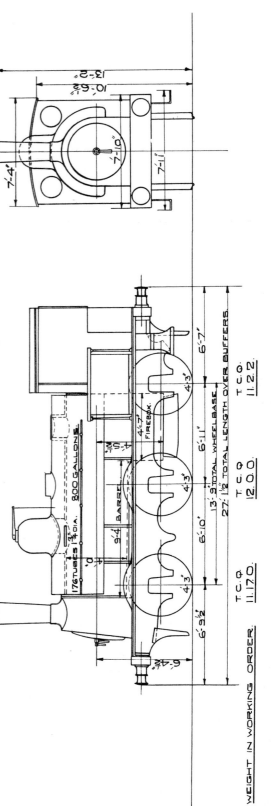

Class 0330 0-6-0ST. (Eastleigh dwg No.E7)

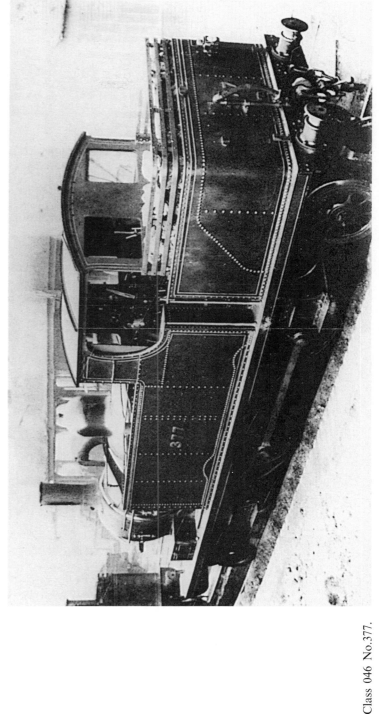

Class 0330 No.0334 at Eastleigh in 1931.

Class 0330 No.0331, Eastleigh 1926 (RH side).

046 class 4-4-2T

The bogie tank engine originally classified 46, was the first of Adams' designs to be built for the LSWR when he took over from Beattie in 1878. Built by Beyer, Peacock in 1879, the twelve engines in the order started out as 4-4-0 tanks, with small 2ft 6in solid bogie wheels and 5ft 7in coupled drivers. Boilers were pressed for 160lbs and were 4ft 2in x 10ft 0¾in in the barrel. Between 1883 and 1886, all twelve were converted to the 4-4-2T arrangement by extending the bunker and fitting a pair of trailing radial wheels underneath. This enabled the coal capacity to be increased to 3 tons, whilst a well tank under, pushed up the water capacity to 1,650 gallons in total, together with the side tanks. In staff terms these engines were known as "Ironclads", but later in the Poole area, they took the nickname of "Hamworthy Buses".

Seven engines passed to the SR and were as follows:

LSWR No.	Rebuilt	Duplicate list	Withdrawn
46	1886	046 (1905)	1924
130	1885	0130 (1903)	1924
132	1885	0132 (1903)	1924
374	1886	0374 (1903)	1924
375	1884	0375 (1903)	1925
377	1886	0377 (1903)	1925
378	1885	0378 (1903)	1923

Class 046 No.377.

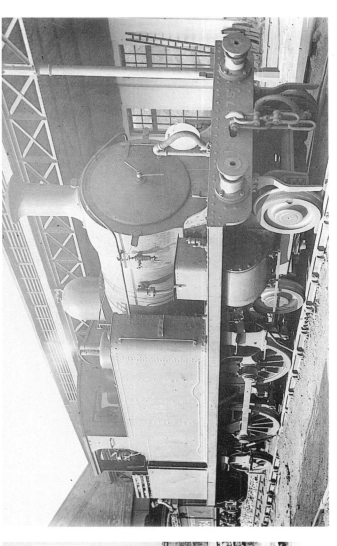

Class 046 No.124 (withdrawn in 1921, prior to Grouping).

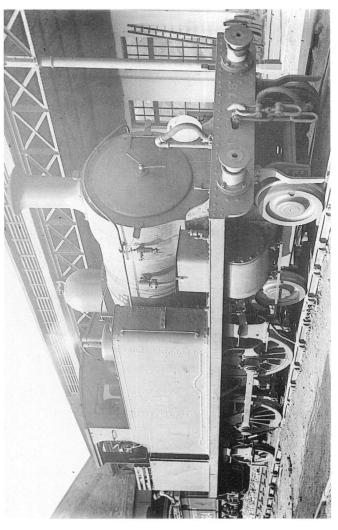

Class 046 No.0375 at Bournemouth, 1924.

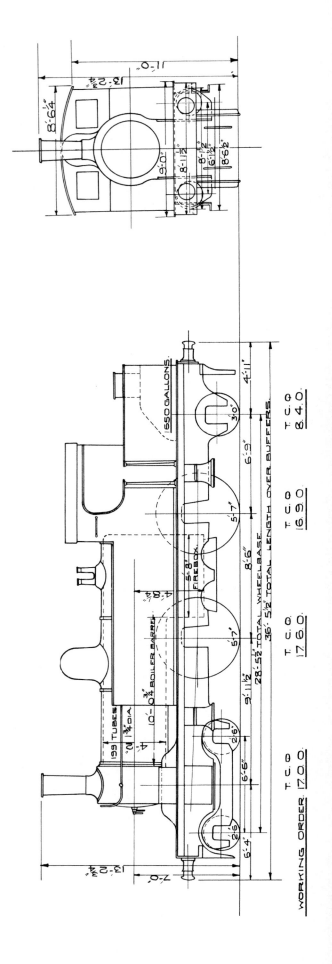

0380 class 4-4-0

The 380 class of twelve engines, were built to Adams' designs in 1879 by Beyer, Peacock & Co. Ltd. They were given the nickname "Steamrollers" by railwaymen because of the solid leading bogie wheels and the tall stove-pipe chimneys.

They were quite small locomotives, and spent most of their working life on goods links, and shunting duties. The boilers were 4ft 6in x 10ft 0¾in working at 160lbs pressure. The outside cylinders being 18in x 24in and driving wheels 5ft 7in dia, with the bogie wheels only 2ft 6in.

The tender had a capacity of 2,500 gallons and 3½ tons and was provided originally with a footboard and handrail to give access to where the water filling orifice and rear tool box were situated. Built with steam brakes, complete vacuum was fitted later.

Only eight of these machines went into SR hands and the details are as under, new boilers being put in by Mr Drummond.

Class 0380 No.337 at Eastleigh, 1924.

Class 0380 No.384 (LH side).

LSWR No.	Duplicate No.	New No. in 1914	Withdrawn
380	0380*		1924
381	0381*		1924
382	0382	0160	1923

LSWR No.	Duplicate No.	New No. in 1914	Withdrawn
384	0384*	0288	1924
385	0385	0277	1924
386	0386	0162	1924
388	0388		1925
390	0390	0337	1924

*Adams boiler

TYPE 4.4.0.

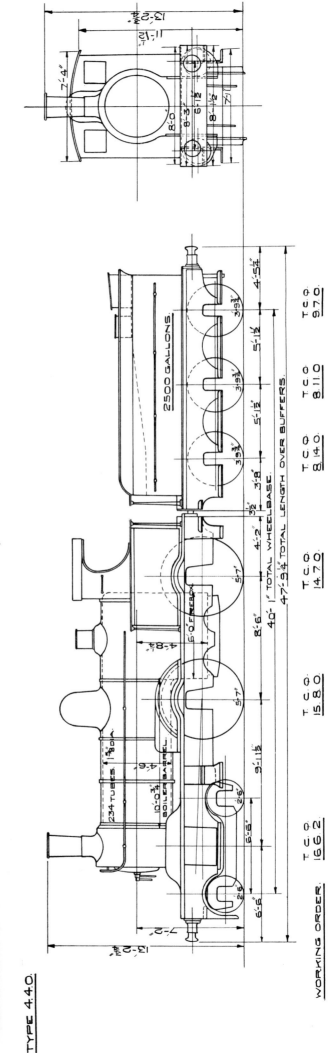

Class 0380 4-4-0. (Eastleigh dwg No.E12)

0307 class 4-4-0

The first series of express passenger engines which Mr Adams built for the LSWR, were the handsome 135 class (later, after 1914, 0307 class). Twelve were built by Beyer, Peacock in 1880 and only three concern this volume, as the other nine engines had been withdrawn before the Grouping. They had outside cylinders 18in x 24in on coupled wheels of 6ft 7in diameter. Bogie wheels were 3ft 4in, the boiler was 4ft 6in x 10ft 0¼in, pressed for 160lbs. The tender held 4 tons of fuel, and water capacity was 2,500 gallons, and originally had the Beattie type footboards and handrails. The engine had a steam brake, and also had a vacuum ejector for operating the brakes on the carriages.

The three survivors at Grouping were:

LSWR No.	1902 No.	1914 No.	Withdrawn
139	0139	0307	1924
140	0140	0310	1924
143	0143	0312	1922

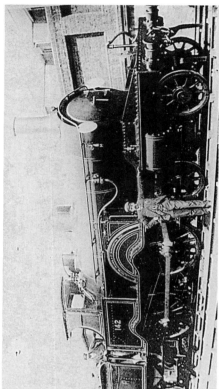

Class 0380 No.162 at Exmouth Junction in 1924.

Class 135 No.142 which was withdrawn in 1913.

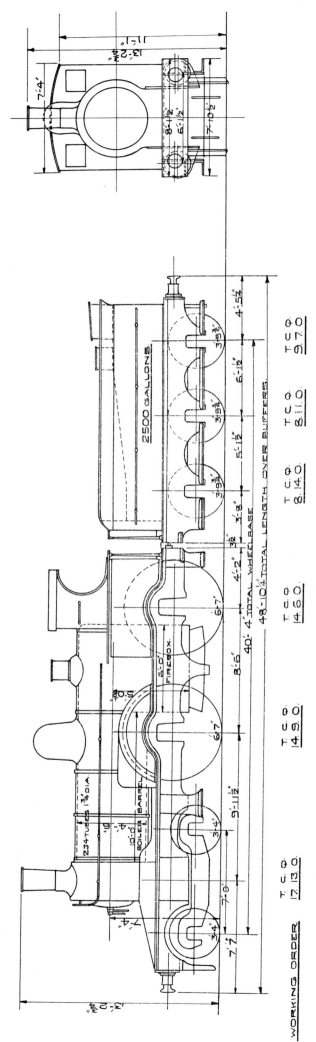

Class 135 No.136 also withdrawn (1913) prior to Grouping.

Class 0395 No.E029 at Eastleigh in 1929 (RH side).

Class 0395 No.3441 at Salisbury in 1945.

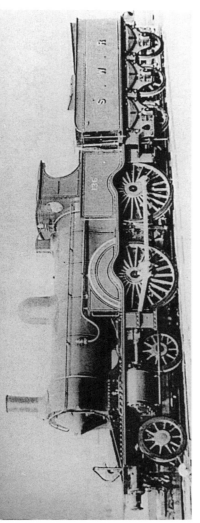

0395 class 0-6-0

In 1878 William Adams left the Great Eastern Railway to become Locomotive Superintendent of the LSWR. As has been already shown, he started on a long-term project of updating the locomotive stud of his new masters. Amongst the many orders that went out to the various contract firms was a large purchase of 70, 395 class 0-6-0 goods tender engines. Neilson & Co. of Glasgow secured this contract and all the engines were delivered between 1881 and 1886. They were very robust and sturdy machines with 5ft 1in diameter coupled wheels, boiler pressure 140lbs, size 4ft 4in x 10ft 6in and with a six-wheeled tender holding

2,500 gallons of water. The last 34 engines built in 1885–86, differed slightly in being 1ft 4in longer at the front end, making them slightly heavier. Only 20 were passed to the Southern Railway at the Grouping, most of the class being sent abroad on military service during the First World War (some never to return!)

A slight break with the Adams design came with these engines, in that the front of the smokebox was not vertical, being sloped backward from bottom to top, whilst the cab sides had no square bottom panels as before. Details of the history of the SR 0395s are as follows:

LSWR No.	Duplicate list	1931 Renumbering	BR No.	Withdrawn
29	029 (1904)	3029	30564	1958
69 (83)	083 (1908)	3083	30565	1953
101	0101 (1908)	3101	30566	1959
153	0153 (1902)	—	—	1933
154	0154 (1903)	3154	30567	1959
155	0155 (1903)	3155	30568	1958
163	0163 (1903)	3163	30569	1956
167	0167 (1904)	3167	30570	1956
397	0397 (1903)	3397	30571	1953
400	0400 (1903)	3400	30572	1957
433	0433 (1905)	3433	30573	1956
436	0436 (1906)	3436	30574	1957
439	0439 (1907)	3439	30575	1958
440	0440 (1907)	3440	30576	1950
441	0441 (1907)	3441	30577	1956
442	0442 (1907)	3442	30578	1957
496	0496 (1921)	3496	30579	1956
506	0506 (1920)	3506	30580	1957
509	0509 (1920)	3509	30581	1953
515	0515 (1921)	—	—	1933

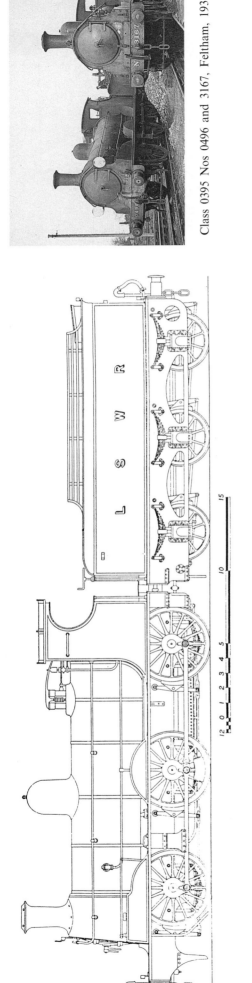

Class 0395 Nos 0496 and 3167, Feltham, 1932.

Class 0395 0-6-0.

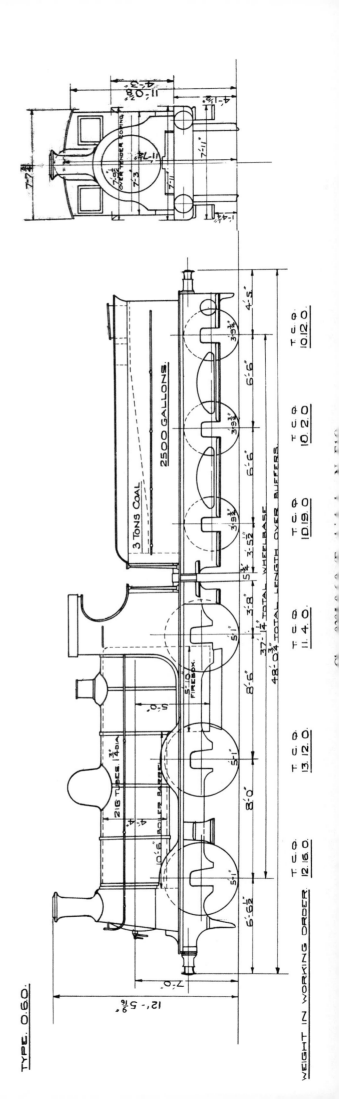

Class 0395 No.3163, Salisbury, 1935.

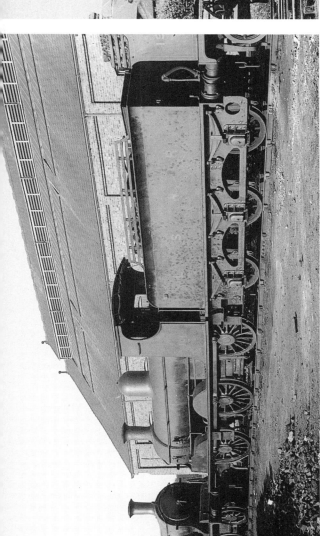

Class 0395 No.101 at Strawberry Hill, 1921.

Class 0395 No.3442, Feltham, 1942.

Class 0395 No.E0155, Feltham, 1925 (LH side).

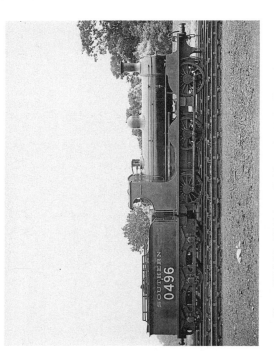

Class 0395 No.0153 at Exmouth Junction in 1924.

Class 0395 LSWR No.397, Strawberry Hill, 1923.

Class 0395 No.E0496 at Feltham in 1924 (RH side).

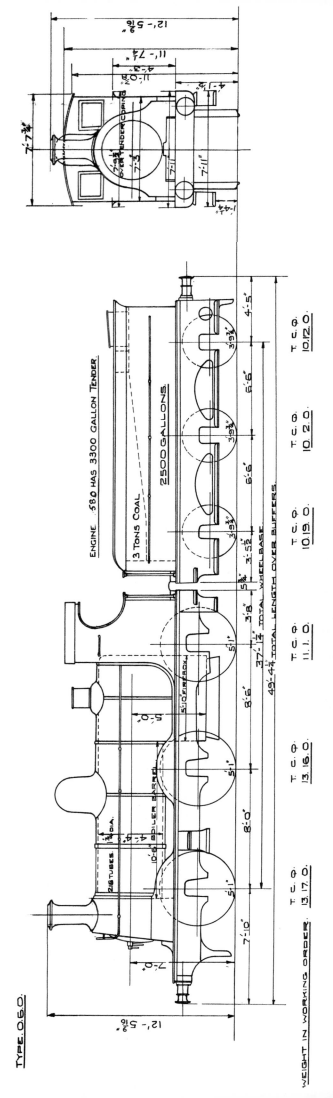

TYPE. O.6.O.

ENGINE .580 HAS 3300 GALLON TENDER.

3 TONS COAL

2500 GALLONS.

216 TUBES. 1½"DIA.

10'-6" BOILER BARREL.

5'-0" FIREBOX

37'-1½" TOTAL WHEELBASE.

49'-4½" TOTAL LENGTH OVER BUFFERS.

| WEIGHT IN WORKING ORDER | T.C.Q.
13.17.0 | T.C.Q.
13.16.0 | T.C.Q.
11.1.0 | T.C.Q.
10.19.0 | T.C.Q.
10.2.0 | T.C.Q.
10.12.0 |

Class 0395 (1885–6) 0-6-0 (Eastleigh dwg. No.E16A)

0415 class 4-4-2T

Following on from the 70 goods engines of the 395 class, Adams ordered 71 Class 415 suburban tank engines of the 4-4-2T configuration in 1882, to meet the ever-increasing London suburban traffic on the LSWR. Again the contracts went outside the railway to the locomotive builders, R. Stephenson, Beyer, Peacock, and Neilson & Co. This class was purely a development of the earlier 46 class of 1879, which had been rebuilt and improved in 1883 by conversion from 4-0T to 4-4-2T.

Handsome and handy little engines, the new 415 class differed from their predecessors by having spoked bogie and radial wheels of 3ft diameter (instead of 2ft 6in) and the side tanks were very much shorter, 320 gallons. The main body of water was carried in a well tank under the bunker, (680 gallons) all of which improved the riding qualities of the machines. Although records show that 49 of this class were passed into the Southern Railway at the Grouping, in fact, only 30 engines actually went onto the stock book but another was acquired later, in 1946. A point of interest to note is that during their existence several machines were given double slide bars and crossheads in place of the original single bars. These were Nos 0419/047/052/057/0129/0415/0486/0428/0520/0522/0523/0525.

A brief history of the 31 engines taken into stock is as under.

LSWR No.	Builder	Year	Duplicate list	BR No.	Withdrawn
45	Stephenson	1883	045 (1905)		1924
50	Stephenson	1883	050 (1905)		1927
54	Stephenson	1883	054 (1905)		1927
55	Stephenson	1883	055 (1905)		1924
58 (68)	Stephenson	1885	058 (1906)		1925
59 (77)	Stephenson	1885	059 (1906)		1925

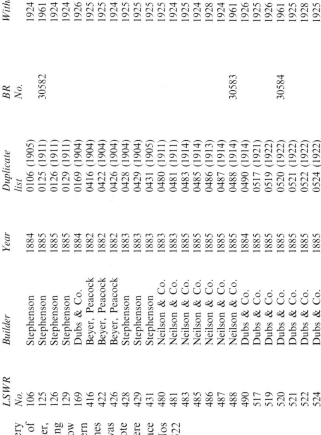

LSWR No.	Builder	Year	Duplicate list	BR No.	Withdrawn
106	Stephenson	1884	0106 (1905)		1924
125	Stephenson	1885	0125 (1911)	30582	1961
126	Stephenson	1885	0126 (1911)		1924
129	Stephenson	1885	0129 (1911)		1924
169	Dubs & Co.	1884	0169 (1904)		1926
416	Beyer, Peacock	1882	0416 (1904)		1925
422	Beyer, Peacock	1882	0422 (1904)		1925
426	Beyer, Peacock	1882	0426 (1904)		1924
428	Stephenson	1883	0428 (1904)		1925
429	Stephenson	1883	0429 (1904)		1925
431	Stephenson	1883	0431 (1905)		1925
480	Neilson & Co.	1883	0480 (1911)		1925
481	Neilson & Co.	1883	0481 (1911)		1924
483	Neilson & Co.	1885	0483 (1914)		1925
485	Neilson & Co.	1885	0485 (1914)		1924
486	Neilson & Co.	1885	0486 (1913)		1928
487	Neilson & Co.	1885	0487 (1914)		1924
488	Neilson & Co.	1885	0488 (1914)	30583	1961
490	Dubs & Co.	1884	0490 (1914)		1926
517	Dubs & Co.	1885	0517 (1921)		1925
519	Dubs & Co.	1885	0519 (1922)	30584	1961
520	Dubs & Co.	1885	0520 (1922)		1925
521	Dubs & Co.	1885	0521 (1922)		1925
522	Dubs & Co.	1885	0522 (1922)		1928
524	Dubs & Co.	1885	0524 (1922)		1925

No. 488 was sold in 1917 but acquired by the SR in 1946 and given the number 3488. Now preserved on the Bluebell Railway.

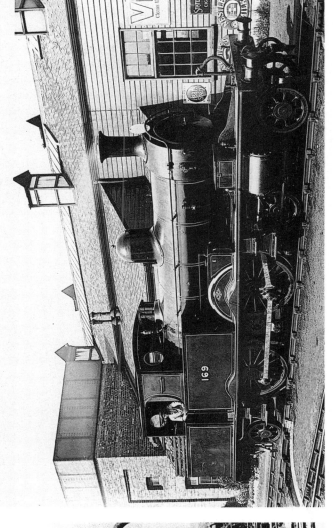

Class 0415 No.169, Wadebridge, 1922. (RH side).

Class 0415 No.517 in LSWR livery (LH side).

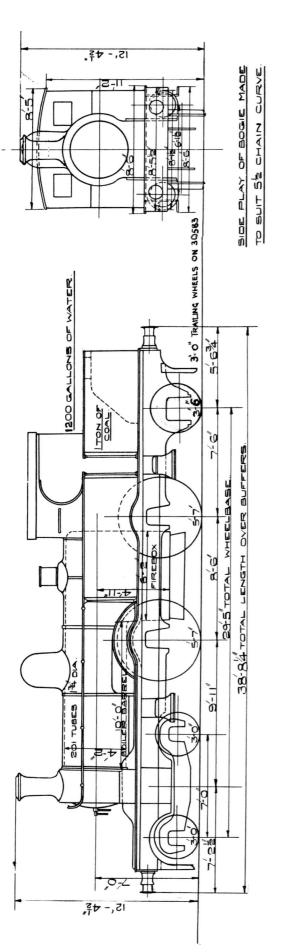

SIDE PLAY OF BOGIE MADE TO SUIT 5½ CHAIN CURVE.

Class 0415 4-4-2T. (Eastleigh dwg No.E15A)

1200 GALLONS OF WATER.

1 TON OF COAL

FIREBOX

201 TUBES

BOILER BARREL

3'-0" TRAILING WHEELS ON 30583

29'-5" TOTAL WHEELBASE.

38'-8¼" TOTAL LENGTH OVER BUFFERS.

Class 0415 BR No.30583 at Axminster in 1954.

Class 0415 4-4-2T.

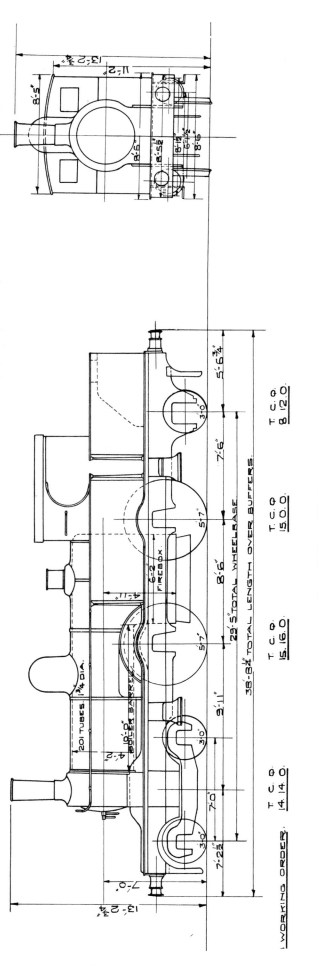

WORKING ORDER. | T.C.Q. 14.14.0. | T.C.Q. 15.16.0. | T.C.Q. 15.0.0. | T.C.Q. 8.12.0.

Class 0415 4-4-2T. (Eastleigh dwg No.E15)

Class 0415 No.3488.

Class 0415 No.3520 in 1937.

Class 0415 BR No.30583.

Class 0415 BR No.30582.

0445 class 4-4-0

Three years after the appearance of the 135 class, Adams produced an enlarged version in the shape of the 445 class. Built by R. Stephenson & Co. in 1883, this series consisted of twelve engines, numbered consecutively from 445 to 456. The wheels were larger, the coupled drivers being 7ft 1in diameter and the bogies were 3ft 7in. The boiler was slightly narrower, being 4ft 4in, but longer than the 135's by 2in. Pressure was increased to 160lbs and the boiler centre line was 5in higher than the previous series. A larger tender was attached, capable of carrying 2,800 gallons of water including 300 gallons in a well tank. Five of the engines were rebuilt with new boilers between 1893 and 1896, and all twelve saw service on the SR.

LSWR No.	Rebuilt	Renumbered	Withdrawn
445	–	0445 (1911)	1925
446	1907	0446 (1911)	1925
447	1896	0447 (1911)	1925
448	1894	0448 (1910)	1924
449	1893	0449 (1910)	1925
450	–	0450 (1911)	1925
451	1896	0451 (1911)	1924
452	–	0452 (1911)	1925
453	–	0453 (1908)	1924
454	–	0454 (1908)	1924
455	1895	0455 (1908)	1925

Class 0445 No.448 at Guildford in 1922.

Class 0445 4-4-0.

Class 0445 No.453, Eastleigh, 1924 (LH side).

Class 0445 No.450 at Eastleigh in 1922 (RH side).

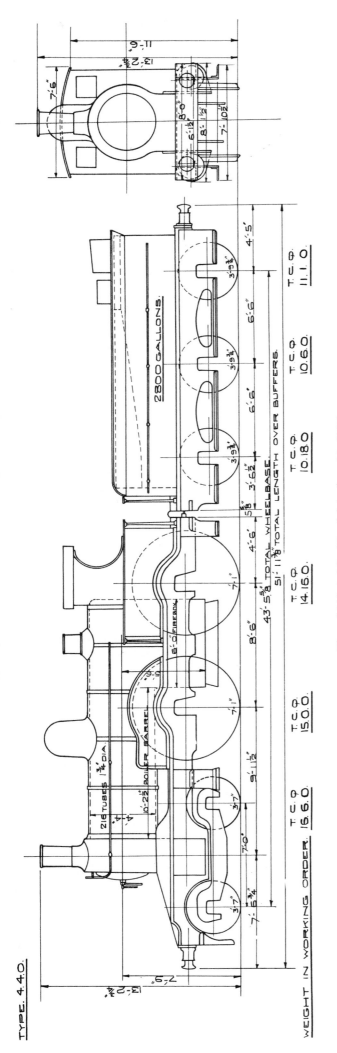

Class 0445 4-4-0. (Eastleigh dwg No.E17)

LSWR No.	New No.	Withdrawn
147	0147 (1906)	1927
460	0460 (1912)	1929
461	0461 (1912)	1926
462	0462 (1912)	1926
463	0463 (1912)	1929
464	0464 (1912)	1924
465	0465 (1912)	1928
466	0466 (1912)	1929
467	0467 (1912)	1928
468	0468 (1912)	1927
469	0469 (1912)	1929
470	0470 (1912)	1928
471	0471 (1913)	1928
472	0472 (1913)	1927
473	0473 (1923)	1928
474	0474 (1923)	1928
475	0475 (1924)	1926
476	0476 (1924)	1926
477	0477 (1924)	1927
478	0478 (1924)	1928
526	—	1928

No. 526. Built 1886

0460 class 4-4-0

Following the 445 class, the next batch of express passenger engines built for the LSWR was the 460 class. Adams placed orders with Neilson & Co. for ten of these engines, and a further ten were built by R. Stephenson & Co. from the middle of 1884 onwards. In the event, Stephenson's must have liked the design, because in 1886-7 they constructed an extra locomotive at their own expense, which they exhibited at a Jubilee exhibition in Newcastle of 1887. Later the engine was bought by the LSWR and made the class up to 21 machines.

This class was very similar to the Adams 135 series being 2½ tons lighter, although the adhesive weight on the coupled wheels was greater. Perhaps a better comparison is to regard them as a 445 class with 3ft 4in bogie and 6ft 7in driving wheels. The slightly smaller boiler, and the cutting down of weight on both engine and tender, gave them a much wider traffic availability, especially in the West Country.

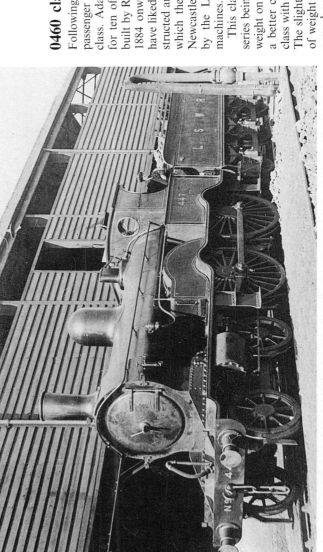

Class 0445 No 447 Eastleigh in 1922

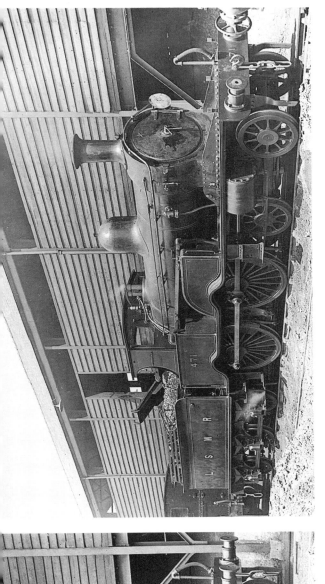

Class 0460 No.471 at Eastleigh, 1921.

Class 0460 No.477 at Eastleigh, 1923.

Class 0460 No.0470, Exmouth Juction in 1926.

Class 0460 No.E526 at Wadebridge, 1926.

Class 0460 No.0477, Eastleigh, 1924 (RH side).

Class 0460 No.475, Barnstaple in 1925.

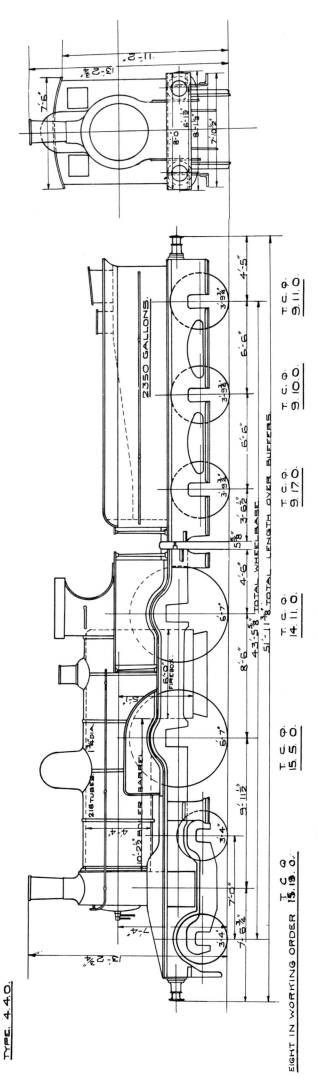

TYPE. 4.4.0.

Class 0460 4.4.0. (Eastleigh drg. No.E19)

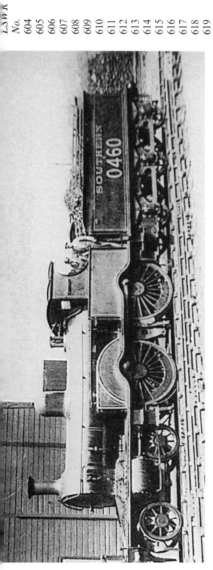

Class 0460 No.E0460 in 1929 (LH side).

A12 (and O4) class 0-4-2

In 1887, locomotives once again were built at the LSWR workshops at Nine Elms, after a lapse of 13 years. The first engines ordered were the A12 class, better known as the 'Jubilees', as 1887 was the 50th year of the reign of Queen Victoria. They were rather unusual in being of 0-4-2 configuration, similar to the 'Gladstones' of the LBSCR with which they were contemporary. The LSWR version, however, had the trailing wheels 4ft diameter running in outside axleboxes, whereas the Brighton engines had inside bearings. Driving wheels were 6ft diameter, cylinders were 18in x 26in and the boiler was 4ft 4in x 11ft, pressed at 160lb. Altogether, 90 engines were constructed to this design: 50 at Nine Elms and 40 by Neilson & Co. at Glasgow.

After the first 30 had been built by LSWR, Adams altered the motion slightly, in having the steam chest between, instead of below the cylinders, also the reversing was by lever, instead of the original system of screw reversing. This later batch was on the order books as the O4 class, but this was seldom used in traffic. The first 20 machines were vacuum braked, the remainder having steam brake and vacuum ejector. Six locomotives were fitted with Westinghouse pump, with a large cylinder between the trailing drivers and trailing truck on the right-hand side. They were Nos 529, 534, 538, 543, 555 and 556. All 90 engines entered the Southern Railway at the Grouping and several lasted until 1948. The tenders allocated to this class were many and various, from "Large Beyer" 2,500 gallons, "Small Beyer", Beattie 1,950 gallon, and the Standard and Large Adams of 3,000 and 3,500 gallon capacity.

LSWR No.	Built	Withdrawn
527	1887	1930
528	1887	1929
529	1887	1928
530	1887	1931
531	1887	1929
532	1887	1929
533	1887	1929
534	1887	1931
535	1887	1928
536	1887	1929
537	1888	1929
538	1888	1931
539	1888	1930
540	1888	1929
541	1888	1931
542	1888	1928
543	1888	1929
544	1888	1929
545	1888	1931
546	1888	1930
547	1889	1929
548	1889	1928
549	1888	1929
550	1889	1929
551	1889	1932
552	1889	1928
553	1889	1928
554	1889	1931
555	1889	1944
556	1889	1929
597	1893	1947
598	1893	1947
599	1893	1946
600	1893	1946
601	1894	1934
602	1894	1933
603	1894	1935

LSWR No.	Built	Withdrawn
604	1894	1933
605	1894	1936
606	1894	1946
607	1892	1932
608	1892	1932
609	1892	1947
610	1892	1932
611	1892	1937
612	1892	1946
613	1892	1947
614	1892	1946
615	1892	1946
616	1892	1936
617	1892	1938
618	1892	1948
619	1892	1937
620	1892	1946
621	1892	1935
622	1893	1936
623	1892	1946
624	1893	1947
625	1893	1947
626	1893	1933
627	1893	1948
628	1893	1938
629	1893	1948
630	1893	1947
631	1893	1933
632	1893	1937
633	1893	1933
634	1893	1947
635	1893	1935
636	1893	1948

LSWR No.	Built	Withdrawn
637	1893	1946
638	1893	1947
639	1893	1933
640	1893	1937
641	1893	1945
642	1893	1947
643	1893	1947
644	1893	1946
645	1893	1933
646	1893	1939
647	1894	1933
648	1894	1947
649	1894	1946
650	1895	1938
651	1895	1933
652	1895	1947
653	1895	1932
654	1895	1947
655	1895	1936
656	1895	1932

Nos 527-606 and 647-656 LSWR Nine Elms Works.
Nos 607-646 Neilson & Co., Glasgow.
Tenders:
Standard Adams 3,000 gallons Nos 554-600
Large Adams 3,300 gallons Nos 607-646
Large Beyer 2,500 gallons Nos 527, 530, 531, 534, 535 and 536
Small Beyer 2,000 gallons No. 545
Beattie Standard 1,950 gallons Nos 528, 529, 532, 533, 537-544
348 class 2,250 gallons Nos 546-553

Class A12 LSWR No.555 (RH side).

Class A12 No.555 at Nine Elms in 1924.

Class A12 No.E614 in 1928.

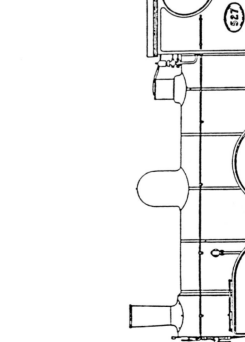

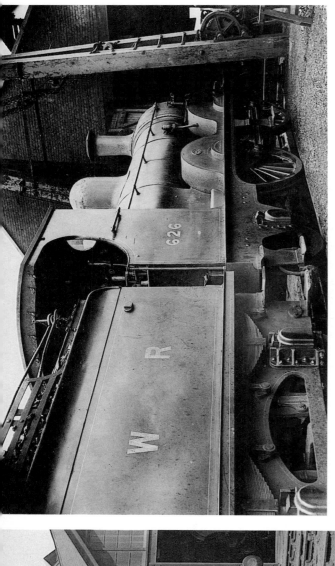

Class A12 No.626 at Reading in 1924.

Class A12 No.E528, Guildford, 1927.

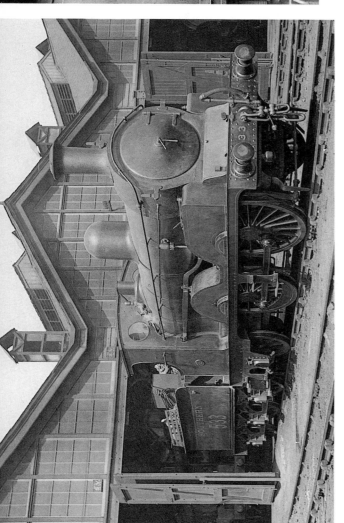

Class A12 No.E533, Salisbury, 1929.

Class A12 No.636 at Eastleigh in 1947 (LH side).

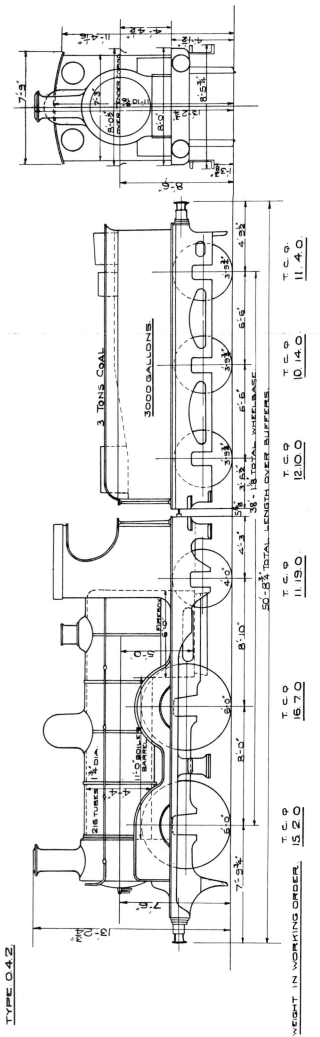

TYPE. 0.4.2.

WEIGHT IN WORKING ORDER.

T.C.Q.	T.C.Q.	T.C.Q.	T.C.Q.	T.C.Q.	T.C.Q.
15. 2. 0	16. 7. 0	11. 19. 0	12. 10. 0	10. 14. 0	11. 4. 0

Class A12 0-4-2. (Eastleigh dwg No.E19)

Class A12 No.E548 shunts at Guildford in 1927.

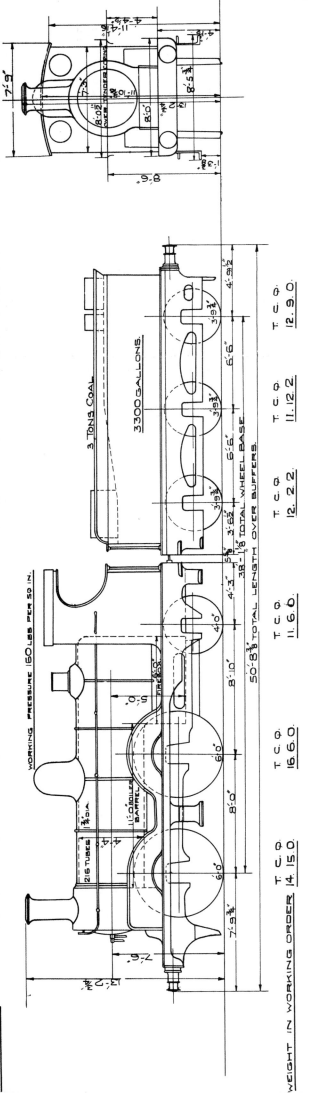

WORKING PRESSURE 150 LBS PER SQ IN.

216 TUBES | 1¾ DIA.

11' 0 BOILER BARREL

FIRE BOX

3 TONS COAL

3300 GALLONS.

50'-8⅜ TOTAL LENGTH OVER BUFFERS.

38'-1⅛ TOTAL WHEEL BASE.

Class O4 0-4-2. (Eastleigh dwg No.E19A)

WEIGHT IN WORKING ORDER 14. 15. 0.

T.C.Q.
16. 6. 0.

T.C.Q.
11. 6. 6.

T.C.Q.
12. 2. 2.

T.C.Q.
11. 12. 2.

T.C.Q.
12. 9. 0.

Class O4 No.612 in 1935.

Class O4 No.617 in 1938.

T1 (and F6) class 0-4-4T

Just 15 months after the appearance of the first A12 series from Nine Elms, came the 'tank' version of this design, in the form of an 0-4-4T to be classified as T1. Boilers, cylinders and motion followed the A12 class, the exception being in the driving wheels which were 5ft 7in diameter as compared to the A12's 6ft coupled wheels. The bogie had wheels of 3ft diameter on a 5ft wheelbase, and as with the previous class, the first 20 (Nos 61-80) had the steam chests below the cylinders. The second order for a further 30 engines had the steam chests between the cylinders, which initially made them F6 class. However, in traffic the F6s were officially referred to as T1s after 1898. It should be noted that engines Nos 1 to 20, built between 1894-95 had smaller side tanks than the predecessors, the extra water being carried in a well tank under the bunker.

Summary of the two classes T1 and F6 is as follows:

LSWR No.	Built Nine Elms	Withdrawn
13	1895	1949
14	1895	1933
15	1895	1944
16	1895	1946
17	1895	1945
18	1895	1935
19	1895	1935
20	1895	1937
61	1888	1951
62	1888	1932
63	1888	1933
64	1888	1933
65	1888	1932
66	1888	1934
67	1888	1932
68	1888	1931
69	1889	1931
70	1889	1931
71	1889	1934
72	1889	1936
73	1889	1933
74	1889	1936
75	1889	1934
76	1890	1935
77	1890	1933
78	1890	1932
79	1890	1933
80	1890	1936
358	1896	1944
359	1896	1943
360	1896	1944
361	1896	1949
362	1896	1939
363	1896	1948
364	1896	1944
365	1896	1938
366	1896	1948
367	1896	1951

LSWR No.	Built Nine Elms	Withdrawn
1	1894	1949
2	1894	1949
3	1894	1948
4	1894	1946
5	1894	1950
6	1894	1947
7	1894	1951
8	1894	1949
9	1894	1948
10	1894	1948
11	1895	1944
12	1895	1933

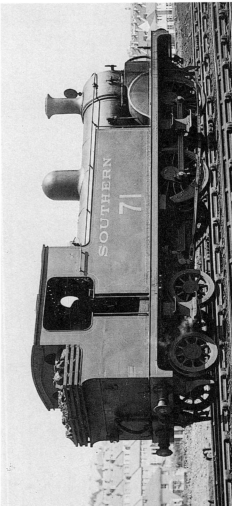

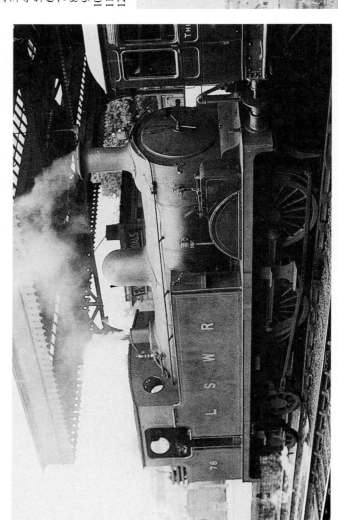

Class O4 No.644, Eastleigh 1939 (RH side).

Class T1 No.78 at Woking in 1925.

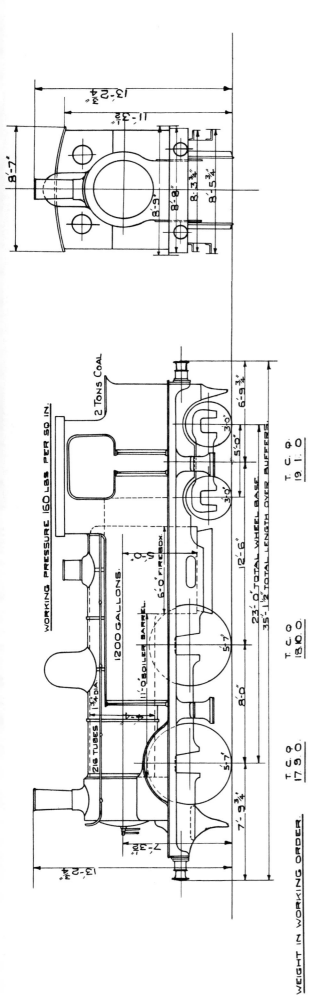

WORKING PRESSURE 160 LBS PER SQ IN.

2 TONS COAL

1200 GALLONS.

11'0" BOILER BARREL

6'0" FIREBOX

216 TUBES

1¾" DIA

13'-2¾"

7'-3¼"

8'-0"

12'-6"

23'-0" TOTAL WHEEL BASE.

35'-1½" TOTAL LENGTH OVER BUFFERS.

3'0"   5'0"   6'-9¾"

5'-7"   5'-7"   3'0"

8'-7"

11'-3½"

13'-2¾"

8'-9"   8'-8"   8'-3¾"   8'-5¼"

WEIGHT IN WORKING ORDER.

T.C.Q.	T.C.Q.	T.C.Q.	T.C.Q.
17. 3. 0.	18.10. 0.	19. 1. 0.	

Class T1 0-4-4T. (Eastleigh dwg No.E20)

Class T1 No.E80 at Salisbury, 1931.

Class T1 No.70 at Bournemouth, 1933.

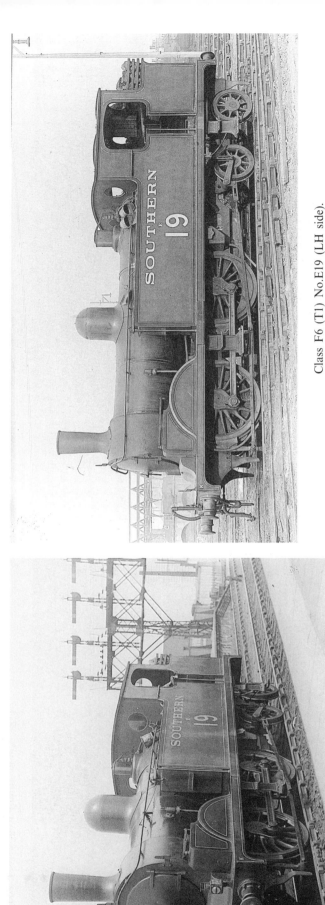

Class F6 (T1) No.E19 (LH side).

Class F6 (T1) No.E19 at Clapham Junction, 1928.

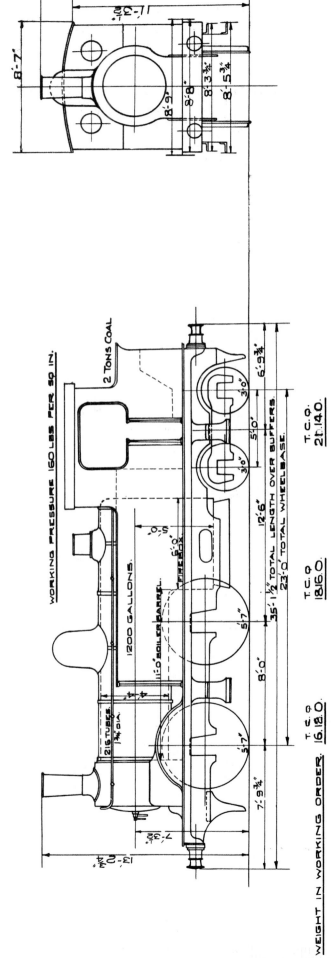

WORKING PRESSURE 160 LBS PER SQ IN.

2 TONS COAL

1200 GALLONS.

11'-0" BOILER BARREL.

216 TUBES 1¾" DIA.

6'-0" FIRE BOX.

5'-0"

5'-7"

5'-7"

7'-9¾"

8'-0"

12'-6"

35'-1½" TOTAL LENGTH OVER BUFFERS.

23'-0" TOTAL WHEELBASE.

6'-9¾"

3'-0"

3'-0"

13'-2¼"

7'-3⅜"

T.C.O.
16.18.0.

T.C.O.
18.16.0.

T.C.O.
20.14.0.

WEIGHT IN WORKING ORDER.

8'-7"

13'-2¼"

11'-3¼"

8'-9"

8'-8"

8'-3¾"

8'-5¾"

Class F6 LSWR No.361 at Strawberry Hill, 1921.

Class F6 (T1) No.1 at Eastleigh in 1945.

Class F6 (T1) LSWR No.18, Guildford, 1921.

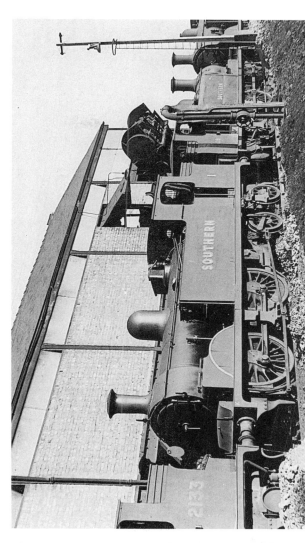

Class F6 (T1) No.15, Eastleigh in 1939.

Class F6 (T1) No.10 at Salisbury, 1937.

Class F6 (T1) No 17 Salisbury 1935

Class F6 (T1) No.359 (RH side), Plymouth in 1938.

Class F6 (T1) No.367 at Eastleigh in 1938.

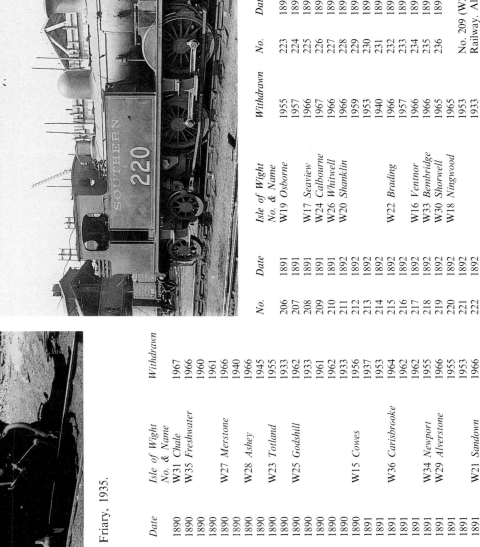

Class O2 No.232, Eastleigh, 1938 (LH side).

Class O2 No.E220, Exmouth Junction in 1925 (RH side).

No.	Date	Isle of Wight No. & Name	Withdrawn
206	1891	W19 Osborne	1955
207	1891		1957
208	1891	W17 Seaview	1966
209	1891	W24 Calbourne	1967
210	1891	W26 Whitwell	1966
211	1892	W20 Shanklin	1966
212	1892		1959
213	1892		1953
214	1892		1940
215	1892	W22 Brading	1966
216	1892		1957
217	1892	W16 Ventnor	1966
218	1892	W33 Bembridge	1955
219	1892	W30 Shorwell	1966
220	1892	W18 Ningwood	1965
221	1892		1953
222	1892		1933
223	1892		1961
224	1892		1958
225	1892		1962
226	1892	W32 Bonchurch	1964
227	1894		1933
228	1894		1943
229	1894		1961
230	1894		1956
231	1894		1953
232	1895		1959
233	1895		1958
234	1895		1937
235	1895		1933
236	1895		1960

No. 209 (W24) is preserved on the Isle of Wight Steam Railway. All were built at Nine Elms Works.

Class O2 No.231, Plymouth Friary, 1935.

O2 class 0-4-4T

The next large batch of engines to be built at Nine Elms Works was the short, sturdy and powerful O2 class. Initially, these engines were constructed to take the place of the old Beattie well tanks, but proved so versatile that the 60 erected between 1889 and 1895 were soon at work all over the LSWR system. These engines are still remembered by hundreds of holidaymakers who saw the class at work on the Isle of Wight until the end of steam traction in 1966. Some of the dimensions are as follows: Boilers pressed for 160lbs were 4ft 2in x 9ft 5in long. Coupled wheels 4ft 10in, with bogie wheels 3ft. Cylinders finally settled at 17½in x 24in and the overall length was 30ft 8½in. Water tank capacity was 800 gallons. During the Southern Railway era 1923-1947, 23 engines of this class were transferred to the Isle of Wight and further details are to be found in the Isle of Wight (W) section.

No.	Date	Isle of Wight No. & Name	Withdrawn
180	1890	W31 Chale	1967
181	1890	W35 Freshwater	1966
182	1890		1960
183	1890		1961
184	1890	W27 Merstone	1966
185	1890		1940
186	1890	W28 Ashey	1966
187	1890		1945
188	1890	W23 Totland	1955
189	1890		1933
190	1890	W25 Godshill	1962
191	1890		1933
192	1890		1961
193	1890		1962
194	1890		1933
195	1890	W15 Cowes	1956
196	1891		1937
197	1891		1953
198	1891	W36 Carisbrooke	1964
199	1891		1962
200	1891		1962
201	1891	W34 Newport	1955
202	1891	W29 Alverstone	1966
203	1891		1955
204	1891		1953
205	1891	W21 Sandown	1966

No.	Date	Isle of Wight No. & Name	Withdrawn
177	1889		1959
178	1889	W14 Fishbourne	1966
179	1890		1959

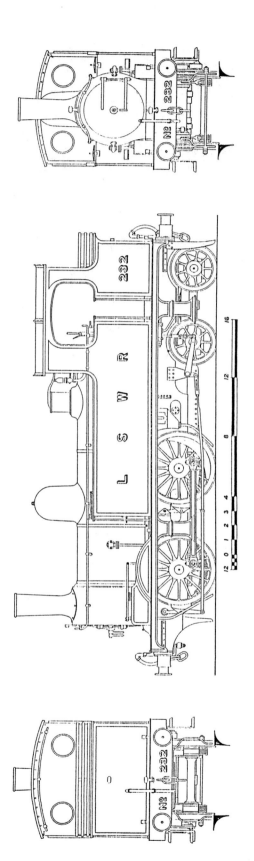

Class O2 0-4-4T

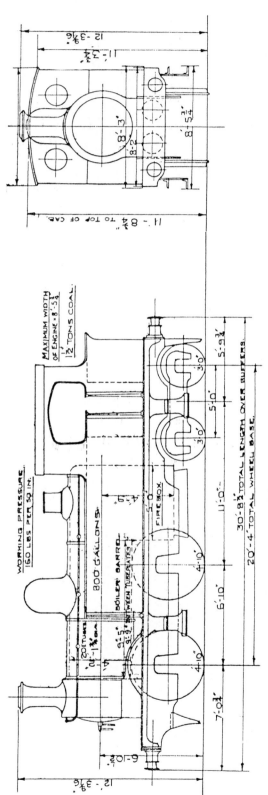

Class O2 0-4-4T (Feltham loco. No. E223)

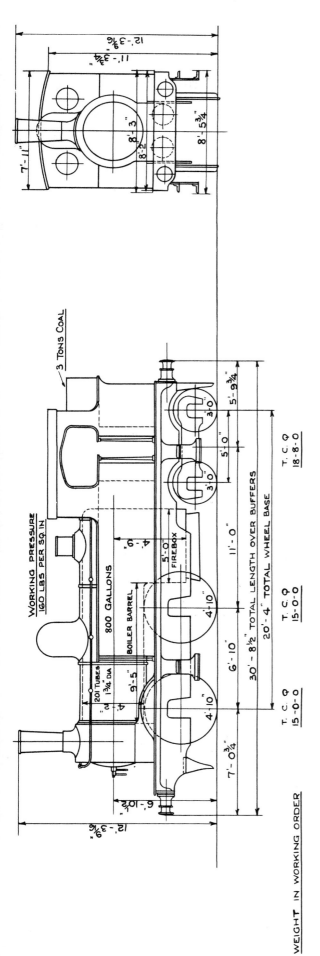

WORKING PRESSURE
160 LBS PER SQ.IN

800 GALLONS

3 TONS COAL

201 TUBES 1¾" DIA

BOILER BARREL

FIREBOX

WEIGHT IN WORKING ORDER

Class O2 0-4-4T. (Eastleigh dwg No.E22A)

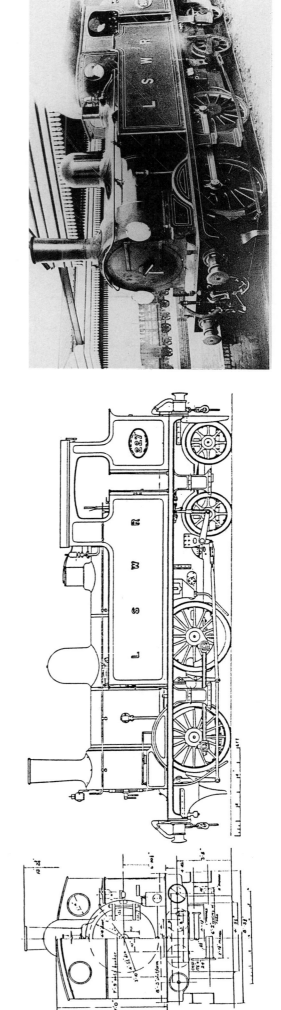

Class O2 LSWR No.208 at Plymouth.

Class O2 0-4-4T

X2 class 4-4-0

William Adams was at the height of his career as Locomotive Superintendent of the LSWR when he produced his superb 4-4-0 express passenger engine series in 1890. In effect, these 60 locomotives were enlarged versions of the previous 445-460 classes, and very handsome machines they were. Divided into four distinct lots, the X2 and T6 had large 7ft 1in driving wheels, and were intended for the Bournemouth expresses, whilst the T3 and X6s were designed for services west of Salisbury, being fitted with 6ft 7in coupled wheels. The first 20 X2s appeared between 1890 and 1892; the first engine, No. 577, being given a six months' workout, before the rest of the order left the works. During these trials, W.F. Pettigrew, the Works Manager, declared the X2s to be the most economical and powerful locomotives in the world. (Well he would, wouldn't he!) The runs in traffic proved the cabs to be too narrow, the firebox too small and the need for a larger tender. In the light of these findings, although Nos 577 to 582 originally had narrow cabs and small tenders, the remaining 14 were built with wider cabs and 3,300 gallon tenders. Eventually, the whole series conformed.

All 20 engines entered the Southern Railway, and from 1924 onwards, were painted in the Maunsell green livery and given the 'E' prefix. Summary is as follows.

LSWR No.	Built	'E' Prefix & Maunsell livery	Withdrawn
577	1890	1924	1933
578	1890	1924	1933
579	1890	1926	1932
580	1890	1925	1933
581	1890	1926	1932
582	1891	1926	1931
583	1891	1924	1931
584	1891	1924	1933
585	1891	1924	1931
586	1891	1926	1942
587	1891	1924	1937
588	1891	1924	1932
589	1891	1924	1931
590	1891	1925	1937
591	1891	1927	1931
592	1892	1924	1936
593	1892	1925	1931
594	1892	1926	1931
595	1892	1924	1930
596	1892	1924	1931

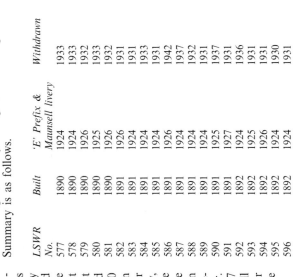

Class O2 No.E235 at Clapham Junction, 1925.

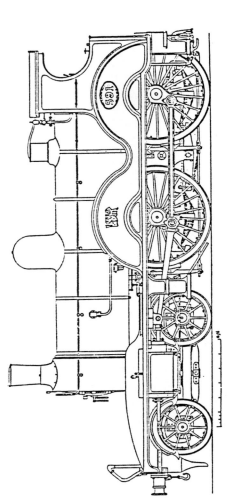

Class X2 4-4-0.

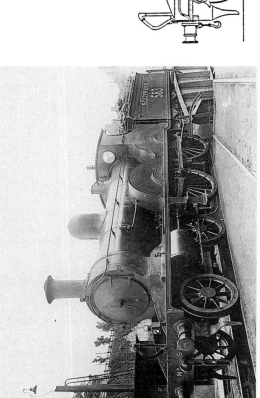

Class X2 No.E583 at Guildford in 1924.

Class X2 No.E585, Eastleigh, 1931.

Class X2 No.E592, Nine Elms, 1924.

Class X2 No.E595 at Guildford in 1927.

Class X2 No.590, Eastleigh, 1937.

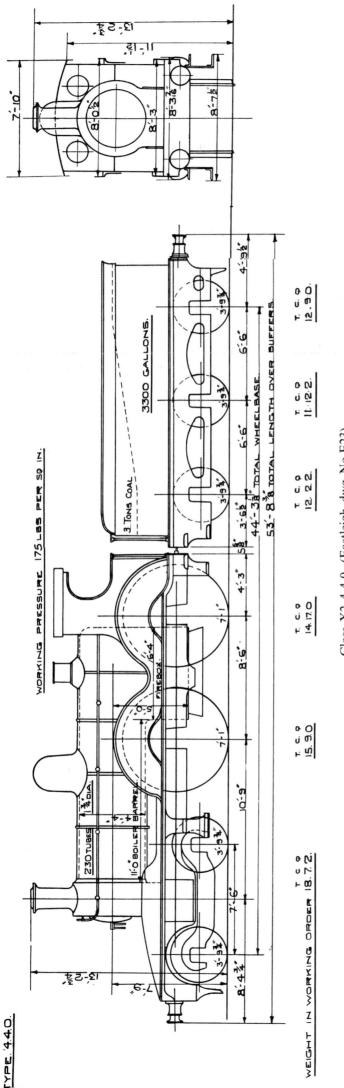

TYPE. '4.4.0.

7'-10"

13'-2¾"
11'-1½"
8'-0½"
8'-3"
8'-3⅜"
8'-7½"

WORKING PRESSURE 175 LBS PER SQ IN.

3300 GALLONS.

3 TONS COAL

230 TUBES
¾ DIA
1'-6"
11'-0" BOILER BARREL.
FIREBOX.

13'-2¾"
6'-4"

4'-9½"
3'-9¾"
6'-6"
3'-9¾"
6'-6"
3'-9¾"
3'-6½"
5'-8"
4'-3"
7'-1"
8'-6"
7'-1"
10'-9"
3'-9¾"
7'-6"
8'-4¼"
3'-9¾"
6'-0"

44'-3⅞" TOTAL WHEELBASE.
53'-8⅜" TOTAL LENGTH OVER BUFFERS.

T.C.O   T.C.O   T.C.O   T.C.O   T.C.O   T.C.O   T.C.O
12.9.0. 11.12.2. 12.2.2. 14.17.0 15.9.0 18.7.2.

WEIGHT IN WORKING ORDER 18.7.2.

Class X2 4-4-0. (Eastleigh dwg No.E23)

Class X2 No.587, Eastleigh, 1935.

Class X2 LSWR No.591 at Basingstoke, 1926 (LH side).

Class X2 No.592,
Salisbury, 1925.

T3 class 4-4-0

As designed, Adams intended the T3 class to be just a smaller wheeled version of the X2s. However, trials revealed that a larger firebox would give better steaming, so the wheelbase between the coupled drivers of the T3s was increased to 9ft which permitted these engines to have the biggest firebox of any of the Adams designs. In addition, the bogie wheels were smaller by 2¾in, and they could be identified from their big sisters by the short, straight sections between those huge splashers. (The X2 and T6 had a reverse curve between the two wheel arches, and the X6 had a little straight section, but almost on the running plate.) Wide cabs were fitted to all 20 of the class, and steaming so freely, the engines were always popular with crews. Details of building, etc. as follows.

No.	Built (Nine Elms)	'E' Prefix & Maunsell livery	Withdrawn
557	1892	1924	1936
558	1892	1924	1931
559	1892	1926	1931
560	1893	1926	1932
561	1893	1924	1930
562	1893	1925	1931
563	1893	1924	1945
564	1893	1924	1931
565	1893	1924	1933
566	1893	1925	1931
567	1893	1925	1933
568	1893	1926	1932

Class X2 No.E586 at Eastleigh in 1931.

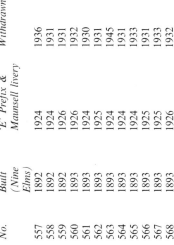

No.	Built (Nine Elms)	'E' Prefix & Maunsell livery	Withdrawn
569	1893	1925	1932
570	1893	1924	1931
571	1893	1924	1943
572	1893	1926	1931
573	1893	1926	1931

No.	Built (Nine Elms)	'E' Prefix & Maunsell livery	Withdrawn
574	1893	1926	1933
575	1893	1923	1932
576	1893	1924	1933

No. 563 is now preserved in the National Collection.

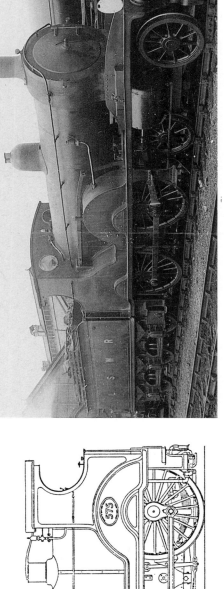

Class T3 No.568 at Eastleigh in 1925 (LSWR livery).

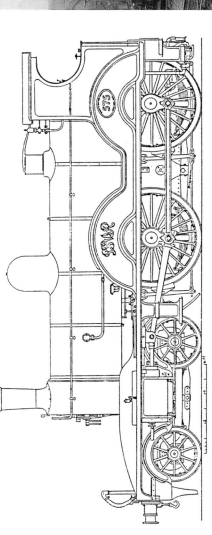

Class T3 4-4-0.

Class T3 No.570, Eastleigh, 1931.

Class T3 No.E568 at Eastleigh in 1926 (LH side).

Class T3 No.563 as restored, Nine Elms, 1948.

Class T3 No.566 (LSWR livery), Dorchester, 1925 (RH side).

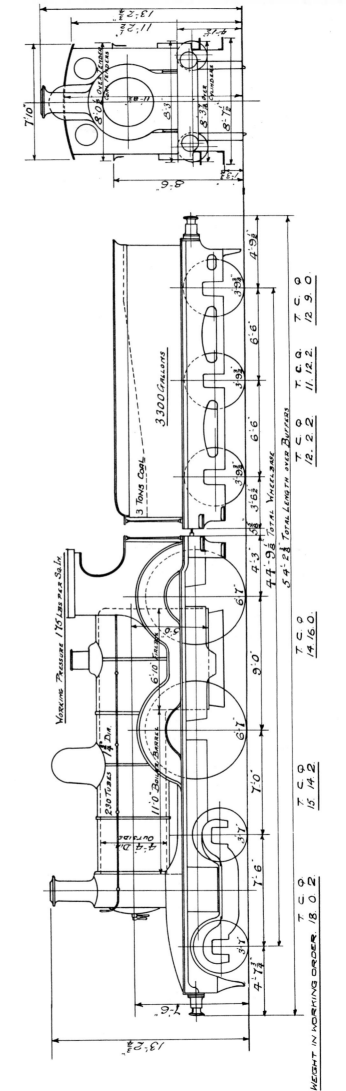

Class T3 4-4-0. (Eastleigh dwg No.E24)

B4 0-4-0T

At the beginning of the Adams era on the LSWR, much of the shunting work at large stations and depots was carried out by the old 330 class of Beyer, Peacock 0-6-0ST engines, several elderly Manning, Wardle saddle tanks, and horses. As traffic increased, both in volume and weight, the need arose for a class of locomotive built mainly for shunting duties. Mr Adams created the B4 class to meet this requirement, and 20 machines, in two batches of ten, were erected at Nine Elms between 1891 and 1893. Later, in Drummond's reign, five more similar engines were built in 1908, one of them, No. 84, being the last locomotive to be constructed at Nine Elms in June 1908, all LSWR locomotive building thereafter being concentrated at Eastleigh Works.

The Drummond order for the extra five shunters was known as K14, but after 1913 the whole class was referred to as B4. These powerful 0-4-0 side tanks had outside horizontal 16in x 22in cylinders, connected to coupled driving wheels 3ft 9¾in on a 7ft wheelbase. Boilers were 3ft 9in x 10ft 8in, the pressure was 140lbs and tanks held 600 gallons. Cabs were tiny, and those for the docks were cut away to give better vision on quayside curves.

Coal was stowed at footplate level in the cab under each side tank, cramped working conditions indeed, yet crews liked them and all 25 lasted to see the Southern Railway handed over to British Railways.

The LSWR took over the Southampton Docks in 1893, and eventually 14 of the class were transferred to the Docks Department and painted 'invisible' green. Later, at the Grouping they were given a livery of dark green with red lining. The remainder of the class after 1893, allocated to the Running Dept. were painted dark green goods livery. After the Grouping, the Southern Railway painted these eleven engines black, lined in red with the 'E' prefix to the numbers. As can be seen in the summary, only the engines attached to the Docks and Marine Department received names. Two are preserved, No. 96 on the Bluebell Railway, and No. 102 at Bressingham Steam Museum, Norfolk.

All the Dock locomotives were fitted with linseed filtrators for preventing scale in the boilers. This feature resembled a motorcycle engine behind the dome. All were removed in 1941 except for those upon Nos 85, 90, 98 and 147.

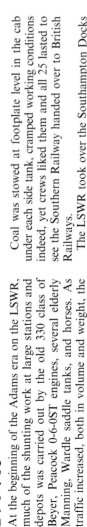

Class T3 No.575, Eastleigh, 1928.

Class T3 No.E563, Feltham, 1924.

No.	Built	Date to Docks	Name	SR livery	'E' prefix removed	Withdrawn
81	1893	1893	Jersey	1924	1936	1949
82	1908	-	-	1924	-	1957
83	1908	-	-	1924	1933	1959
84	1908	-	-	1925	1933	1959
85	1891	1900	Alderney	-	-	1949
86	1891	1896	Havre	-	-	1959
87	1891	-	-	1926	1931	1958
88	1892	-	-	1926	1935	1959
89	1892	1901	Trouville	-	-	1963
90	1892	1901	Caen	-	-	1948
91	1892	-	-	1926	1935	1948
92	1892	-	-	1926	1932	1949
93	1892	1896	St. Malo	-	-	1969
94	1892	-	-	1923	-	1957
95	1893	1896	Honfleur	-	-	1949
96	1893	1893	Normandy	-	-	1963
97	1893	1893	Brittany	-	-	1949
98	1893	1900	Cherbourg	-	-	1949
99	1893	-	-	1926	1936	1949
100	1893	-	-	1937	1931	1949
102	1893	1896	Granville	-	-	1963
103	1893	-	-	1924	1935	1949
176	1893	1893	Guernsey	-	-	1948
746	1908	1908	Dinan	-	-	1948
747	1908	1908	Dinard	-	-	1949

Nos 96 and 102 are now preserved.

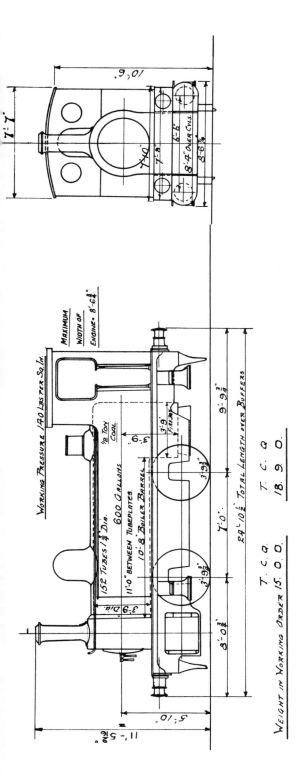

Class B4 0-4-0T. (Eastleigh dwg No.E25)

Class B4 No.100 at Plymouth Friary, 1935.

Class B4 No.94 in 1935.

Class B4 No.99 with spark arrester, Eastleigh, 1945.

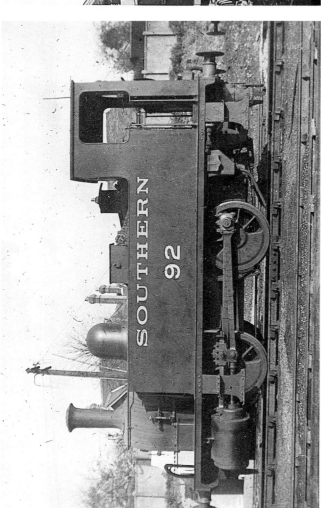

Class B4 No.92, Bournemouth, 1937 (LH side).

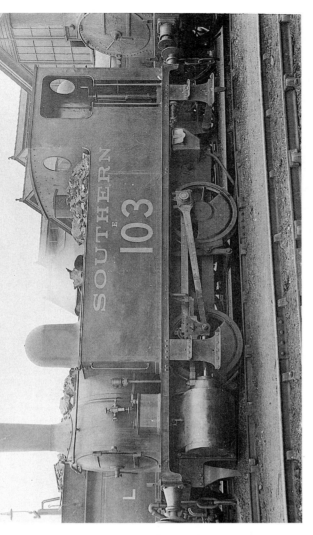

Class B4 No.E103, Eastleigh 1924.

Class B4 No.E82 c1925 (RH side).

Class B4 No.92 at Bournemouth, 1937.

Class B4 No.82 at Eastleigh in 1928.

G6 class 0-6-0T

Discounting the old 330 class of saddle tanks built by Beyer, Peacock to their design, to the order of Beattie, and later Adams, the G6 class of goods tanks were really the one and only class of 0-6-0T that Adams planned. In fact, he retired during the production of the first ten machines. In essence they were an 0-6-0T version of the O2 class 0-4-4T engines, having the same size coupled wheels, boiler, cylinders and motion, whilst the bunker, side tanks and cab were very similar to the O2's pattern.

Although designed primarily for goods work, they were all fitted with vacuum pipes and ejectors, and were utilised for carriage shunting work at many depots.

These engines must have proved themselves, as, after Adams retired, Drummond ordered a further 24, using many spare boilers which were available, resulting in various boiler fittings in various positions. The lot which used these old spare boilers were originally recorded as M9 class, but this soon lapsed, and the whole series generally became G6. All were built at Nine Elms Works, dates as follows.

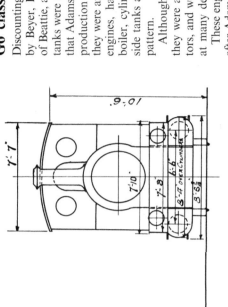

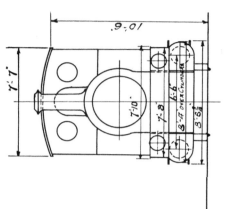

(Eastleigh dwg No.E25A)

Class B4, (ex-LSWR Class K14) 0-4-0T.

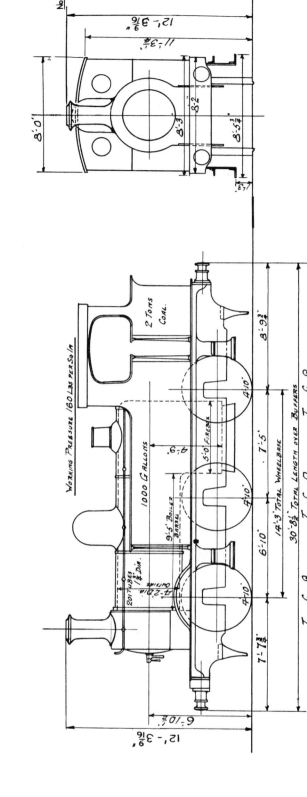

Class G6 0-6-0T. (Eastleigh dwg No.E26)

Class G6 0-6-0T. (Eastleigh dwg No.E26A)

No.	Built	To SR black livery & prefix 'E'	Withdrawn
160	1900	1925	1959
162	1900	1923	1958
237	1898	1925	1949
238	1898	1925	1962
239	1898	1926	1948
240	1898	1925	1949
257	1894	1925	1949
258	1894	1925	1961
259	1894	1926	1950
260	1894	1924	1958
261	1894	1925	1948
262	1894	1925	1949
263	1894	1925	1949
264	1894	1925	1949
265	1894	1924	1949
266	1894	1925	1960
267	1896	1924	1949
268	1896	1925	1950
269	1896	1925	1949
270	1896	1925	1959
271	1897	1923	1948
272	1898	1925	1960
273	1898	1924	1949
274	1898	1926	1960
275	1898	1925	1949
276	1900	1926	1949
277	1900	1925	1961
278	1900	1926	1948
279	1898	1926	1949
348	1900	1927	1948
349	1900	1926	1961
351	1900	1926	1949
353	1900	1925	1951
354	1900	1924	1949

No. 30238 Transferred to service stock No. DS682 1960 at Meldon Quarry.

No. 30272 Transferred to service stock No. DS3152 1950 at Meldon Quarry.

Class G6 No.E272, Exmouth Junction in 1925 (LH side).

Class G6 No.351 at Eastleigh in 1927.

Class G6 No.257 in 1930 (LH side).

Class G6 No.276 at Yeovil in May 1935.

T6 class 4-4-0

The ten engines which comprise the T6 class were virtually the X2, with the benefit of lessons learnt in traffic. As built, with their huge 7ft 1in coupled wheels, which were spaced at 9ft apart, together with the larger firebox of the T3, wider cabs, larger tenders, and the leading bogie was placed 3in further ahead of the drivers. The small mudguards over the bogie wheels had vanished, as had piston tailrods, and coal rails permitted more fuel on the tender.

These machines worked the Bournemouth and Salisbury expresses for many years before being relegated to the semi-fasts and cross-country services. As constructed, the T6 class had single slide bars, but from 1912 onward, all except No. 684 were rearranged with double slide bars and crossheads, which necessitated much strengthening around and behind the cylinders. The whole class entered Southern Railway service and details are overleaf:

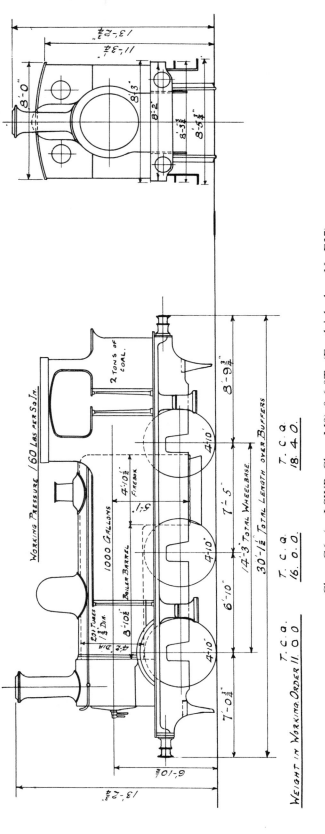

Class G6, (ex-LSWR Class M9) 0-6-0T. (Eastleigh dwg No.E37)

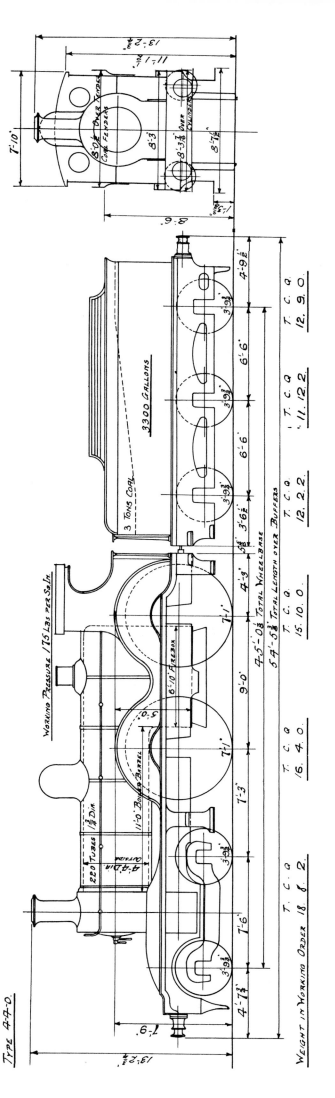

Class T6 4-4-0. (Eastleigh dwg No.E28)

Class T6 No.679, Reading, 1933.

Class T6 No.681, Basingstoke, 1933.

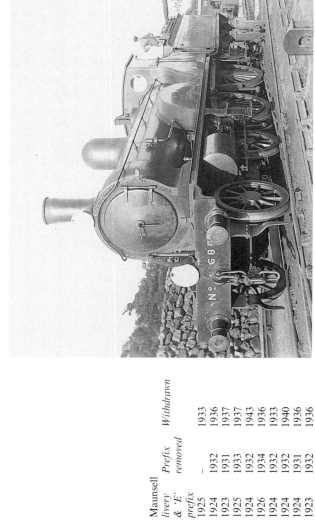

LSWR No.	Built Nine Elms	Maunsell livery & 'E' prefix	Prefix removed	Withdrawn
677	1895	1925	–	1933
678	1895	1924	1932	1936
679	1895	1923	1931	1937
680	1895	1925	1933	1937
681	1895	1924	1932	1943
682	1895	1926	1934	1936
683	1896	1924	1932	1933
684	1896	1924	1932	1940
685	1896	1924	1931	1936
686	1896	1923	1932	1936

Class T6 No.E681, Bournemouth, 1925.

Class X6 No.661, Eastleigh in 1937.

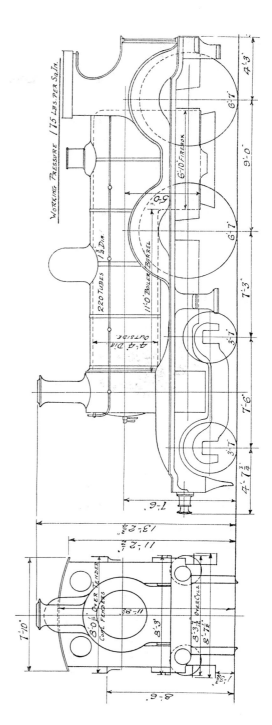

Class X6 4-4-0. (Eastleigh dwg No.E27)

X6 class 4-4-0

The final batch of the big 4-4-0 passenger express engines of the Adams regime, were the ten classed as X6. They were virtually the T6 class, with 6ft 7in coupled wheels and 3ft 7in bogie wheels. They were the first engines to have the abbreviated initials 'S.W.R.' painted on the tenders and saw the use of the Drummond cabside numberplates. Many of the class in latter days were fitted with Drummond boilers and chimneys with No. 658 lasting until 1946.

LSWR No.	Built Nine Elms	Maunsell livery & 'E' prefix	Prefix removed	Withdrawn
657	1895	1924	1932	1940
658	1895	1926	1932	1946
659	1895	1924	1932	1943
660	1895	1924	1932	1936
661	1895	1925	1933	1936
662	1895	1925	–	1933
663	1896	1925	1932	1936
664	1896	1924	1935	1942
665	1896	1934	–	1933
666	1896	1926	1932	1943

Class X6 No.E666, Basingstoke, 1931.

Class X6 No.657 at Basingstoke in 1939.

Class X6 No.662, Eastleigh, 1924 (LH side)

5in x 10ft 6in. The firebox was 4in longer and the grate was inclined, being 6in lower at the front end. The cylinders were larger, being 18½in x 26in and the engines were driven from the left-hand side.

Some of the 1897 lot were built with conical smokebox doors, namely Nos 242 to 256, but these were removed long before the Grouping. From 1903 onwards, further engines of the class were built, until by 1911 a total of 105 machines had been constructed to this design, the last ten at the Eastleigh factory newly opened.

Naturally with such a large class, there were small differences between batches; for instance, 25 were built with a long overhang in front, being approximately 1ft 3in longer than the remainder. Some did not have the splasher-sandbox combined feature over the leading drivers, later versions had steam reversing, and so on. (Full details can be obtained in Don Bradley's excellent works). Suffice it to state that all the class (except No. 126 which was the 'guinea pig' for Urie's superheating experiments) not only went into Southern Railway ownership, but saw service with British Railways after 1948. The boiler pressure of the M7s was originally 175lbs but later reduced to 150lbs per sq inch.

M7 class 0-4-4T

W. Adams retired from the LSWR in August 1895 and his position was offered to Mr. Drummond, who had already spent five years in the Brighton Works of the LBSCR. Having accepted the top job as the Locomotive Superintendent of the LSWR (which in 1905 was re-phrased as 'Chief Mechanical Engineer') one of his first tasks was to consider the purchase of 25 passenger tank engines. At that time 20 T1 class tanks were on order at Nine Elms, being Nos 358 to 377. However, only ten were built, Nos 368 to 377 being cancelled, whilst Drummond sought competitive tenders for 0-4-4Ts of his own design.

Expecting a cost of £1,600 each, he was appalled by an average quote of £2,475 from the contract firms, so obtained sanction from the Locomotive Committee to put the order through the Company's own works at Nine Elms. The first order was increased to 25 machines and Nos 242-256, 667-676 were delivered in 1897, and a further 30 followed between 1897 and 1900. This Drummond design differed from the Adams T1 class in many ways. The coupled wheels remained at 5ft 7in diameter, but the bogie wheels were larger by 7in. The boiler was shorter but larger in diameter, 4ft

Full summary is as follows:

LSWR No.	Built	SR livery	'E' prefix removed	Push-Pull gear fitted	Withdrawn
21	1904	1924	1932	1930	1964
22	1899	1923	1933	–	1958
23	1899	1925	1933	–	1961
24	1899	1924	1931	–	1963
25	1899	1924	1931	–	1964
26	1899	1925	1931	–	1959
27	1904	1924	1932	1930	1959
28	1904	1924	1932	1930	1962
29	1904	1924	1933	1930	1964
30	1904	1924	1931	–	1959
31	1898	1924	1931	1961	1963
32	1898	1925	1931	–	1963
33	1898	1925	1933	–	1962
34	1898	1926	1933	–	1963
35	1898	1924	1934	–	1963
36	1898	1925	1934	–	1964
37	1898	1926	1932	–	1958
38	1898	1925	1932	–	1958
39	1898	1925	1932	–	1963
40	1898	1925	1933	–	1961
41	1899	1924	1932	–	1957
42	1899	1924	1934	–	1957
43	1899	1924	1932	–	1961
44	1899	1924	1932	–	1961
45	1905	1924	1932	1930	1962
46	1905	1924	1931	1930	1959
47	1905	1926	1932	1930	1960
48	1905	1924	1931	1937	1964
49	1905	1924	1931	1930	1962
50	1905	1924	1932	1930	1962
51	1905	1925	1933	1937	1962
52	1905	1925	1932	1930	1964
53	1905	1923	1932	1930	1964
54	1905	1926	1932	1930	1959
55	1905	1923	1931	1931	1963
56	1906	1926	1934	1930	1963
57	1906	1924	1932	1930	1963
58	1906	1925	1933	1930	1960
59	1906	1925	1933	1930	1961
60	1906	1924	1932	1930	1961
104	1905	1925	1933	1931	1961
105	1905	1924	1932	1930	1963
106	1905	1926	1933	1930	1964
107	1905	1925	1933	1930	1964
108	1904	1924	1933	1930	1964
109	1904	1926	1934	1930	1961
110	1904	1924	1933	1930	1963
111	1904	1925	1932	1930	1964
112	1900	1924	1931	–	1963
123	1903	1925	1934	–	1959
124	1903	1925	1936	–	1961
125	1911	1924	1931	1930	1962
126	1911	1925	1932	–	1937
127	1911	1926	1931	–	1963
128	1911	1924	1931	1930	1961
129	1911	1925	1933	1930	1963
130	1903	1924	1932	–	1959
131	1911	1926	1932	1930	1962

LSWR No.	Built	SR livery	'E' prefix removed	Push-Pull gear fitted	Withdrawn
132	1903	1925	1932	1960	1962
133	1903	1926	1931	–	1964
241	1899	1926	1931	–	1963
242	1897	1925	1934	–	1958
243	1897	1924	1931	–	1958
244	1897	1924	1931	–	1957
245	1897	1925	1931	–	1962
246	1897	1924	1931	–	1961
247	1897	1924	1932	–	1961
248	1897	1926	1935	–	1961
249	1897	1923	1931	–	1963
250	1897	1925	1934	–	1957
251	1897	1925	1931	–	1963
252	1897	1924	1934	–	1959
253	1897	1926	1931	–	1961
254	1897	1925	1932	–	1964
255	1897	1925	1932	–	1960
256	1897	1925	1935	–	1959
318	1900	1924	1931	–	1959
319	1900	1925	1932	–	1960
320	1900	1924	1933	–	1963
321	1900	1927	1933	–	1962
322	1900	1924	1934	–	1958
323	1900	1923	1934	–	1959
324	1900	1924	1932	–	1959
328	1911	1924	1934	1937	1963
356	1900	1924	1932	–	1958
357	1900	1925	1934	–	1961
374	1903	1926	1933	–	1959
375	1903	1925	1932	–	1962
376	1903	1925	1934	–	1959
377	1903	1924	1934	–	1962
378	1903	1925	1932	1962	1962
379	1904	1924	1932	1937	1963
479	1911	1924	1931	–	1961
480	1911	1926	1931	1937	1964
481	1911	1924	1934	1930	1959
667	1897	1926	1933	1961	1960
668	1897	1924	1934	–	1961
669	1897	1925	1933	–	1961
670	1897	1924	1931	–	1963
671	1897	1926	1932	–	1959
672	1897	1926	1933	–	1948
673	1897	1924	1934	–	1960
674	1897	1925	1934	–	1961
675	1897	1924	1933	–	1958
676	1897	1925	1934	–	1961

All auto-fitted locomotives had long frames to provide space under the front platform for air reservoir.

Note. No. 126 superheated in 1921 and re-classified X14.

Note. Various changes of identity took place during the period 1960-62.

No. 30031 withdrawn as No. 30128.

No. 30128 renumbered 30031.

No. 30667 renumbered 30106; scrapped in February 1961.

No. 30106 renumbered 30667 in March 1961.

No. 30053 preserved by the Swanage Railway, following a period of preservation in the USA.

No. 30245 is preserved in the National Collection.

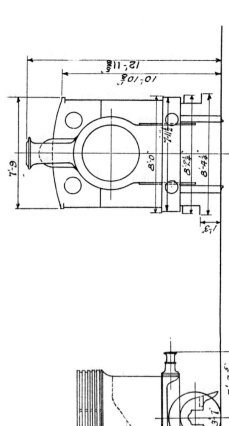

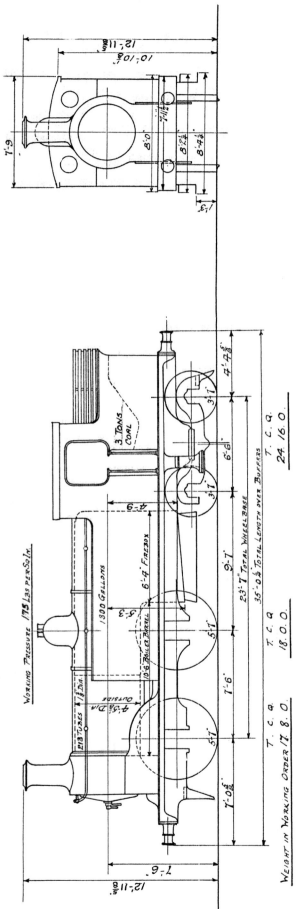

WORKING PRESSURE 175 LBS PER SQ IN.

3 TONS COAL

1300 GALLONS

2 PISTONES 18½ DIA OUTSIDE

4'-5⅜ DIA

10'-6 BOILER BARREL

6'-4 FIREBOX

5'-3

23'-7" TOTAL WHEELBASE

35'-0½ TOTAL LENGTH OVER BUFFERS

T. C. Q.
24. 16. 0.

T. C. Q.
18. 0. 0.

T. C. Q.
17. 8. 0.

WEIGHT IN WORKING ORDER 17. 8. 0.

Class M7 0-4-4T. (Eastleigh dwg No.E3)

Class M7 No.245 lettered S.W.R.

Class M7 LSWR No.318 (LH side).

Class M7 No.111 with Westinghouse brake. (RH side).

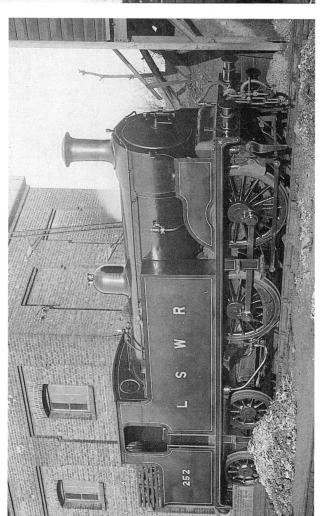

Class M7 No.255, Bournemouth in 1933.

Class M7 No.669 in 1922.

Class M7 LSWR No.252 at Strawberry Hill in 1922.

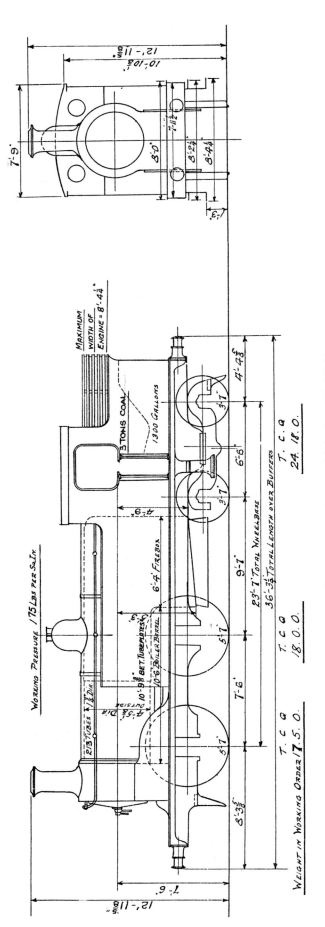

Class M7 0-4-4T. (Eastleigh dwg No.E2A)

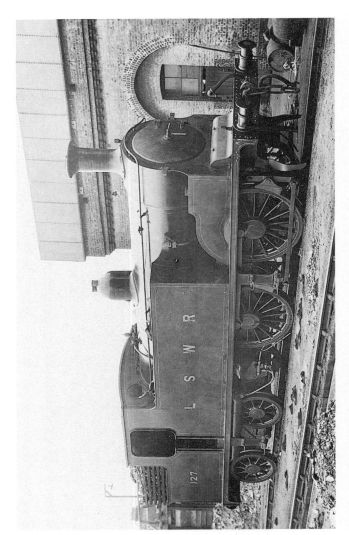

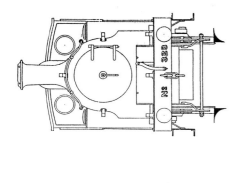

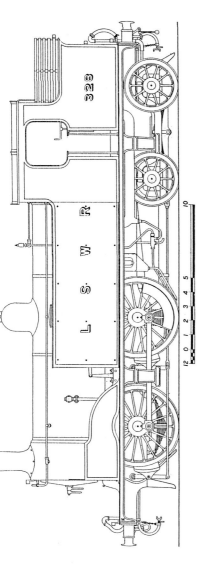

Class M7 0-4-4T.

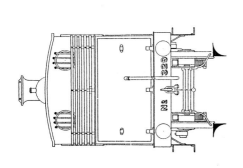

Class M7 No.E480, Eastleigh in 1929.

Class M7 No.374 in 1936.

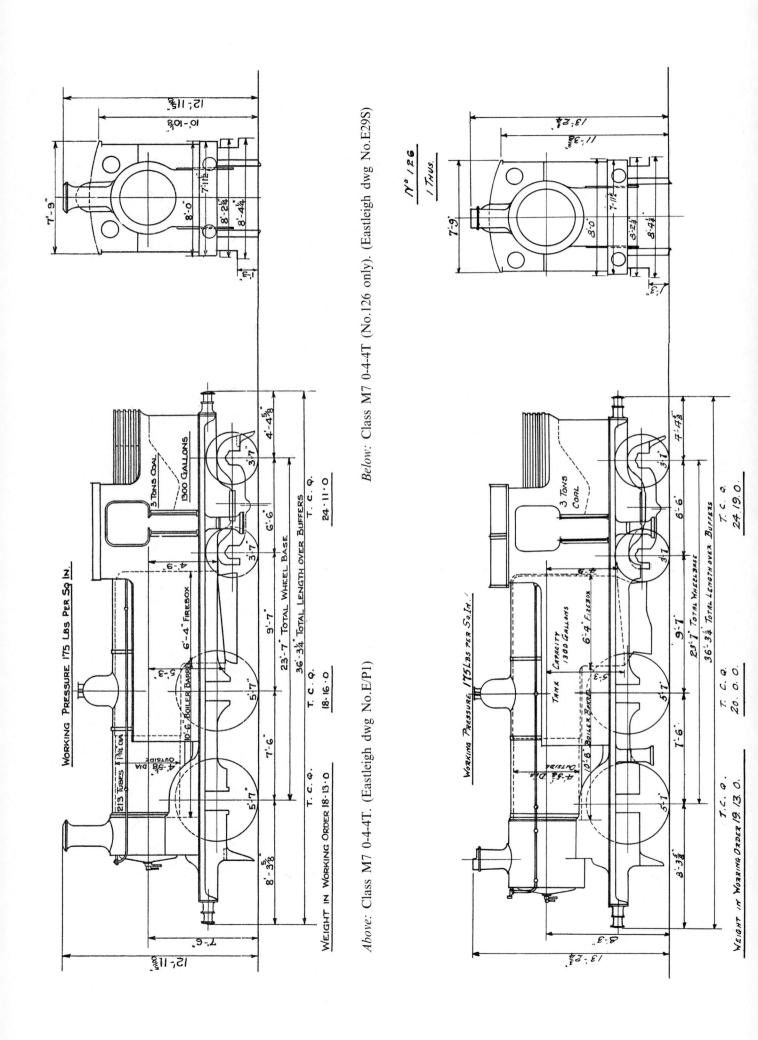

Above: Class M7 0-4-4T. (Eastleigh dwg No.E/P1)

Below: Class M7 0-4-4T (No.126 only). (Eastleigh dwg No.E29S)

Class M7 No.126 as rebuilt and reclassified X14.

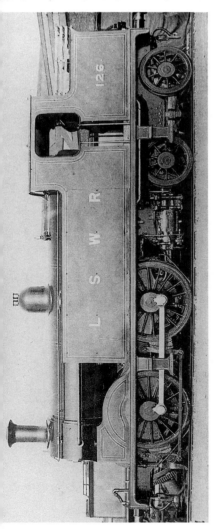

Class M7 No.126 as built (LH side).

X14 class 0-4-4T

One engine of the M7 class, No. 126, was used by Urie, Drummond's successor, in 1921 as an experiment in the modernisation of some of the older engines. This particular locomotive was taken into Eastleigh Works and fitted with a superheater, enlarged 19in cylinders, a four-feed Detroit lubricator, a higher and more rounded cab, and an extended smokebox resting on a saddle. To compensate for the extra weight at the front end, a large cast balance weight was fixed at the rear end to prevent any nose-heavy hunting. Unfortunately, although an improvement on the standard M7 class, No. 126 proved too heavy for suburban traffic and was dismantled in 1937, the parts being used on other engines.

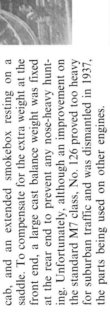

Class M7 (X14) No.E126 at Feltham in 1925 (LH side).

Class M7 (X14) No.126 in 1935 (RH side).

T7 4-2-2-0

Having at last a free hand in the design and construction of locomotives for the LSWR, Drummond went off at a tangent with his next opus for express passenger work. No. 720, the famous (or perhaps infamous!) engine, was really a 4-cylinder double simple single, which all sounds a bit odd, but what he was after was the free running of the single-wheelers with the tractive effort of four driving wheels. No. 720 was built at Nine Elms in 1897. It had the conventional bogie under the smokebox, and a pair of inside cylinders between the bogie wheels, worked by Stephenson link motion, and driving the leading pair of driving wheels through the inside crankshaft. The second set of cylinders were outside and behind the bogie, and powered the trailing driving wheels, being operated by a system of Joy's valve gear fixed to the frame between the two *separate* pairs of driving wheels, and below the cylinders.

Thus, this machine had two separate engines, one inside-cylindered working the leading 6ft 7in drivers, and an outside cylindered engine driving the trailing wheels via an extremely long piston rod. As built, this engine had a narrow cab and splashers, and single slide bars to the outside cylinders, but later was given a full width cab and double slide bars. However this was to no avail and the machine spent more time on shed, or laid aside than it did in traffic, and although passed into SR ownership in 1923, it was withdrawn in 1927.

One important factor worth recording, however, is that this was the first LSWR locomotive to use the 8-wheeled double-bogied 'water cart' tender. This was similar to those Peter Drummond brought into use on the Highland Railway, adopting the inside bearings for the wheels, so that old engine carrying wheels could have a second lease of life under tenders.

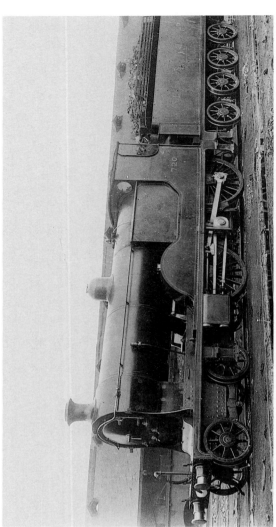

Class T7 No.720 when new (LH side).

Class T7 No.720 at Nine Elms in 1927.

Class T7 No.720 at Nine Elms in 1921.

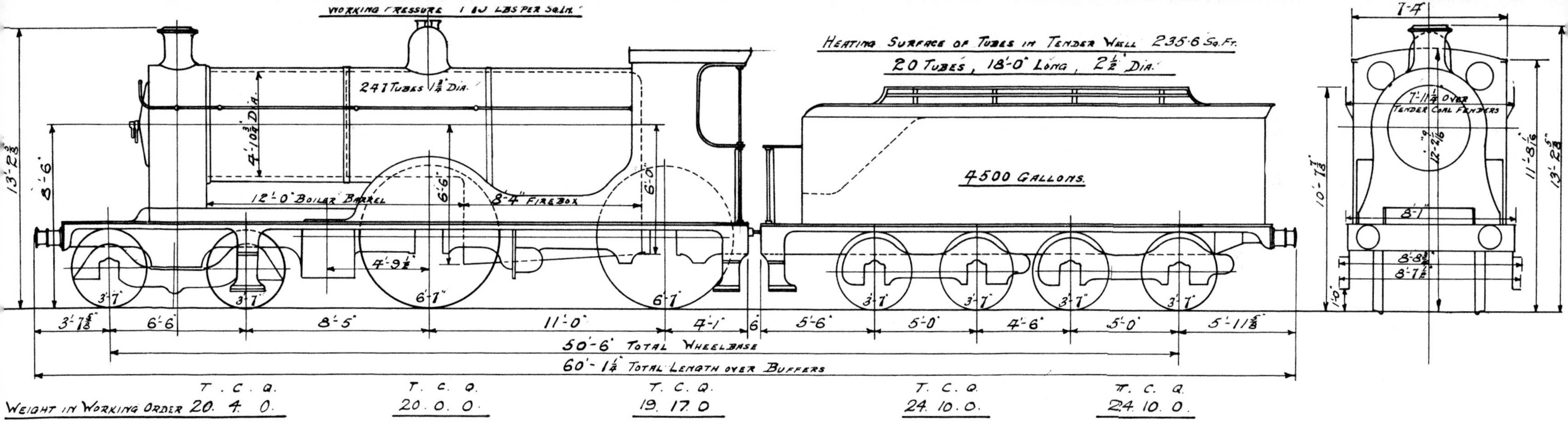

Class T7 4-2-2-0. (Eastleigh dwg No.E31)

Drawing labels:

HEATING SURFACE OF TUBES IN TENDER 235.6 SQ.FT.
20 TUBES, 18'-0" LONG, 2¼" DIA.
4500 GALLONS.
WORKING PRESSURE 175 LBS PER SQ.IN.
241 TUBES 1¾" DIA.
8'-4" FIREBOX
12'-0" BOILER BARREL
4'-10⅜" DIA.
WEIGHT IN WORKING ORDER 20.4.0
T.C.Q. 20.0.0
T.C.Q. 19.17.0
T.C.Q. 24.10.0
50'-6" TOTAL WHEELBASE
60'-1¾" TOTAL LENGTH OVER BUFFERS

LSWR No.	Re No.	Superheated Urie	Maunsell	'E' prefix removed	SR livery	Withdrawn
687		1923	1932	1932	1926	1960
688			1927	1933	1924	1957
689		1922	1931	1931	1925	1962
690			1926	1932	1926	1962
691			1926	1932	1926	1961
692			1926	1932	1926	1962
693			1926	1932	1925	1961
694		1922	1931	1934	1926	1961
695			1926	1932	1925	1962
696			1926	1931	1923	1961
697			1925	1931	1925	1962
698			1925	1933	1925	1962
699			1927	1931	1924	1961
700		1923	1929	1932	1926	1962
701			1927	1932	1924	1961
702	306		1929	1932	1925	1962
703	308	1922	1931	1931	1925	1961
704	309		1925	1934	1925	1962
705	315		1925	1932	1925	1962
706	317		1925	1933	1925	1961
707	325		1925	1933	1925	1962
708	326	1923	1931	1933	1926	1962
709	327		1926	1931	1926	1961
710	339	1924	1931	1933	1924	1962
711	346	1923	1933	1933	1926	1962
712	350	1922	1929	1933	1926	1962
713	352		1927	1933	1924	1959
714	355		1929	1932	1924	1961
715	368	1922	1930	1932	1925	1962
716	316	1920	1931	1933	1925	1962

700 class 0-6-0

As can be envisaged, Nine Elms in 1897 was fully occupied in producing M7s and other orders, so much so that when Mr. Drummond required a series of goods tender engines, he had to place the order with one of the contract firms. Dubs & Co. of Glasgow were the successful tenderers, and 30 0-6-0 machines were constructed and delivered in the year of 1897. Nicknamed the "Black Motors", many of the parts were interchangeable with the contemporary M7 class, the motion, boiler and cylinders being identical. Coupled wheels were 6in smaller in diameter, and this brought the boiler centre line 3in lower, consequently reducing the overall height of the machines. Six-wheeled tenders were attached, 4 tons of coal and a water capacity of 3,500 gallons.

As first built, conical smokebox doors were fitted, but these had all been replaced before SR days. Although classed as 'goods' engines, these handy locomotives, fitted with vacuum braking, were often used for passenger work. Nos 687 and 700 were dual fitted for working exchange traffic. As with the one M7 example, Urie decided to superheat and update No. 316, and the result was so satisfactory that ten more were rebuilt between 1922 and 1924, and later Maunsell modernised the whole class. The different photographs show the changed appearance of the superheated engines.

Class 700 No.306, Feltham in 1948 (LH side).

Class 700 No.316 at Feltham in 1924 (RH side).

Class 700 No.700 at Nine Elms in 1923.

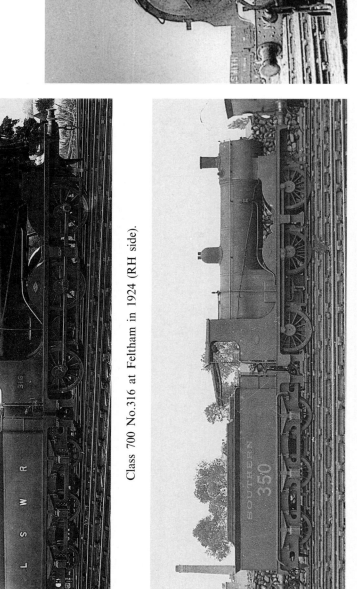

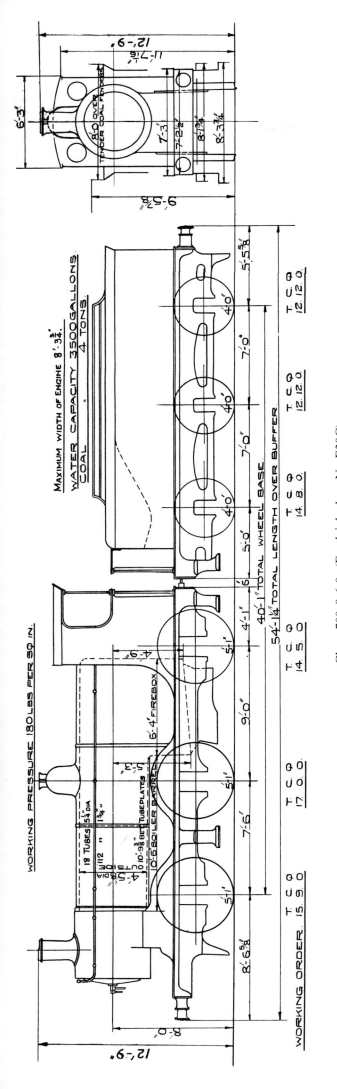

Class 700 0-6-0. (Eastleigh dwg No.E30C)

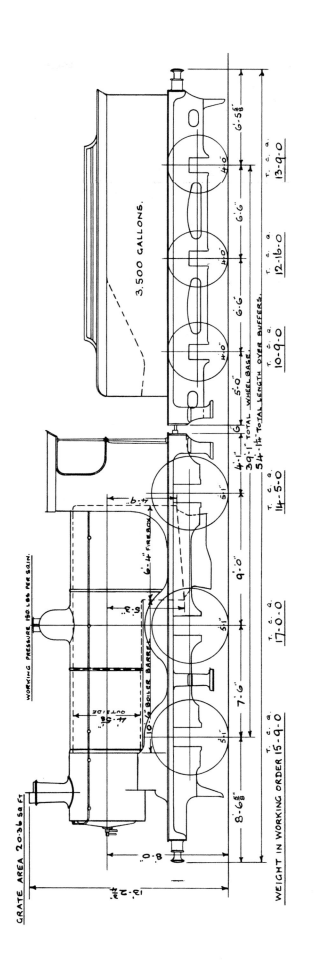

Class 700 0-6-0. (Eastleigh dwg No.E30A)

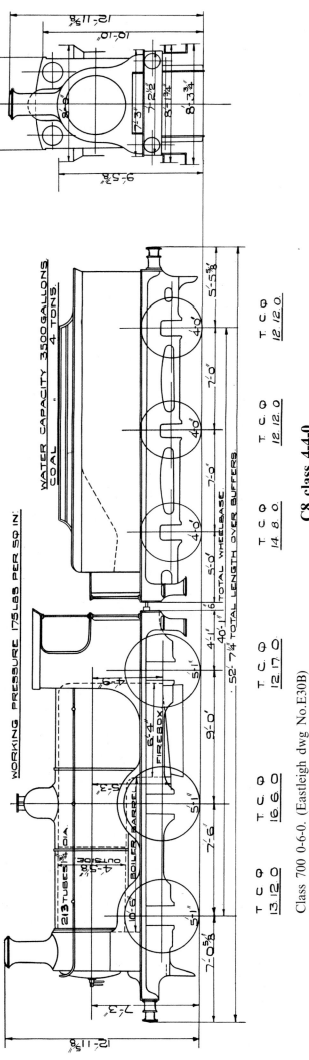

Class 700 0-6-0. (Eastleigh dwg No.E30B)

0-6-0s and the M7 tanks. Coupled driving wheels were 6ft 7in diameter on a 9ft wheelbase, bogie wheels 3ft 7in. The tender attached was the same pattern as that supplied to the 700 class, namely six-wheeled, with outside bearings, coal capacity 4 tons, and a water tank capable of holding 3,500 gallons. Later on, between 1903 and 1907, these tenders were removed, passed over to the K10 and L11 classes and replaced by large double-bogied 4,000 gallon 'water carts'. (Eventually these tenders finished up on the Urie S15s.)

Splasher-sandboxes were removed from nine of the class in SR days. Ten engines formed the C8 class, numbered 290-299, all were built in 1898 and all entered the SR in 1923. I feel their main importance in the chain of locomotive events is that they led directly on to the formation of those well-known machines, the T9s.

C8 class 4-4-0

Whilst experimenting with his theory of a double-single locomotive, Drummond still had the responsibility for increasing the stock of efficient passenger engines to cope with the ever-growing traffic on the LSWR. With this in view, he designed a straightforward inside cylindered 4-4-0 machine which was very similar to the engines he had provided for the Caledonian and North British railways in Scotland, before he came South. (Readers are advised to look at the 'Carbrook' class of the Caledonian Railway).

The order for the new engines, to be known as C8 class, was placed in 1896, but work did not commence until two years later. This was due to pressure on the Nine Elms Works, and only then because Beyer, Peacock & Co. supplied the boilers, frames, cylinders and other various parts, all of which were interchangeable with the 700 class

LSWR No.	4,000 gallon tender	'E' prefix & Maunsell livery	'E' prefix removed	Withdrawn
290	1906	1924	–	1933
291	1903	1925	–	1935
292	1903	1925	1931	1936
293	1907	1924	1932	1935
294	1902	1925	–	1933
295	1907	1925	–	1935
296	1903	1925	–	1935
297	1904	1925	1931	1936
298	1904	1925	1931	1938
299	1903	1923	1931	1937

Class 700 No S316 in early BR livery, Eastleigh 1948

Class C8 No.290 in LSWR livery (LH side).

Class C8 No.293 at Strawberry Hill in 1920 (RH side).

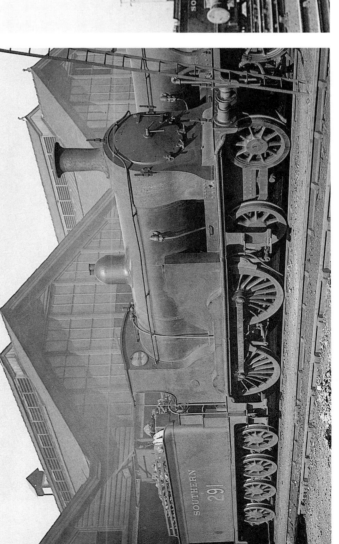

Class C8 No.298 at Feltham, 1937.

Class C8 No.E291 at Eastleigh in 1930.

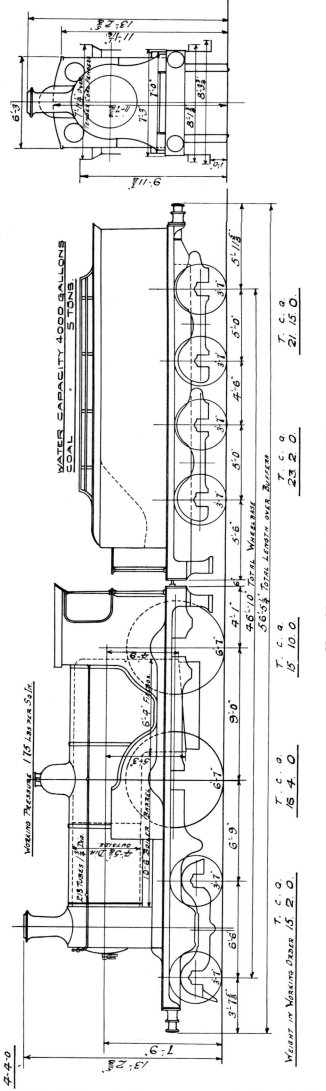

Class C8 4-4-0. (Eastleigh dwg No.E32)

Class C8 No E144 at Eastleigh in 1933 (RH side)

Class C8 No E294 at Eastleigh in June 1933 (3 rear RH side)

Class C8 No.E298 at Salisbury in June 1926.

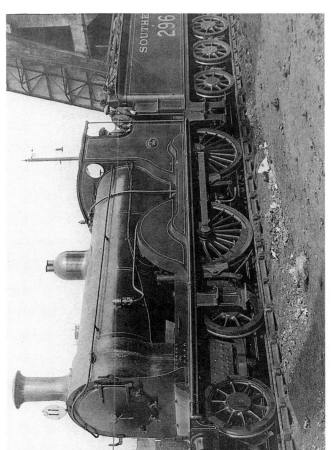

Class C8 No.E296, Nine Elms, 1931.

Class C8 No.E293, Eastleigh in September 1931.

Class C8 No.296 at Salisbury in 1929 (LH side).

T9 class 4-4-0

Even whilst the C8 class were being built, Drummond was concerned about their ability to steam freely and handle the heavy trains of the LSWR. With these doubts in mind, he prepared drawings for an improved version of 4-4-0 engine in 1898, and so the famous T9 came into being.

To outward appearances, the first engines in the new series had a marked family likeness to the C8s, but to get better steaming, Drummond increased the coupled wheelbase to 10ft, so that a really large firebox could be used between the axles. The boilers were fitted with 280 x 1¾in tubes instead of 216 x 1¾in, and 30 of the class were equipped with firebox water tubes. The engines were very solidly built with 1in thick steel frames, left-hand drive with steam reversing, and everything with a view to simple operation and reliable service, and so it proved. The T9s were a credit to Dugald Drummond.

Sixty-six machines were built over two years, 1899 to 1901, in three distinct groups:

Nos	Built
'A' – 113-122 and 280-9	Nine Elms (20)
'B' – 702-719 and 721-32	Dubs & Co. (30)
'C' – 300-5/7/10-4/36-8	Nine Elms (15)

One extra, (group 'B') was built by Dubs for exhibition and bought in 1901 by the LSWR. As built this was No. 773, but it became SR No. 733. The three groups differed slightly as follows:

'A' series – narrow cabs and six-wheeled tenders.
'B' series – all fitted with water tubes in the firebox.
'C' series – as 'B', but with wide cab and splashers, sandboxes not on leading splashers, and running with 4,000 gallon tenders with 8 wheels.

All engines had vacuum braking and Nos 337 and 338 were dual fitted. In 1922, Urie rebuilt No. 314 with a superheater (Eastleigh pattern), removed the firebox water tubes, extended the smokebox and replaced the Drummond chimney with a 'stove-pipe' version. The result was obviously a success, as the remaining 65 were also rebuilt in a like manner, with many receiving Maunsell superheaters. The whole class passed into the SR and a summary is as follows:

No.	Built	SR livery	'E' prefix removed	Eastleigh Superheater	Maunsell Superheater	Withdrawn
113*	1899	1923 (a)	1932			1951
114*	1899	1925 (a)	1933			1951
115*	1899	1925 (a)	1933			1951
116	1899	1925	1931			1951
117	1899	1925	1931			1961
118*	1899	1925 (a)	1931		1928	1951
119	1899	1925 (a)	1931		1925	1952
120	1899	1925 (a)	1932		1927	1963
121*	1899	1923 (a)	1932		1927	1951
122	1899	1926	1933		1926	1951
280*	1899	1924 (a)	1932		1927	1951
281	1899	1924 (a)	1933		1928	1951
282	1899	1925	1932	1923	1925	1954
283	1899	1925	1933		1925	1957
284	1899	1926	1932	1923	1925	1958
285	1900	1924 (a)	1932		1926	1958
286*	1900	1923 (a)	1931		1926	1951
287	1900	1923	1931	1923	1925	1961
288	1900	1924 (a)	1932		1926	1960
289	1900	1925 (a)	1931		1927	1959
300	1900	1924	1932	1922	1925	1961
301	1900	1925	1932	1923	1925	1959
302	1900	1925	1932	1923	1925	1952
303*	1901	1926	1933	1923	1926	1951
304	1901	1925	1932	1922	1925	1957
305*	1901	1924	1933	1922	1925	1951
307	1901	1924	1932	1924	1925	1952
310	1901	1925	1933	1923	1925	1959
311	1901	1925	1933	1922	1925	1952

No.	Built	SR livery	'E' prefix removed	Eastleigh Superheater	Maunsell Superheater	Withdrawn
313	1901	1924	1934	1922	1925	1961
314*	1901	1925	1931	1922	1925 •	1951
336	1901	1925	1931	1923	1925	1953
337	1901	1925	1933		1925	1958
338	1901	1924	1932	1923	1925	1961
702	1899	1925	1931	1923	1925	1959
703	1899	1924 (a)	1933		1926	1952
704	1899	1925	1932		1925	1951
705	1899	1925	1932	1924	1925	1958
706	1899	1924 (a)	1931		1925	1959
707	1899	1924	1931		1924	1961
708	1899	1924 (a)	1932		1927	1957
709	1899	1925	1932	1923	1925	1961
710	1899	1925 (a)	1931		1929	1959
711	1899	1924 (a)	1932		1927	1959
712	1899	1925 (a)	1931		1928	1958
713*	1899	1925	1932		1925 •	1951
714	1899	1924	1932	1924	1925	1951
715	1899	1923	1932	1923	1925	1961
716	1899	1924 (a)	1932		1927	1951
717	1899	1925 (a)	1931		1927	1961
718	1899	1925 (a)	1933		1928	1961
719	1899	1925 (a)	1932		1926	1961
721	1899	1925	1932	1923	1925	1958
722*	1899	1925 (a)	1932	1923	1928 •	1951
723	1899	1925 (a)	1932		1928	1951
724	1899	1926	1932	1923	1926	1959
725	1899	1925 (a)	1933		1926	1952
726	1899	1924	1933	1924	1926	1959
727	1899	1925	1931		1925	1958
728	1900	1926	1931		1926	1956
729	1900	1926	1932	1923	1927	1961
730	1900	1925 (a)	1932		1927	1957
731*	1900	1924 (a)	1932		1925 •	1951
732	1900	1924 (a)	1933		1927	1959
773/733	1901	1926	1932	1923	1925	1952

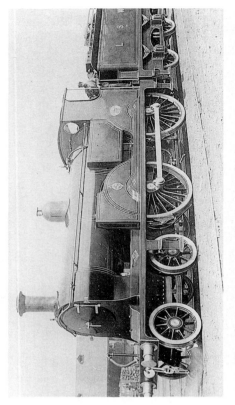

No. 120 is preserved in the National Collection. No. 773 renumbered 733 in 1924. Fitted with Maunsell superheater before receiving SR livery.

(a) Southern livery before superheated.

* Fitted electric lighting and oil burning apparatus in 1947.

• Did not carry BR numbers.

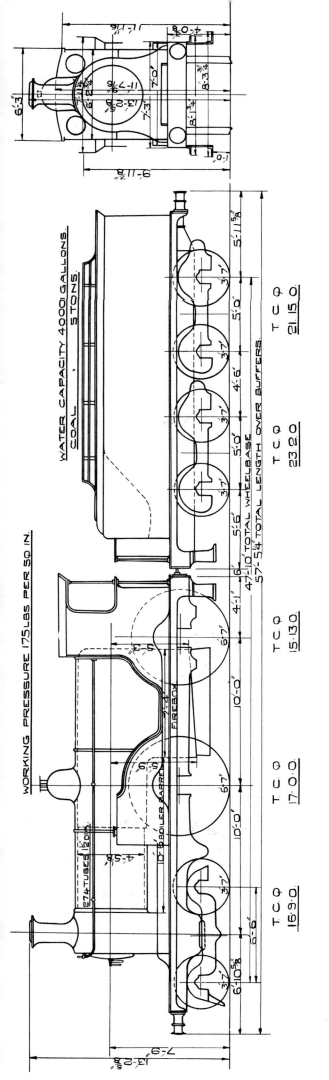

Class T9 4-4-0. (Eastleigh dwg No.E34)

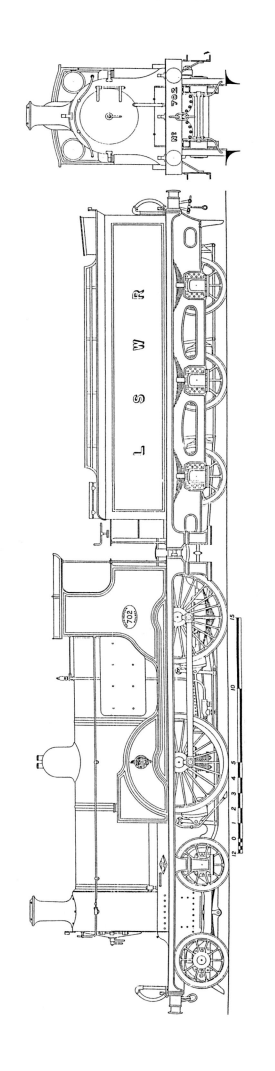

Class T9 4-4-0.

Class T9 No.314 at Nine Elms in 1920 (RH side).

Class T9 No.709 at Nine Elms in 1921 (LH side).

Class T9 No.313 at Brighton in 1931 (?) ... (LH side).

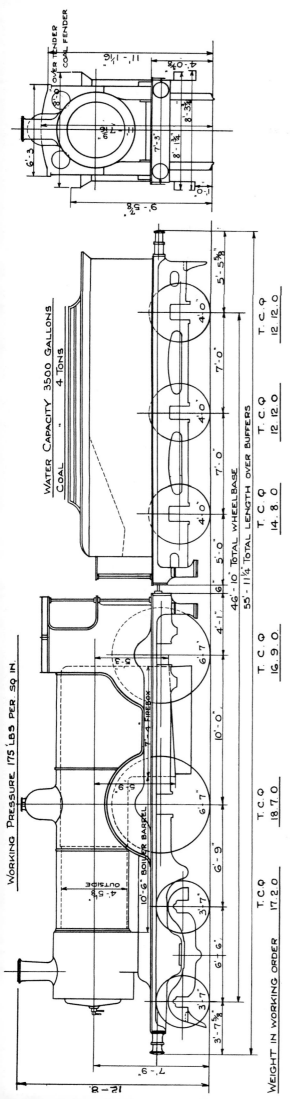

WORKING PRESSURE 175 LBS PER. SQ IN.

WATER CAPACITY 3500 GALLONS
COAL   „   4 TONS

WEIGHT IN WORKING ORDER	T.C.Q. 17. 2. 0	T.C.Q. 18. 7. 0	T.C.Q. 16. 9. 0	T.C.Q. 14. 8. 0	T.C.Q. 12. 12. 0	T.C.Q. 12. 12. 0

46'-10" TOTAL WHEELBASE
55'-11¼" TOTAL LENGTH OVER BUFFERS

Class T9 4-4-0. (Eastleigh dwg No.E34B)

Class T9 No.703 in 1937.

Class T9 No.119, Nine Elms, September 1945.

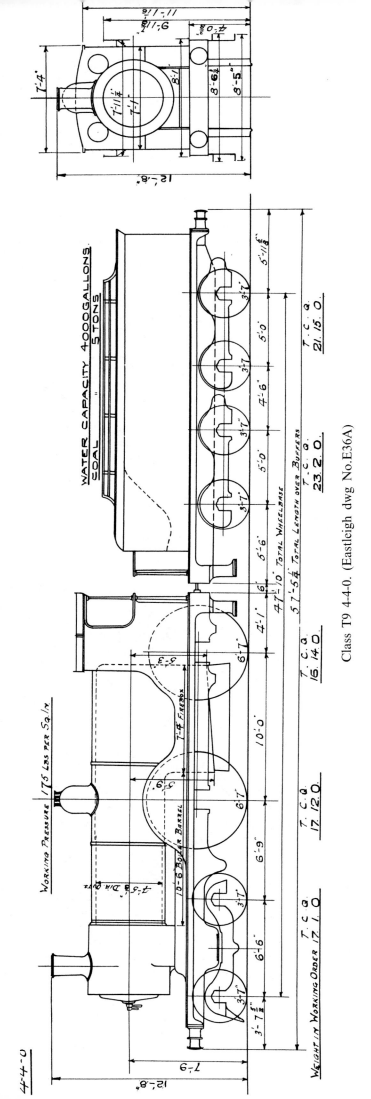

Class T9 4-4-0. (Eastleigh dwg No.E36A)

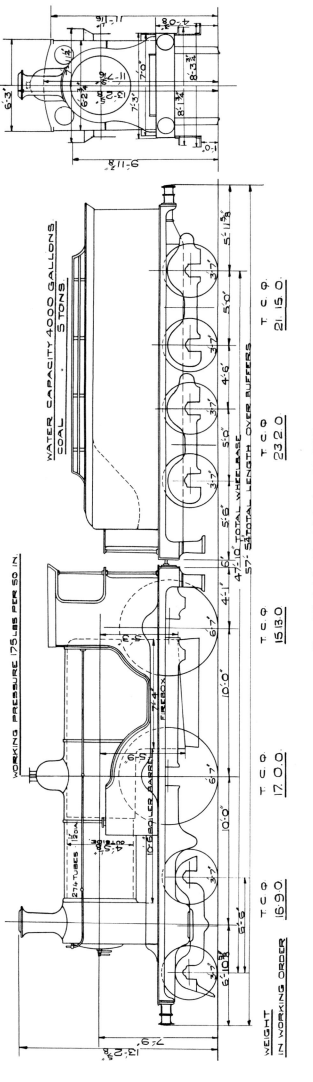

Class T9 4-4-0. (Eastleigh dwg No.E33)

WATER CAPACITY 4000 GALLONS
COAL 5 TONS

WORKING PRESSURE 175 LBS PER SQ IN.

WEIGHT IN WORKING ORDER

Class T9 No.E710 at Exmouth Junction in 1928.

Class T9 No.715 at Nine Elms in 1922.

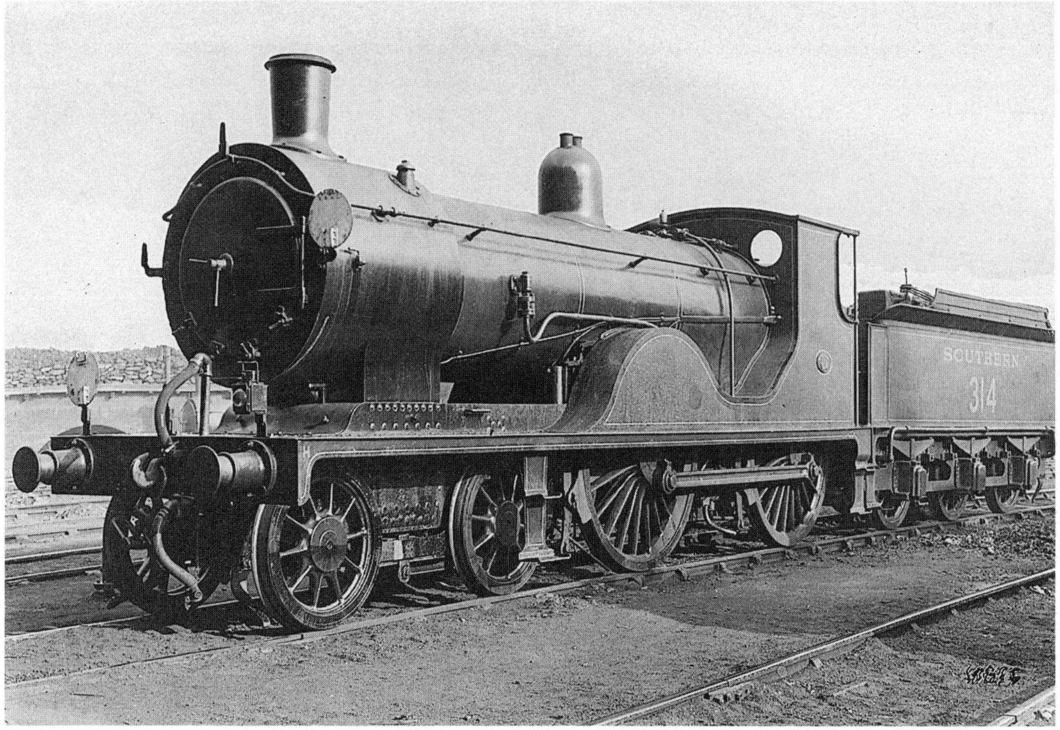

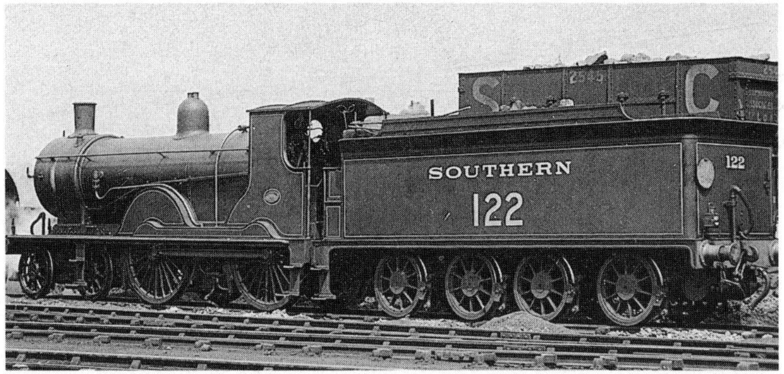

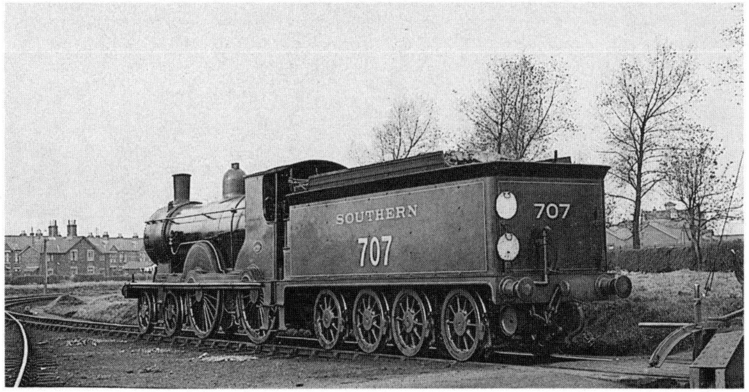

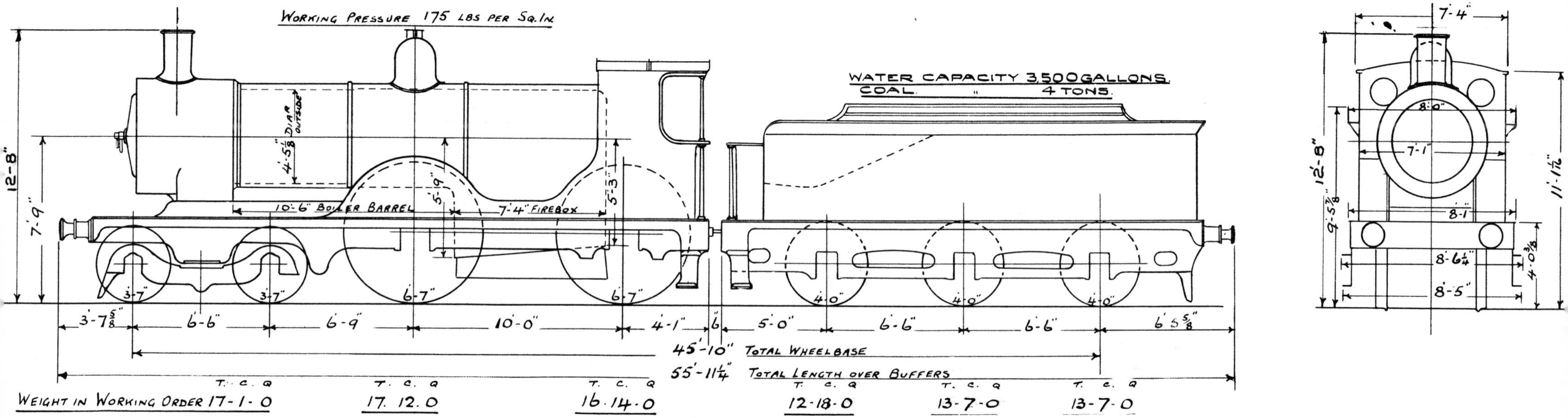

Class T9 No.314 in 1936 (LH side).

Class T9 No.122, Salisbury in May 1935.

Class T9 No.707, Eastleigh in October 1938.

WORKING PRESSURE 175 LBS PER SQ.IN.
WATER CAPACITY 3,500 GALLONS.
COAL " 4 TONS.
4'-5⅝" DIAR OUTSIDE
10'-6" BOILER BARREL
7'-4" FIREBOX
45'-10" TOTAL WHEELBASE
55'-11¼" TOTAL LENGTH OVER BUFFERS
WEIGHT IN WORKING ORDER 17-1-0
17.12.0
16.14.0
12-18-0
13-7-0
13-7-0

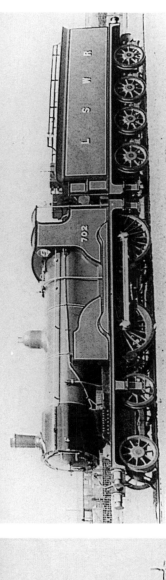

Class T9 No.702 as built (LH side).

Class T9 No.702 showing cab detail.

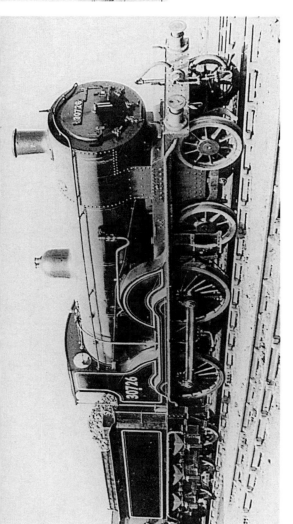

Class T9 No.30726 in BR lined black livery.

Class T9 No.116 at Eastleigh in 1936.

Class T9 No.114 at Eastleigh in 1947 when converted to oil burning.

Class T9 No.30119 in early BR days.

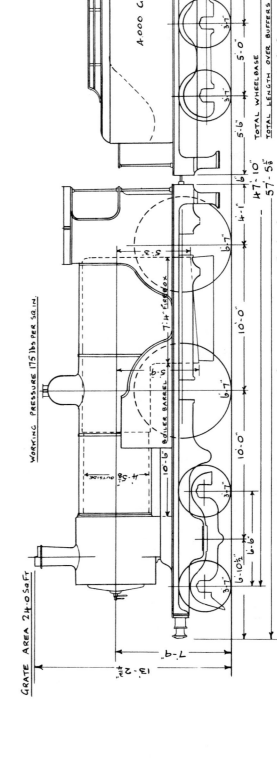

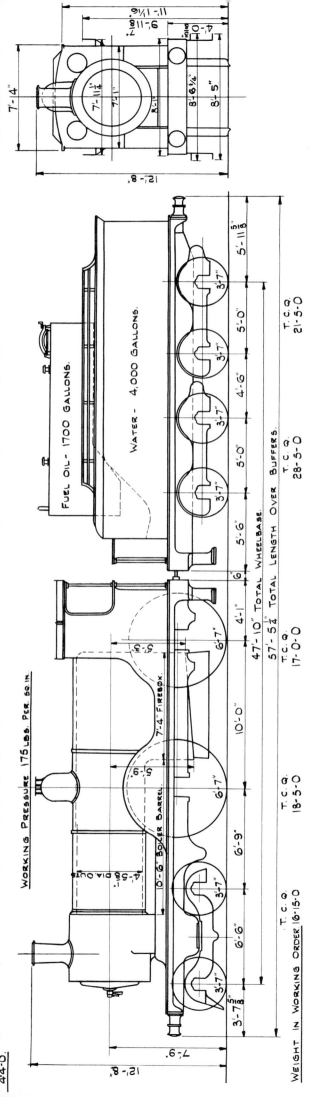

WORKING PRESSURE 175 LBS. PER. SQ. IN.

FUEL OIL - 1700 GALLONS.

WATER - 4,000 GALLONS.

7'-4" FIREBOX.

10'-0" BOILER BARREL.

4'-5⅝" DIA. O/S.

3'-7⅝"   6'-6"   6'-9"   10'-0"   6'-7"   6'-7"   4'-1"   6"   5'-6"   3'-7"   5'-0"   3'-7"   4'-6"   3'-7"   5'-0"   3'-7"   5'-11⅛"

47'-10" TOTAL WHEELBASE.

57'-5¼" TOTAL LENGTH OVER BUFFERS.

T.C.Q. 16·15·0   T.C.Q. 18·5·0   T.C.Q. 17·0·0   T.C.Q. 28·5·0   T.C.Q. 21·5·0

WEIGHT IN WORKING ORDER 16·15·0

Class T9 4-4-0. (Eastleigh dwg No.E36C)

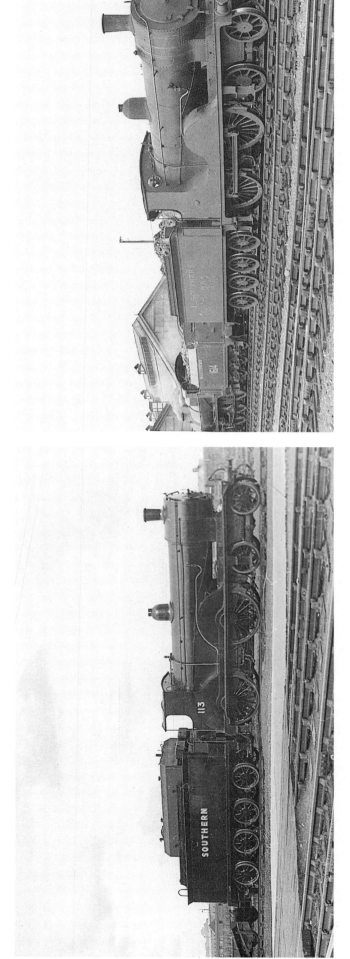

Class T9 No.302 at Eastleigh, 1939. (As built with wider splashers and cab.)

Class T9 No.113 (oil burner) at Eastleigh, 1947.

F9 class 4-2-4 Inspection Saloon

Specially constructed and designed for his own personal use, Drummond's Car was a small single-driver engine with a leading bogie, having a small carriage built on to the extended frame and supported by an 8ft wheelbase trailing bogie. In the period at the turn of the century, Locomotive Superintendents were autocratic figures indeed, and Victorian Scots were more autocratic than most!

Therefore, it was probably fitting that the 'Chief' should have his own private conveyance. Living then at Surbiton, this car was used to commute between there, the Company's workshops and indeed anywhere, that Dugald dictated. When it is realised that between 1900 and 1912, the "Bug" as it was known, covered in excess of 171,000 miles, it shows that many were the visits, scheduled or otherwise, that Drummond paid to outlying sheds, etc. It was built in 1899, and the dimensions can be seen on the official diagram (signed by Drummond himself). Coal, 1 ton, was carried on the footplate in the cab, under the side tanks, which held 600 gallons. Vacuum brake was fitted, but only operated through two brake shoes on the leading edge of the driving wheels. All the bogie wheels had splashers or mudguards. The saloon itself was supplied with some easy chairs, a table, a buffet and a toilet, lighting was by gas, and although there was electric bell communication between saloon and cab, this was largely ignored, as the Chief issued his instructions through a glazed porthole in the bulkhead between engine and saloon.

This little outfit entered SR stock at the Grouping and gave its number 733 to a T9 No. 773, which was then used in the 'King Arthur' class. After 1924 the "Bug" was No. 58S. Its last years were spent conveying guests and engineers around the newly-built Southampton Docks and in 1936 was transferred to the Marine Department. However, the firebox went in 1937, and the unit was withdrawn in 1940. Although subsequently broken up, the saloon body survives today, privately preserved in Hampshire.

Class F9 Inspection saloon No.58S, Eastleigh, 1927.

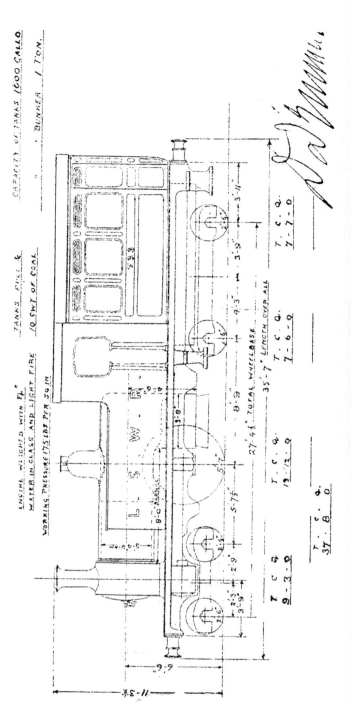

Class F9 4-2-4T. Drummond's official diagram of his Inspection Engine.

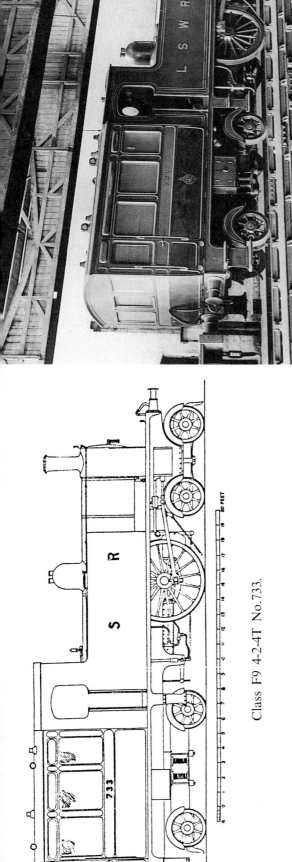

Class F9 Inspection saloon in LSWR livery as No.733, 1922.

Class F9 4-2-4T No.733.

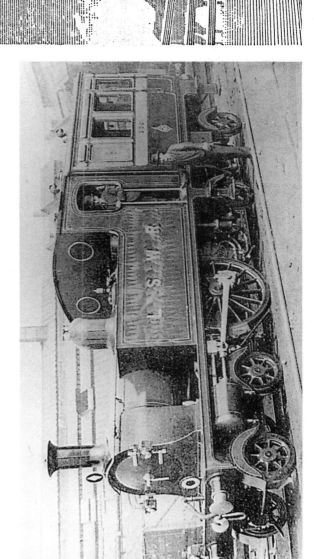

Class F9 No.733 in 1912 – better known as "Drummond's Bug".

Class E10 No.372 at Nine Elms in 1924.

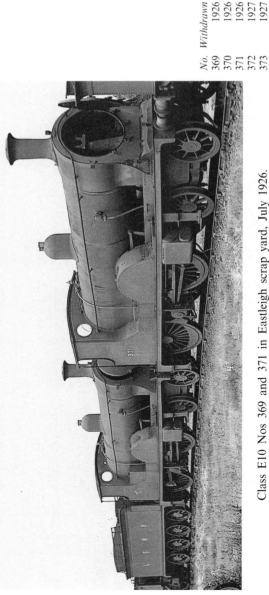

Class E10 Nos 369 and 371 in Eastleigh scrap yard, July 1926.

E10 class 4-2-2-0

Notwithstanding all the problems, pitfalls, and poor performance of No. 720, Drummond went ahead and built five more 'improved' engines of the same, double-single style, in 1901. The improvements were in fitting double slide bars to

the outside cylinders, with a more robust Joy valve gear. Full width cab and splashers were fitted and the cross water tubes had rectangular access covers on the outside of the firebox. Reversing was by steam, as was sanding, but this was to the bogie

No.	Withdrawn
369	1926
370	1926
371	1926
372	1927
373	1927

rosters. As a lot of their existence, especially in winter, was spent on shed, these five acquired the staff name of "Butterflies"!

An extra 1 ton wheels (this was changed later). An extra 1 ton was loaded onto each pair of drivers, but all these extras did little to improve their performance and by 1904 all five had been relegated to lighter

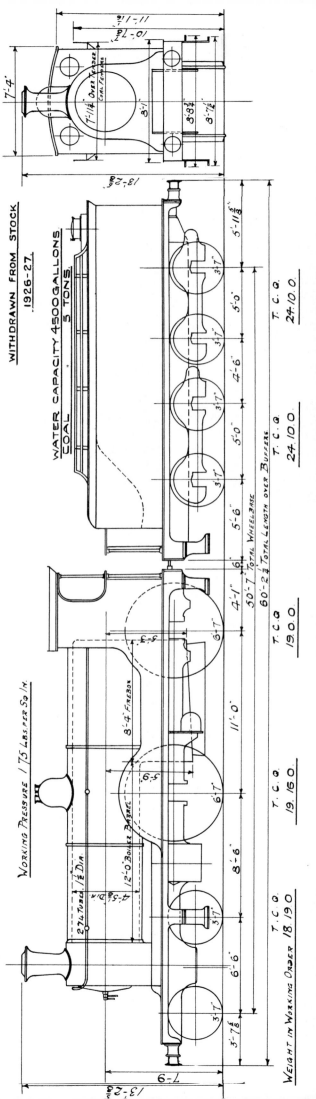

Class E10 4-4-0 (Eastleigh dwg No F38)

Class E10 No.370, Nine Elms, 1924.

Class E10 No.373 as built (LH side).

K10 class 4-4-0

With a large stud of reliable passenger engines in the 66 T9 class locomotives, Drummond now turned his attention to providing motive power for mixed traffic duties. Up to this time the A12 class 0-4-2s had been doing yeoman work, but something a little heavier was now required. Following his usual practice, Drummond produced a smaller version of an existing satisfactory machine, namely, the C8s. Known as the K10 class, or "Small Hoppers" to the trade, the new engines had the same boiler, cylinders and firebox as the C8, but the coupled wheels were 5ft 7in, instead of 6ft 7in, although the bogies were identical. As built, 40 water tubes were located in the firebox, but Urie soon removed these when he took over. All 40 engines were attached to Drummond six-wheeled tenders, but in later days could be seen with the 4,000 gallon eight-wheeled bogie water-carts. In 1925, ten engines had their Drummond chimneys replaced with 'stove pipe' types and were sent to the Eastern section to replace redundant M3s, but were ousted in their turn by F1s.

The whole class entered the Southern Railway and were painted SR green and given the 'E' prefix. Only 31 went into BR but were scrapped so fast that only one, No. 382, was renumbered.

No.	Built (Nine Elms)	SR livery	'E' prefix removed	Withdrawn
135*	1902	1924	1932	1949
136	1902	1924	1933	1947
137	1902	1925	1932	1949
138	1902	1925	1931	1947
139	1902	1924	1935	1948
140	1902	1925	1932	1950

No.	Built (Nine Elms)	SR livery	'E' prefix removed	Withdrawn
141	1902	1925	1931	1949
142	1902	1924	1932	1950
143	1902	1924	1932	1948
144*	1902	1924	1934	1949
145	1902	1926	1934	1948
146	1902	1926	1933	1948
149	1902	1924	1934	1947
150	1902	1925	1933	1948
151	1902	1924	1935	1950
152	1902	1924	1935	1949
153	1902	1924	1931	1949
329	1901	1924	1933	1950
340	1901	1924	1934	1948
341	1901	1924	1933	1949
342	1919	1924	1934	1947
343	1901	1925	1932	1948
344	1901	1926	1934	1947
345	1902	1925	1934	1949
347	1902	1924	1934	1947
380*	1902	1925	1934	1949
381	1902	1924	1932	1947
382*	1902	1925	1931	1950
383	1902	1924	1934	1949
384	1902	1924	1934	1951
385	1902	1924	1931	1949
386*	1902	1926	1932	1949
387	1902	1926	1934	1947
388	1902	1925	1933	1947
389	1902	1924	1934	1951
390	1902	1924	1934	1950
391*	1902	1926	1934	1949
392*	1902	1925	1934	1948
393	1902	1924	1932	1949
394	1902	1925	1935	1949

* 8-wheeled tender attached.

Class K10 No.151 at Salisbury in May 1935.

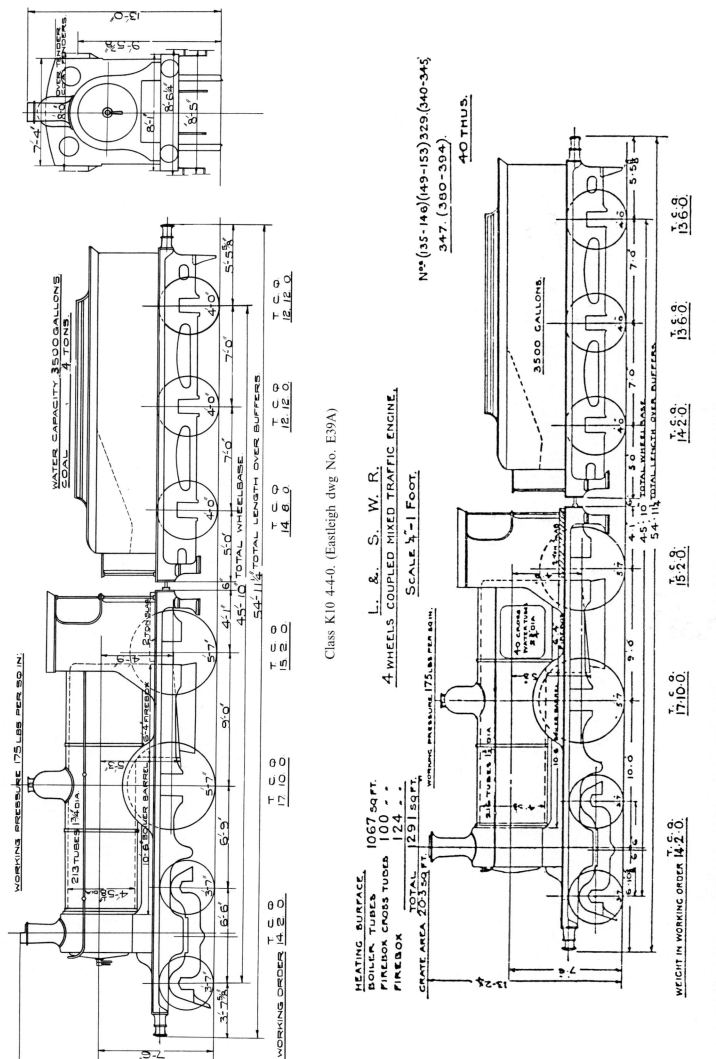

Class K10 4-4-0. (Eastleigh dwg No. E39A)

L. & S. W. R.

4 WHEELS COUPLED MIXED TRAFFIC ENGINE.

SCALE ¼″ = 1 FOOT.

HEATING SURFACE.

BOILER TUBES	1067 SQ.FT.
FIREBOX CROSS TUBES	100 „ „
FIREBOX	124 „ „
TOTAL	1291 SQ.FT.

GRATE AREA 20·35 SQ.FT.

Class K10 4-4-0. (LSWR diagram)

Class K10 No.149 in 1920.

Class K10 No.329 at Eastleigh in 1933 (RH side).

Class K10 No.384 c1936 (LH side).

Class K10 No.151 at work at Reading, July 1949.

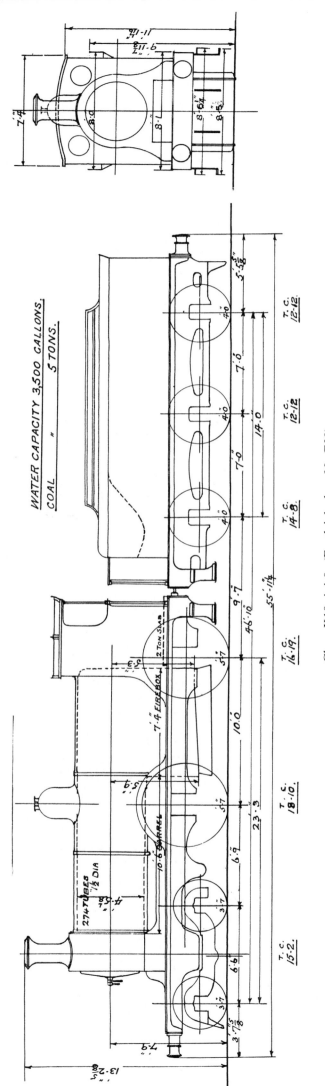

WATER CAPACITY 3,500 GALLONS.
COAL   "   5 TONS.

Class K10 4-4-0. (Eastleigh dwg No.E39)

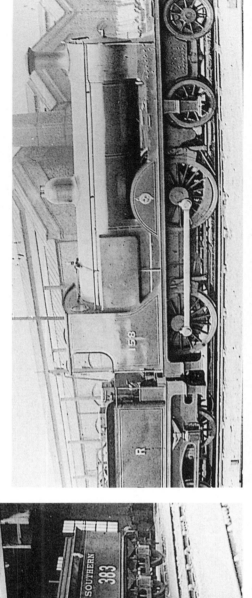

Class I.11 No.158 as built (RH side)

Class K10 No.383 Salisbury in 1937 (LH side)

L11 class 4-4-0

As the K10 was the smaller version of the C8 design, so the L11 was a smaller wheeled edition of the T9. Imagine a T9 with new 5ft 7in coupled drivers, plus the 7ft 4in firebox, and 10ft coupled wheelbase, and you have got the L11. This all meant that they were bigger engines than the K10s, so they were known as the "Large Hoppers". Starting off with the outside framed 6-wheel tenders, over their lives they had many other types. Nos 174/175, 405-413, had 8-wheeled 4,000 tenders, and 164/166/405/435/39 were attached to the big 4,500 gallon bogie tenders of Drummond circa 1911. Built with the cross firebox water tubes, these were eventually removed, although ten still had these fittings on entering the Southern Railway. In 1947, eight of the class were converted to oil burning, but by September 1948 oil had become too expensive, so these engines were laid aside. All entered BR stock in 1948, but only 16 were renumbered.

No.	Built (Nine Elms)	SR livery	'E' prefix removed	Double bogie tender	Withdrawn
134	1904	1928	1934	1925	1951
148*	1904	1923	1932	1925	1952
154*	1903	1925	1931	1925	1951
155*	1903	1925	1932	1925	1951
156	1903	1925	1933	1925	1951
157*	1903	1925	1933	1926	1952
158	1903	1926	1933	1925	1950
159	1903	1924	1933	1925	1951
161	1903	1924	1933	1925	1950
163	1903	1925	1932	1925	1951
164	1903	1926	1931	1925	1951
165	1903	1925	1933	1925	1951
166	1904	1924	1935	1927	1950
167	1904	1924	1931	1925	1949

No.	Built (Nine Elms)	SR livery	'E' prefix removed	Double bogie tender	Withdrawn
168	1904	1924	1933	1925	1950
169	1904	1923	1933	1926	1949
170*	1904	1923	1934	1925	1952
171	1904	1927	1932	1925	1951
172*	1904	1925	1935	1925	1952
173	1904	1923	1932	1925	1951
174	1906	1927	1933	(when built)	1951
175	1906	1924	1934	(when built)	1951
405	1906	1925	1934	1925	1951
406	1906	1925	1933	(when built)	1951
407	1906	1926	1931	(when built)	1950
408	1906	1924	1934	(when built)	1951
409	1906	1926	1934	(when built)	1951
410	1906	1924	1932	(when built)	1949
411*	1906	1926	1934	(when built)	1952
412	1906	1924	1932	(when built)	1950
413	1906	1926	1934	(when built)	1951
414	1906	1924	1932	1926	1951
435	1906	1926	1931	1925	1949
436	1906	1926	1932	1926	1951
437*	1906	1923	1933	1926	1952
438	1906	1925	1931	1925	1951
439	1907	1924	1933	1925	1949
440	1907	1926	1933	1925	1949
441	1907	1924	1934	-	1951
442	1907	1925	1935	1925	1951

* Fitted with electric lighting and oil burners 1947-8.

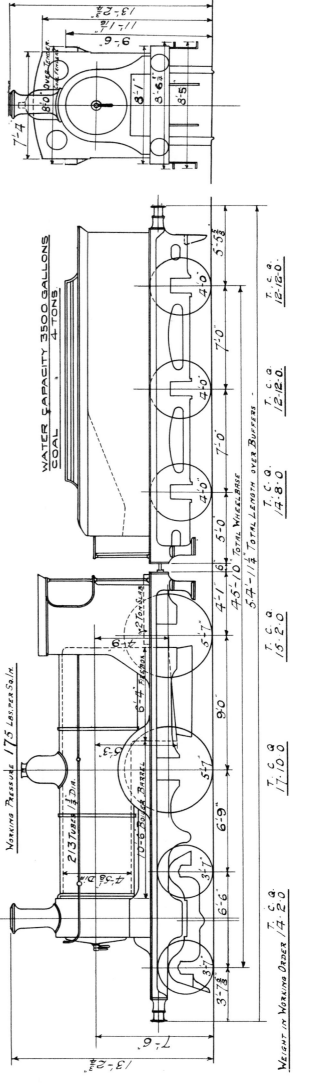

Class L11 4-4-0. (Eastleigh dwg No.E41)

Class L11 No.442 at Eastleigh in 1938.

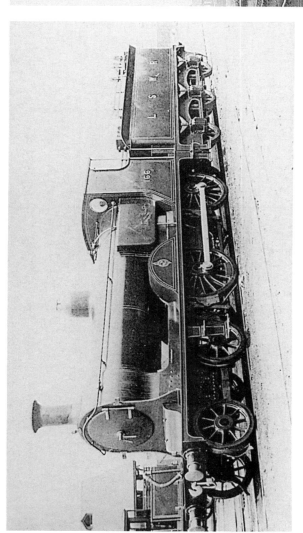

Class L11 No.166 in LSWR days (LH side).

Class L11 No.161 at Fratton, April 1928.

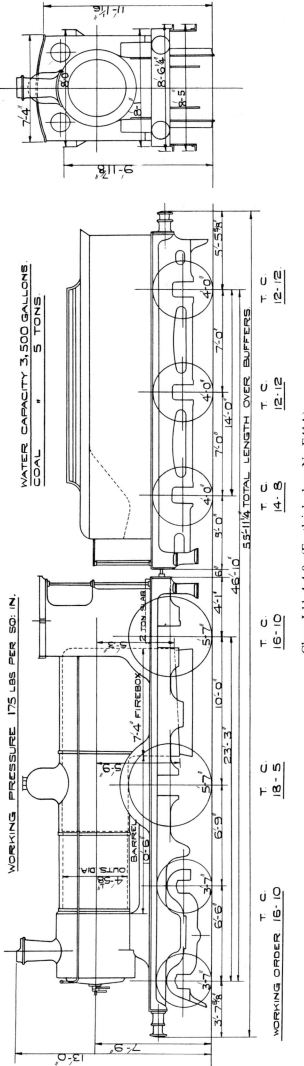

WATER CAPACITY 3,500 GALLONS.
COAL " 5 TONS.

WORKING PRESSURE 175 LBS PER SQ: IN.

Class L11 4-4-0. (Eastleigh dwg No.E41A)

Class L11 No.157, Nine Elms, June 1924.

Class L11 No.441, Nine Elms, 1923 with Westinghouse brake.

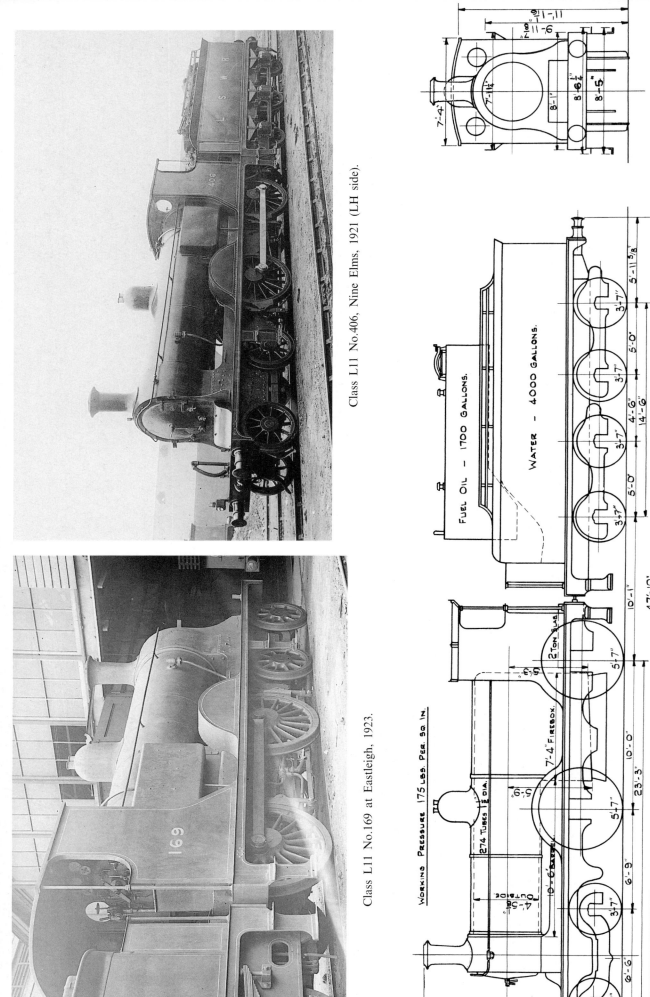

Class L11 No.406, Nine Elms, 1921 (LH side).

Class L11 No.169 at Eastleigh, 1923.

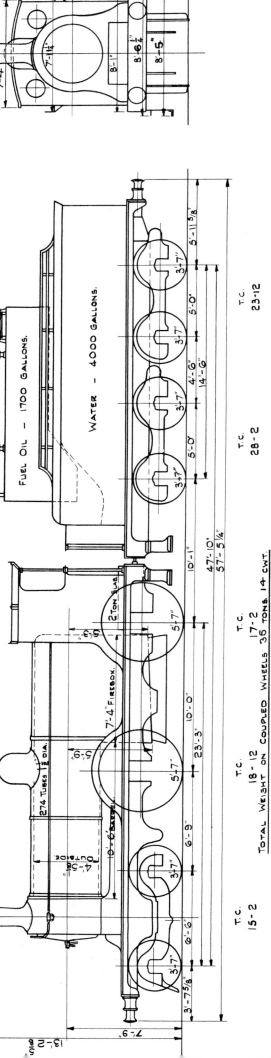

FUEL OIL — 1700 GALLONS.

WATER — 4000 GALLONS.

WORKING PRESSURE 175 LBS. PER SQ. IN.

274 TUBES 1⅝ DIA.

7'-4" FIREBOX.

2 TON SLAB.

TOTAL WEIGHT ON COUPLED WHEELS 35 TONS. 14 CWT.

T.C.
15-2

T.C.
18-12

T.C.
17-2

T.C.
28-2

T.C.
23-12

Class L11 No.155 as an oil burner, Eastleigh, 1948.

Class L11 No.440 at Nine Elms, 1926.

Class L11 No.437, Plymouth, 1924 (RH side).

Class L11 No.438 at Bournemouth in 1933.

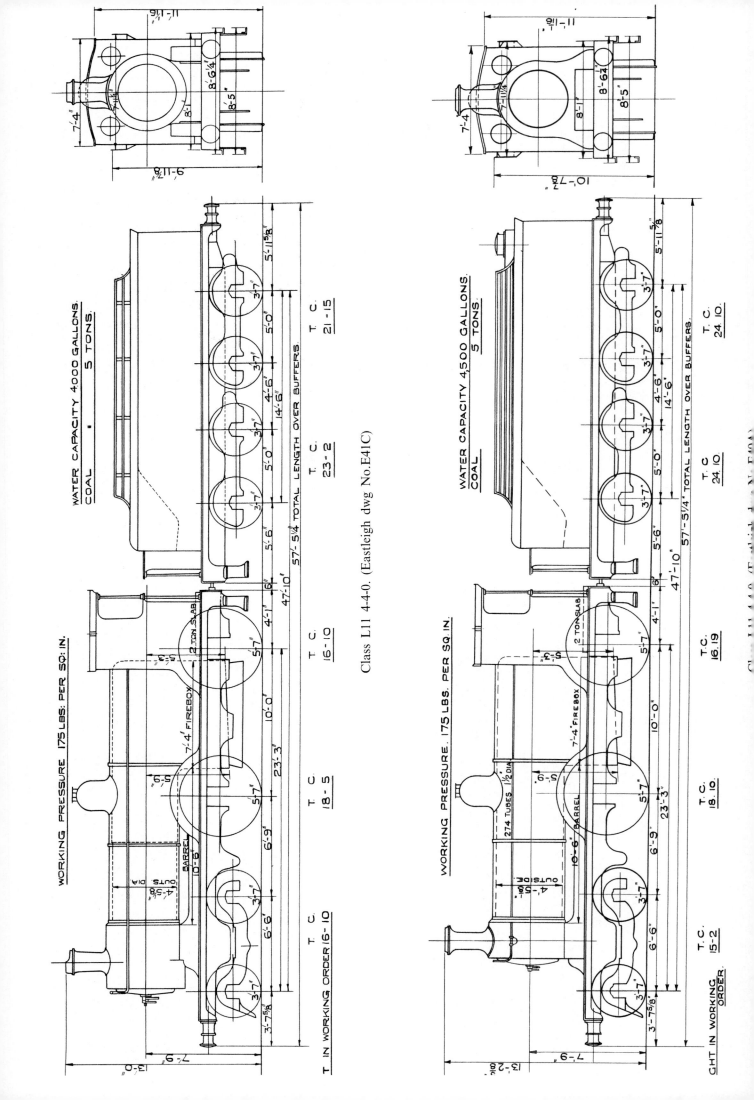

Class L11 4-4-0. (Eastleigh dwg No.E41C)

S11 Class 4-4-0

The S11 series was a T9 frame, 19in x 26in cylinders, 6ft driving wheels and a large boiler – a 'souped-up' T9 with the four coupled wheels 7in smaller in diameter than that class. The boiler was larger, being 5ft in diameter against the T9's 4ft 5in, although the same length. Firebox water tubes were fitted when built in 1903, but these were all removed by Southern Railway absorption. What was different was the built-up balanced crank axle, which did away with the need of balance weights on the wheels, a Drummond invention and these were the first British engines to be so fitted.

In 1920-22 the engines were superheated and given an extended smokebox. All entered Southern Railway ownership to be given the 'E' prefix and painted Maunsell green. All started out with 8-wheeled tenders, but in 1947 Nos 395 and 397 were given 6-wheeled tenders when they lost their 4,000 gallon type to T9s.

No.	'E' prefix removed	Superheated Eastleigh	Maunsell	Withdrawn
395	1932	1921	1930	1951
396*	1933	1922	1925	1951
397*	1933	1921	1931	1951
398	1932	1922	1930	1951
399*	1933	1920	1931	1951
400*	1932	1921	1931	1954
401*	1932	1922	1930	1951
402	1931	1922	1929	1951
403*	1931	1921	1929	1951
404	1933	1921	1931	1951

All built at Nine Elms Works in 1903. Disposal: No. 400 was broken up at Ashford Works, the remainder at Eastleigh Works.
* Fitted stove pipe chimneys from 1943 on.

Class S11 No.395 at Nine Elms in 1934.

Class L11 No.171, Eastleigh, July 1925.

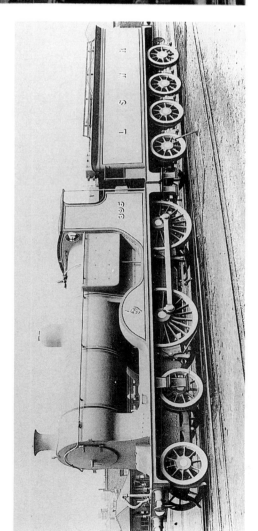

Class S11 No.395 as built (LH side).

Class S11 No.400 c1945.

Class S11 No.395 c1939 (LH side).

Class S11 No.30400 in BR days.

Class S11 No.E403 c1927.

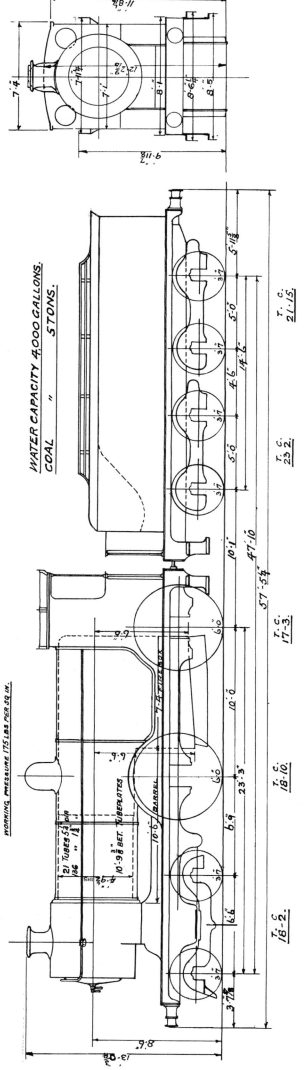

Class S11 4-4-0. (Eastleigh dwg No.E42A)

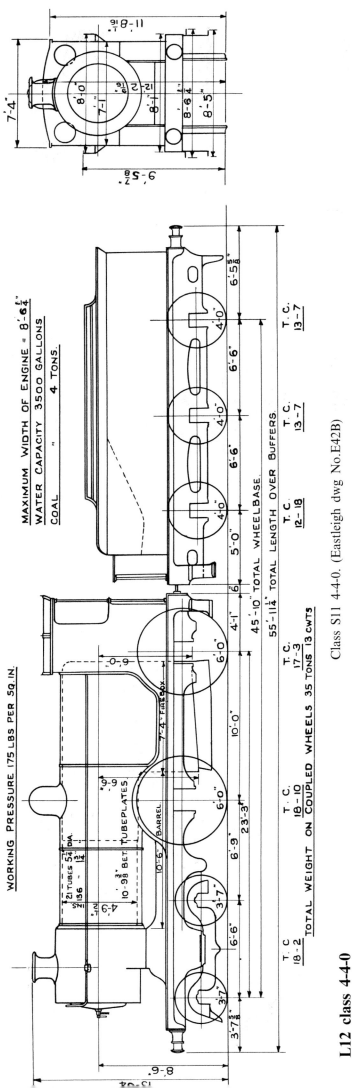

Class S11 4-4-0. (Eastleigh dwg No.E42B)

L12 class 4-4-0

The S11 4-4-0 locomotives, having proved their worth, were used as a pattern for the subsequent class, the L12s. This class of 20 engines, built between 1904 and 1905 at Nine Elms, had the boiler, cylinders, motion, bogie and tender of the S11 class, all mounted on a 1901 series of T9 type chassis. Driving wheels were 6ft 7in diameter on a 10ft wheelbase, with a 7ft 4in firebox. Like the S11, the engine was balanced-crank, without any weights in the coupled wheels. As built they had the water tube firebox, but upon being superheated, this system was removed by Urie in the early 1920s. The whole class was fitted with the Maunsell superheater in SR days and three were fitted for oil burning in 1921 and again in 1926. All survived into both SR and BR records.

No.	Built	Superheated Eastleigh	Maunsell	SR livery	'E' prefix removed	Withdrawn
415	1904	1920	1927	1924	1933	1953
416	1904	1918	1925	1925	1932	1951
417	1904	1921	1925	1925	1931	1951
418	1904	1919	1929	1924	1932	1951
419	1904	1919	1925	1925	1932	1951
420	1904	1922	1926	1923	1932	1951
421	1904	1915	1925	1924	1931	1951
422	1904	1920	1925	1925	1932	1951
423	1904	1919	1926	1923	1931	1951
424	1904	1918	1925	1925	1932	1951
425	1904	1920	1925	1924	1931	1951
426	1904	1919	1926	1924	1933	1951
427	1904	1922	1925	1924	1933	1951
428	1905	1920	1925	1925	1933	1951
429	1905	1922	1927	1924	1931	1951
430	1905	1919	1925	1925	1931	1951
431	1905	1921	1925	1923	1931	1951
432	1905	1920	1925	1924	1931	1951
433	1905	1919	1925	1925	1933	1951
434	1905	1922	1928	1923	1933	1955

Class L12 No.421 as built (LH side).

Class L12 No.423 at Exmouth Junction in 1930.

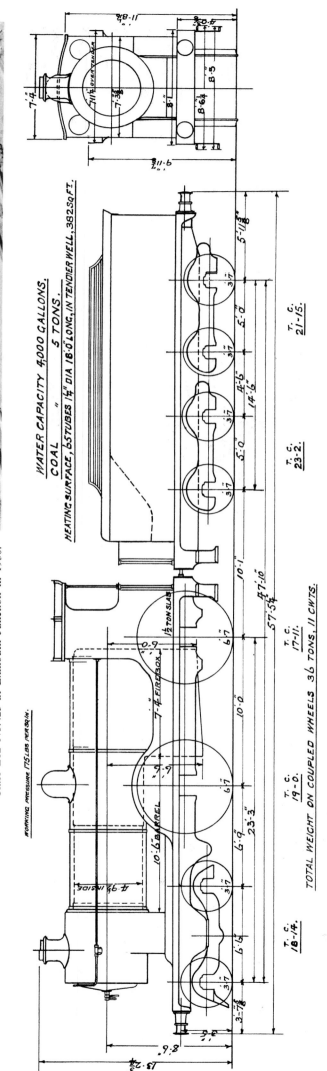

WATER CAPACITY 4,000 GALLONS.
COAL   „   5 TONS.
HEATING SURFACE, 65 TUBES 1¾" DIA 18'·0" LONG, IN TENDER WELL, 382 SQ.FT.

WORKING PRESSURE 175 LBS. PER SQ.IN.

TOTAL WEIGHT ON COUPLED WHEELS 36 TONS, 11 CWTS.

Class L12 4-4-0. (Eastleigh dwg No.E59)

Class L12 No.425, Salisbury, 1924.

Class L12 No.E431 at Nine Elms, January 1924.

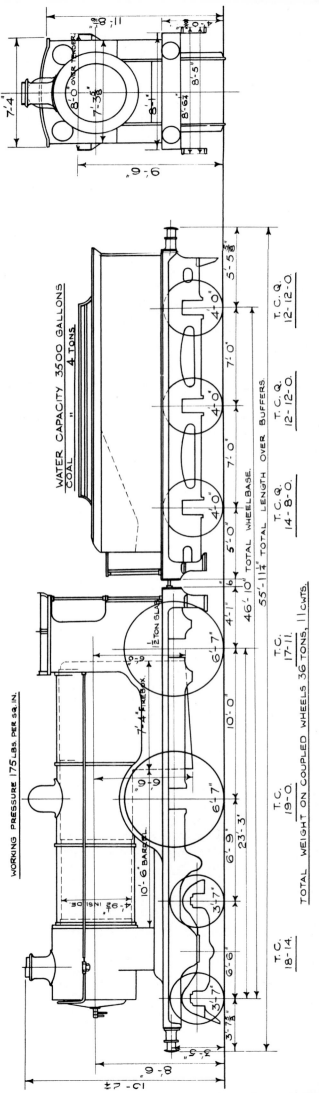

WATER CAPACITY 3500 GALLONS
COAL " 4 TONS.

WORKING PRESSURE 175 LBS. PER SQ. IN.

TOTAL WEIGHT ON COUPLED WHEELS 36 TONS, 11 CWTS.

Class L12 4-4-0 (English Arr.) No.E504.

Class L12 balanced crank axle.

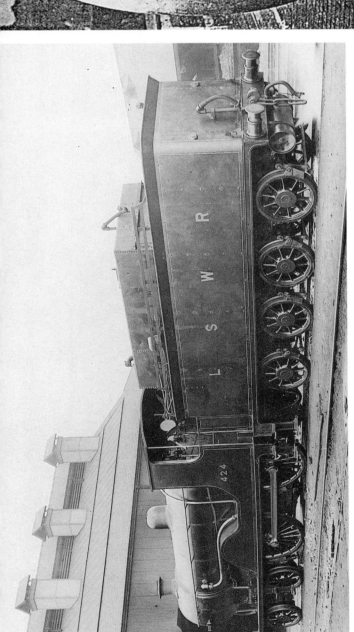

Class L12 No.424 at Nine Elms in 1921 as an oil burner.

Class C14 No.736 as built (LH side).

C14/S14 2-2-0T/0-4-0T

The C14 class of 2-2-0T engines were built originally for working with motor train services. Very small machines, and single-wheelers in effect, Nos 736 and 743 were constructed in 1906 and two others Nos 744-745 a year later in 1907.

No. 741 was rebuilt as an 0-4-0T in 1913, and No. 745 in 1922, No. 745 in 1913, and it was only similarly treated in 1923; and it was only these three that survived into SR ownership, in fact, also lasting to see BR days.

The S14 class, which resembled the rebuilt C14s, were always distinguishable by having 3ft 8in driving wheels against the 3ft diameter wheels of the earlier motor engines. There were only two in this class, Nos 101 and 147, both built in 1910, but although their life was quite short, (they did not enter into SR stock), they deserve a mention as being the first two locomotives to be constructed at the then new works at Eastleigh. Both were sold in 1917 to the Ministry of Munitions.

LSWR No.	Built	Rebuilt	Duplicate list	1931 SR list	BR No.	Withdrawn
741	1906	1922	1918	3741	30588	1957
744	1907	1923	1918	3744	30589	1957
745	1907	1913	1918	3745	77S	1959

Class C14 No.3744 at Eastleigh in 1947 (RH side).

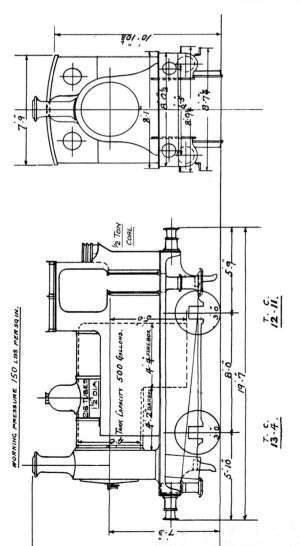

WORKING PRESSURE 150 LBS PER SQ IN.

½ TON COAL.

TANK CAPACITY 500 GALLONS.

26 TUBES 1½" DIA

4' 2" BARREL 4' 4" FIREBOX

Class C14 0-4-0T. (Eastleigh dwg No.E48)

Class C14 No.3744, Eastleigh, 1933.

Class S14 No.101 as built (LH side).

Class C14 No.3744 at Eastleigh, June 1933.

Class C14 No.3744 at Eastleigh in September 1947.

Class C14 No.741 at Strawberry Hill, May 1921.

F13/E14/G14/P14/T14 class 4-6-0

Faced again with ever-increasing traffic, with trains of heavier, corridor and steam heated stock, Drummond, as with other CMEs in the UK, had to think of more powerful locomotives. The next logical step up from the 4-4-0 configuration was a 4-6-0 class with four cylinders. Thus came about the notorious LSWR monsters which were divided into five classes, but were really only variations of an original theme. The first five, built in 1905, were classed F13. They were massive engines, but their performance did not live up to their appearance.

Drummond was no doubt married to his design of No. 720 (the double-single) because the motion of these new machines followed the pattern of two inside cylinders, worked by Stephenson valve gear on to the leading drivers, with two outside cylinders operated by Walschaerts gear driving the centre pair of wheels. The difference now being

that there were six drivers and all coupled together to obtain maximum adhesion. The F13, E14, G14 and P14 classes all had coupled wheels of 6ft diameter, but the final ten, classed T14, were fitted with 6ft 7in drivers.

The main differences between the series was in the cylinder sizes, and the final T14s had their outside cylinders moved forward to a position where they were in line with the inside cylinders. This configuration, together with the continuous splashers, gave this class the nickname of "Paddleboxes". Some of the class were given bogie tenders fitted with water scoops, but there being no water troughs on the system, these otherwise useful additions were never required!

The life of the F13, E14, G14 and P14s was quite short, as although Urie had a go at rebuilding No. 333 in 1920, and the records show these engines being rebuilt as H15s, in fact, only a few

Class F13 4-6-0. (LSWR diagram)

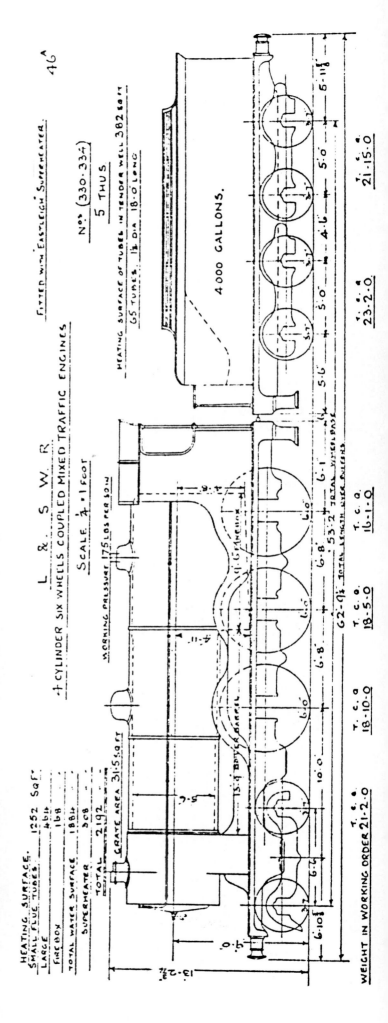

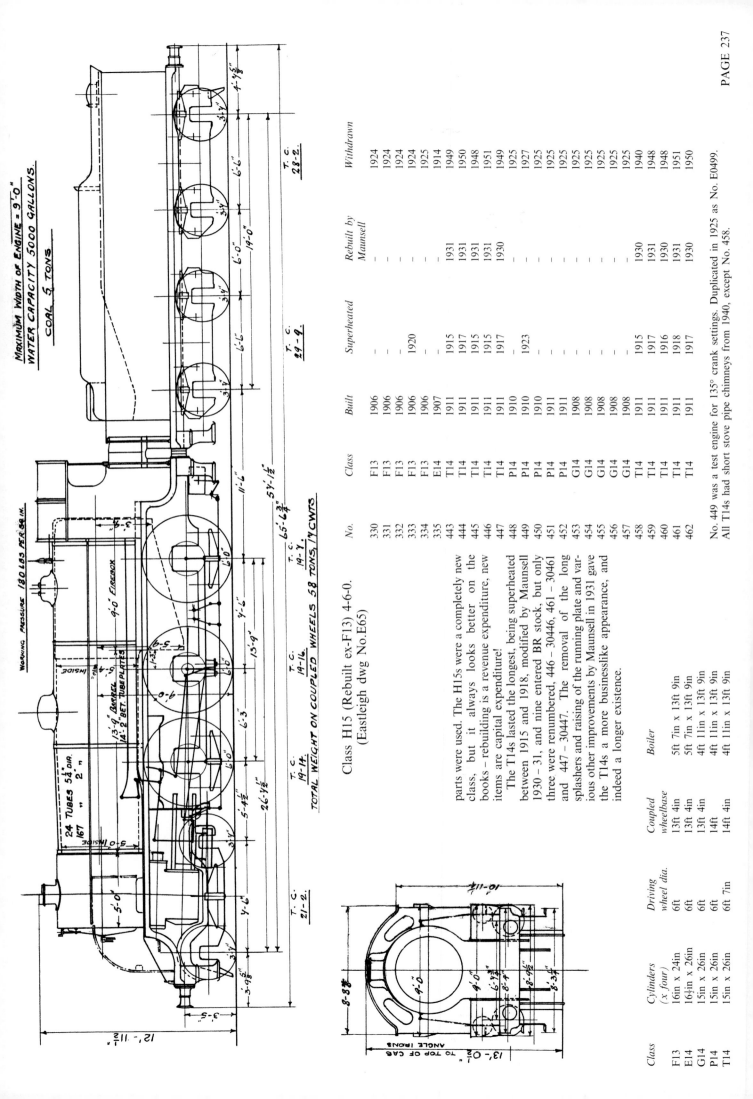

MAXIMUM WIDTH OF ENGINE = 9'-0"
WATER CAPACITY 5000 GALLONS.
COAL 5 TONS.

WORKING PRESSURE 180 LBS PER SQ.IN.

TOTAL WEIGHT ON COUPLED WHEELS 58 TONS, 14 CWTS.

No.	Class	Built	Superheated	Rebuilt by Maunsell	Withdrawn
330	F13	1906	—	—	1924
331	F13	1906	—	—	1924
332	F13	1906	—	—	1924
333	F13	1906	—	—	1924
334	E14	1906	—	—	1925
335	E14	1907	1920	—	1914
443	T14	1911	1915	—	1949
444	T14	1911	1917	1931	1950
445	T14	1911	1915	1931	1948
446	T14	1911	1915	1931	1951
447	T14	1911	1917	1931	1949
448	P14	1910	—	—	1925
449	P14	1910	1923	—	1927
450	P14	1910	—	—	1925
451	P14	1911	—	—	1925
452	P14	1911	—	—	1925
453	G14	1908	—	—	1925
454	G14	1908	—	—	1925
455	G14	1908	—	—	1925
456	G14	1908	—	—	1925
457	G14	1908	—	—	1925
458	T14	1911	1915	1930	1940
459	T14	1911	1917	1931	1948
460	T14	1911	1916	1930	1948
461	T14	1911	1918	1931	1951
462	T14	1911	1917	1930	1950

Class H15 (Rebuilt ex-F13) 4-6-0. (Eastleigh dwg No.E65)

parts were used. The H15s were a completely new class, but it always looks better on the books – rebuilding is a revenue expenditure, new items are capital expenditure!

The T14s lasted the longest, being superheated between 1915 and 1918, modified by Maunsell 1930–31, and nine entered BR stock, but only three were renumbered, 446–30446, 461–30461 and 447–30447. The removal of the long splashers and raising of the running plate and various other improvements by Maunsell in 1931 gave the T14s a more businesslike appearance, and indeed a longer existence.

Class	Cylinders (x four)	Driving wheel dia.	Coupled wheelbase	Boiler
F13	16in x 24in	6ft	13ft 4in	5ft 7in x 13ft 9in
E14	16½in x 26in	6ft	13ft 4in	5ft 7in x 13ft 9in
G14	15in x 26in	6ft	13ft 4in	4ft 11in x 13ft 9in
P14	15in x 26in	6ft	14ft	4ft 11in x 13ft 9in
T14	15in x 26in	6ft 7in	14ft 4in	4ft 11in x 13ft 9in

No. 449 was a test engine for 135° crank settings. Duplicated in 1925 as No. E0499.
All T14s had short stove pipe chimneys from 1940, except No. 458.

Class H15 No.331 at Nine Elms in 1925.

Class F13 No.333 at Exmouth Junction, July 1924.

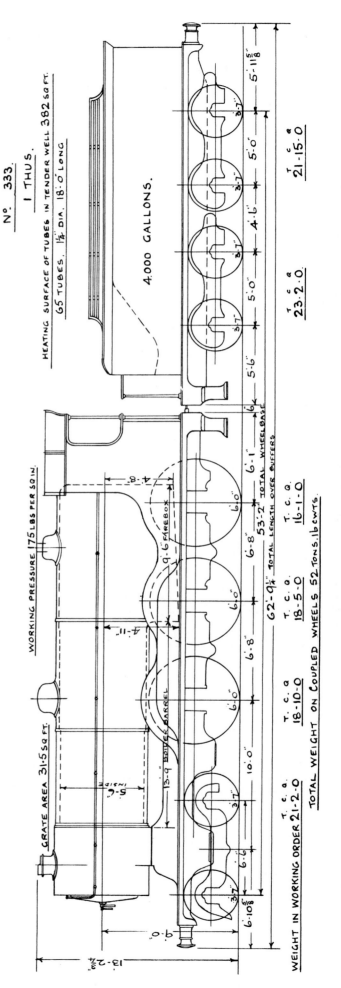

Class F13 4-6-0 No.333 (LSWR diagram)

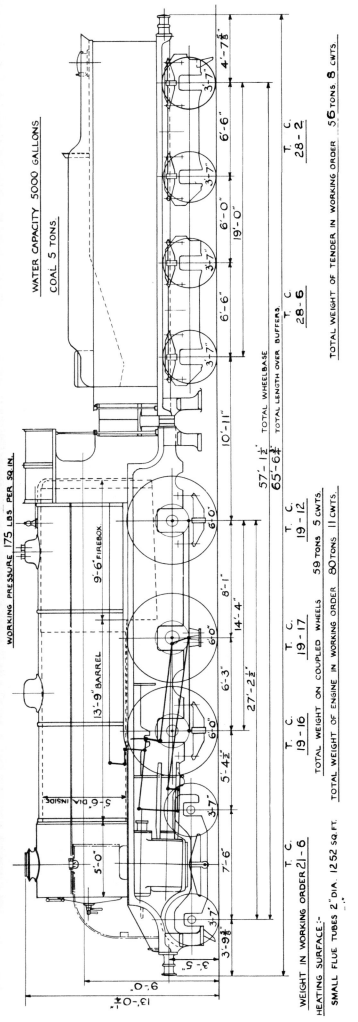

WATER CAPACITY 5000 GALLONS

COAL 5 TONS

WORKING PRESSURE 175 LBS PER SQ. IN.

9'-6" FIREBOX

13'-9" BARREL

5'-6" DIA INSIDE

5'-0"

7'-6"

3'-9⅝"

3'-7"

5'-4½"

6'-3"

6'-0"

14'-4"

6'-0"

8'-1"

6'-0"

27'-2½"

3'-7"

6'-6"

3'-7"

6'-0"

19'-0"

3'-7"

6'-6"

3'-7"

4'-7⅝"

10'-11"

57'-1½" TOTAL WHEELBASE

65'-6¾" TOTAL LENGTH OVER BUFFERS

T.C. 21-6   T.C. 19-16   T.C. 19-17   T.C. 19-12   T.C. 28-6   T.C. 28-2

WEIGHT IN WORKING ORDER

TOTAL WEIGHT ON COUPLED WHEELS 59 TONS 5 CWTS.

TOTAL WEIGHT OF ENGINE IN WORKING ORDER 80 TONS 11 CWTS.

TOTAL WEIGHT OF TENDER IN WORKING ORDER 56 TONS 8 CWTS.

HEATING SURFACE:-

SMALL FLUE TUBES 2" DIA. 1252 SQ.FT.

13'-0"±¼"

9'-0"

Class H15 (Rebuilt ex-F13) 4-6-0. (Eastleigh dwg No.E68A)

13'-0½" TO TOP OF CAB

ANGLE IRONS

8'-8⅛"

10'-11 1/16"

9'-0"

8'-5¼"

8'-3¾"

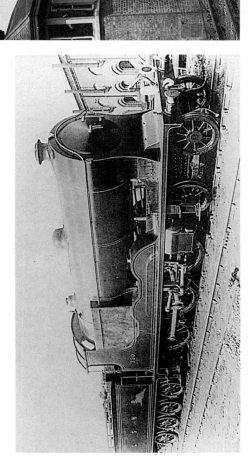

Class H15 No.330 at Hewish Gates in August 1928. PAGE 239

Class F13 No.330 as built (RH side).

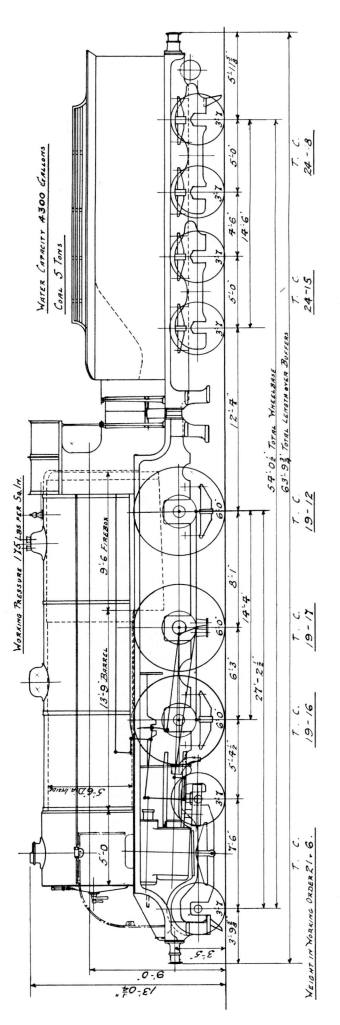

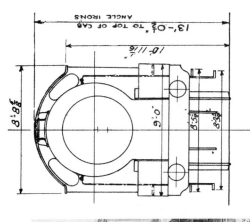

Class H15 (Rebuilt ex-F13) 4-6-0. (Eastleigh dwg No.E65A)

Class H15 No.30334 in BR livery at Feltham, 1950.

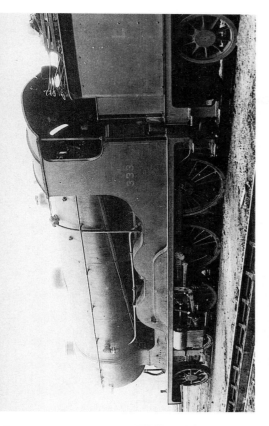

Class E14 No.335 at Exmouth Junction in 1924 (RH side).

Class F13 No.333 at Exmouth Junction in 1924. (LH side).

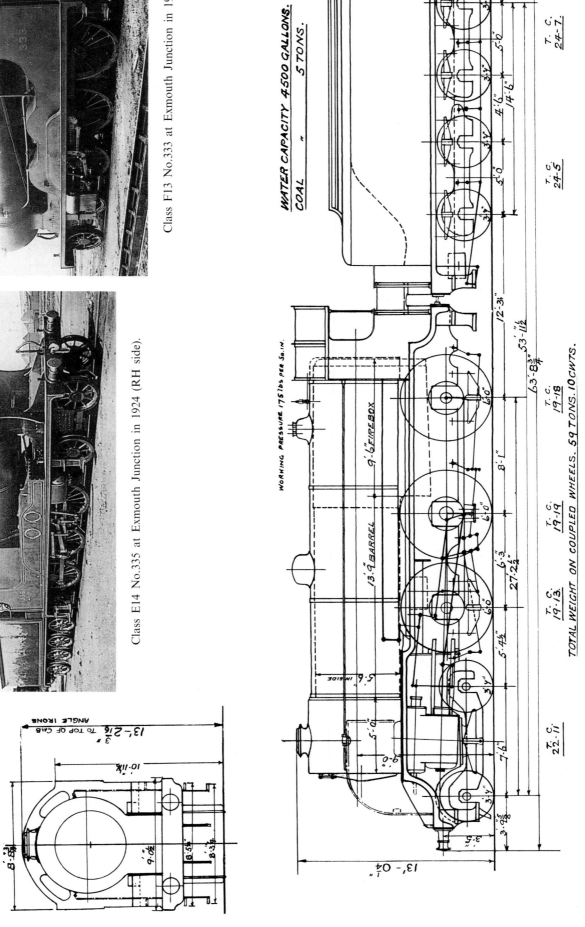

Class H15 4-6-0. (Eastleigh dwg No.E51)

Class G14 4-6-0.
(Eastleigh dwg No.E52A)

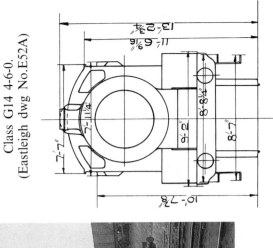

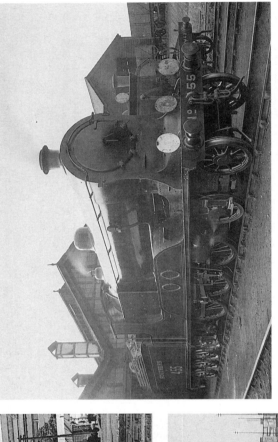

Class H15 No.30335 at Eastleigh in 1949.

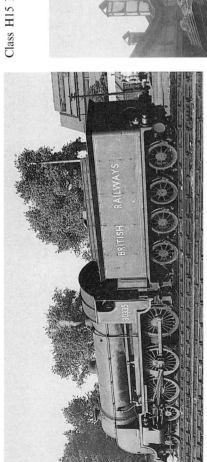

Class G14 No.E455 at Salisbury, 1924.

Class G14 No.457 at Clapham Junction in 1920 (RH side).

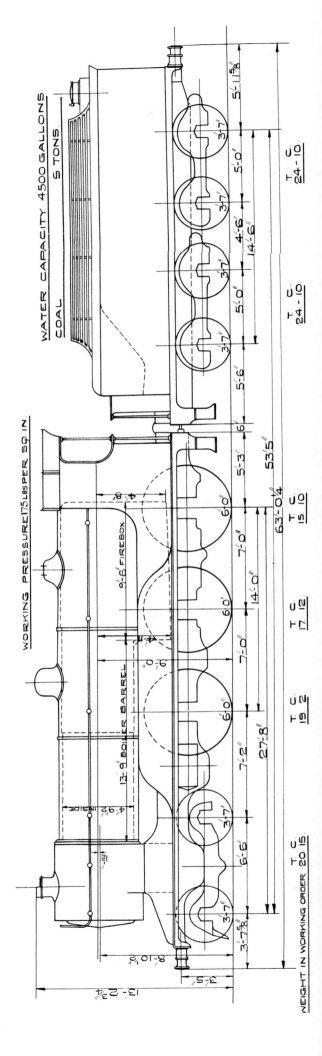

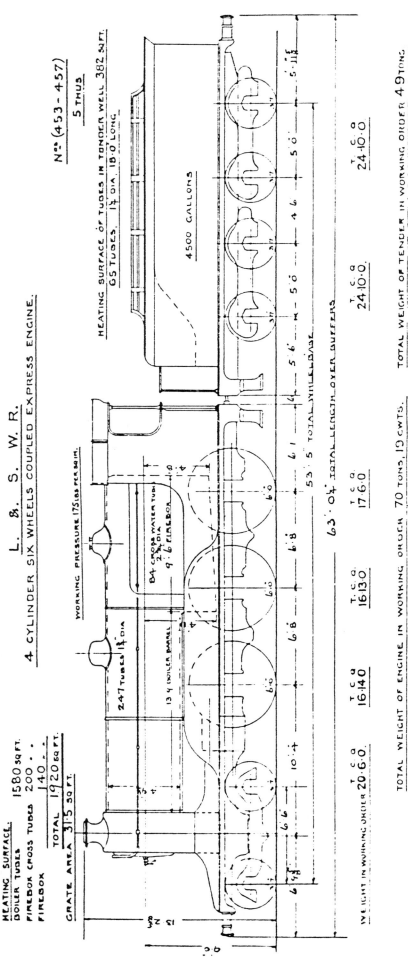

L. & S. W. R.

4 CYLINDER SIX WHEELS COUPLED EXPRESS ENGINE.

Nᵒˢ (453 - 457)
5 THUS

WORKING PRESSURE 175 lbs PER SQ IN.

HEATING SURFACE.
BOILER TUBES . . . . . 1580 SQ FT.
FIREBOX CROSS TUBES 200 . . .
FIREBOX . . . . 140 . .
TOTAL 1920 SQ FT.
GRATE AREA 31·5 SQ FT.

247 TUBES 1⅞ DIA

13·4 BOILER BARREL

34 CROSS WATER TUBES 2" DIA
9·6 FIREBOX

HEATING SURFACE OF TUBES IN TENDER WELL 382 SQ FT.
65 TUBES, 1⅞ DIA 18·0 LONG

4500 GALLONS

63·0¼ TOTAL LENGTH OVER BUFFERS

53·5 TOTAL WHEELBASE

WEIGHT IN WORKING ORDER
20·6·0 T.C.Q.
16·14·0 T.C.Q.
16·13·0 T.C.Q.
17·6·0 T.C.Q.
24·10·0 T.C.Q.
24·10·0 T.C.Q.

TOTAL WEIGHT OF ENGINE IN WORKING ORDER 70 TONS, 19 CWTS.
EMPTY 64 · 12

TOTAL WEIGHT OF TENDER IN WORKING ORDER 49 TONS
EMPTY 24 · 14 CWT

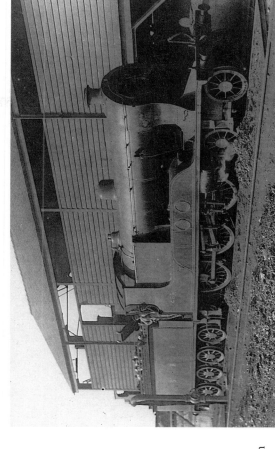

Above: Class G14
4-6-0 Nos 453-457.
(LSWR diagram)

Left: Class G14
No.457, Nine Elms,
June 1920 (LH side).

Right: Class G14
No.456 at Eastleigh in
1922 (RH side).

L. & S. W. R.

4 CYLINDER SIX WHEELS COUPLED EXPRESS ENGINE

Nos (448-452)
5 THUS.

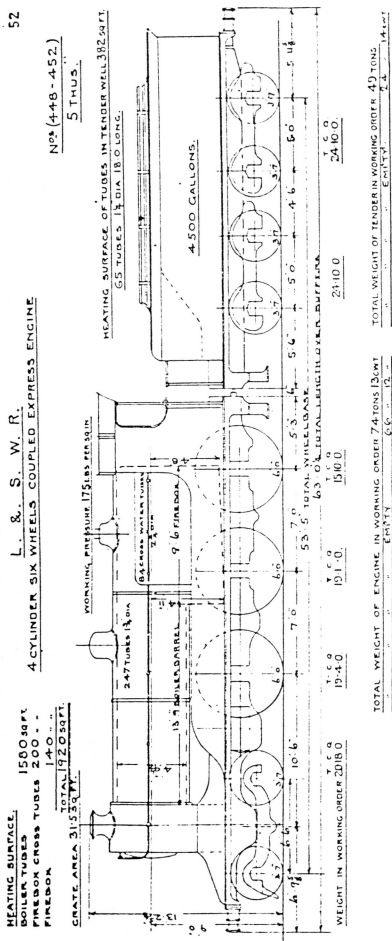

HEATING SURFACE.
BOILER TUBES   1580 sq ft
FIREBOX CROSS TUBES   200 - -
FIREBOX   140 - -
TOTAL 1920 sq ft

GRATE AREA 31.53 sq ft

WORKING PRESSURE 175 LBS PER SQ IN

HEATING SURFACE OF TUBES IN TENDER WELL 382 sq ft
65 TUBES 1¾ DIA 18.0 LONG.

4500 GALLONS.

247 TUBES 1¾ DIA
8 CROSS WATER TUBES 7¼ DIA
9' 6" FIREBOX
15' 9" BOILER BARREL

WEIGHT IN WORKING ORDER 2018.0

TOTAL WEIGHT OF ENGINE IN WORKING ORDER 74 TONS 13 CWT
EMPTY 66 .. 12

TOTAL WEIGHT OF TENDER IN WORKING ORDER 49 TONS
EMPTY 24 .. 14 cwt

TOTAL WEIGHT OF ENGINE AND TENDER IN WORKING ORDER 123 TONS 13 CWT
EMPTY 91 .. 6

DIAMETER OF CYLINDERS 15" (FOUR)
STROKE 26"
TRACTIVE FORCE = 24200 LBS.

TYPE 4.6.0

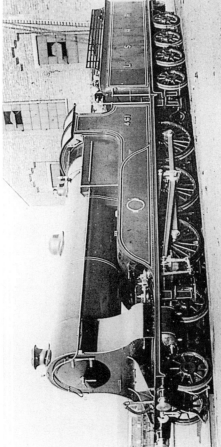

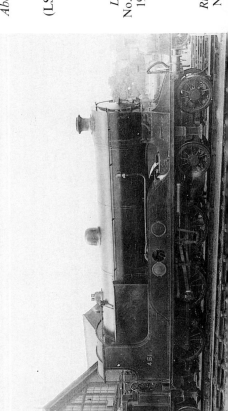

Above: Class P14
4-6-0 Nos
448-452.
(LSWR diagram)

Left: Class P14
No.451 at Salisbury
1924 (RH side).

Right: Class T14
No.461 as built

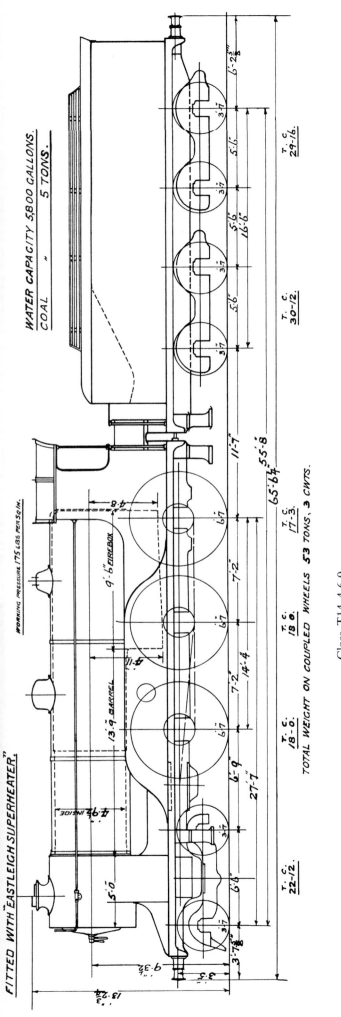

FITTED WITH "EASTLEIGH SUPERHEATER".

WORKING PRESSURE 175 LBS PER SQ IN.

WATER CAPACITY 5,800 GALLONS.
COAL ~ 5 TONS.

TOTAL WEIGHT ON COUPLED WHEELS 53 TONS, 3 CWTS.

Class T14 4-6-0.

Class T14 No.460 at Salisbury, 1926 (RH side).

Class T14 No.446 under repair at Nine Elms, June 1925.

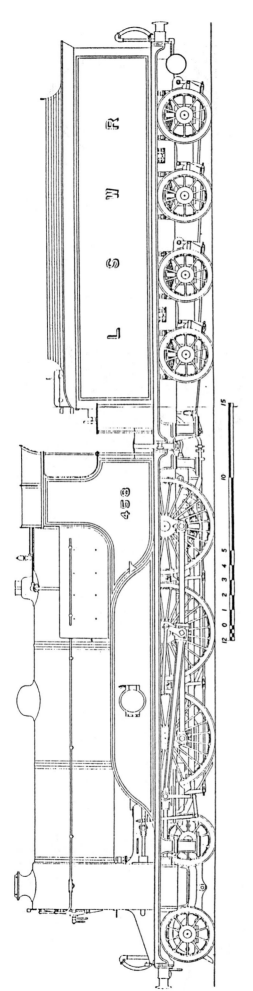

Class T14 4-6-0.

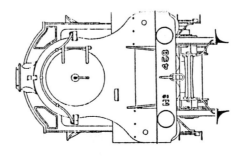

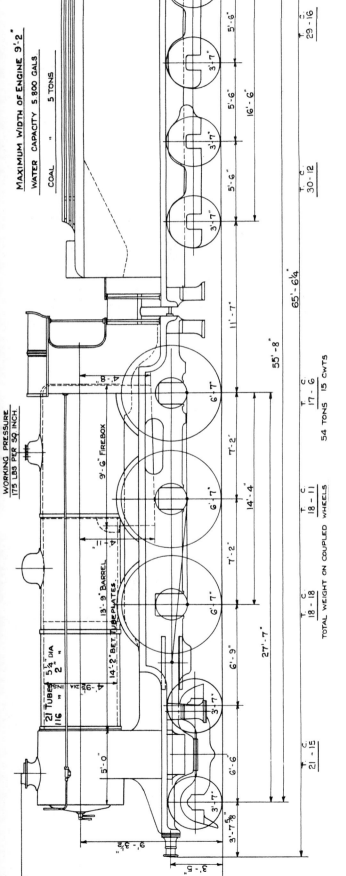

MAXIMUM WIDTH of ENGINE 9'-2"

WATER CAPACITY 5,800 GALS
COAL " 5 TONS

WORKING PRESSURE
175 LBS PER SQ INCH

Class T14 4-6-0. (Eastleigh dwg No.E60A)

Class T14 No.461 at Exmouth Junction in 1926.   PAGE 247

Class T14 No.E445 at Nine Elms in 1931.

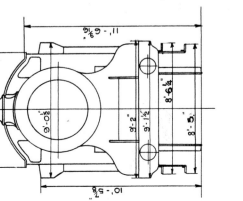

COUPLED AXLEBOXES FITTED WITH
MECHANICAL LUBRICATION.

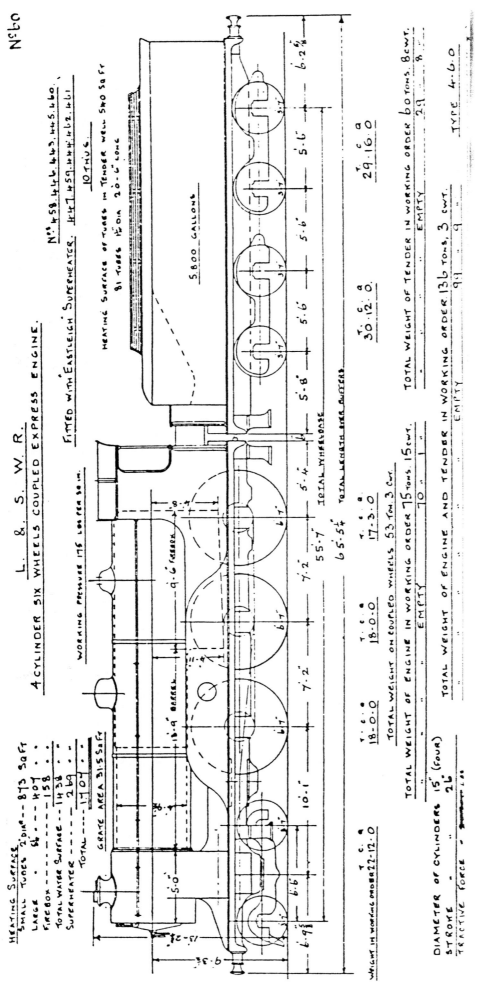

Class T14 Rebuilt 4-4-0. (LSWR diagram No.60)

Left: Class T14 No.E460 at Clapham Junction, 1931 (RH side).

Right: Class D15 No.467 as rebuilt in 1917

D15 class 4-4-0

The last design of locomotive which Drummond provided for the LSWR was the large 4-4-0 express passenger class known as the D15. No doubt disillusioned, not only by the performance of his own 4-6-0 engines, but also by the experiences of his native Scottish contemporaries, he settled for a solid, robust 4-coupled machine of simple design and with generous bearing surfaces. In previous 4-coupled inside-cylindered engines, using Stephenson valve gear with its four eccentric sheaves as well as the cranks, space for wide axle bearings was at a premium. In the D15s, Drummond overcame this by using a modified form of Walschaerts valve gear on the crankshaft, which enabled 9in bearings to be fitted, which effectively did away with 'hot box' trouble so many previous engines had been plagued with. The steam chests were sited above the cylinders, instead of between, with 10in piston valves working the 19½in x 26in cylinders. All this, of course, meant a high boiler centre line, which can be seen

on any front view of the D15 class.

The boiler was of a pattern similar to that on No.720, the T7, but the firebox, being too long to fit between the axles, was sloped so that the cab end cleared the trailing axle. Water tubes in the firebox followed Drummond's standard, but were removed after his death in 1912. Ten engines were built in two batches of five, but their designer only lived to see the first batch in traffic, sadly, because these ten engines were the fastest runners and easiest steamers of all the Drummond engines. During the First World War, Urie rebuilt the class by removing the firebox water tubes, superheating and extending the smokebox so that a saddle was necessary. Also the cylinders were increased to 20in. In SR days the engines were fitted with Maunsell superheaters and had their 8-wheel 'water carts' replaced by 3,500 gallon, 6-wheel, Drummond type tenders. All ten entered SR service and survived to carry BR numbers, except one, No.463.

Class D15 No.30466 in BR days.

No.463 was fitted with electric lighting and oil burners.

No.	Built	Rebuilt with Superheater Eastleigh	Maunsell	'E' prefix Applied	Removed	Withdrawn
463	1912	1916	1926	1924	1931	1951
464	1912	1915	1926	1925	1933	1954
465	1912	1915	1926	1924	1932	1956

No.	Built	Rebuilt with Superheater Eastleigh	Maunsell	'E' prefix Applied	Removed	Withdrawn
466	1912	1916	1926	1923	1933	1952
467	1912	1917	1925	1924	1932	1955
468	1912	1916	1926	1924	1932	1952
469	1912	1916	1925	1924	1934	1951
470	1912	1917	1925	1925	1933	1952
471	1913	1917	1926	1924	1932	1954
472	1913	1916	1926	1924	1932	1952

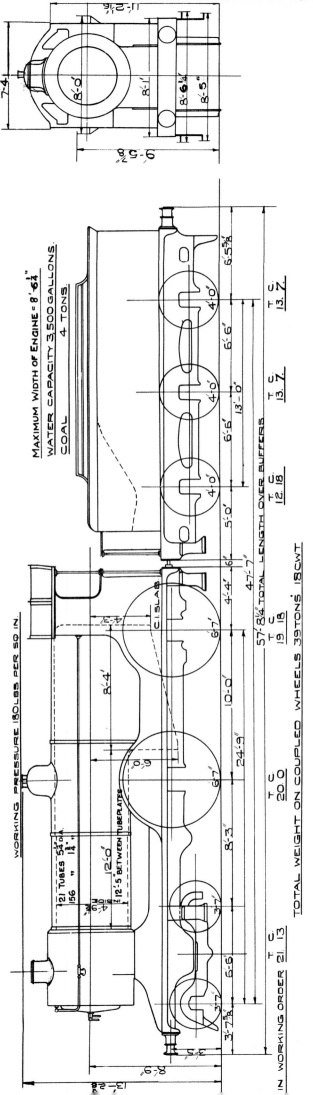

Class D15 4-4-0. (Eastleigh dwg No.E58A)

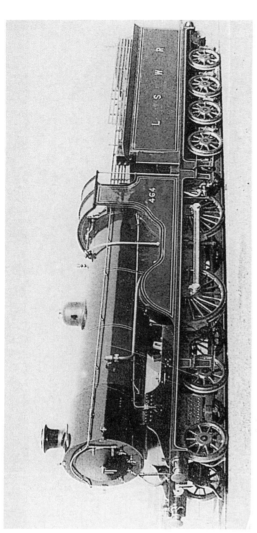

Class D15 No.464 in 1915.

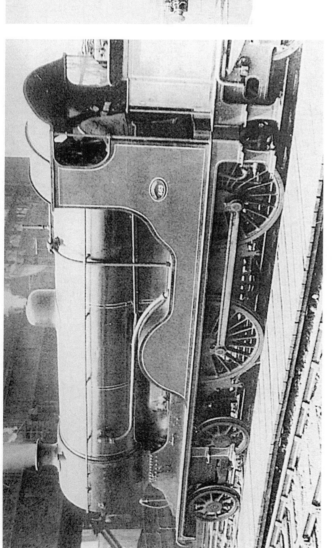

Class D15 No.463 in 1913.

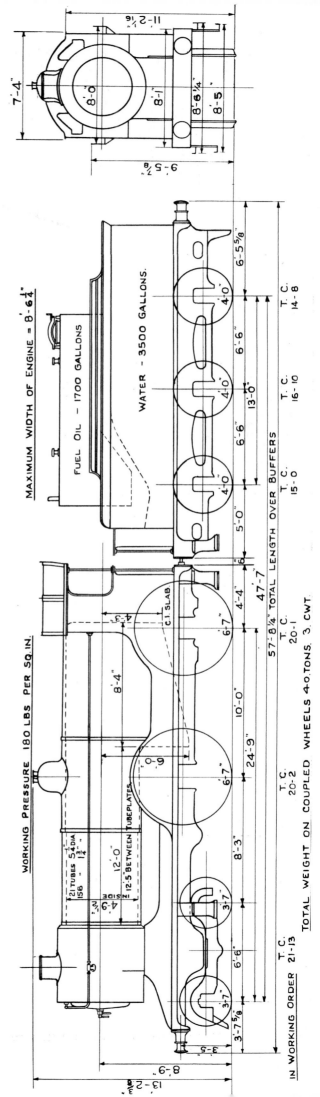

MAXIMUM WIDTH OF ENGINE = 8'-6¼"

WORKING PRESSURE 180 LBS PER SQ. IN.

FUEL OIL — 1700 GALLONS.

WATER — 3500 GALLONS.

21 TUBES 5¼" DIA
156 " 1¾"

12'-0"
12'-5 BETWEEN TUBEPLATES

8'-4"

C.I. SLAB

57'-8¼" TOTAL LENGTH OVER BUFFERS
47'-7"

T.C. 21-13
T.C. 20-2
T.C. 20-1
T.C. 15-0
T.C. 16-10
T.C. 14-8

IN WORKING ORDER

TOTAL WEIGHT ON COUPLED WHEELS 40 TONS. 3. CWT.

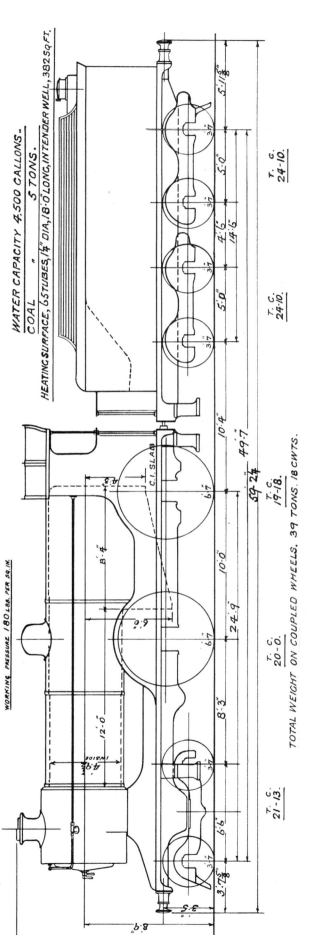

WATER CAPACITY 4,500 GALLONS..

COAL " 5 TONS.

HEATING SURFACE, 65 TUBES, 1¾" DIA, 18'-0 LONG, INTENDER WELL, 382 SQ FT.

WORKING PRESSURE 180 LBS. PER SQ.IN.

Class D15 4-4-0. (Eastleigh dwg No.E58)

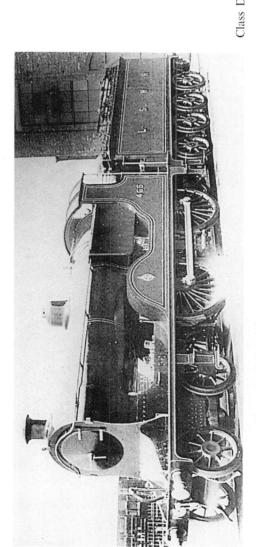

Class D15 No.465 (LH side).

Class D15 No.467 in 1913.

Class H15 No.E475 at Bournemouth in 1925.

Class D15 No.469 in 1913.

No.	Original Class	Rebuilt/Built	'E' prefix removed	Short chimney fitted	Maunsell chimney fitted	Withdrawn
330	F13	1924	1932	1952		1957
331	F13	1924	1931	1941		1961
332	F13	1924	1932	1947		1956
333	F13	1924	1932	1952		1958
334	F13	1925	1932	1953		1958
335	E14	1914	1932	1952		1959
473		1924	1931	–	1927	1959
474		1924	1931	–	1931	1960
475		1924	1932	–	1930	1961
476		1924	1932	–	1929	1961
477		1924	1931	–	1931	1959
478		1924	1932	–	1928	1959
482		1914	1932	1932	–	1959
483		1914	1934	1943	–	1957
484		1914	1931	1934	–	1959
485		1914	1932	1932	–	1955
486		1913	1932	1932	–	1959
487		1914	1931	1935	–	1957
488		1914	1933	1939	–	1959
489		1914	1932	1932	–	1961
490		1914	1931	1936	–	1955
491		1914	1931		1927	1961
521		1924	1931		1927	1961
522		1924	1932		1929	1961
523		1924	1931		1927	1961
524		1924	1932		1928	1961

No. 488 fitted with '330' series chimney 1925-39.

H15 class 4-6-0

Upon the death of Drummond in 1912, the post of Chief Mechanical Engineer of the LSWR was given to Robert Urie, who had been Works Manager at Nine Elms and later at Eastleigh for 15 years. A close associate of Drummond, not only on the LSWR, but previously in Scotland with the Caledonian, Urie was well aware of the good and the bad in the ex-chief's designs. His immediate task was to design a successful six-coupled locomotive to handle both freight and passenger traffic which was increasing all the time.

His first venture into the 'big engine' programme was for ten 2-cylinder 4-6-0s with 6ft driving wheels, to be known as the H15 class. Unlike any previous LSWR engines, these robust machines had a boiler 5ft 6in x 13ft 9in with a firebox 9ft long. The two outside cylinders 21in x 28in were operated by standard Walschaerts valve gear. All but two were superheated as built, Nos 482 to 485 with the Schmidt pattern, 486 to 489 with Robinson superheaters, while Nos 490 and 491 were left saturated. For comparison, All were eventually

refitted with Urie's own design, which became known as the 'Eastleigh' type, after trials on other 4-6-0s etc already mentioned.

In SR days, Maunsell superheaters were installed. The one E14 class engine, No. 335, was rebuilt as an H15 to join the class, and in 1924 the F13 engines, Nos 330 – 334 were also reconstructed, and in 1924 Maunsell built ten more machines, making a grand total in SR days of 26. Note: The engines numbered 473 to 478, 521 to 524, and the 'rebuilt' Nos 330 – 334, all had straight running plates in Maunsell days; all others had an upward step over the cylinders and splashers. As built, the H15s were attached to Drummond 8-wheeled 'water carts', but in later SR days, had the Urie 5,000 gallon pattern tender. Another item which appeared in the 1929 – 31 period was the Maunsell smoke deflector plates, which were fitted to the smokebox sides. They were obviously successful, as from then on, the majority of the Southern main line engines carried them.

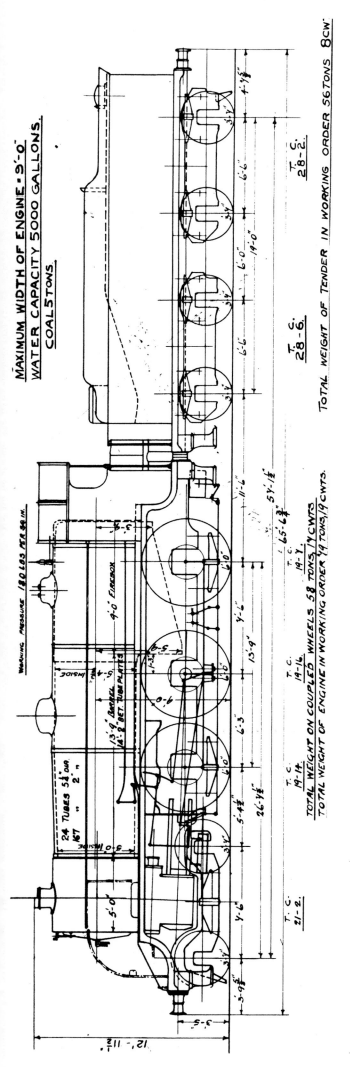

Class H15 4-6-0. (Eastleigh dwg No.E65)

No.	Name	Built	Urie chimney replaced by Maunsell	Maunsell Superheater	'E' prefix removed	Withdrawn
736	Excalibur†	1918	1928	1930	1932	1956
737	King Uther†	1918	1925	1929	1932	1956
738	King Pellinore	1918	1928	1930	1932	1958
739	King Leodegrance	1919	1927	1930	1931	1957
740	Merlin**	1919	1925	1929	1931	1955
741	Joyous Gard†	1919	1925	1929	1932	1956
742	Camelot	1919	1925	1930	1932	1957
743	Lyonnesse	1919	1925	1930	1933	1955
744	Maid of Astolat	1919	1927	1930	1932	1956
745	Tintagel**	1919	1928	1930	1932	1956
746	Pendragon	1922	1929	1932	1932	1955
747	Elaine	1922	1925	1929	1932	1956
748	Vivien**	1922	1929	1929	1932	1957
749	Iseult**	1922	1925	1928	1932	1957
750	Morgan le Fay	1922	1928	1930	1931	1957
751	Etarre	1922	1928	1929	1931	1957
752	Linette†**	1922	1928	1930	1932	1955
753	Melisande	1923*	1926	1928	1931	1957
754	The Green Knight	1923*	1925	1930	1932	1953
755	The Red Knight†	1923*	1927	1929	1932	1957

No. 755 fitted 21in cylinders.
* Built at Eastleigh by SR.
** Fitted electric light and oil burners.
† Fitted large diameter chimney.

N15 class (Urie) 4-6-0

The success of the H15 class of mixed traffic engine led directly to the building of an express passenger design, which was in effect a larger version of the Urie Opus I. Now known as the 'King Arthur' class, after the naming of these engines based on the Round Table legends, the design was formulated in 1916, but due to war difficulties, construction of the machines was not started until 1918. Apart from the fact that these 20 new engines had 6ft 7in coupled drivers, the main innovations were, a cylinder size of 22in x 28in, and a taper boiler, the taper being in the front ring only.

The cabs were of the same Drummond pattern as that on the H15s, and the tenders were the 8-wheeled double bogie with outside axleboxes, with a capacity of 5,000 gallons of water and 5 tons of coal. (It should be noted that the 54 Maunsell 'Arthurs' belong to the *Southern Railway* section of this work, so do not feature here). Smoke deflectors were fitted between 1927 and 1929.

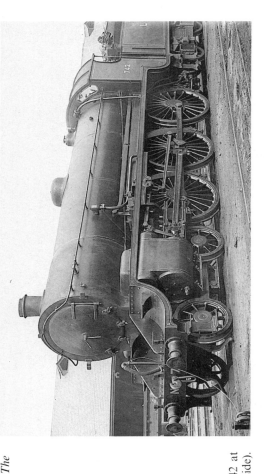

Class N15 (Urie) No.755 *The Red Knight* at Nine Elms, 1923.

Class N15 (Urie) No.742 at Nine Elms, 1923 (LH side).

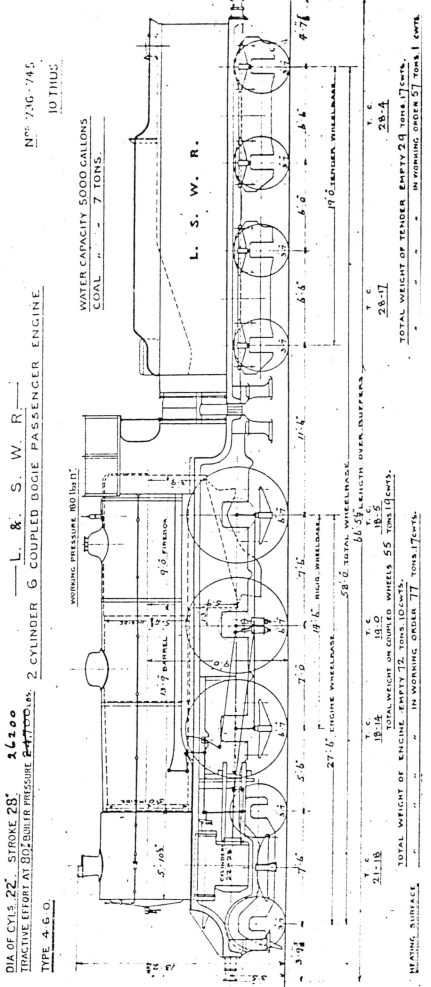

DIA OF CYLS. 22″. STROKE 28″. 26200
TRACTIVE EFFORT AT 80% BOILER PRESSURE 24,700 LBS.

TYPE 4-6-0.

———— L. & S. W. R. ————

2 CYLINDER 6 COUPLED BOGIE PASSENGER ENGINE

N⁰⁵ 736-745.

10 THUS

WATER CAPACITY 5000 GALLONS
COAL   „   7 TONS.

L. S. W. R.

WORKING PRESSURE 180 lbs □″

9′.0″ FIREBOX

13′.9″ BARREL

5′.10½″

27′.6″ ENGINE WHEELBASE

14′.6″ RIGID WHEELBASE

58′.0″ TOTAL WHEELBASE

66′.5¾″ LENGTH OVER BUFFERS

19′.0″ TENDER WHEELBASE

| T.C. 21·18 | T.C. 18·14 | T.C. 19·0 | T.C. 18·5 | T.C. 28·17 | T.C. 28·4 |

TOTAL WEIGHT OF ENGINE. EMPTY 72 TONS. 10 CWTS.
„   „   „   IN WORKING ORDER 77 TONS. 17 CWTS.

TOTAL WEIGHT ON COUPLED WHEELS 55 TONS. 19 CWTS.

TOTAL WEIGHT OF TENDER EMPTY 29 TONS. 17 CWTS.
„   „   „   IN WORKING ORDER 57 TONS. 1 CWTS.

HEATING SURFACE

Class N15 (Urie) 4-6-0. (LSWR diagram No 61)

Class N15 (Urie) No.E754 *The Green Knight*, Salisbury, 1926.

Class N15 (Urie) No.E752 *Linette* at Eastleigh in 1927.

Class N15 (Urie) No.30736 *Excalibur* in BR days.

Class N15 (Urie) No.749 *Iseult*, Eastleigh, 1938.

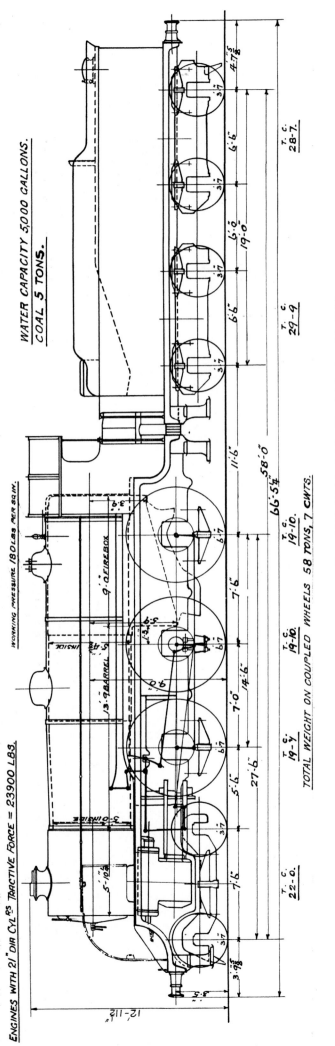

WATER CAPACITY 5,000 GALLONS.
COAL 5 TONS.

WORKING PRESSURE 180 LBS. PER SQ.IN.

ENGINES WITH 21" DIA CYL.PS TRACTIVE FORCE = 23900 LBS.

TOTAL WEIGHT ON COUPLED WHEELS 58 TONS, 7 CWTS.

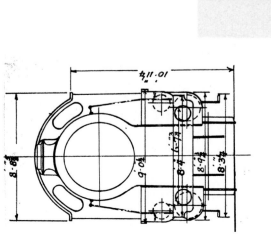

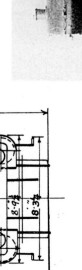

Class N15 (Urie) 4-6-0. (Eastleigh dwg No.E61)

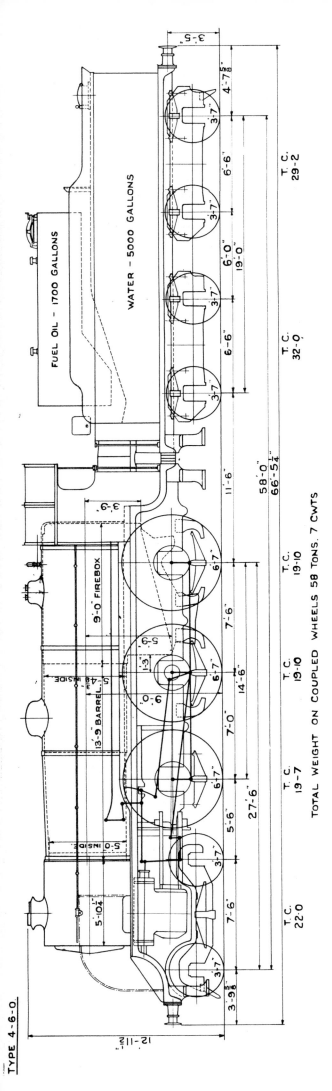

TYPE 4-6-0.

FUEL OIL - 1700 GALLONS

WATER - 5000 GALLONS

9'-0 FIREBOX

13'-9 BARREL

4'-8 INSIDE

5'-0 INSIDE

TOTAL WEIGHT ON COUPLED WHEELS 58 TONS. 7 CWTS

Class N15 (Urie) Oil burning 4-6-0. (Eastleigh dwg No.E61A)

PAGE 257

Right: Class S15 class (Urie) No.E501 in 1927 (LH side).

S15 class (Urie) 4-6-0

The third locomotive design, which Robert Urie prepared for the LSWR was for 20 'little' N15s to be used for freight traffic. Built at Eastleigh in 1920–21, these engines differed from the Urie 'Arthurs' in that the coupled wheels were 5ft 7in, which brought the boiler centre line down 4½in, the cylinders were 21in x 28in, and of course with smaller wheels, the total wheelbase was shorter. The running plates were stepped, similar to the H15s and they had a taller 'stove-pipe' chimney. (25 further S15s were built by Maunsell between 1926 and 1936. See *Southern Railway* section). Standard Urie 5,000 gallon bogie tenders were attached originally, but later some were replaced by redundant tenders from scrapped C8 class engines.

The 20 Urie S15s went into SR ownership at the Grouping and were painted black, lined out, but as many were used on passenger services, they later had the SR green. Between 1929 and 1932 smoke deflectors were fitted, and the 'Eastleigh' superheaters replaced by the Maunsell type. All went into BR and were painted plain black and worked on until the mid-1960s.

No.	Built	Green livery	'E' prefix removed	Withdrawn
496	1921	1930	1933	1963
497	1920	1929	1932	1963
498	1920	1930	1932	1963
499	1920	1931	1934	1964
500	1920	1930	1933	1963
501	1920	1928	1931	1963
502	1920	1930	1932	1962
503	1920	1931	1934	1963
504	1920	1929	1932	1962
505	1920	1929	1931	1962
506	1920	1930	1932	1964

No.	Built	Green livery	'E' prefix removed	Withdrawn
507	1920	1932	1932	1963
508	1920	1932	1932	1963
509	1920	1929	1932	1963
510	1921	1931	1933	1963
511	1921	1930	1933	1963
512	1921	1928	1931	1964
513	1921	1931	1932	1963
514	1921	1934	1934	1963
515	1921	1928	1931	1963

Nos 499 and 506 are preserved on the Mid-Hants Railway.

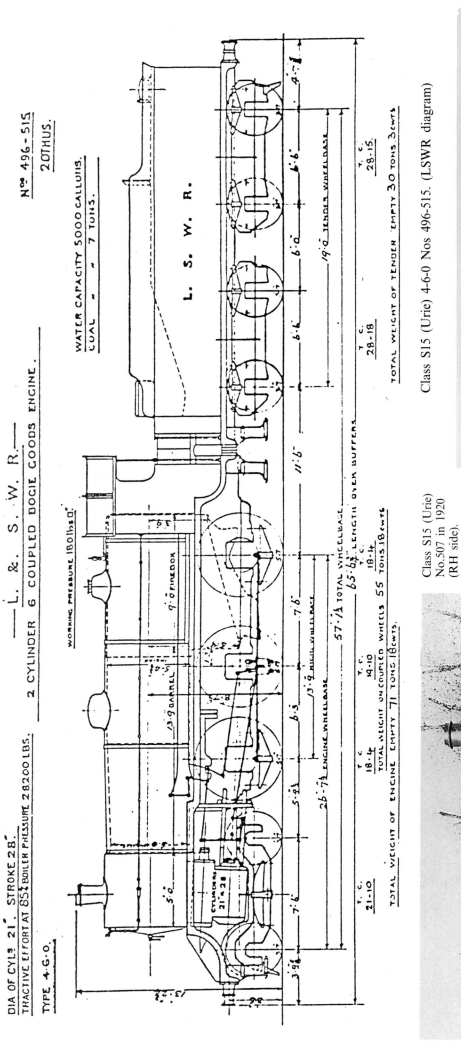

DIA OF CYL⁵ 21". STROKE 28".

TRACTIVE EFFORT AT 85% BOILER PRESSURE 28 200 LBS.

TYPE 4·6·0.

— L. & S. W. R. —

2 CYLINDER 6 COUPLED BOGIE GOODS ENGINE.

Nᵒˢ 496 - 515

20 THUS.

WORKING PRESSURE 180 lbs □".

L. S. W. R.

WATER CAPACITY 5000 GALLONS.

COAL " 7 TONS.

TOTAL WEIGHT OF TENDER EMPTY 30 TONS. 3 cwts.

TOTAL WEIGHT ON COUPLED WHEELS 55 TONS. 18 cwts.

TOTAL WEIGHT OF ENGINE EMPTY 71 TONS. 18 cwts.

Class S15 (Urie) 4-6-0 Nos 496-515. (LSWR diagram)

Class S15 (Urie)
No.507 in 1920
(RH side).

Class S15 (Urie)

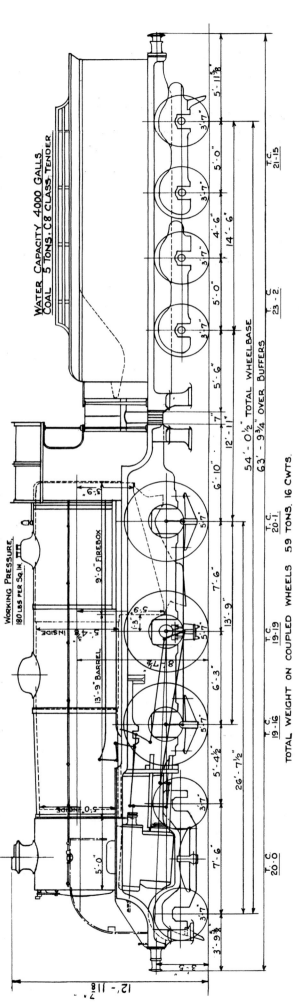

WATER CAPACITY 4000 GALLS
COAL 5 TONS. C8 CLASS TENDER

WORKING PRESSURE,
180 LBS PER SQ. IN.

Class S15 (Urie) 4-6-0. (Eastleigh dwg No.E62A)

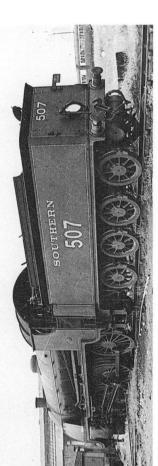

Class S15 (Urie) No.487 at Nine Elms in 1923 (LH side).

Class S15 (Urie) No.507 at Fratton in May 1937.

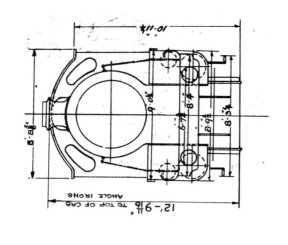

Class S15 (Urie) No.30506 in BR days.

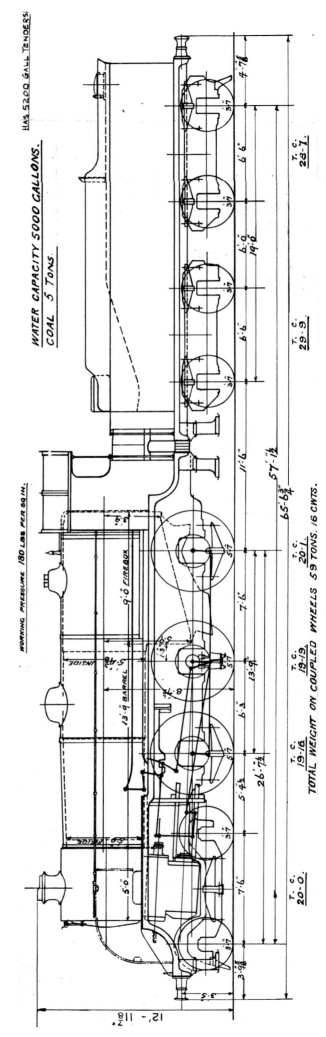

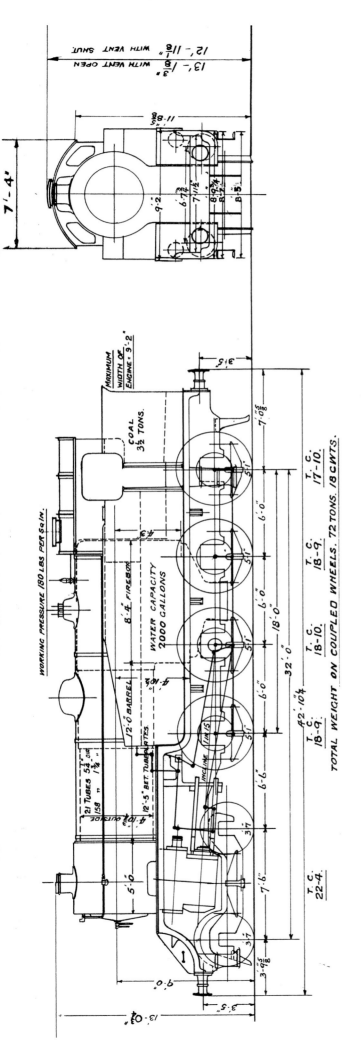

Class G16 4-8-0T. (Eastleigh dwg No.E63)

Class G16 No.492 at Strawberry Hill in 1923 (LH side).

G16 class 4-8-0T

At the end of the First World War, the LSWR completed the construction of a large marshalling yard at Feltham, built to handle the increasing freight traffic of the time. Arranged as a 'hump', where wagons run into respective sidings by gravitation, these yards needed powerful locomotives to propel trains forward up to the apex of the 'hump' before vehicles start to drop away. At that time the only shunting engines available were the G6 0-6-0Ts, which were incapable of continuously moving heavy trains at a slow pace for humping. To meet this requirement, Urie, after putting forward an abortive 4-6-0 tank design, produced drawings for a large 4-8-0 tank locomotive, which was accepted by the Locomotive Committee, and four of the new class G16 were

ordered from Eastleigh and started work in 1921.

The general design was based on the 4-6-0 S15 class of goods engine, but with 8-coupled wheels of 5ft 1in diameter, a smaller boiler and firebox, and large side tanks holding 2,000 gallons. A large cab was provided with a coal bunker having a capacity of 3½ tons. The running plate was raised over the cylinders, but dropped over the coupled wheels and ran straight to the rear buffer beam. The side tanks were sloped off at the forward end to improve sighting, and this always gave the impression of the engines having tapered boilers, which was not so. Large, 22in x 28in cylinders and small driving wheels gave these four machines the highest tractive effort of any LSWR engines. All four entered both SR and BR stock and the summary is as under.

No.	Built	Cab vents fitted	'E' prefix removed	Stove pipe chimneys	Withdrawn
492	1921	1938	1932	1941	1959
493	1921	1939	1931	1939	1959
494	1921	1941	1931	1941	1962
495	1921	1938	1932	1940	1962

Class H16 No.E519 at Feltham in 1925 (LH side).

Class H16 No.518 at Eastleigh, October 1938 (RH side).

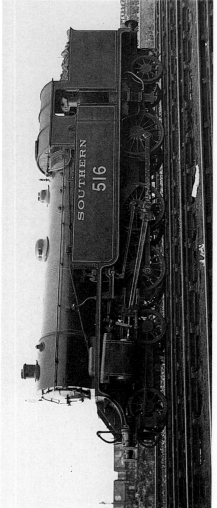

Class H16 No.516 Feltham March 1933

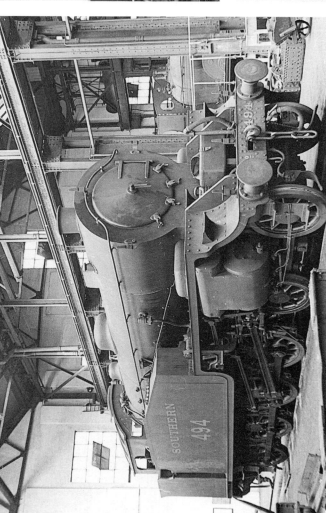

Class G16 No.494 at Eastleigh in 1937 (RH side).

H16 class 4-6-2T

Having produced a design for a heavy 'hump' shunting locomotive in the G16, Urie also had to consider the movement of heavy freight between Brent Sidings on the Midland Railway and Willesden on the LNWR over to the LSWR yards at Feltham. With this need in view he produced what was to be his last locomotive design, the large 4-6-2T for goods work. Classified as H16, these five engines were very similar to the G16 'hump' shunters, except that the cylinders were 21in diameter

instead of 22in, and the six coupled wheels were 5ft 7in. The wider spacing between the centre and trailing drivers allowed a larger ashpan to the firebox, which gave better steaming. The side tanks were not so large as those on the G16s, but the deficiency in water capacity was made up by a well tank under the enlarged bunker. Although mainly used on freight traffic, these machines were painted in passenger green in SR days and passed into BR ownership, all being withdrawn in 1962.

No.	Built	'E' prefix removed	Cab vents fitted	Stove pipe chimneys
516	1921	1931	1938	1935
517	1921	1932	1938	1935
518	1921	1932	1938	1935
519	1922	1931	1937	1935
520	1922	1932	1938	1935

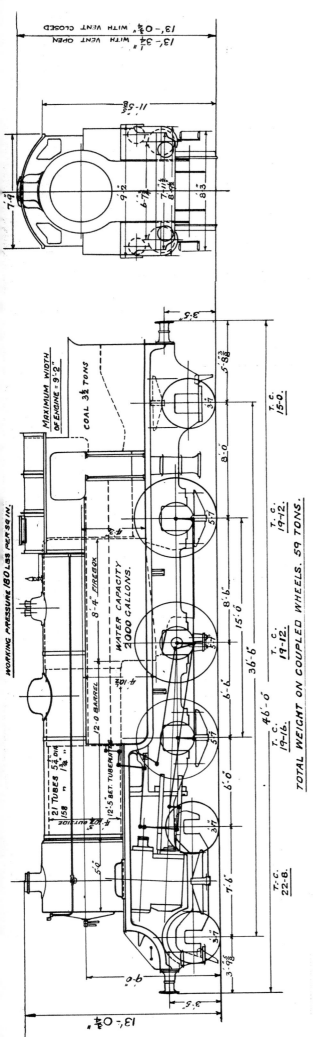

WORKING PRESSURE 180 LBS PER SQ IN.

MAXIMUM WIDTH OF ENGINE = 9'-2"

COAL 3½ TONS

8'-4" FIREBOX

WATER CAPACITY 2000 GALLONS.

12'-0 BARREL

221 TUBES 5½ DIA
158 1¾ OUTSIDE

13'-0¾"

TOTAL WEIGHT ON COUPLED WHEELS. 59 TONS.

T.C. 15-0.

T.C. 19-12.

T.C. 19-12.

T.C. 19-16.

T.C. 22-8.

13'-1¾" WITH VENT OPEN
13'-0¾" WITH VENT CLOSED

Class H16 4-6-2T. (Eastleigh dwg No.E64)

Class 0458 *Bretwalda* at Guildford in October 1922.

Class H16 No.30518 in BR days.

0111 and 0458 class 0-4-0T

These four small dock tanks were originally owned by the Southampton Dock Company, which was absorbed into the LSWR in 1892. There were other little shunters, but only four passed on into Southern Railway stock lists. The 0111 class consisted of two engines, both made by Vulcan Foundry in 1878. No. 118 named *Vulcan*, renumbered 111 in 1899, and put on the duplicate list in 1904 as 0111. Her sister, No. 408 *Bretwalda* was identical and became No. 0408 in 1906, also withdrawn in 1924 and sold to Messrs J. Wood & Co. and scrapped in 1935.

The 0458 class were two similar dock tanks, built by Hawthorn, Leslie & Co. in 1890. No. 457 *Clausentum* received its number in 1901, was renumbered 0457 in 1913, became 734 in 1914 and was withdrawn in 1945. *Ironside*, numbered 458 in 1901, renumbered 0458 in 1913, and 3458 in 1931. This small locomotive ended her working days as shed pilot at Guildford in 1954.

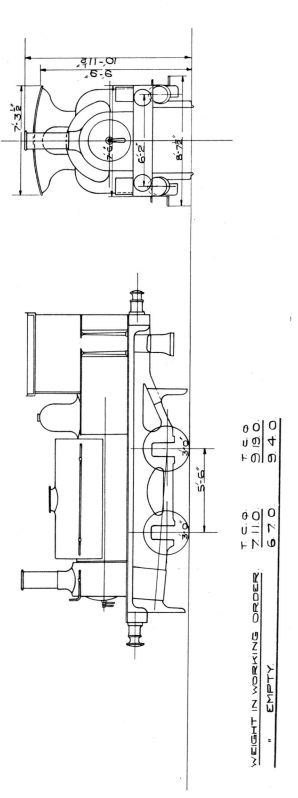

WEIGHT IN WORKING ORDER.	T.C.Q. 7 11 0	T.C.Q. 9 19 0
" EMPTY.	6 7 0	9 4 0

Class 0458 0-4-0ST. (Eastleigh dwg No.E10)

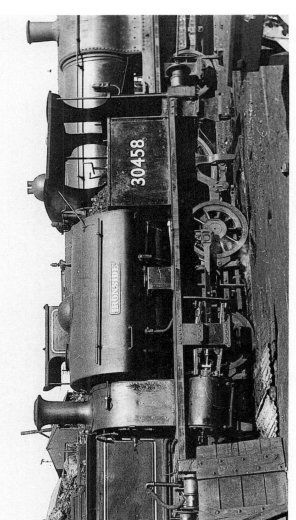

Class 0458 No. 30458 *Ironside* at Guildford in 1952 (M.J. HW-)

Class 0458 *Vulcan* in 1923

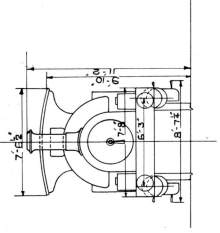

WORKING PRESSURE 120 LBS PER SQ IN.

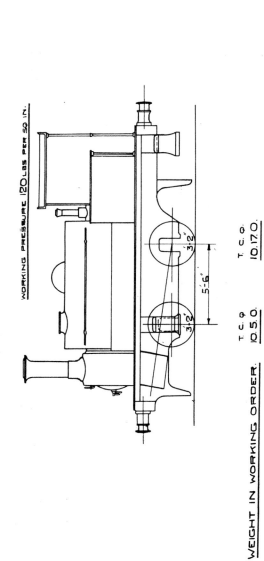

WEIGHT IN WORKING ORDER.

	T. C. Q.	T. C. Q.
	10. 5. 0.	10. 17. 0.

Class 0458 0-4-0ST. (Eastleigh dwg No.E21)

Class 0458 No.E0458 *Ironside* at Guildford in 1929 (RH side).

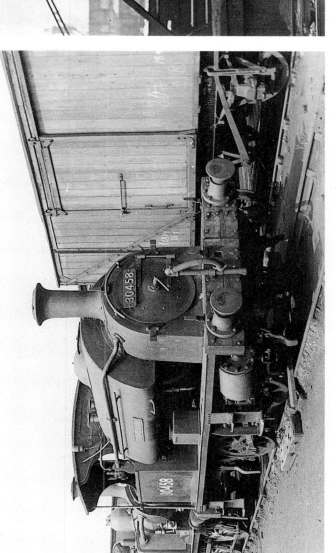

Class 0458 No.30458 *Ironside* at Eastleigh in 1954 (RH side).

Class 0458 No.30458 *Ironside* at Guildford in 1951.

735 class 0-6-0T
(ex-LBSCR A1 class)

There were two engines in the 735 class, both being Stroudley 'Terriers' which the LSWR bought from the LBSCR in 1903 for working the Axminster – Lyme Regis branch which was opened in that year and could only accept a light axle loading.

No. 734 was originally LBSCR No. 46 *Newington* built in 1876. Rebuilt in 1912 with a Drummond boiler and sold the following year to the FYNR on the Isle of Wight, becoming No. 2. Taken into the Southern

Railway at the Grouping, the engine stayed on the Island to become eventually No. W8 *Freshwater*, and today is preserved at Haven Street on the Isle of Wight.

No. 735, which started life in 1874 as No. 68 *Clapham* had a Drummond boiler in 1912, plus a stove pipe chimney in 1920. It worked for some time on the Lee-on-Solent branch, and spent its last days at Ashford Works, being withdrawn finally in 1936.

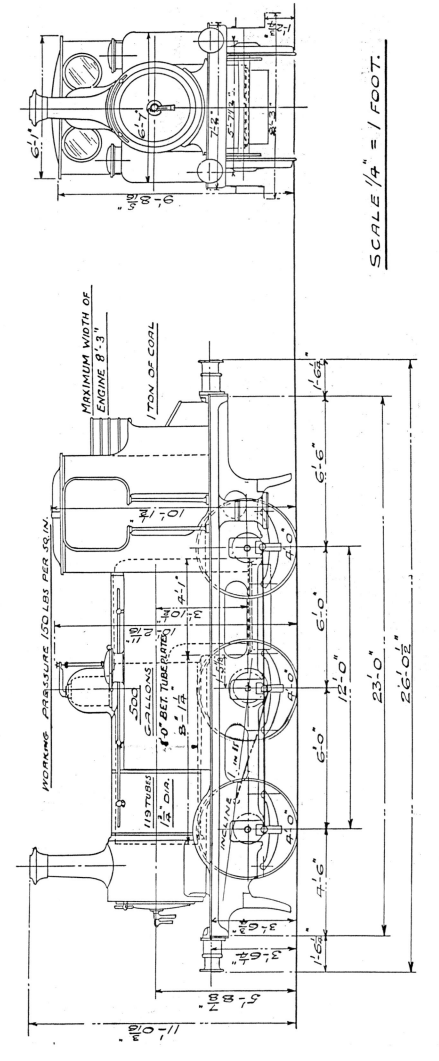

Part Four

Locomotives built by the Southern Railway and BR (SR), 1923 onwards

N15 'King Arthur' class (Maunsell) 4-6-0

Three of the Urie 'Arthurs', Nos 753-755, although being ordered in LSWR days were actually constructed at Eastleigh by the Southern Railway in 1923. R.E.L. Maunsell, who became the CME of the SR at the Amalgamation, realised the soundness of Urie's design, and arranged a series of trials and tests to ascertain how best to improve the performance of the 'Arthurs'. As a direct result of these findings, many modifications were made to the order for 54 Maunsell N15s built by the SR between 1925 and 1927. Amongst the alterations made, was the fitting of long travel valves, outside steam pipes, Ashford N class smokebox, Maunsell superheaters, an improved ashpan, a flared top chimney, and a cab roof which could accommodate the new 'composite' gauge, which would allow the new engines to work over the whole three sections of the SR. Also, the boiler pressure was increased to 200 lbs per sq.in.

The total of 54 locomotives can be divided up into three groups. The first batch of ten were the so-called reconstructed P14 and G14 classes, but about the only things from the old Drummonds used, were the 4,500 gallon bogie tenders, and the running numbers, 448-457! These Maunsell N15s were outshopped from Eastleigh in 1925. The second order for 30 engines of this class was built by the North British Locomotive Co. later in 1926, and numbered 763-792. (For this reason, these engines were always referred to by the staff as the "Scotch Arthurs"). Finally, the last 14 were erected at Eastleigh between 3/1926 and 1/1927, and fitted with Ashford pattern 6-wheeled tenders. The whole class were given names of Arthurian legend, and equipped with smoke deflectors between 1927 and 1929. It should be noted that although the Urie 'Arthurs' eventually received some modifications, they were always relegated to lighter duties than those of the Maunsells.

SR No.	Name	Built	Prefix removed	Withdrawn
785	Sir Mador de la Porte	1925	1932	1959
786	Sir Lionel	1925	1932	1959
787	Sir Menadeuke	1925	1931	1959
788	Sir Urre of the Mount	1925	1932	1962
789	Sir Guy	1925	1932	1959
790	Sir Villiars	1925	1932	1961
791	Sir Uwaine	1925	1931	1960
792	Sir Hervis de Revel	1925	1932	1959
"Eastleigh" 'Arthurs' (with 6-wheel tenders)				
793	Sir Ontzlake	1926	1932	1962
794	Sir Ector de Maris	1926	1932	1960
795	Sir Dinadan	1926	1932	1962
796	Sir Dodinas le Savage	1926	1931	1962
797	Sir Blamor de Ganis	1926	1932	1959
798	Sir Hectimere	1926	1933	1962
799	Sir Ironside	1926	1932	1961
800	Sir Meleaus de Lile	1926	1932	1961
801	Sir Meliot de Logres	1926	1932	1959
802	Sir Durnore	1926	1931	1961
803	Sir Harry le Fise Lake	1926	1932	1961
804	Sir Cador of Cornwall	1926	1932	1962
805	Sir Constantine	1927	1933	1959
806	Sir Galleron	1927	1933	1961

No. 777 is preserved in the National Collection.

"Eastleigh" 'Arthurs'

SR No.	Name	Built	Prefix removed	Withdrawn
448	Sir Tristram	1925	1933	1960
449	Sir Torre	1925	1933	1959
450	Sir Kay	1925	1932	1960
451	Sir Lamorak	1925	1932	1962
452	Sir Meliagrance	1925	1931	1959
453	King Arthur	1925	1931	1961
454	Queen Guinevere	1925	1932	1958
455	Sir Launcelot	1925	1932	1959
456	Sir Galahad	1925	1931	1960
457	Sir Bedivere	1925	1932	1961

"Scotch" 'Arthurs'

SR No.	Name	Built	Prefix removed	Withdrawn
763	Sir Bors de Ganis	1925	1932	1960
764	Sir Gawain	1925	1932	1961
765	Sir Gareth	1925	1933	1962
766	Sir Geraint	1925	1931	1958
767	Sir Valence	1925	1931	1959
768	Sir Balin	1925	1932	1961
769	Sir Balan	1925	1931	1960
770	Sir Prianius	1925	1932	1962
771	Sir Sagramore	1925	1932	1961
772	Sir Percivale	1925	1932	1961
773	Sir Lavaine	1925	1932	1962
774	Sir Gaheris	1925	1931	1960
775	Sir Agravaine	1925	1932	1960
776	Sir Galagars	1925	1932	1959
777	Sir Lamiel	1925	1932	1961
778	Sir Pelleas	1925	1931	1959
779	Sir Colgrevance	1925	1932	1959
780	Sir Persant	1925	1932	1959
781	Sir Aglovale	1925	1933	1962
782	Sir Brian	1925	1931	1962
783	Sir Gillemere	1925	1932	1961

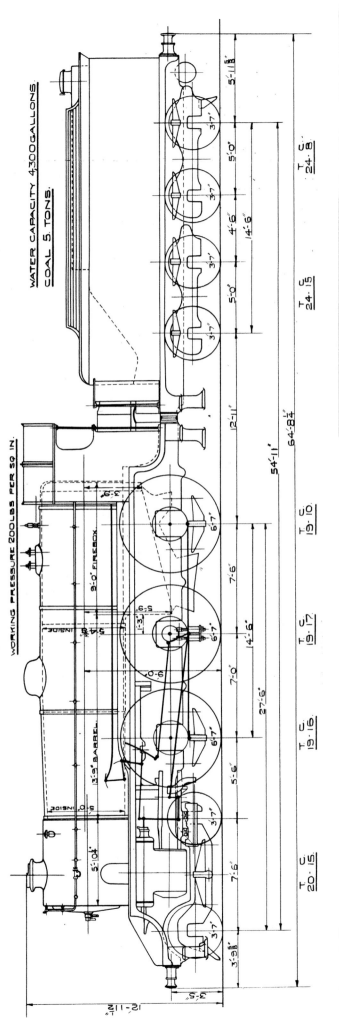

WATER CAPACITY 4300 GALLONS.
COAL 5 TONS.
WORKING PRESSURE 200 LBS PER SQ. IN.

Class N15 (Urie) 4-6-0. (Eastleigh dwg No.SR71)

Class N15 (Maunsell) No.774 *Sir Gaheris* at Waterloo in April 1927.

Class N15 (Maunsell) No.792 *Sir Hervis de Revel* at Eastleigh, 1938.

Class N15 (Maunsell) 4-6-0.
Scale 3mm: 1ft

Class N15 4-6-0. (Eastleigh dwg No.SR72A)

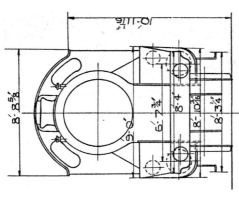

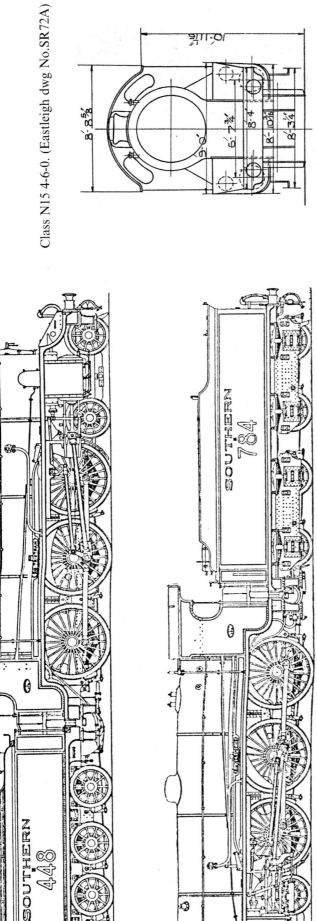

SOUTHERN
448

SOUTHERN
784

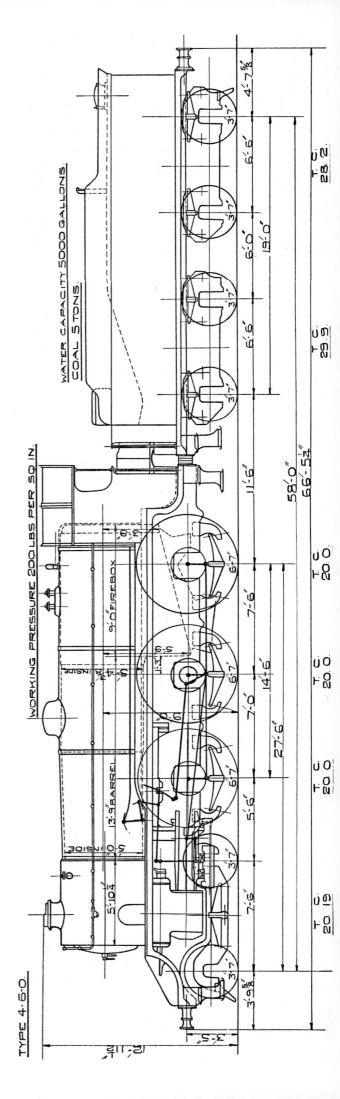

WATER CAPACITY 5000 GALLONS.
COAL 5 TONS.

WORKING PRESSURE 200 LBS PER SQ IN.

TYPE 4-6-0.

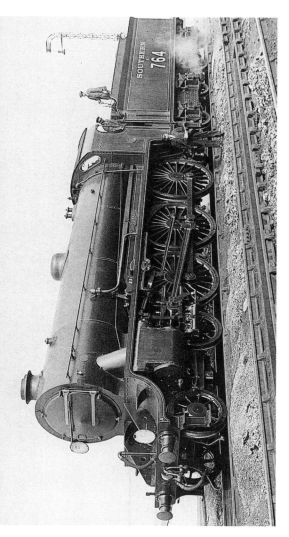

Class N15 (Maunsell) No.E764 *Sir Gawain* c1927.

Class N15 (Maunsell) No.30448 *Sir Tristram* (RH side).

Class N15 (Maunsell) No.E763 *Sir Bors de Ganis* c1925 (LH side).

Class N15 (Maunsell) No.30456 *Sir Galahad* in BR days.

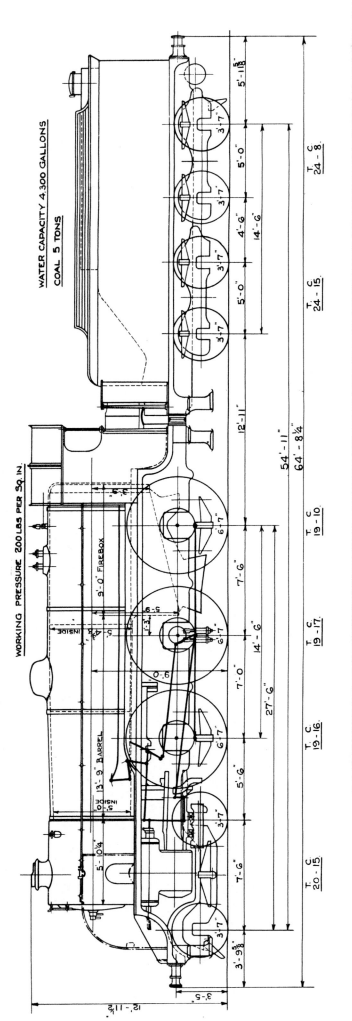

WATER CAPACITY 4,300 GALLONS

COAL 5 TONS

WORKING PRESSURE 200 LBS PER SQ. IN.

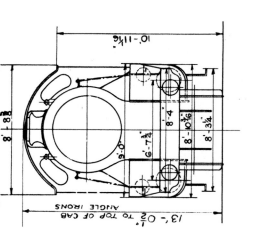

Class N15 4-6-0. (Eastleigh dwg
No.SR71A)

TYPE 4-6-0

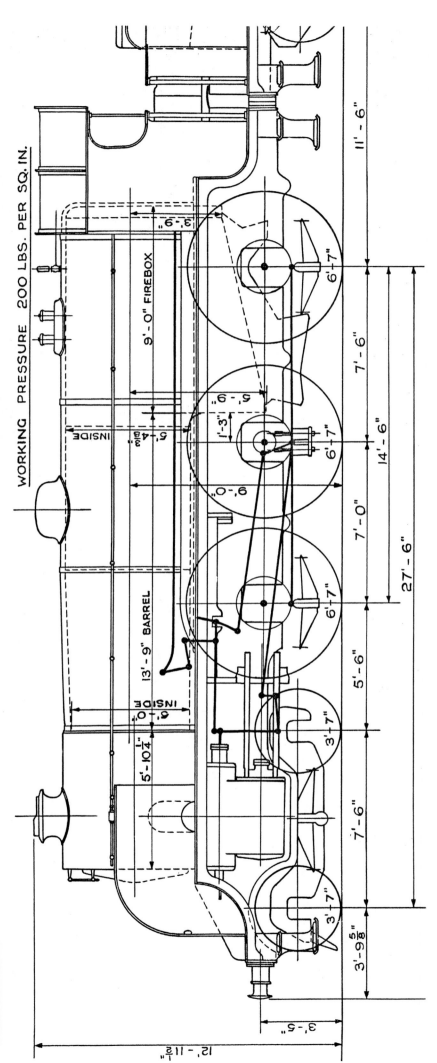

WORKING PRESSURE 200 LBS. PER SQ. IN.

9'-0" FIREBOX

13'-9" BARREL

INSIDE

INSIDE

5'-4⅜"

9'-0"

1'-3"

5'-6"

6'-0" INSIDE

5'-10¼"

3'-9"

6'-7"

6'-7"

6'-7"

3'-7"

3'-7"

11'-6"

7'-6"

14'-6"

7'-0"

27'-6"

5'-6"

7'-6"

3'-9⅝"

3'-5"

12'-11½"

Class N15 4-6-0. (Eastleigh dwg No.SR71B)

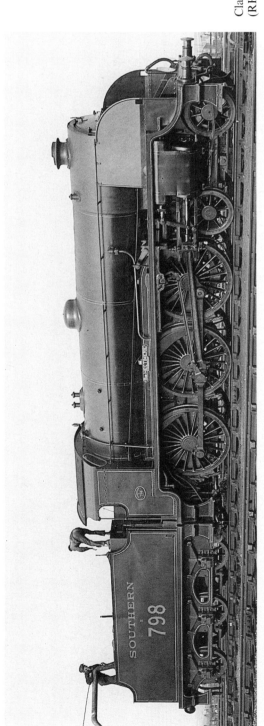

SOUTHERN
798

Class N15 (Maunsell) No.E798 *Sir Hectimere* c1926
(RH side).

PAGE 273

Class N15 4-6-0.
Scale 3mm: 1ft

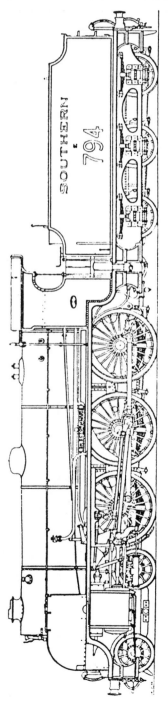

Cab fittings of Class N15.

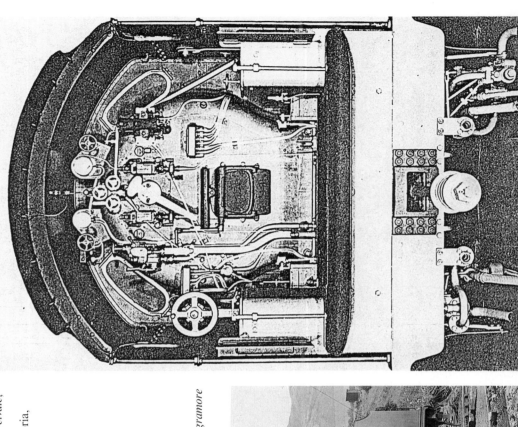

Class N15 (Maunsell) No.E772 *Sir Percivale*, another view of the locomotive with experimental smoke deflectors at Victoria, 18th February 1928.

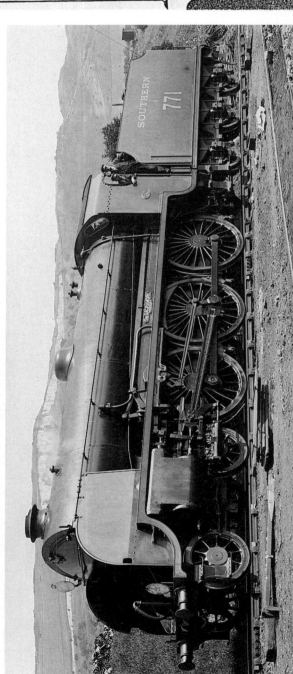

Class N15 (Maunsell) No.E771 *Sir Sagramore* (LH side).

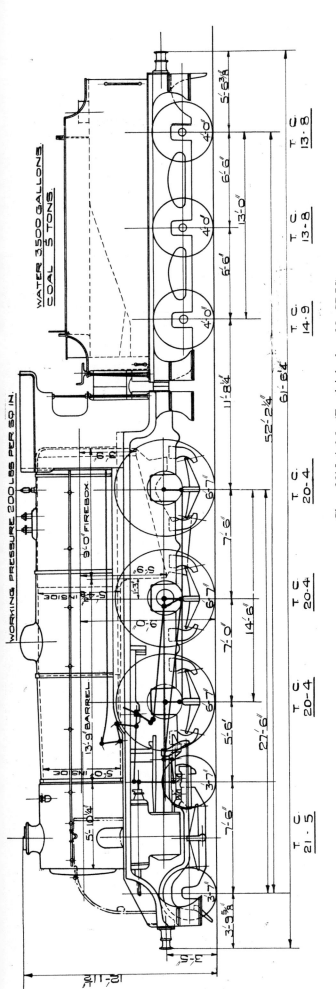

Class N15 4-6-0. (Eastleigh dwg No.SR75)

WATER 3500 GALLONS
COAL 5 TONS

WORKING PRESSURE 200 LBS PER SQ IN.

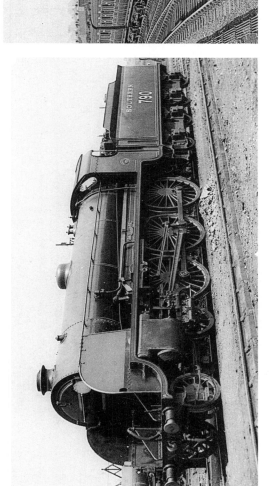

Class N15 (Maunsell) No.E799 *Sir Ironside.*

Class N15 (Maunsell) No.790 *Sir Villiars.*

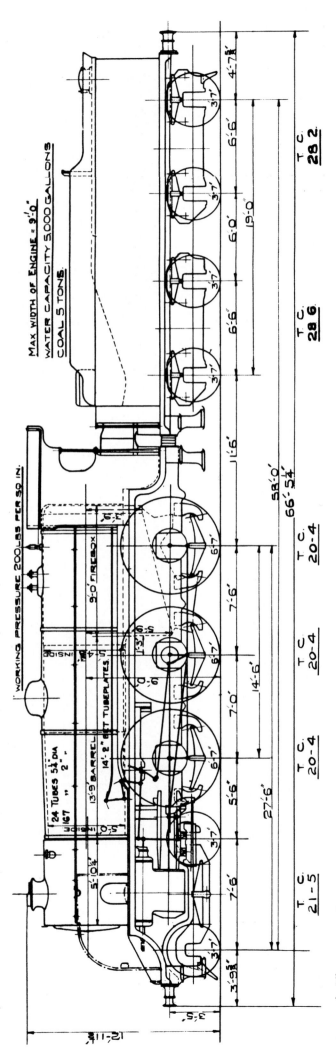

MAX WIDTH OF ENGINE = 9'-0"

WATER CAPACITY 5,000 GALLONS

COAL 5 TONS.

WORKING PRESSURE 200 LBS PER SQ IN.

24 TUBES 5¼ DIA

167 " 2 "

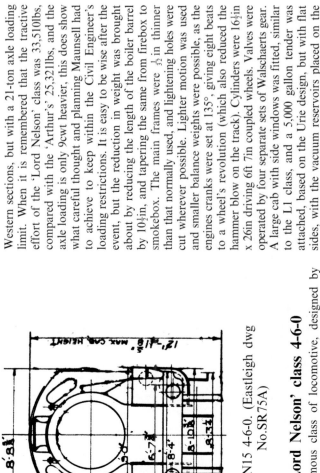

Class N15 4-6-0. (Eastleigh dwg No.SR75A)

LN 'Lord Nelson' class 4-6-0

This famous class of locomotive, designed by Maunsell in 1925, was a masterpiece in the art of balancing weight versus strength. The CME's problem was to produce a large 4-cylinder express locomotive capable of handling the 500-ton Con-

Western sections, but with a 21-ton axle loading limit. When it is remembered that the tractive effort of the 'Lord Nelson' class was 33,510lbs, compared with the 'Arthur's' 25,321lbs, and the axle loading is only 9cwt heavier, this does show what careful thought and planning Maunsell had to achieve to keep within the Civil Engineer's loading restrictions. It is easy to be wise after the event, but the reduction in weight was brought about by reducing the length of the boiler barrel by 10½in, and tapering the same from firebox to smokebox. The main frames were 1/32in thinner than that normally used, and lightening holes were cut wherever possible. Lighter motion was used and smaller balance weights were possible, as the engines cranks were set at 135°, giving eight beats to a wheel's revolution (which also reduced the hammer blow on the track). Cylinders were 16½in x 26in driving 6ft 7in coupled wheels. Valves were operated by four separate sets of Walschaerts gear. A large cab with side windows was fitted, similar to the L1 class, and a 5,000 gallon tender was attached, based on the Urie design, but with flat sides, with the vacuum reservoirs placed on the tank top to the rear alongside the water fillers.

Only one machine was erected in 1926, No. 850 Lord Nelson, which Maunsell put into top link duty to find any faults which could be rectified

After two years running, and being satisfied that the LN was reliable and a good steamer, if fired by first-class crews, Maunsell ordered the construction of a further 15 engines for delivery in 1928-29. All were built at Eastleigh.

Several modifications were tried out on the class. No. 859 Lord Hood was fitted with 6ft 3in driving wheels, but no advantage could be detected, and No. 860 Lord Hawke, was built with a special boiler, having 10in extra length in the barrel, but again, no improvement in performance could be ascertained. Also, in 1937 No. 857 Lord Howe had an extended firebox, which protruded into the round topped boiler to act as a combustion chamber, but again, the idea was not pursued and it was replaced in 1945.

In 1934, experiments with Kylchap blastpipe and chimney were carried out on No. 862 Lord Collingwood and although good results were obtained, the system was not followed up at that time. In 1938 No. 865 Sir John Hawkins was also altered. Both were removed in 1942. As originally built, Lord Nelson did not carry smoke deflectors, but eventually all 16 were so fitted, Lord Howe carrying a special bevelled, experimental type.

With regard to tenders attached to the 'Lord Nelson' class, briefly, they were all the large 5,000 gallon style, some with flat sides, modified to self-

gallon tenders which were coupled to Nos 852 and 853, from building date until 1929 and 1930 respectively, when they were changed for the big bogie 'water carts'. The reason for the small tenders was that distances on the Eastern section did not call for all that coal and water. However, they did not look well with the 'Lord Nelsons' and were given to 'hunting' at speed, and so were removed. Eventually all were fitted with Lemaitre type chimneys.

SR No.	Name	Built	Withdrawn
850	Lord Nelson	1926	1962
851	Sir Francis Drake	1928	1961
852	Sir Walter Raleigh	1928	1962
853	Sir Richard Grenville	1928	1962
854	Howard of Effingham	1928	1961
855	Robert Blake	1928	1962
856	Lord St. Vincent	1928	1962
857	Lord Howe	1928	1962
858	Lord Duncan	1929	1961
859	Lord Hood	1929	1961
860	Lord Hawke	1929	1962
861	Lord Anson	1929	1962
862	Lord Collingwood	1929	1962
863	Lord Rodney	1929	1962
864	Sir Martin Frobisher	1929	1962
865	Sir John Hawkins	1929	1961

No. 850 is preserved in the National Collection. No. 30852 was fitted with a MN class chimney in 1956.

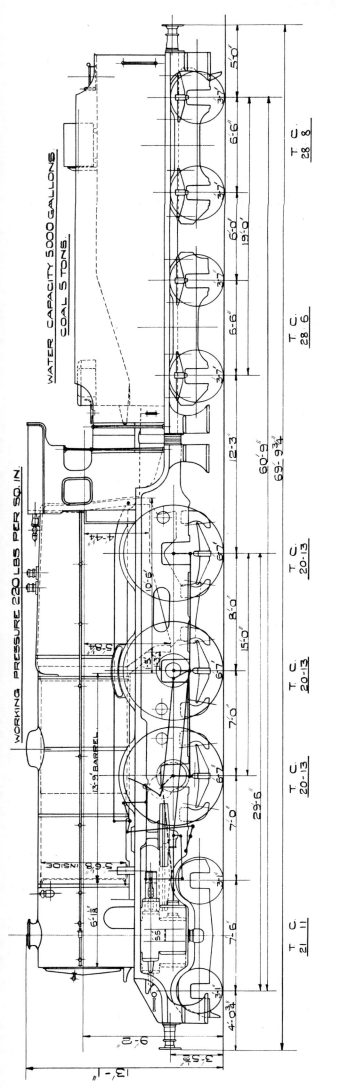

WATER CAPACITY 5000 GALLONS
COAL 5 TONS.

WORKING PRESSURE 220 LBS PER SQ. IN.

Class LN No.850 *Lord Nelson* as built.

Class LN No.E852 *Sir Walter Raleigh*.

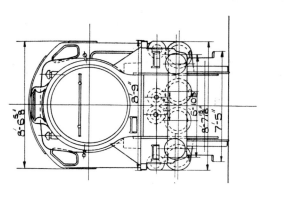

Class LN 4-6-0. (Eastleigh dwg
No.SR76)

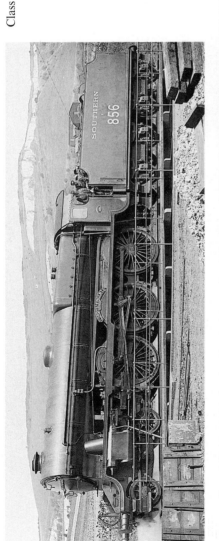

Class LN No.E856 *Lord St Vincent* when new (LH side).

Class LN No.E850 *Lord Nelson* with smoke deflectors (LH side).

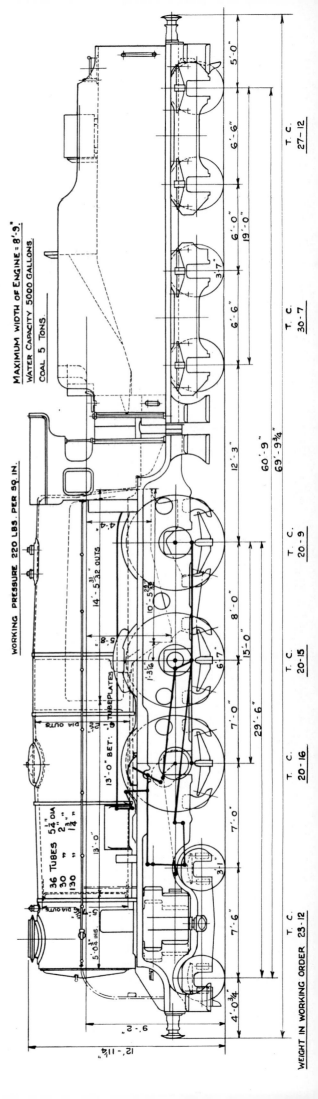

Class LN 4-6-0. (Eastleigh dwg No.SR76BX)

MAXIMUM WIDTH OF ENGINE = 8'-9".
WATER CAPACITY 5000 GALLONS
COAL 5 TONS.

WORKING PRESSURE 220 LBS. PER SQ. IN.

WEIGHT IN WORKING ORDER	23·12		20·16		20·15		20·9		30·7		27·12

T. C.

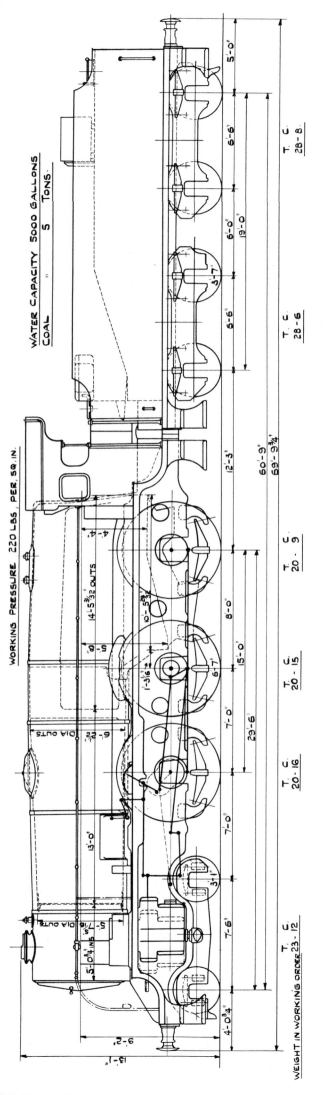

WATER CAPACITY 5000 GALLONS
COAL " 5 TONS.

WORKING PRESSURE 220 LBS., PER. SQ. IN.

WEIGHT IN WORKING ORDER 23-12

Class LN 4-6-0. (Eastleigh dwg No.SR76B)

Class LN No.857 *Lord Howe* in 1946.

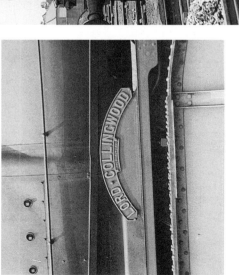

Class LN Nameplate of No.862
Lord Collingwood.

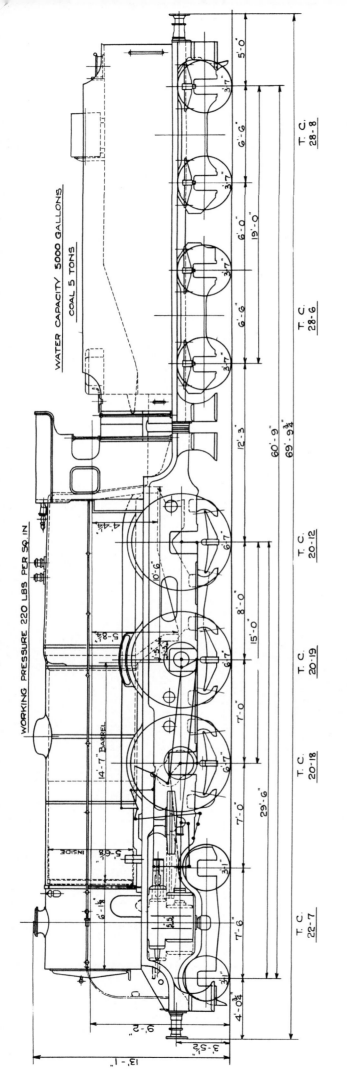

WATER CAPACITY 5000 GALLONS

COAL 5 TONS

WORKING PRESSURE 220 LBS PER SQ. IN

Class LN 4-6-0. (Eastleigh dwg No.SR76A)

Class LN No.857 *Lord Howe* in works grey.

Class LN No.860 *Lord Hawke* (RH side)

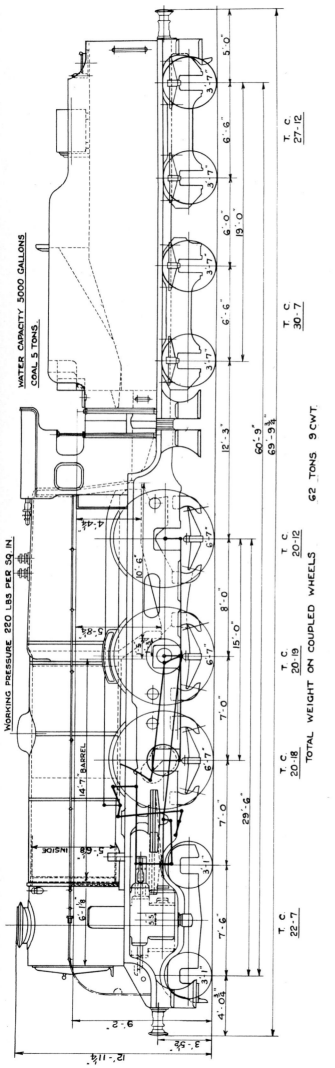

WATER CAPACITY 5000 GALLONS
COAL 5 TONS.

WORKING PRESSURE 220 LBS PER SQ. IN.

TOTAL WEIGHT ON COUPLED WHEELS   62 TONS   9 CWT.

Class LN 4-6-0. (Eastleigh dwg No.SR76AX)

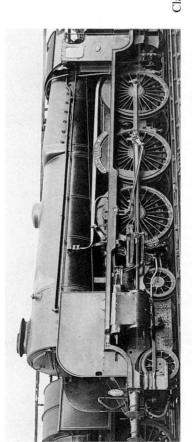

Class LN No.862 *Lord Collingwood* at Nine Elms, September 1934.

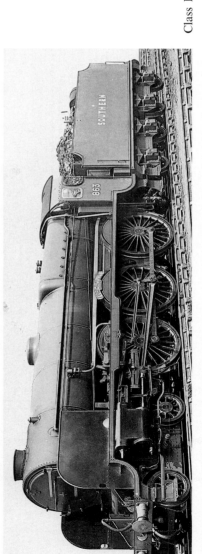

Class LN No.863 *Lord Rodney.*

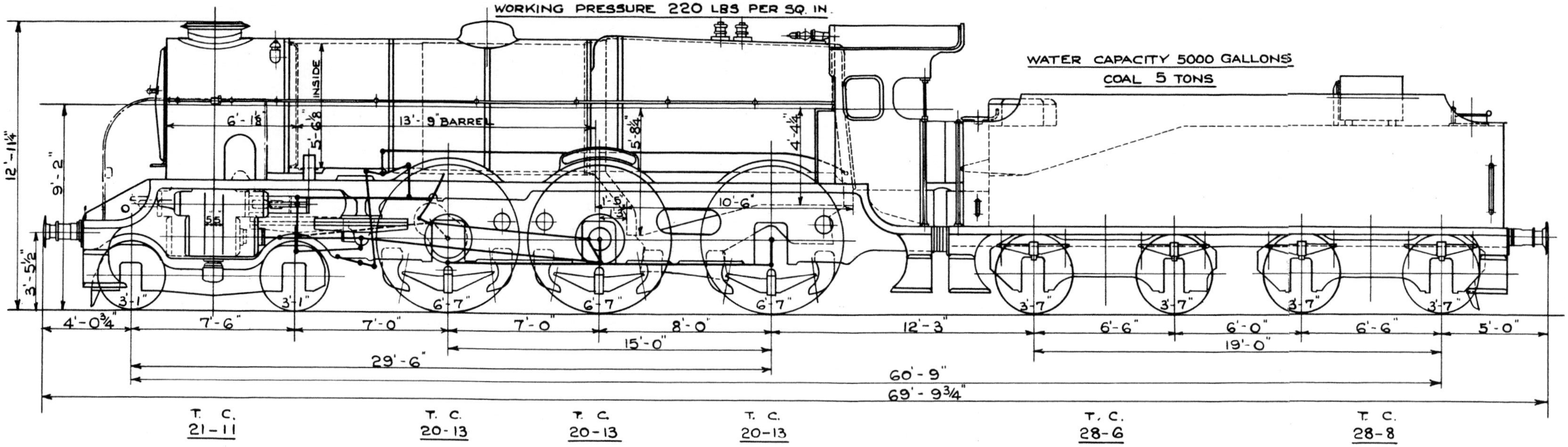

WORKING PRESSURE 220 LBS PER SQ. IN.

WATER CAPACITY 5000 GALLONS

COAL 5 TONS

13' 9 BARREL

10'-6"

5'-8¾"

4'-4"

5'-9⅝ INSIDE

6'-1⅛"

5-5

3'-5½"

9'-2"

12'-1½"

4'-0¾"

3'-1"

3'-1"

3'-7"

3'-7"

3'-7"

3'-7"

6'-7"

6'-7"

6'-7"

5'-0"

6'-6"

6'-0"

6'-6"

3'-7"

12'-3"

8'-0"

7'-0"

7'-0"

15'-0"

29'-6"

19'-0"

60'-9"

69'-9¾"

T.C. 21-11

T.C. 20-13

T.C. 20-13

T.C. 20-13

T.C. 28-6

T.C. 28-8

8'-6½"

8'-6"

9'-5½"

8'-1½"

7'-5"

Class LN 4-6-0.
(Eastleigh dwg No.SR76X)

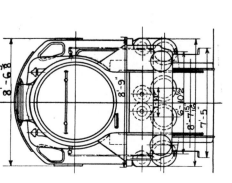

Class LN No.852 Sir Walter Raleigh at Eastleigh in 1946

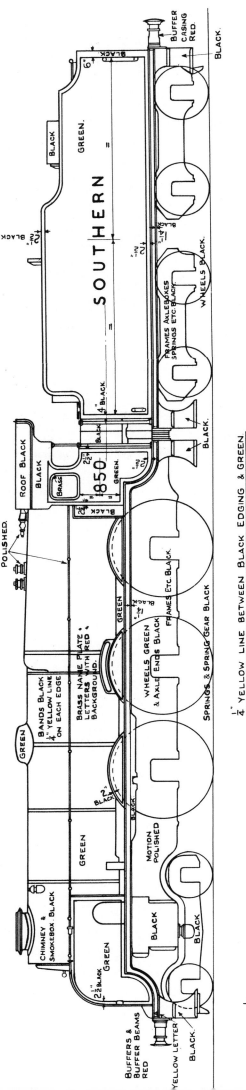

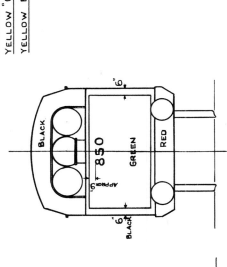

¼" YELLOW LINE BETWEEN BLACK EDGING & GREEN
YELLOW "GILL SANS" LETTERS 9" ON SIDE OF TENDER
YELLOW FIGURES 9" ON CAB SIDE.
6" ON FRONT BUFFER BEAM AND BACK OF TENDER.

	THE RAILWAY EXECUTIVE.	
SOUTHERN REGION C.M.E. LOCO. OFF. EASTLEIGH.		
	TITLE.	
	DIAGRAM OF PAINTING SHOWING LINING	
	LORD NELSON CLASS.	
CORR. REF.		E.40297.
D.	J.E. T. 14-1-48	
C.	P	

Class LN 4-6-0. Eastleigh painting diagram.

L1 class 4-4-0

At the time of the Grouping in 1923, the London-Folkstone express trains were getting too heavy for the L class locomotives to keep to the fast timing. Although the Traffic Department had asked for more L class locomotives to be built, Maunsell decided to modify and update the design to achieve the necessary increase in power. However it was not possible to construct these engines in any of the Company's workshops, so the contracts for the 15 L1s, as they were known, went to the North British Locomotive Company in 1925 and all were built in 1926.

These very useful engines were a sort of amalgam of the old Ls and the N classes. They had an increased boiler pressure of 180lbs, but smaller cylinders of 19½in x 26in. The running plate was stepped up to clear the coupling rods and crank pins, and the cabs were fitted with windows. Maunsell superheaters were fitted, the smokebox was the standard N class, as were the chimneys.

The whole class of 15 engines passed into BR ownership and were numbered 31753-59, 31782-89.

They had been painted in malachite green after the war, but in BR days were repainted lined black, although some remained green until 1953.

No. as built	No. after 1931	Withdrawn	No. as built	No. after 1931	Withdrawn
A753	1753		A782	1782	1962
A754	1754	1962	A783	1783	1962
A755	1755	1959	A784	1784	1960
A756	1756	1962	A785	1785	1960
A757	1757	1962	A786	1786	1962
A758	1758	1959	A787	1787	1962
A759	1759	1962	A788	1788	1960
			A789	1789	1962

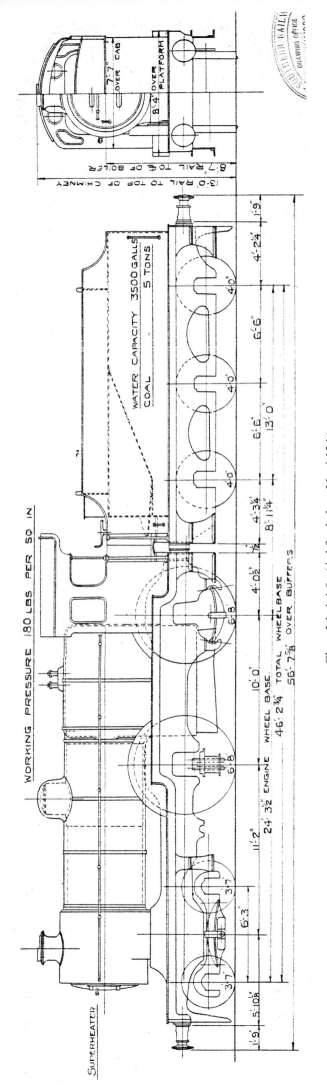

Class L1 4-4-0. (Ashford dwg No.A13A)

WORKING PRESSURE 180 LBS PER SQ IN

WATER CAPACITY 3500 GALLS
COAL 5 TONS

SUPERHEATER

7'7" OVER CAB

8'4" OVER PLATFORM

13'0" RAIL TO TOP OF CHIMNEY

8'7" RAIL TO ⊄ OF BOILER

24'3½" ENGINE WHEEL BASE

46'2¾" TOTAL WHEELBASE

56'7⅝" OVER BUFFERS

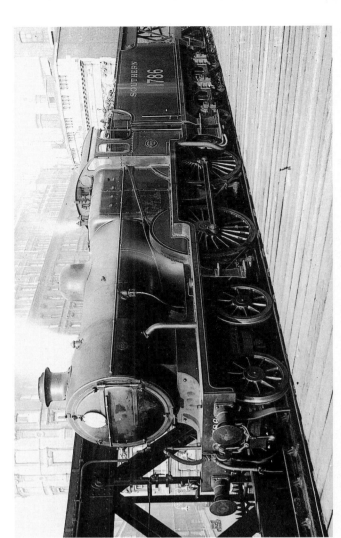

Class L1 No.1786 in 1938 (LH side).

Class L1 No.1783 in August 1937 (RH side).

Class L1 No.1788 in 1938 (LH side).

H15 class 4-6-0

For full details of the H15 class, see Part Three. As however, several of the class were built in Southern Railway days, and others rebuilt at Eastleigh with straight running plates and Maunsell fittings, this page of diagrams and photographs illustrate the various differences quite well.

Class L1 No.31785 at Ramsgate in July 1949.

Class H15 4-6-0. (Eastleigh dwg No.SR56)

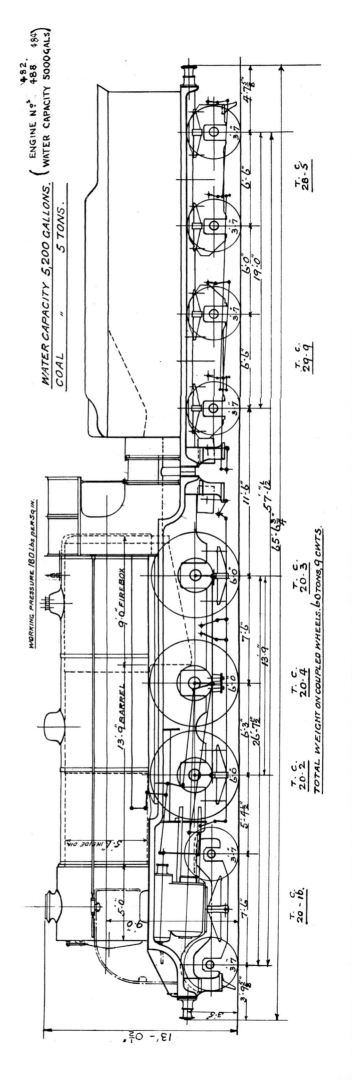

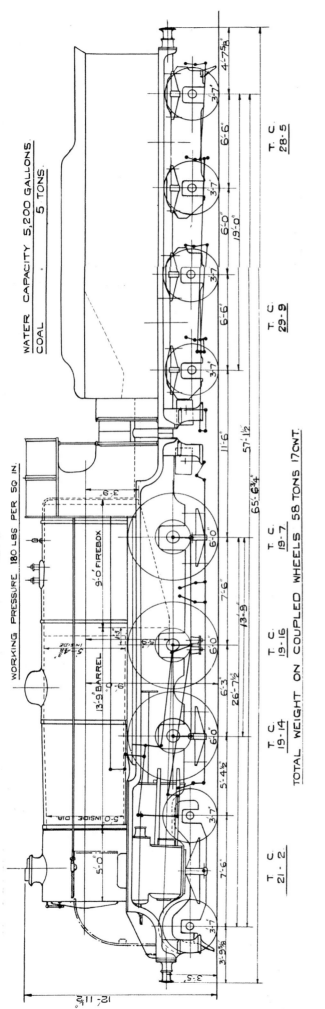

Class H15 4-6-0. (Eastleigh dwg No.SR56A)

Class H15 (Maunsell) No 30476 at Salisbury in July 1949 (RH side)

U Class 2-6-0

As previously mentioned in the *Eastern* section, the 'River' class tank engines were found to be unstable, and when one particular engine, No. A800 *River Cray*, ran off the road at Sevenoaks in August 1927, resulting in the deaths of 13 passengers and seriously injuring 40 others, the outcome was, not only to rectify track faults, but to withdraw the whole K class and rebuild them as 2-6-0 tender engines. So the U class came into being in 1927, when it had been decided to build a further 20 additional K class 2-6-4Ts. Due to the adverse publicity of the accident-prone 'Rivers', this new order was changed to a 2-6-0 machine which was almost identical with the successful N class. The only major difference being in the retaining of the 7ft 9in wheelbase between the centre and rear coupled wheels, as prevailed on the 2-6-4Ts. The first ten were constructed at Brighton Works in 1928, and the other ten were erected at Ashford between 1928 and 1931. The conversions of the already-built 'Rivers' into 2-6-0s took place in 1928, and the rebuilding was divided between Ashford, Brighton and Eastleigh.

U class summary

SR No.	Rebuilt	Date	Withdrawn
A790	Eastleigh	1928	1965
A791	Eastleigh	1928	1966
A792	Eastleigh	1928	1964
A793	Eastleigh	1928	1964
A794	Eastleigh	1928	1963
A795	Eastleigh	1928	1963
A796	Eastleigh	1928	1964
A797	Ashford	1928	1964
A798	Ashford	1928	1964
A799	Ashford	1928	1965
A800	Ashford	1928	1965
A801	Ashford	1928	1964
A802	Ashford	1928	1964
A803	Brighton	1928	1966
A804	Brighton	1928	1964
A805	Ashford	1928	1963
A806	Brighton	1928	1964
A807	Brighton	1928	1964
A808	Brighton	1928	1964
A809	Brighton	1928	1966

All the above converted from K class 2-6-4T

SR No.	Built new	Date	Withdrawn
A610	Brighton	1928	1962
A611	Brighton	1928	1963
A612	Brighton	1928	1963
A613	Brighton	1928	1964
A614	Brighton	1928	1963
A615	Brighton	1928	1963
A616	Brighton	1928	1964
A617	Brighton	1928	1964
A618	Brighton	1928	1964
A619	Brighton	1928	1965
A620	Ashford	1928	1965
A621	Ashford	1928	1964
A622	Ashford	1929	1964
A623	Ashford	1929	1963
A624	Ashford	1929	1964
A625	Ashford	1929	1964
A626	Ashford	1929	1964
A627	Ashford	1929	1965
A628	Ashford	1929	1964
A629	Ashford	1929	1964
A630	Ashford	1931	1962
A631	Ashford	1931	1963
632	Ashford	1931	1964
633	Ashford	1931	1963
634	Ashford	1931	1963
635	Ashford	1931	1963
636	Ashford	1931	1963
637	Ashford	1931	1963
638	Ashford	1931	1964
639	Ashford	1931	1966

Nos 1806; 1618; 1625 and 1638 are all preserved. No. A628 was equipped for burning pulverised fuel 1929-32.

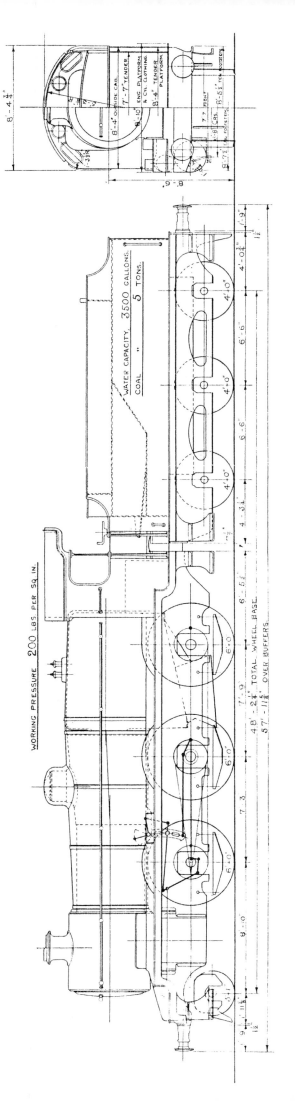

Class U No.1808, Salisbury, 1937. Ex-K class 2-6-4T (LH side).

Class U 2-6-0 (Rebuilt ex-Class K 2-6-4T). (Ashford dwg No.A29A)

WATER CAPACITY, 3500 GALLONS.
COAL ″ 5 TONS.
WORKING PRESSURE 200 LBS. PER SQ. IN.

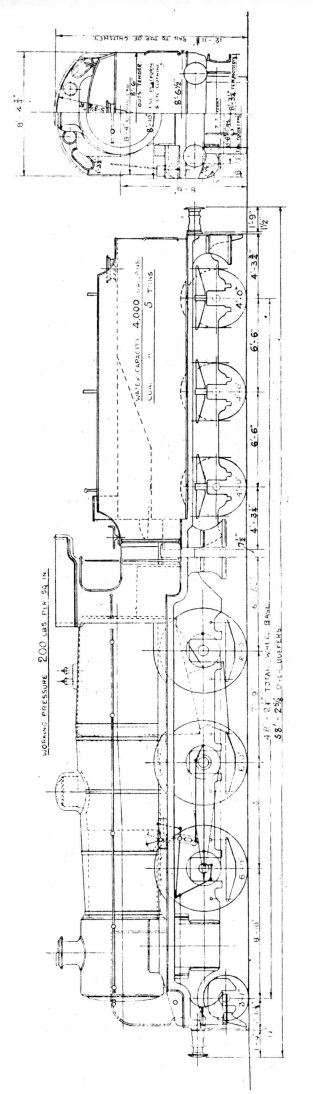

Class U 2-6-0 (Rebuilt ex-Class K 2-6-4T). (Ashford dwg No.A29G).

Class U No.A622 as built (LH side).

Class U (ex-Class K)
No.1797 as an oil-burner
in 1948, Fratton.

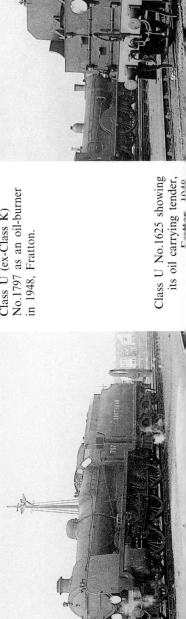

Class U No.1625 showing
its oil carrying tender,
Fratton, 1948.

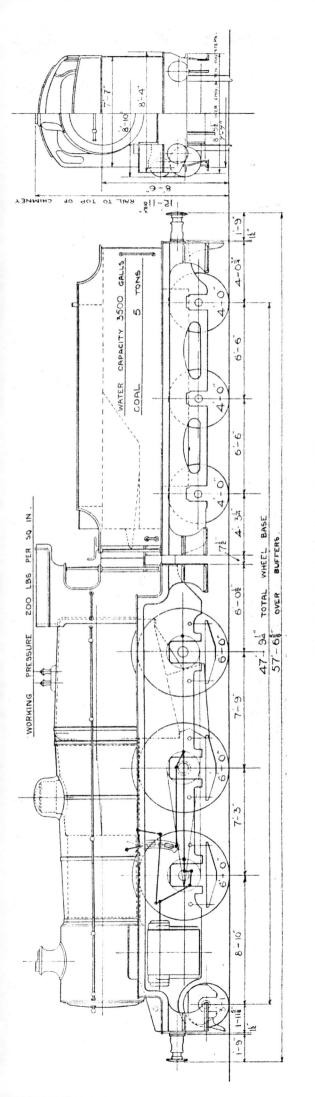

Class U 2-6-0. (Ashford dwg No.A29)

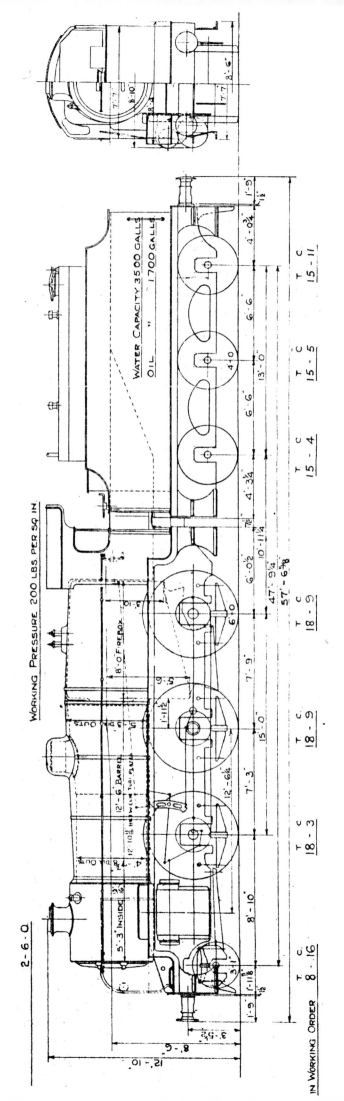

Class U 2-6-0. (Ashford dwg No.A29E)

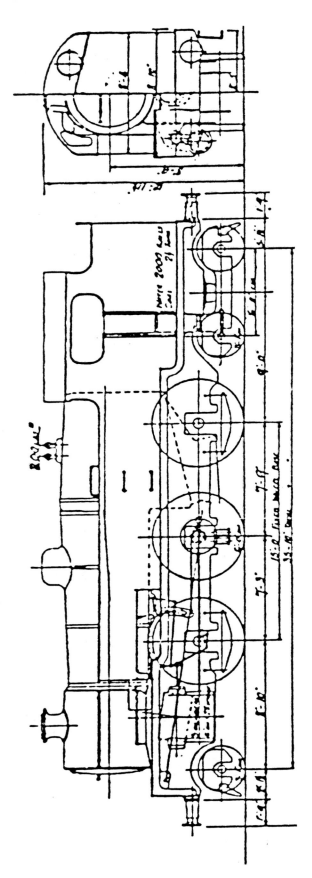

U1 class 2-6-0
(K1 class 2-6-4T)

The one 3-cylinder 'River' class,
No. A890 *River Frome*, was also
changed into a 2-6-0 engine, but
retained its conjugated valve gear
and became class U1, which was
virtually an N1 with 6ft coupled
wheels. In 1930 a further 20
engines were ordered from Eastleigh, and like the N1s, differed
only from the prototype in having
three sets of Walschaerts gear operating the three cylinders, instead of
the conjugated system. Also they
were given 4,000 gallon tenders
with in-turned tops.

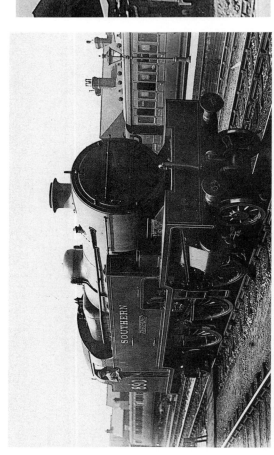

Class K1 2-6-4T. (Ashford dwg)

3-Cylinder U1 class

SR No.	Rebuilt	Date	Withdrawn
A890	Ashford From 2-6-4T	1928	1963
	Built new		
891	Eastleigh	1931	1963
892	Eastleigh	1931	1962
893	Eastleigh	1931	1962
894	Eastleigh	1931	1962
895	Eastleigh	1931	1962
896	Eastleigh	1931	1962
897	Eastleigh	1931	1962
898	Eastleigh	1931	1962
899	Eastleigh	1931	1962
900	Eastleigh	1931	1962
901	Eastleigh	1931	1963
902	Eastleigh	1931	1962
903	Eastleigh	1931	1962
904	Eastleigh	1931	1962
905	Eastleigh	1931	1962
906	Eastleigh	1931	1962
907	Eastleigh	1931	1962
908	Eastleigh	1931	1962
909	Eastleigh	1931	1962

SCALE :– $\frac{1}{4}$ = 1 FT.

WORKING PRESSURE 200LBS PER SQ.IN.

1'-9" 1⅝" 1½" 8'-10" 7'-3" 7'-9" 6'-5½" 4' 7½"

3'-1" 6'-0" 6'-0" 6'-0"

48' - 2¼" TOTAL WHEEL BASE.

57'- 11⅝" OVER BUFFERS.

Class U1 No.1908.

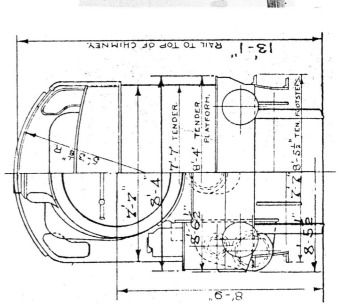

Class K1 No.A890 *River Frome* in works grey (LH side).

Class U1 2-6-0 (Rebuilt ex-Class K1 2-6-4T).

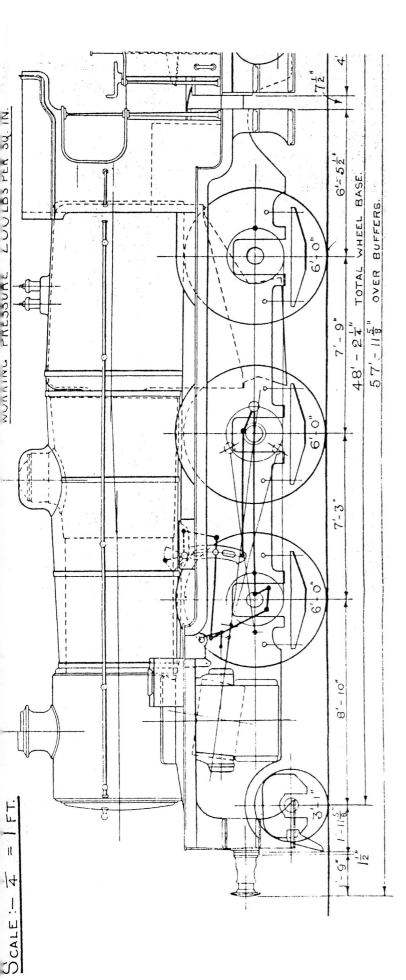

13'-1" RAIL TO TOP OF CHIMNEY.

7'-7" 8'-4" 8'-6½" 8'-5½" TEN. FOOTSTEPS.

7'-7" TENDER. 8'-4" TENDER PLATFORM. 7'-7" 8'-5½"

8'-6"

5'-3½" R.

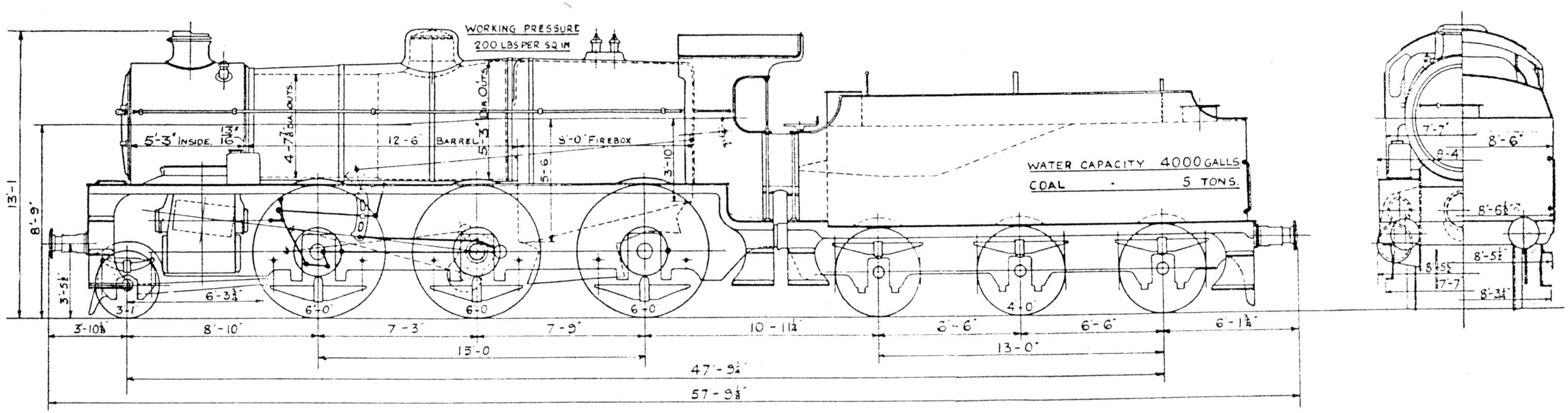

WORKING PRESSURE
200 LBS PER SQ IN

WATER CAPACITY 4000 GALLS.
COAL - 5 TONS.

5'-0" FIREBOX

BARREL

12-6

5'-3" INSIDE

8'-9"

13'-1"

3'-10⅝"

8'-10"

6'-3¼"

7'-3"

15'-0"

7'-9"

3'-10"

10'-11¼"

47'-9½"

57'-9⅞"

6'-0"

6'-0"

6'-0"

6'-0"

4'-0"

6'-6"

6'-6"

13'-0"

9'-0"

6'-1¾"

3'-5¼"

3-1

3-10

8'-6"

8'-5⅝"

8'-5⅜"

8'-3¼"

7'-7"

Class U1 2-6-0. (Ashford dwg No.A29C)

Left: Class U1 No.A895 when new (LH side).

Above: Class U1 No.1906 in 1938.

Left: Class U1 No.1902 (RH side).

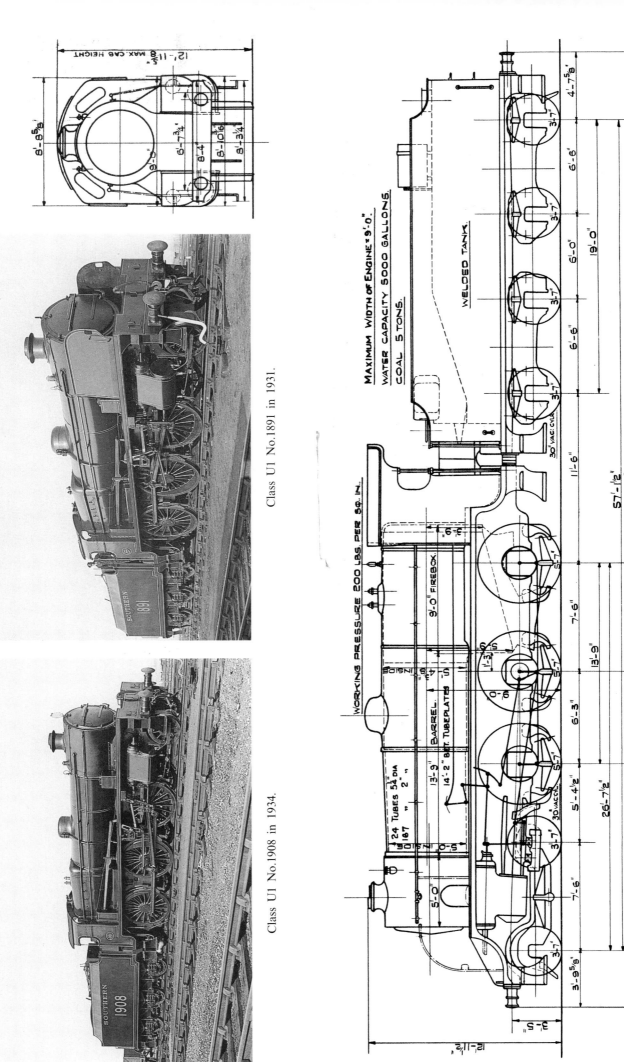

Class U1 No.1891 in 1931.

Class U1 No.1908 in 1934.

Class S15 4-6-0. (5,000 gallon tender.) (Eastleigh dwg No.SR74A)

S15 class (Maunsell) 4-6-0

In 1925, the Southern Railway Running Department demanded more heavy duty goods engines, and Maunsell, taking heed of the 1924 trials, decided to order ten of the S15 class, suitably modified and improved. These were to follow along the lines of the 'King Arthur' class, which were being built at that time. Ten of the new engines were put into service in 1927, five more in 1928, and then a gap of eight years due to economic depression, when the last ten engines were built in 1936.

The Maunsell S15s differed from the original Urie engines visually by the Maunsell boiler mountings, outside steam pipes, and the straight running plate. Mechanically the machines were fitted with 20½in cylinders, longer valve travel, and larger steam pipes and parts. Bigger ashpans and better draughting, and a Maunsell superheater, all improved the steaming qualities and there is no doubt these later S15s were the finest freight engines to see service on the Southern Railway.

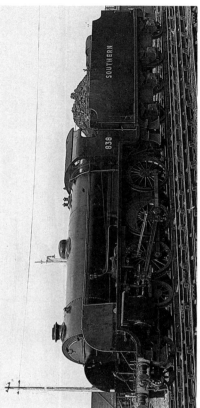

SR No.	Built	Date	Painted black	Withdrawn
831	Eastleigh	1927	1950	1963
832	Eastleigh	1927	1948	1964
833	Eastleigh	1927	1950	1965
834	Eastleigh	1927	1949	1964
835	Eastleigh	1927	1950	1964
836	Eastleigh	1927	1950	1965
837	Eastleigh	1928	1948	1965
838	Eastleigh	1936	1948	1965
839	Eastleigh	1936	1949	1964
840	Eastleigh	1936	1949	1964

SR No.	Built	Date	Painted black	Withdrawn
841	Eastleigh	1936	1948	1964
842	Eastleigh	1936	1949	1968
843	Eastleigh	1936	1949	1964
844	Eastleigh	1936	1950	1964
845	Eastleigh	1936	1948	1964
846	Eastleigh	1936	1948	1963
847	Eastleigh	1936	1948	1964

All were prefixed 'E' until 1931-32. Nos 825, 828, 830, 841 and 847 are all preserved.

SR No.	Built	Date	Painted black	Withdrawn
823	Eastleigh	1927	1948	1964
824	Eastleigh	1927	1950	1965
825	Eastleigh	1927	1948	1964
826	Eastleigh	1927	1949	1962
827	Eastleigh	1927	1949	1964
828	Eastleigh	1927	1949	1964
829	Eastleigh	1927	1949	1963
830	Eastleigh	1927	1950	1964

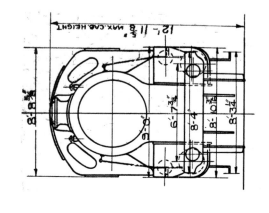

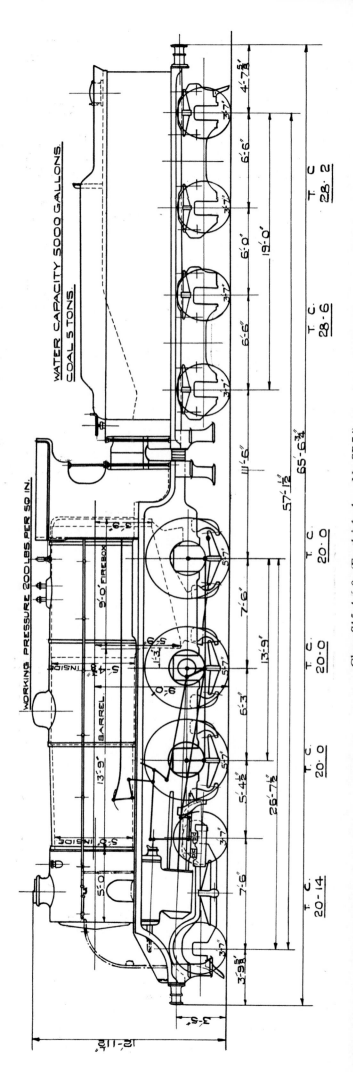

Class S15 (Maunsell) No.838 in 1945 (LH side).

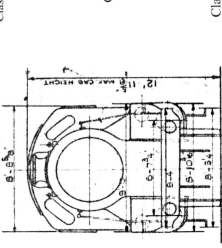

Class S15 (Maunsell) No.E825 as built (LH side).

Class S15 (Maunsell) No.E825 showing cab detail.

Class S15 4-6-0. (Eastleigh dwg No.SR74C)

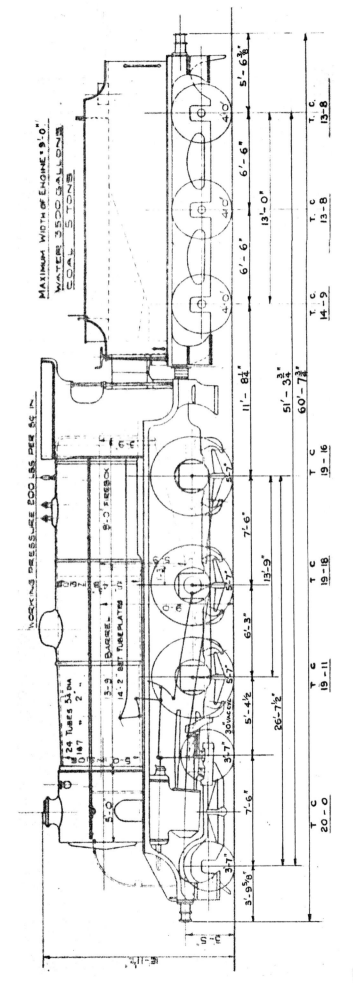

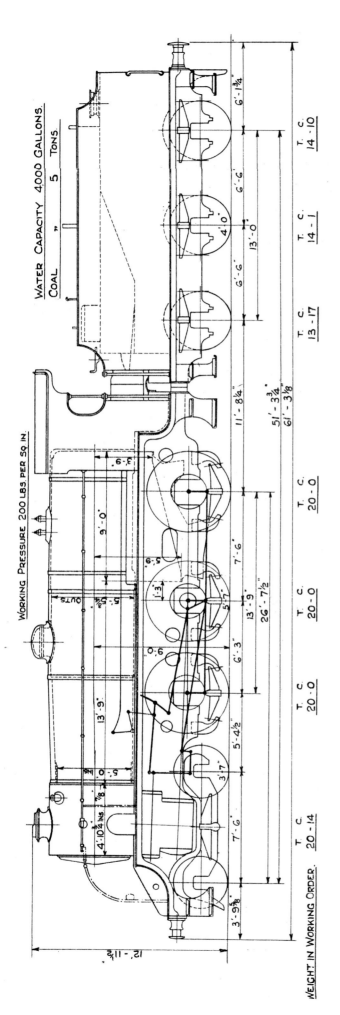

WATER CAPACITY 4,000 GALLONS.
COAL " 5 TONS.

WORKING PRESSURE 200 LBS. PER SQ. IN.

WEIGHT IN WORKING ORDER.

Class S15 4-6-0. (Eastleigh dwg No.SR74B)

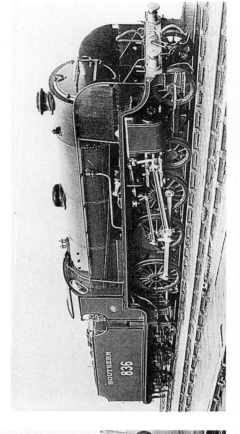

Class S15 (Maunsell) No.836 in 1929.

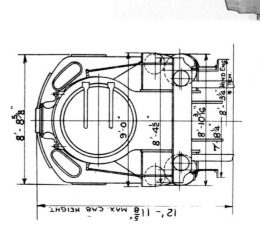

Class S15 (Maunsell) No.835 in 1936.

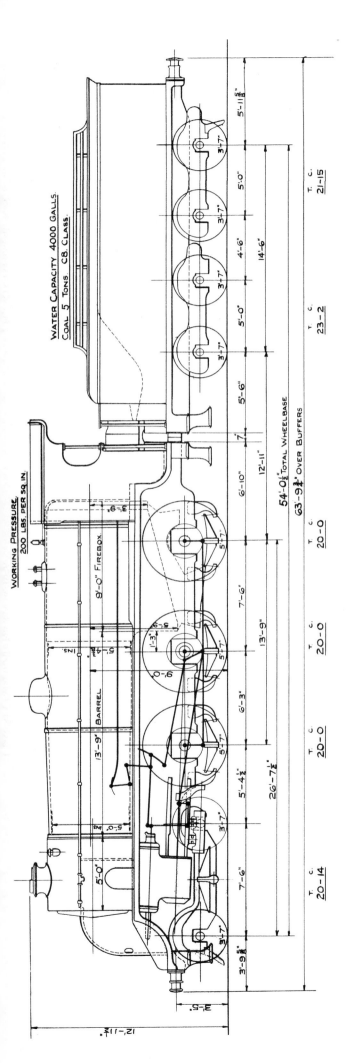

Class S15 4-6-0. (4,000 gallon tender.) (Eastleigh dwg No.SR74A)

WATER CAPACITY 4000 GALLS.
COAL 5 TONS C8. CLASS.

WORKING PRESSURE, 200 LBS. PER SQ. IN.

N and N1 class 2-6-0

As previously described in the *Eastern* section, the N class of mixed traffic engines was to a design of Maunsell when he was CME of the SECR, and 15 of this class were built at Ashford Works. At the formation of the Southern Railway, circumstances due to the war years ruled out the railway workshops being in a position to build the large quantities of locomotives which were needed at that time. On the other hand, Woolwich Arsenal, having stopped the manufacture of munitions, were only too pleased to employ their skilled workers in making complete sets of parts for locomotives. Therefore, Maunsell ordered 50 N class machines, the boilers from the North British Locomotive Co., and everything else from Woolwich Arsenal. All to be assembled at Ashford Works, which was achieved between 1924 and 1925.

Later, between 1932 and 1933, a further 15 engines were completed at Ashford, which brought the grand total for this class to 80. All the locomotives in the Woolwich Arsenal group were always known to railwaymen as the "Woolworths" and were to be seen all over the Southern Railway network, from the Kent coast to Ilfracombe in North Devon. The numbering of the class was from 810 of 1917 to 875 of 1925, and 1400 to 1414 in the

1932-34 series, and it should be noted that the 'A' prefix was used on the 800 series until 1932.

One of the Ashford built engines. No. 822, was turned out with three cylinders of 16in x 28in and became the 'guinea-pig' for Harry Holcroft to try out his conjugated valve gear. This design eventually became the N1 class. Proving a success, five more similar engines were ordered from Ashford in 1931 and became Nos 1876 to 1880 after 1931. From 1933 onward, both the N and N1 class were fitted with smoke deflectors and all were passed into BR ownership at the Nationalisation, when several also received outside steam pipes.

It should be noted that the 1931 N1s did not have the conjugated valve gear, but the three cylinders each had an independent set of Walschaerts gear.

SR No.	Built	Date	Withdrawn
817	Ashford	1922	1964
818	Ashford	1922	1963
819	Ashford	1922	1964
820	Ashford	1922	1963
821	Ashford	1922	1964
823	Ashford	1923	1963
824	Ashford	1923	1963
A825	Ashford	1923	1963
A826	Woolwich Arsenal/	1924	1964
A827	Ashford	1924	1964
A828	Woolwich Arsenal/	1924	1964
	Ashford		
A829	Woolwich Arsenal/	1924	1964
A830	Ashford	1924	1965
	Woolwich Arsenal/		
A831	Ashford	1924	1964
A832	Woolwich Arsenal/	1924	1964
A833	Ashford	1924	1964
A834	Woolwich Arsenal/	1924	1964
A835	Ashford	1924	1964

N class

SR No.	Built	Date	Withdrawn
810	Ashford	1917	1964
811	Ashford	1920	1965
812	Ashford	1920	1964
813	Ashford	1920	1963
814	Ashford	1920	1964
815	Ashford	1920	1963
816	Ashford	1922	1966

SR No.	Built	Date	Withdrawn
A836	Woolwich Arsenal/ Ashford	1924	1963
A837	Woolwich Arsenal/ Ashford	1924	1964
A838	Woolwich Arsenal/ Ashford	1924	1964
A839	Woolwich Arsenal/ Ashford	1924	1963
A840	Woolwich Arsenal/ Ashford	1924	1964
A841	Woolwich Arsenal/ Ashford	1924	1964
A842	Woolwich Arsenal/ Ashford	1924	1965
A843	Woolwich Arsenal/ Ashford	1924	1964
A844	Woolwich Arsenal/ Ashford	1924	1963
A845	Woolwich Arsenal/ Ashford	1924	1964
A846	Woolwich Arsenal/ Ashford	1925	1964
A847	Woolwich Arsenal/ Ashford	1925	1963
A848	Woolwich Arsenal/ Ashford	1925	1964
A849	Woolwich Arsenal/ Ashford	1925	1964
A850	Woolwich Arsenal/ Ashford	1925	1964
A851	Woolwich Arsenal/ Ashford	1925	1963

SR No.	Built	Date	Withdrawn
A852	Woolwich Arsenal/ Ashford	1925	1963
A853	Woolwich Arsenal/ Ashford	1925	1964
A854	Woolwich Arsenal/ Ashford	1925	1964
A855	Woolwich Arsenal/ Ashford	1925	1964
A856	Woolwich Arsenal/ Ashford	1925	1964
A857	Woolwich Arsenal/ Ashford	1925	1964
A858	Woolwich Arsenal/ Ashford	1925	1964
A859	Woolwich Arsenal/ Ashford	1925	1964
A860	Woolwich Arsenal/ Ashford	1925	1963
A861	Woolwich Arsenal/ Ashford	1925	1963
A862	Woolwich Arsenal/ Ashford	1925	1965
A863	Woolwich Arsenal/ Ashford	1925	1963
A864	Woolwich Arsenal/ Ashford	1925	1963
A865	Woolwich Arsenal/ Ashford	1925	1966
A866	Woolwich Arsenal/ Ashford	1925	1964
A867	Woolwich Arsenal/ Ashford	1925	1963

SR No.	Built	Date	Withdrawn
A868	Woolwich Arsenal/ Ashford	1925	1964
A869	Woolwich Arsenal/ Ashford	1925	1964
A870	Woolwich Arsenal/ Ashford	1925	1964
A871	Woolwich Arsenal/ Ashford	1925	1963
A872	Woolwich Arsenal/ Ashford	1925	1963
A873	Woolwich Arsenal/ Ashford	1925	1966
A874	Woolwich Arsenal/ Ashford	1925	1964
A875	Woolwich Arsenal/ Ashford	1925	1964
1400	Woolwich Arsenal/ Ashford	1925	1964
1401	Woolwich Arsenal/ Ashford	1932	1965
1402	Woolwich Arsenal/ Ashford	1932	1963
1403	Woolwich Arsenal/ Ashford	1932	1963
1404	Woolwich Arsenal/ Ashford	1932	1963
1405	Woolwich Arsenal/ Ashford	1932	1966
1406	Woolwich Arsenal/ Ashford	1933	1964
1407	Woolwich Arsenal/ Ashford	1933	1963

SR No.	Built	Date	Withdrawn
1408	Woolwich Arsenal/ Ashford	1933	1966
1409	Woolwich Arsenal/ Ashford	1933	1962
1410	Woolwich Arsenal/ Ashford	1933	1964
1411	Woolwich Arsenal/ Ashford	1933	1966
1412	Woolwich Arsenal/ Ashford	1933	1964
1413	Woolwich Arsenal/ Ashford	1934	1964
1414	Woolwich Arsenal/ Ashford	1934	1962

No. 812 fitted with stove-pipe chimney 1921-25.
No. 1831 was an oil burner 1947-48.
No. A866 was exhibited at the British Empire Exhibition, Wembley, from May to November 1925.
No. 31874 is preserved on the Mid-Hants Railway. Fitted BR Std Class 4 chimney.
Nos 31815/17/25/26/28/34/41/47/57/65/67/70/73/75/3140/2/10/12/14 were fitted with BR Standard Class 4 chimneys.

N1 class

SR No.	Built	Date	Withdrawn
822	Ashford	1922	1962
1876	Ashford	1930	1962
1877	Ashford	1930	1962
1878	Ashford	1930	1962
1879	Ashford	1930	1962
1880	Ashford	1930	1962

Class N 2-6-0 (Ashford dwg. No. A144)

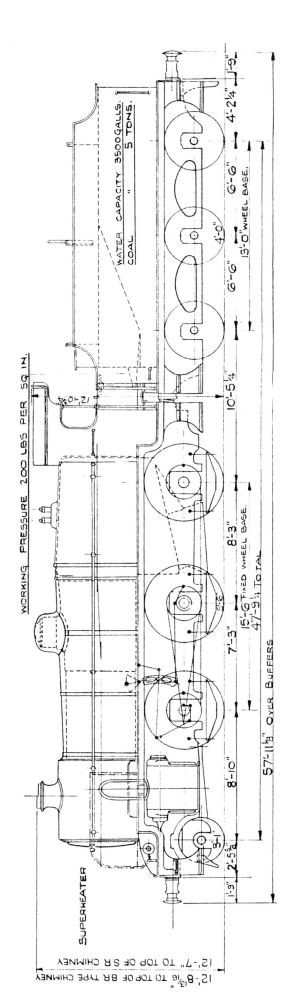

Class N 2-6-0. (Ashford dwg No.A14)

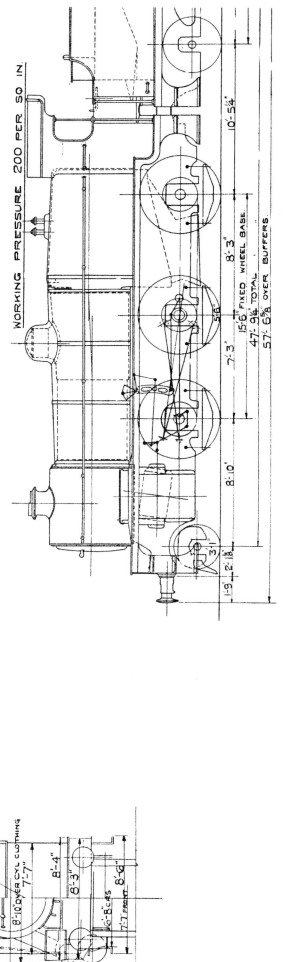

Class N1 2-6-0. (Ashford dwg No.A14B)

Class N No.1414 at Salisbury in 1937.

Class N No.A816 as built (LH side).

N15x 'Remembrance' class 4-6-0

Although slightly out of date sequence, the classification of N15x inferred that the engines fit in here. As has been noted in the *Central* section, L.B. Billinton designed and built seven large 4-6-4Ts for the LBSCR between 1914 and 1922 for express passenger services.

In SR days electrification soon made these big tank engines redundant, however, instead of scrapping, it was found that the frames and boilers were in such good condition that Maunsell decided to rebuild all seven as 4-6-0 tender engines. Known

as the 'Remembrance' class, or N15x, they had their side tanks removed, new cabs after the 'Lord Nelson' pattern, Ross pop safety valves, 'King Arthur' chimneys and dome covers, and were attached to tenders of the double bogie type, carrying 5,000 gallons of water, which previously had been coupled to Urie S15 class locomotives.

They retained their old numbers, and although originally only three had carried names, after rebuilding and following a suggestion by Holcroft, all seven were given names commemorating the early railway engineers.

LBSCR No.	Original Name	Built	SR No.	Rebuilt	SR name	Withdrawn
327	Charles C.Macrae	1914	2327	1935	Trevithick	1956
328		1914	2328	1936	Hackworth	1955
329	Stephenson	1921	2329	1934	Stephenson	1956
330		1921	2330	1935	Cudworth	1955
331		1921	2331	1936	Beattie	1957
332		1922	2332	1935	Stroudley	1956
333	Remembrance	1922	2333	1935	Remembrance	1956

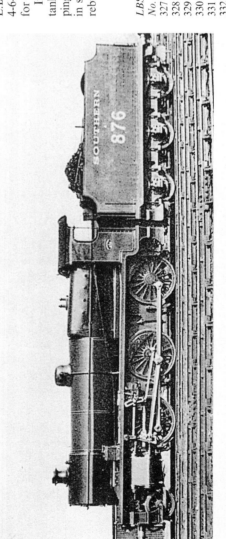

Class N1 No.A876 (LH side).

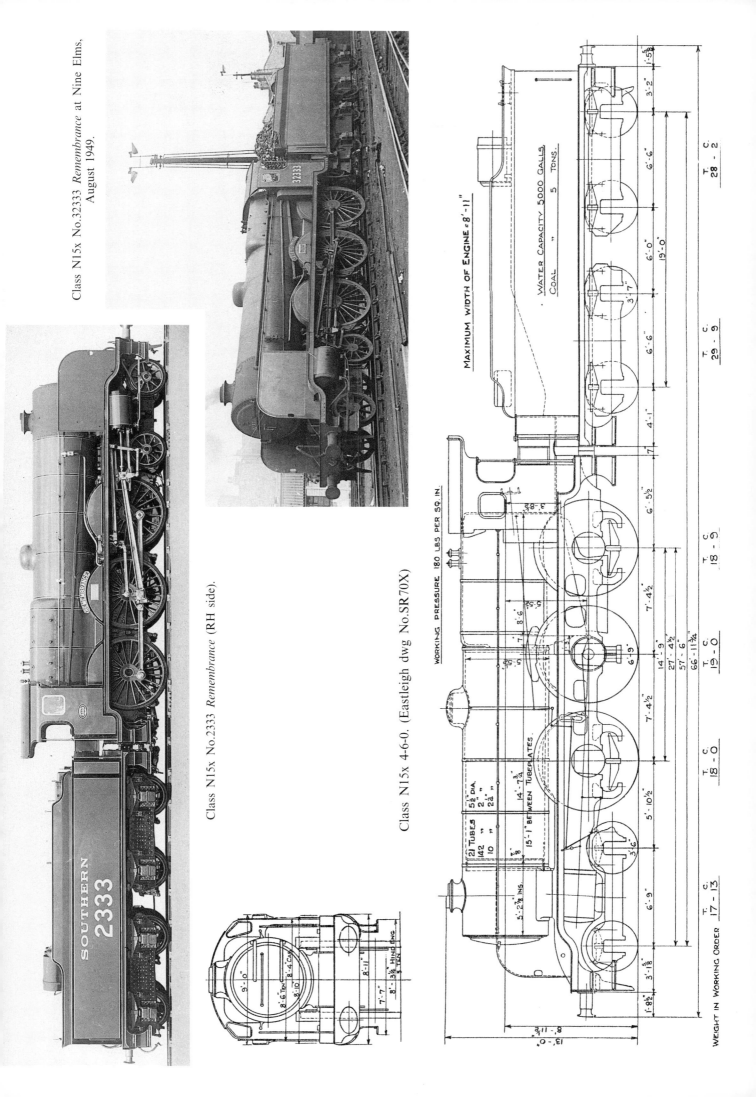

Class N15x No.32333 *Remembrance* at Nine Elms, August 1949.

Class N15x No.2333 *Remembrance* (RH side).

Class N15x 4-6-0. (Eastleigh dwg No.SR70X)

MAXIMUM WIDTH OF ENGINE = 8'-11"

WORKING PRESSURE 180 LBS PER SQ. IN.

WATER CAPACITY 5000 GALLS.
COAL   "   5 TONS.

21 TUBES 5⅛" DIA.
142   "   2" "
10   "   2¼" "

15'-1" BETWEEN TUBEPLATES.

14'-7¾"

5'-2⅞ INS.

WEIGHT IN WORKING ORDER

T. C.   T. C.   T. C.   T. C.   T. C.   T. C.   T. C.
17 - 13 18 - 0   19 - 0   18 - 9   18 - 9   29 - 9   28 - 2

SOUTHERN 2333

Class N15x No.2329 *Stephenson* in works grey.

Class N15x No.2332 *Stroudley* (LH side).

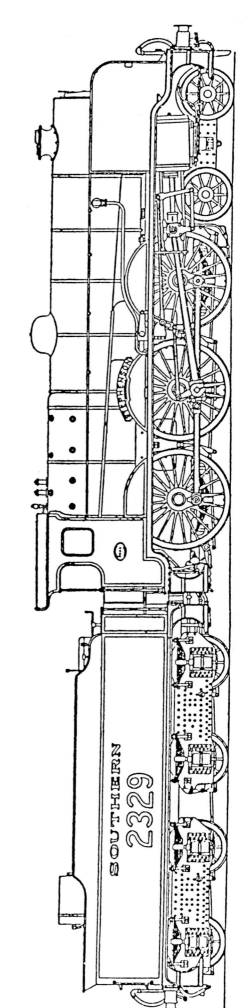

Class N15x 4-6-0.

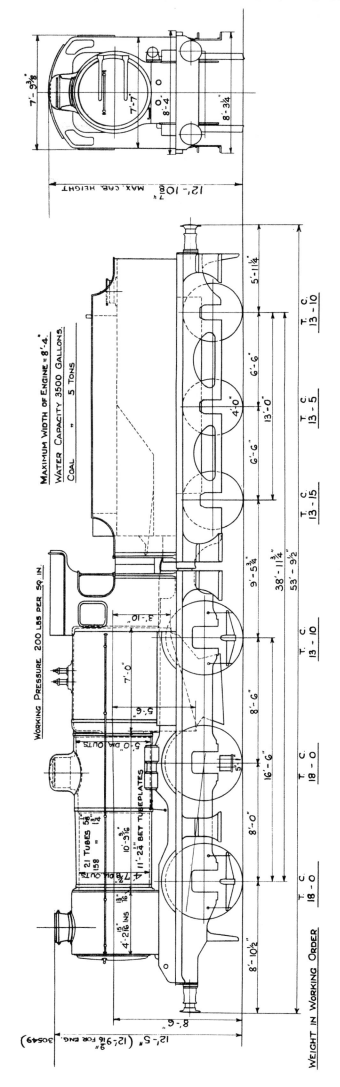

In the mid-thirties, the accent on the Southern Railway was for the main line electrification, and funding for steam locomotive construction was severely restricted. Nevertheless, many of the older classes of freight engines were nearing the end of long and useful lives, which made it imperative to order replacements. In an effort to keep costs down to a minimum, Maunsell designed what was to be his last steam engine, and in fact, he retired before the new engines, the Q class, were constructed.

These 0-6-0 tender engines were based generally on the Ashford design of N and L1 locomotives, with inside cylinders 19in x 26in, driving 5ft 1in coupled wheels. They had many Maunsell items in their make-up, such as chimney, smokebox top sniffing valves, large cab with side windows, Belpaire firebox and superheaters. The tenders attached to these engines were the 6-wheeled 3,500 gallon type which had previously run with the U class 2-6-0 engines, those machines receiving 4,000 gallon tenders. So it can be seen that the Q class was a straightforward, no frills locomotive, but was not a very good steamer. In later years, Bulleid experimented with various blast pipes and chimneys, but to no great improvement.

Following draughting and steaming trials at Swindon a BR Class 4 blastpipe and a stove-pipe chimney was fitted to No. 30549 in 1955, with excellent results!

One small point of interest, the first engine, No. 530, had the front framing protruding beyond the smokebox with lifting holes in the convex curve. All subsequent engines had this extended framing in a concave curve, so losing the lifting holes. I wonder why?

Eleven were built at Eastleigh in 1938, and a further nine in 1939. All entered BR stock and had 30,000 added to their numbers.

SR No.	Date	Withdrawn
530*	1938	1964
531	1938	1964
532	1938	1964
533	1938	1963
534	1938	1962
535	1938	1965
536*	1938	1964
537	1938	1962
538*	1938	1963
539*	1938	1963
540	1938	1962
541	1939	1964
542*	1939	1964

SR No.	Date	Withdrawn
543*	1939	1964
544	1939	1964
545	1939	1965
546*	1939	1964
547*	1939	1964

SR No.	Date	Withdrawn
548	1939	1965
549*	1939	1963

* Fitted with BR Class 4 chimney, 1958 onwards
No. 541 is preserved on the Bluebell Railway.

Class Q No.530 as built, 1938 (RH side).

MAXIMUM WIDTH OF ENGINE = 8'-4"
WATER CAPACITY 3500 GALLONS
COAL " 5 TONS

WORKING PRESSURE 200 LBS PER SQ. IN.

WEIGHT IN WORKING ORDER

Class Q 0-6-0. (Eastleigh dwg No.SR80)

Class Q No.30536 at Eastleigh in 1950.

Class Z No.950 at Ashford in 1948.

Class Q No.535 at Eastleigh in 1938 (LH side).

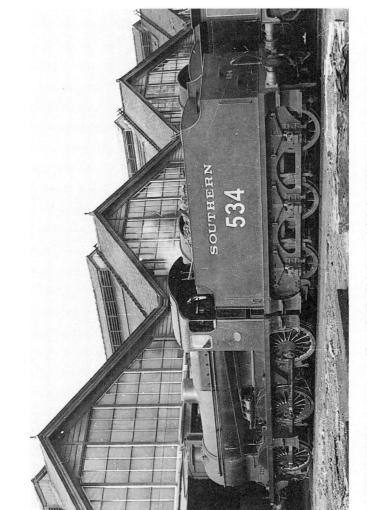

Class Q No.534 at Eastleigh in 1938.

Z Class 0-8-0T

Known to railwaymen as the "Maggies", these heavy shunting tanks were designed by Maunsell to replace the many six-coupled shunters which were at work on the Eastern and Central sections. The Western section was endowed with the massive G16s, the 4-8-0 tanks built by Urie in 1921, and more of this class were on order in 1922.

However, experience had shown that superheaters were wasteful on shunting engines, as was a large grate area as a lot of time was spent standing. The order was cancelled and a new one placed for eight 3-cylinder tank engines of 0-8-0T classification.

Built in 1929, they were, in fact, the last heavy duty steam shunting engines to be constructed by the Southern Railway as diesel-electric locomotives were beginning to take over in the mid-thirties. The Z class had three cylinders of 16in x 28in similar to those on the U1, No. 890, and the N1, No. 822, but the conjugated valve gear was not used on the inside cylinder, there being instead a set of Walschaerts gear, operated by two eccentrics on the crank axle. The two outside cylinders had the standard Walschaerts gear and drove on to the third driving axle, whilst the inside inclined cylinder was connected to the second axle. The wheels were 4ft 8in in diameter set at a short wheelbase of 17ft 6in, very useful for short radius curves in shunting yards, play being allowed in the leading and trailing wheels.

Needing a boiler of large capacity, with a small fire, to avoid losses whilst standing, a standard Brighton boiler similar to those on the C3 class was used. Braking was by steam, although a vacuum system was available if needed. Large Ashford style cabs were fitted, with a bunker capacity of 3 tons, and cut away water tanks that could hold 1,500 gallons. Although all were built at Brighton (in 1929), they carried the 'A' prefix, as all the design work had been carried out at Ashford. This was removed in the 1931 period, but not replaced with the 1000, the eight engines were then treated as Western section stock and kept their 950-957 numbers! After the war, sliding vents were fitted in the cab roofs, and all eight entered BR stock, adding 30,000 to their numbers.

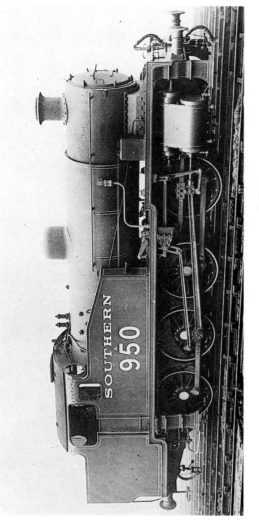

Class Z No.A950 as built (RH side).

SR No.	Built (Brighton)	Withdrawn	SR No.	Built (Brighton)	Withdrawn
950	1929	1962	954	1929	1962
951	1929	1962	955	1929	1962
952	1929	1962	956	1929	1962
953	1929	1962	957	1929	1962

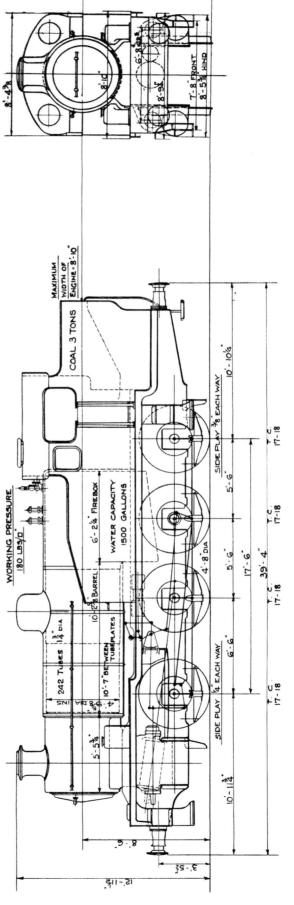

Total Weight of Engine in Working Order   71 Tons. 12 Cwts.
Weight of Engine Empty   56 Tons. 15 Cwts.

Class Z 0-8-0. (Eastleigh dwg No.SR78)

V 'Schools' class 4-4-0

This handsome 4-4-0 passenger engine was perhaps the finest of Maunsell's locomotive designs, and came to fruition through a combination of circumstances. The first of these was the need for a powerful machine to work over the severely restricted Hastings line, which had (and still has!) an 8ft 6½in width limit through a narrow tunnel. This meant larger outside cylinders could not be used. Also Belpaire fireboxes, with the attendant high cabs, were out and a six-coupled engine with its throw-over on curves, was also to be avoided. Therefore, with these restrictions in mind, Maunsell came up with a four-coupled, 3-cylinder engine, with 6ft 7in driving wheels, and with a round-topped firebox to keep the height down, a shortened boiler pressed for 220lbs, and with a maximum 21 tons on each coupled axle. Many railwaymen likened the new class to a "¾ Nelson", but in reality it was more a short version of the "Arthured S15" class, with three 16½in x 26in cylinders.

In order to keep to standardisation as much as possible and keep costs down, many parts were identical with the 'Nelsons', namely, wheel sizes, motion parts and cylinders; the cab was also similar, but the front windows were upside down to those on the 4-6-0 engines. Neat 6-wheeled tenders were attached to these machines, with a water capacity of 4,000 gallons and carrying 5 tons of fuel. This versatile class of locomotive was surely what Ashford Works had been thinking about way back in 1916, and if it had only had the conjugated valve gear, instead of the three separate Walschaerts, it would have been Harry Holcroft's dream engine.

Ten were built in 1930 and were named after famous public schools, and although built for the London-Hastings service, spent their first year on the Eastern and Western main lines, showing and proving what they could do. A further batch of 30 followed at intervals from 1932 through to 1935. One engine, No. 938 *Sevenoaks*, was fitted with plywood streamlining in 1938 from February until March, but the idea was abandoned. After 1931, as engines passed through the shops, the 'E' prefix was omitted and smoke deflectors fitted to all the engines.

SR No.	Name	Built	Withdrawn
905	Tombridge	1930	1961
906	Sherborne	1930	1962
907*	Dulwich	1930	1961
908	Westminster	1930	1961
909*	St. Paul's	1930	1962
910	Merchant Taylors	1932	1961
911	Dover	1932	1962
912	Downside	1932	1962
913	Christ's Hospital	1932	1962
914*	Eastbourne	1932	1961
915*	Brighton	1933	1962
916*	Whitgift	1933	1962
917*	Ardingly	1933	1962
918*	Hurstpierpoint	1933	1961
919*	Harrow	1933	1961
920*	Rugby	1933	1961
921*	Shrewsbury	1933	1962
922	Marlborough	1933	1961
923	Bradfield	1933	1962
924*	Haileybury	1933	1962
925	Cheltenham	1934	1962
926	Repton	1934	1962
927	Clifton	1934	1962
928	Stowe	1934	1962
929*	Malvern	1934	1962
930*	Radley	1934	1962
931*	King's-Wimbledon	1934	1961
932	Blundells	1935	1961
933*	King's-Canterbury	1935	1961
934*	St. Lawrence	1935	1962
935	Sevenoaks	1935	1962
936	Cranleigh	1935	1962
937*	Epsom	1935	1962
938*	St. Olave's	1935	1961
939*	Leatherhead	1935	1961

SR No.	Name	Built	Withdrawn
900*	Eton	1930	1962
901*	Winchester	1930	1962
902	Wellington	1930	1962
903	Charterhouse	1930	1962

Class Z No.30957 at Exmouth Junction depot, 1959.

All built at Eastleigh Works and renumbered in the 30,000 series by BR.

* Lemaître blast pipe and large diameter chimney fitted from 1939.

Nos 30912 and 30921 ran with LN tenders in 1961. No. 923 named *Uppingham* until 1934. Nos 925, 926 and 928 are preserved. (No. 926 was preserved in the USA until 1989.)

Class V No. E901 *Winchester* in 1930, new (LH side)

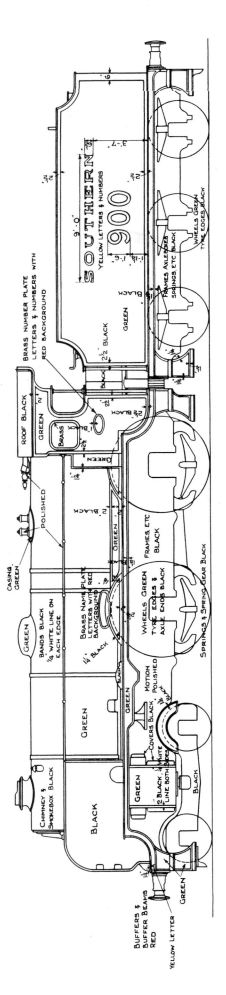

BRASS NUMBER PLATE
LETTERS & NUMBERS WITH
RED BACKGROUND

SOUTHERN

900

GREEN

YELLOW LETTERS & NUMBERS

BLACK

FRAMES AXLEBOXES
SPRINGS ETC BLACK

WHEELS GREEN
TYRE EDGES BLACK

ROOF BLACK

GREEN

BRASS

BLACK

2½ BLACK

2½ BLACK

CASING
GREEN

POLISHED

2 BLACK

BANDS BLACK
¼ WHITE LINE ON
EACH EDGE

GREEN

BRASS NAME PLATE
LETTERS WITH RED
BACKGROUND

¼ BLACK

WHEELS GREEN
TYRE EDGES
& AXLE ENDS BLACK

FRAMES ETC
BLACK

SPRINGS & SPRING GEAR BLACK

GREEN

GREEN

MOTION
POLISHED

COVERS BLACK

2 BLACK ¼ WHITE
LINE BOTH SIDES

GREEN

BLACK

GREEN

CHIMNEY &
SMOKEBOX BLACK

BLACK

BUFFERS &
BUFFER BEAMS
RED

YELLOW LETTER

GREEN

¼ WHITE LINE BETWEEN BLACK EDGING & GREEN

DIAGRAM OF PAINTING
"SCHOOLS" CLASS

YELLOW LETTERS
& NUMBERS WITH
BLACK SHADING.

BLACK

BLACK

GREEN

N° 900

BRASS

GREEN

BLACK

LETTERS & NUMBERS
ON ENGINE BUFFER
BEAM ONLY

Class V 4-4-0. Eastleigh painting diagram.

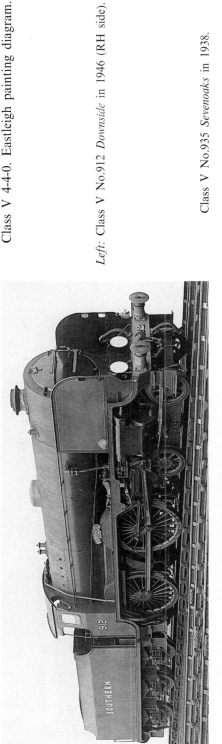

Left: Class V No.912 *Downside* in 1946 (RH side).

Class V No.935 *Sevenoaks* in 1938.

Right: Class V No.905 *Tonbridge* in 1946.

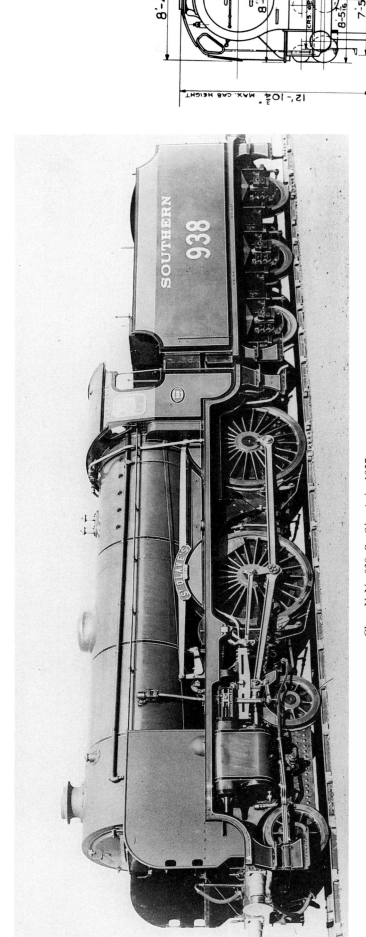

Class V No.938 *St Olave's* in 1937.

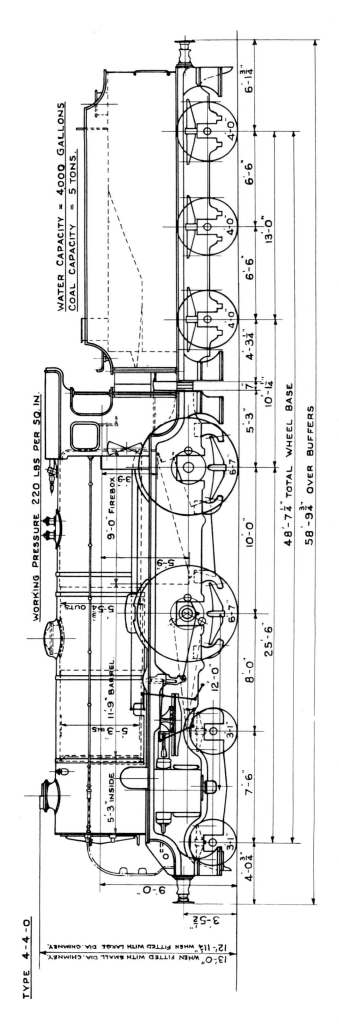

WATER CAPACITY = 4,000 GALLONS
COAL CAPACITY = 5 TONS.

WORKING PRESSURE 220 LBS PER SQ. IN.

48'-7¼" TOTAL WHEEL BASE

58'-9¾" OVER BUFFERS

TYPE 4-4-0

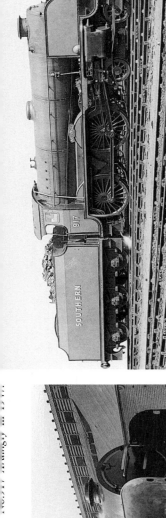

Above: Class V No.936 *Cranleigh* at Bricklayers Arms, April 1936.

Right: Class V No.928 *Stowe* as preserved at Beaulieu, May 1966.

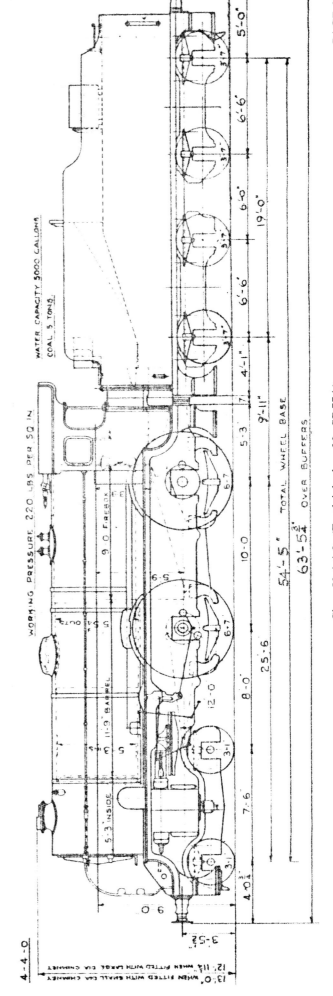

Class V 4-4-0. (Eastleigh dwg No.SR77A)

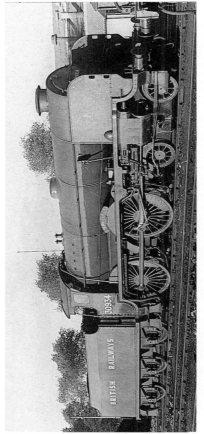

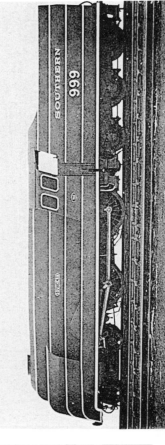

Class V No.909 *St. Paul's.*

Right: Class V No.30934 *St. Lawrence,* Eastleigh, 1948.

Below right: Class V No.999 *Southern* (alias No.935 *Sevenoaks*) with plywood, mock-up streamlining at Eastleigh in March 1938.

ARRANGEMENT OF FOOTPLATE FITTINGS:

Southern Railway "Schools" Class Locomotive

1. Vacuum ejector steam valve.
2. Sight-feed lubricator steam valve.
3. Train-heating steam valve.
4. Live steam injector valve lever.
5. Exhaust injector steam valve lever.
6. Steam to clutch valve.
7. Steam to pressure gauge.
8. Reversing shaft clutch valve.
9. Blower valve hand wheel.
10. Water regulator, exhaust injector.
11. Feed-cock spindle.
12. Whistle wire.
13. Cylinder drain cocks lever.
14. Ashpan front damper lever.
15. Sanding valves lever.
16. Ashpan back damper lever.
17. Whistle lever.

Class V 4-4-0 cab details.

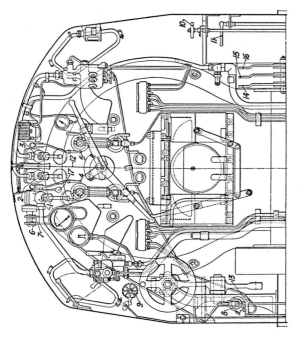

W class 2-6-4T

It seems rather strange that the CME of the newly formed Southern Railway, Maunsell, should order a batch of 2-6-4 tank engines in 1932, after having condemned the K class in 1928! The reason for the new order was the desperate need for a versatile locomotive which could handle the heavy *freight* exchange traffic in the London area.

The 15 engines built, actually used many of the discarded parts of the old K class, such as the pony and bogie wheels, and side tanks, etc. The same type of boiler was used and the 3-cylinder motion layout was similar to that of the N1 class. However, being freight engines, the six coupled wheels were only 5ft 6in in diameter. The first five machines, turned out in 1932, were painted black, with a single green line, but the Ashford series of 1935-36 were unlined black. All 15 entered BR at the Nationalisation, and had the 3xxxx numbering.

SR No.	Built	Date	Withdrawn
1911	Eastleigh	1932	1963
1912	Eastleigh	1932	1964
1913	Eastleigh	1932	1964
1914	Eastleigh	1932	1964
1915	Eastleigh	1932	1963
1916	Ashford	1935	1963
1917	Ashford	1935	1964
1918	Ashford	1935	1963
1919	Ashford	1935	1963
1920	Ashford	1935	1963
1921	Ashford	1935	1963
1922	Ashford	1935	1963
1923	Ashford	1936	1963
1924	Ashford	1936	1964
1925	Ashford	1936	1963

Class W No.1911 in works grey when new (LH side).

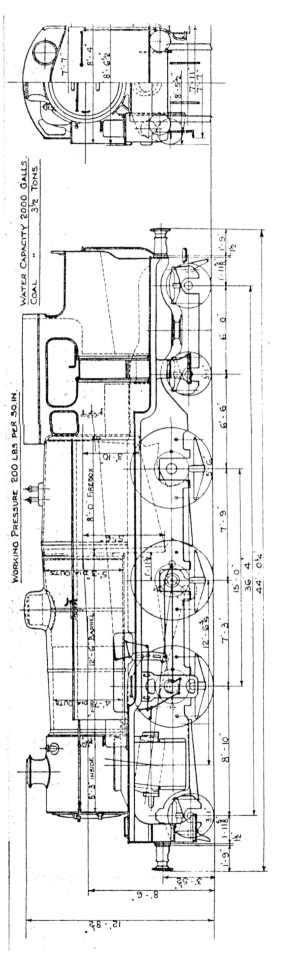

WORKING PRESSURE 200 LBS PER SQ.IN.

WATER CAPACITY 2000 GALLS.
COAL " 3½ TONS.

Class W 2-6-4T. (Eastleigh dwg No.SR35)

Class W No.1924 at Eastleigh in 1963.

Q1 class 0-6-0

The outbreak of hostilities in 1939 brought about an immediate increase in freight traffic on the Southern Railway, due mainly to the network of lines serving the ports linking the UK to France. To deal with all these extra workings more locomotives were needed, especially a large quantity of general-purpose goods machines, which could have a wide availability over the whole system and be powerful enough to handle the heaviest trains.

It would have been easy to have simply ordered more Q class Maunsell-designed engines, but O.V.S. Bulleid, his successor, realised that these locomotives left a lot to be desired, and had a notorious reputation as poor steamers.

To meet this pressing need, he designed the Q1 class of 0-6-0, and in so doing, startled the railway pundits into instant criticism of the stark ugliness of this new creation. Yes, it was different, but so were Churchward's early 4-6-0s, and what the critics seemed to forget was the reasoning behind the design. To quote O.V.S. himself – "An engine was needed to run over as much of the system as possible, not to exceed 54 tons, with a tender restricted to 39½ tons. To get the power needed, the engine must have a large boiler, with a big firebox to generate continuous steam. A shortened form of the 'Lord Nelson' firebox was used, with a grate of 27ft. The wheelbase was to be the same as the Q class, with the cylinders 19in x 26in in the same position. This dictated the length of the boiler, which was 10ft 6in. All this came out to 21¼ tons, only leaving 32¾ tons for the rest of the locomotive".

So now one can see why many of the old frills of earlier engines were dispensed with. For instance, the whole running plate was omitted, the BFB (Bulleid-Firth-Brown) wheel centres were used, being lighter than the normal spoked variety. The frame was lightened where possible, and fabricated parts used instead of castings. Being wartime, the boiler was lagged with Idaglass, which meant light sheet casings. The smokebox had a square bottom, with a clipped door, instead of the heavy dart type. The cab, ashpans and even the tender were fabricated from thin sheet steel, and the end result being an engine of 51 tons 5 cwts, with a tender scaling 38 tons. It was in August 1940 that Bulleid recommended the building of 40 such locomotives, but owing to material shortages in wartime Britain, and Eastleigh being committed to war work and the production of 'Merchant Navy' class locomotives, it was 1942 before Brighton and Ashford Works could produce the engines as required.

It was originally intended to number the class from 550 to 589, but before this could be implemented, Bulleid decided on the Continental system whereby the letter 'C' prefix means six-coupled. Therefore, the Q1 class became Nos C1 through to C40! Upon entering BR stock in 1948, the 'C' was removed and 33,000 was added to their numbers.

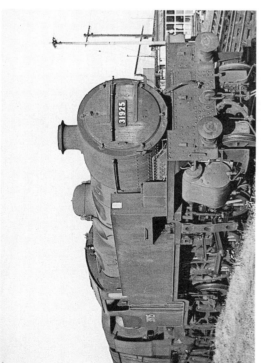

Class W No.31925 at Eastleigh in 1963.

SR No.	Built at Brighton	BR No.	Withdrawn
C1	1942	33001	1964
C2	1942	33002	1963
C3	1942	33003	1964
C4	1942	33004	1965
C5	1942	33005	1963
C6	1942	33006	1966
C7	1942	33007	1964
C8	1942	33008	1963
C9	1942	33009	1965
C10	1942	33010	1964
C11	1942	33011	1963
C12	1942	33012	1964
C13	1942	33013	1963
C14	1942	33014	1964
C15	1942	33015	1964
C16	1942	33016	1963

Class W No.1924 in 1944 (RH side).

SR No.	Built at Ashford	BR No.	Withdrawn
C17	1942	33017	1964
C18	1942	33018	1965
C19	1942	33019	1963
C20	1942	33020	1966
C21	1942	33021	1963
C22	1942	33022	1964
C23	1942	33023	1964
C24	1942	33024	1963
C25	1942	33025	1963
C26	1942	33026	1965
C27	1942	33027	1966
C28	1942	33028	1963
C29	1942	33029	1964
C30	1942	33030	1964
C31	1942	33031	1963
C32	1942	33032	1964
C33	1942	33033	1964
C34	1942	33034	1964
C35	1942	33035	1964
C36	1942	33036	1964
	Brighton		
C37	1942	33037	1963
C38	1942	33038	1964
C39	1942	33039	1964
C40	1942	33040	1964

No. C1 is preserved in the National Collection

Class Q1 No.C1 as built in 1942 (RH side).

Class Q1 No.C1, top view.

WATER : 3700 GALLONS
COAL : 5 TONS.

220 LBS. PER SQ.IN.

Class Q1 0-6-0. (Eastleigh dwg No.SR82)

Class Q1 No.33025 at Eastleigh, May 1948.

Class Q1 No.C18 as built.

MN 'Merchant Navy' class 4-6-2

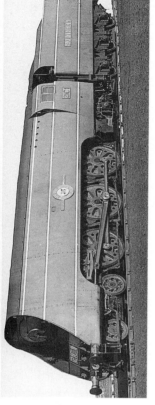

When Mr Bulleid took over from Maunsell, the bulk of the motive power workload was being carried by the 'Lord Nelson', 'Schools', and to a lesser degree, the 'King Arthur' classes, and it soon became apparent that as passenger trains were becoming faster and heavier, newer machines to handle this traffic would be required. This was both a challenge and an opportunity for the new man from the Gresley stable at Doncaster, and after one or two tentative designs, a completely new 4-6-2 'mixed traffic' locomotive was accepted by the Civil Engineer and the Rolling Stock Committee of the Southern Railway in 1938, but restricted to 20 machines. However, war clouds were gathering, and suddenly coal-fired steam engines were the obvious best use of our natural resources, so in October 1939 the Rolling Stock, Locomotive & Electrical Committees, gave way to 30 new engines being constructed. Bulleid tried to keep the innovative design as secret as possible by dividing the preparation work between Brighton, Eastleigh and Ashford in that order.

The heart of any steam locomotive is the boiler, and with the 'Merchant Navy' class, as the new Pacifics were called. Bulleid insisted on a very large modern type fitted with a steel firebox having two thermic syphons and a combustion chamber. The size of this 'steam raiser' was too much for the facilities at Eastleigh and they had to be ordered from the North British Locomotive Co. and pressed for a working pressure of 280lbs. This high pressure enabled three cylinders to be installed, 18in x 24in fed by piston valves of a massive 11in diameter. The main innovation, however, and the one which was to prove the Achilles heel of the design, was the total enclosure of the untried chain-driven radial valve gear, together with the inside connecting rod, crank axle, and crosshead, to form a sort of oil bath commonly used on internal combustion engines. Not only did the chain stretch in service, with dire results to the valve events, but the oil bath leaked down onto the track, causing the engines to slip badly. Another unusual feature was the use of the American style "Box-pox" driving wheels. These were 6ft 2in diameter and were the product of an alliance between Bulleid and Messrs Firth & Brown, a firm of Sheffield steel makers. This avoided paying patent rights, etc. and the wheels became known as the BFB pattern. (They were used also on the Q1 class as previously mentioned.) One of the reasons for the use of these wheels was because a 12% weight saving became effective (see diagram). As a fairly long coupled wheelbase was in

the design, this permitted clasp brakes with two blocks per wheel to be fitted, the braking system being via two steam 8in cylinders which gave a 57 ton pull on the shoes. Again, this preference was because of the weight factor of the engine, as the tender was vacuum braked!

Returning to the large original boilers on the first ten engines, these were 16ft 9¼in in length, tapering from 5ft 9¾in to 6ft 3½in with the first ring tapering underneath, the top being level and the second ring parallel to the firebox, which was 7ft 10½in in length. After the initial ten engines were built, the remaining 20 had slightly different boilers, using ³⁄₃₂in thinner frame plates and with the first ring parallel, and the second ring having the underside taper. This was to save weight in the boiler and lower the water capacity of the boiler. (See diagram.) Three Ross safety valves were fitted on the front ring.

Many people seem to regard these engines as "streamlined"; this was not so, the casing over the lagging was used for easy cleaning, and Bulleid originally wanted the locomotives to follow the pattern of his slab-sided coaching stock. In fact, if one compares the experimental 'boxing-in' of the 'Schools' class, No. 935 Sevenoaks on page 310 with the 'Merchant Navy', it is possible to see the design stemming back from 1939.

There were many other innovations, the describing of which would make this brief description too lengthy, the author would suggest some of the more technical works shown in the bibliography. Suffice it to report that the first ten engines were built at Eastleigh 1941-1942, and the remaining 20 between the years 1944 and 1949. As with any completely new design, there were many shortcomings with the 'Merchant Navys', which showed up in service. The clearance of smoke and steam was a cause of annoyance and many different 'front ends' were tried until the successful pattern evolved. The last twenty engines had changes to their cabs, the side sheets being turned inward for 1ft at the rear to form a slight recess against draughts. Glass windows were fitted in these shields in line with the front windows, and the front of the tender was narrowed so that sighting was improved when reversing.

After the 1948 Nationalisation, and trials in 1947 with No. 21C8 Orient Line, the first twenty engines were fitted with wedge-shaped cab fronts, and the two-section cab side windows were replaced by a wider three-element window set in new cab panels. Another change came about after 1952, when the Ross 'pop' safety valves, which had hitherto been sited on the front boiler ring,

were re-sited between the dome and the firebox, thus avoiding the surge of boiling water through the valves when stopping at stations. (Passengers did not seem to like this downpour and complained bitterly!)

Finally, of course, was the swopping of tenders, as can be seen by the various diagrams, many were the variations of tender attached to these locomotives during service, circumstances often dictating which type and capacity to be used. Eventually, as every enthusiast knows, all 30 'Merchant Navys' were totally rebuilt between 1957 and 1959, but details will appear opposite the drawings of the rebuilds.

Class MN No.21C1 Channel Packet as built in 1941 (LH side).

SR No.	BR No.	Name	Built	Wedge cab fronts fitted	Rebuilt	Withdrawn
21C1	35001	Channel Packet	1941	1950	1959	1964
21C2	35002	Union Castle	1941	1954	1958	1964
21C3	35003	Royal Mail	1941	1950	1959	1967
21C4	35004	Cunard White Star	1941	1950	1958	1965
21C5*	35005*	Canadian Pacific	1941	1950	1959	1965
21C6*	35006*	Peninsular & Oriental S.N. Co.	1941	1951	1959	1964
21C7	35007	Aberdeen Commonwealth	1942	1950	1958	1967
21C8	35008	Orient Line	1942	1947	1957	1967
21C9*	35009*	Shaw Savill	1942	1953	1957	1964
21C10*	35010*	Blue Star	1942	1949	1957	1966
21C11*	35011*	General Steam Navigation	1944	1950	1959	1966
21C12	35012	United States Lines	1945	1949	1957	1967
21C13	35013	Blue Funnel	1945	1952	1956	1967
21C14	35014	Nederland Line	1945	1949	1956	1967
21C15	35015	Rotterdam Lloyd	1945	1949	1958	1964
21C16	35016	Elders Fyffes	1945	1949	1957	1965
21C17	35017	Belgian Marine	1945	1948	1957	1966
21C18*	35018*	British India Line	1945	1948	1956	1964
21C19	35019	French Line C.G.T.	1945	1948	1959	1965
21C20	35020	Bibby Line	1945	1948	1956	1965
	35021	New Zealand Line	1948	1948	1959	1965
	35022*	Holland America Line	1948		1956	1966
	35023	Holland Afrika Line	1948		1957	1967
	35024	East Asiatic Company	1948		1959	1965
	35025*	Brocklebank Line	1948		1956	1964
	35026	Lamport & Holt Line	1948		1957	1967
	35027*	Port Line	1948		1957	1966
	35028*	Clan Line	1948		1959	1967
	35029*	Ellerman Lines	1949		1959	1966
	35030	Elder-Dempster Lines	1949		1958	1967

All built at Eastleigh Works.
No. 35005 fitted with Berkeley stoker 1948-51.
* Preserved. No. 35029 is a sectionalised exhibit in the National Railway Museum.

Class MN No.21C1 *Channel Packet* when new.

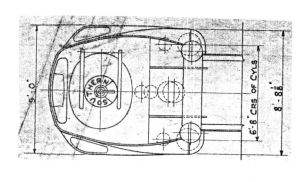

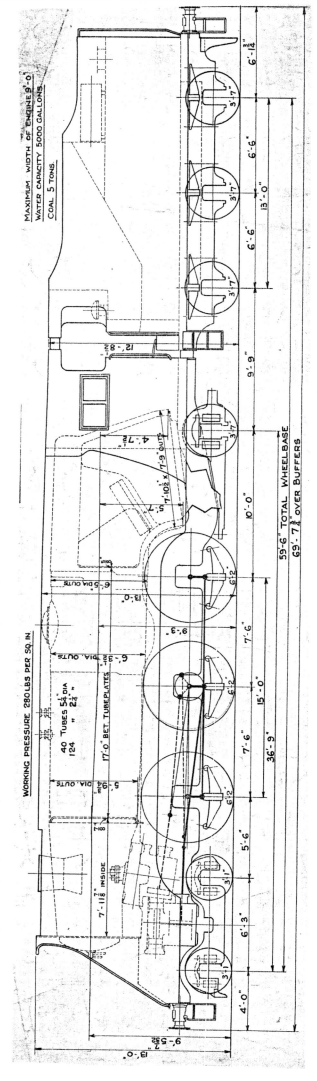

Class MN 4-6-2. (Eastleigh dwg No.SR81)

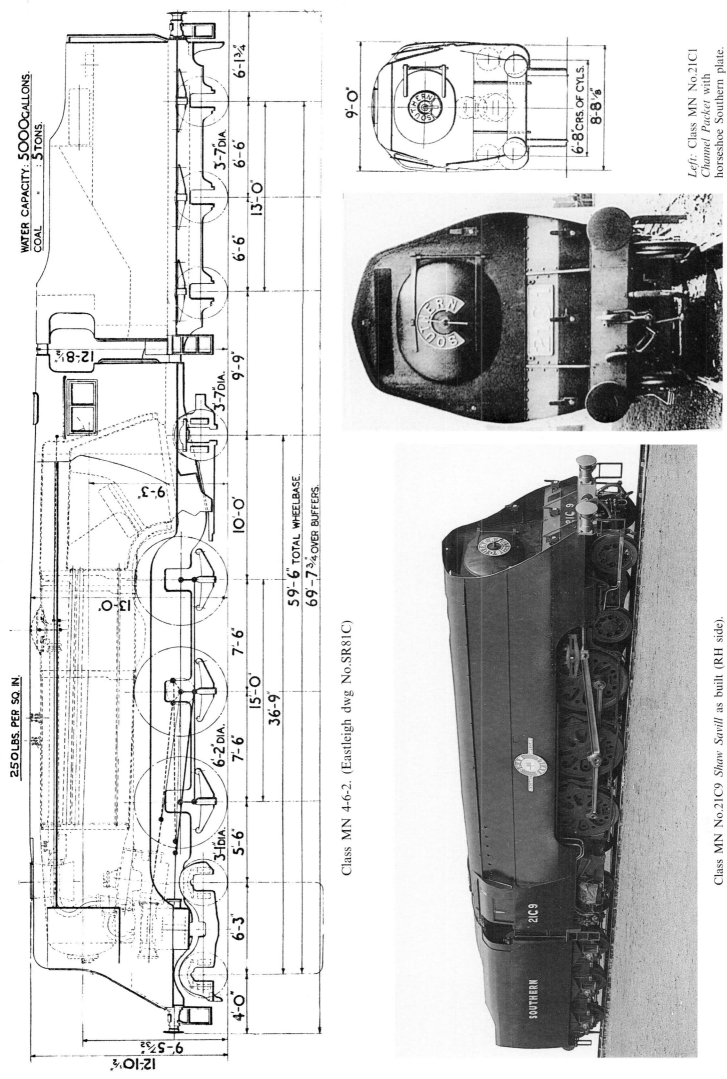

WATER CAPACITY: 5000 GALLONS.
COAL " : 5 TONS.

250 LBS. PER SQ. IN.

12'-8½"

12'-0"

9'-3"

12'-10½"

9'-5 7/32"

4'-0" 6'-3" 5'-6" 7'-6" 7'-6" 10'-0" 9'-9" 6'-6" 13'-0" 6'-6" 6'-1¾"

3'-1" DIA. 6'-2" DIA. 3'-7" DIA. 3'-7" DIA.

15'-0"

36'-9"

59'-6" TOTAL WHEELBASE.

69'-7¾" OVER BUFFERS.

Class MN 4-6-2. (Eastleigh dwg No.SR81C)

9'-0"

6'-8" CRS. OF CYLS.

8'-8⅛"

Left: Class MN No.21C1 *Channel Packet* with horseshoe Southern plate.

Class MN No.21C9 *Shaw Savill* as built (RH side).

WATER CAPACITY 5100 GALLONS
COAL " 5 TONS

280 LBS. PER SQ. IN.

6'-1¾"
3'-7"DIA
6'-6"
13'-0"
6'-6"
11'-2½"
9'-9"
3'-7"DIA
13'-0"
4'-7½"
9'-3"
5'-7"
10'-0"
13'-0"
7'-6"
15'-0"
7'-6"
6'-2"DIA
36'-9"
3'-1"DIA
5'-6"
6'-3"
8'-9/16"
4'-0"
59'-6" TOTAL WHEELBASE
69'-7¾" OVER BUFFERS

Class MN 4-6-2 with 5,100 gallon tender.

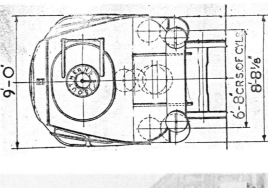

9'-0"
6'-8" CRS. OF CYLS.
8'-8⅛"

Class MN No.21C3 *Royal Mail* with circular Southern plate.

Class MN No.21C7 *Aberdeen Commonwealth.*

Class MN No.35025 *Brocklebank Line* at Wilton.

Class MN No.35021 *New Zealand Line*, left and No.35007 *Aberdeen Commonwealth*, right.

Class MN No.21C19 *French Line C.G.T.* with inverted trough over smokebox.

Class MN No.35011 *General Steam Navigation* heads the Bournemouth Belle.

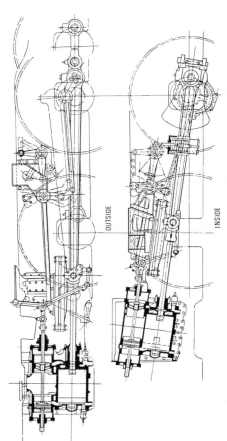

General Arrangement of Bulleid-Firth-Brown driving wheel.

SECTION AA

SECTION BB

SECTION CC

SECTION DD

OUTSIDE

INSIDE

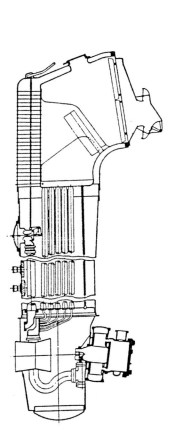

Diagram of Bulleid Pacific boiler.

The 'Merchant Navy' valve gear was of Walschaerts type. In order to cut down the unsprung weight and avoid undue bulk inside the oil bath, Bulleid discarded the use of eccentrics on the crankshaft in favour of a three-throw shaft, driven from the axle by two chains, the longer of which, consisting of 118 links, each 2in in width, was over 11ft in length.

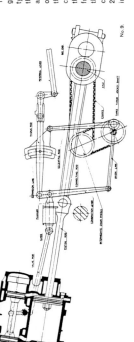

No. 9.

Chain driven valve gear on Merchant Navy class.

VALVE GEAR DESIGNED FOR INSIDE
ADMISSION CONVERTED TO OUTSIDE
ADMISSION BY MEANS OF OPPOSITE
CRANKS ON THE ROCKER SHAFTS.

1. Extreme left-hand valve gear drives middle engine.
2. Second set of valve gear drives left-hand outside cylinder.
3. Third set of valve gear drives right-hand outside cylinder.
4. Chain wheel on main driving axle.
5. Intermediate chain wheels mounted in bracket.
6. Chain wheel driving three-throw jockey shaft.
7. Hanging bracket to offset second valve drive.
8. Both left and right outside cylinder exhaust led back and up into exhaust of middle engine.

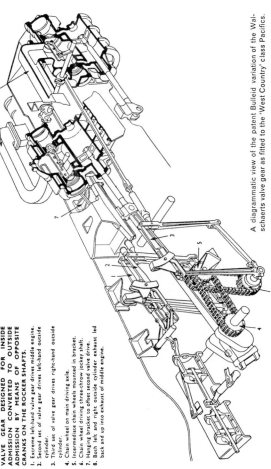

A diagrammatic view of the patent Bulleid variation of the Walschaerts valve gear as fitted to the 'West Country' class Pacifics.

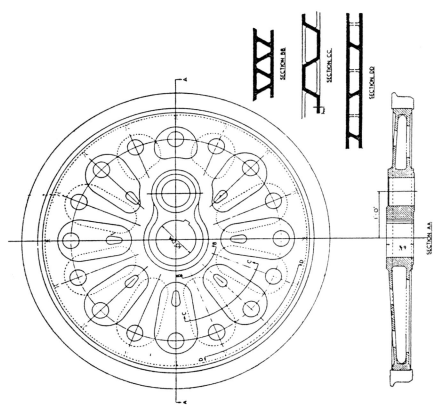

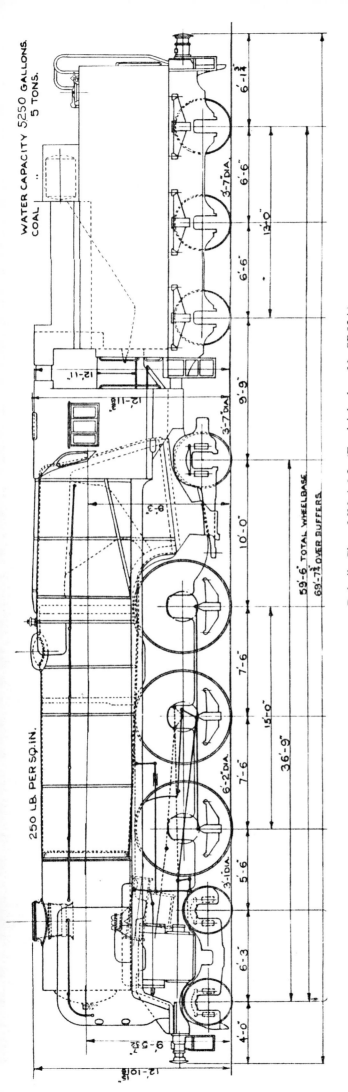

WATER CAPACITY 5250 GALLONS.
COAL 5 TONS.

250 LB. PER SQ.IN.

Rebuilt Class MN 4-6-2. (Eastleigh dwg No.SR92A)

BP 250 LB PER SQ IN

WATER 6000 GALLS

COAL 5 TONS

35018

CYLRS (3) 18" DIA. X 24" STROKE

TOTAL WEIGHT OF ENGINE & TENDER IN WORKING ORDER 151T. 4C

Rebuilt Class MN 4-6-2. Scale 3mm: 1ft

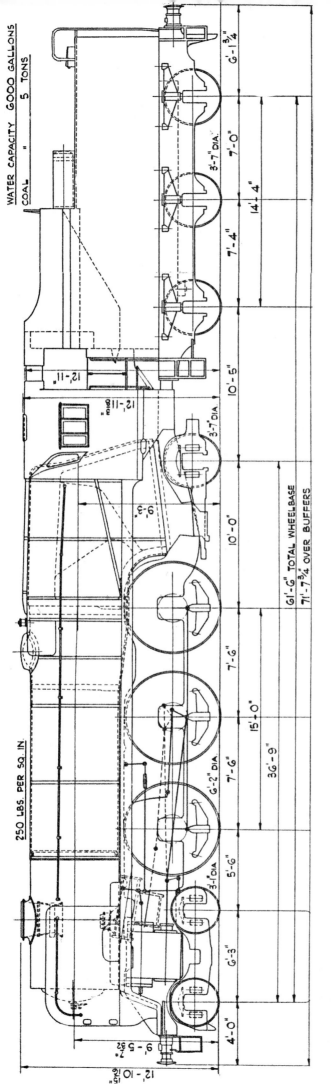

WATER CAPACITY 6000 GALLONS

COAL " 5 TONS

250 LBS. PER SQ. IN.

Rebuilt Class MN 4-6-2 with 6,000 gallon
tender. (Eastleigh dwg No.SR91)

Class MN (Rebuilt). No.35028 Clan Line as
preserved at Longmoor, September 1968.

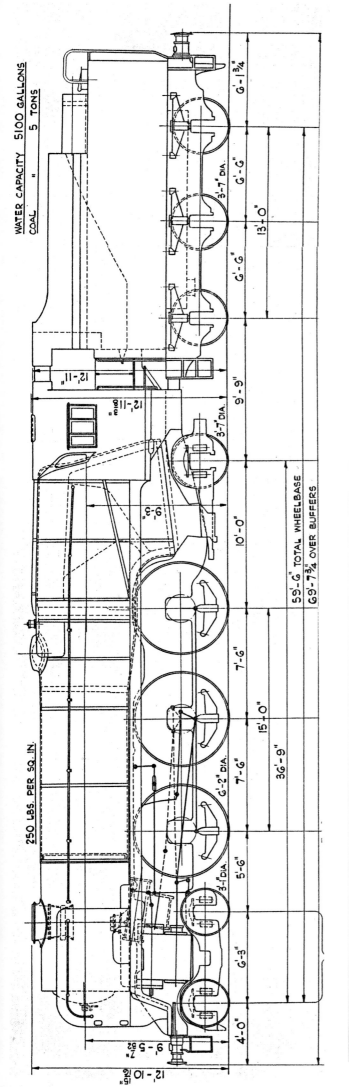

WATER CAPACITY 5100 GALLONS
" COAL " 5 TONS

250 LBS. PER SQ. IN.

59'-6" TOTAL WHEELBASE
69'-7¾" OVER BUFFERS

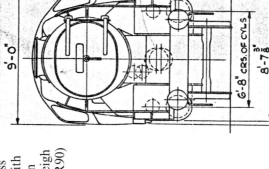

9'-0"
6'-8" CRS.OF CYLS.
8'-7⅞"
8'-11¼"
OVER PLATFORM

Rebuilt Class
MN 4-6-2 with
5,100 gallon
tender. (Eastleigh
dwg No.BRSR90)

Class MN (Rebuilt)
No.35030 Elder-
Dempster lines, at
Tisbury Gates in
August 1958.

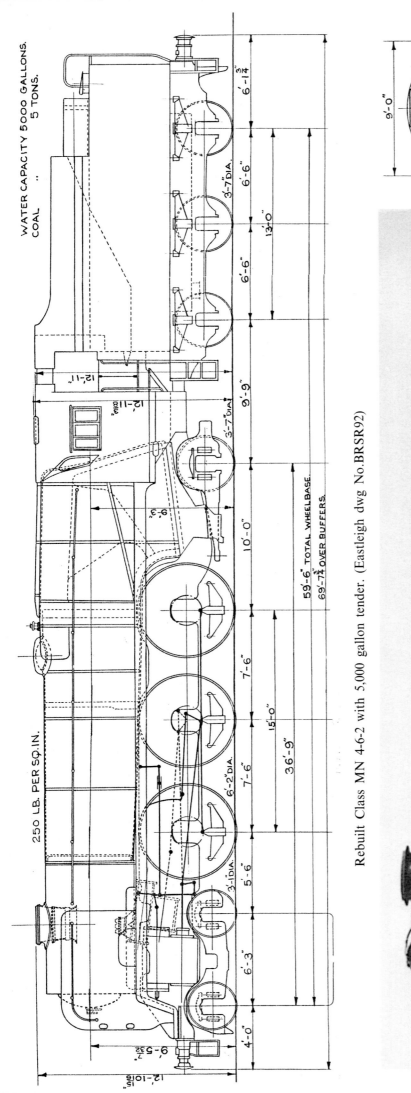

WATER CAPACITY 5000 GALLONS.
COAL .. .. 5 TONS.

250 LB. PER SQ.IN.

12'-11"

12'-11"

3'-7" DIA.

3'-7" DIA.

6'-2" DIA.

3'-1" DIA.

6'-6" 13'-0" 6'-6" 9'-9"

6'-1¾"

10'-0" 7'-6" 15'-0" 7'-6"

36'-9"

59'-6" TOTAL WHEELBASE.
69'-7¾" OVER BUFFERS.

5'-6" 6'-3" 4'-0"

9'-5³²⁄₃₂"

12'-10¹⁵⁄₁₆"

9'-3"

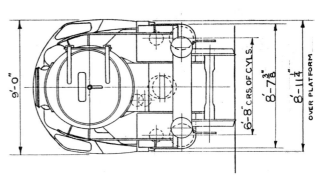

9'-0"

6'-8" CRS. OF CYLS.

8'-7⅜"

8'-11¼"
OVER PLATFORM

35018

Rebuilt Class MN 4-6-2 with 5,000 gallon tender. (Eastleigh dwg No.BRSR92)

WC 'West Country'/BB 'Battle of Britain' class 4-6-2

The success of the 'Merchant Navy' class in traffic and the ability to steam freely, encouraged Bulleid to design a light-weight version of the 'big' Pacifics; a machine which could travel over those sections of the system which were still out of bounds to the MNs. As most of this country was west of Exeter, it was a happy thought to name the class after towns and places in Devon and Cornwall, and as 66 engines were eventually built, this had to be extended to Wiltshire, Somerset and Dorset!

To achieve the route availability, it was necessary to reduce the load on each axle from 21 tons to 18 tons. The width of the cab on the original design trimmed down from 9ft to 8ft 6in for the Hastings line, although it proved an unnecessary alteration, as there was only one recorded occasion when a 'West Country' ever worked over the line.

The batch, Nos 21C101 and 21C170 were so built. In 1948 No. 21C158 *Sir Frederick Pile* was fitted with a 9ft wide 'V'-shaped cab, and similar cabs were fitted to the remainder of the batch as they entered the works. Meanwhile, 'Battle of Britain' class No. 34071 and onwards were built with the new shaped wide cabs and were attached to a 5,500 gallon 9ft wide tender to match.

To the outward appearance, the new light-weights were almost identical to the 'Merchant Navy' class, but under the 'air smoothing' sheets, the boiler, firebox and cylinders were smaller, the three cylinders for instance being 16in x 24in, and the firebox 6ft 11in against the 7ft 10¼in of the MNs.

Following the pattern of the later 'Merchant Navys', the boiler was tapered on the second ring, all of which helped reduce weight and the volume of water carried. Other minor differences included a rocking grate, no dampers to the hopper ash pan, and a smaller tender of 4,500 capacity.

These versatile locomotives proved themselves capable of handling all types of traffic, from the main line expresses right down to heavy freight rosters, and in 1946, after 48 'West Countries' had been put into service, it was decided to build a new series with names commemorating the Battle of Britain. Although more usually referred to as the 'Battle of Britain' class, they were in fact identical to the 'West Country' and were officially classified as such by the SR. These engines, starting at No. 21C149, were built at Brighton from December 1946 onwards, and went up to No. 34090 (BR numbering) plus 34109/10. The 'West Country' class continued to be built by BR from 1949 to 1950, numbers being 34091 to 34108.

SR No.	BR No.	Name	Built	Rebuilt	Withdrawn
21C101	34001	Exeter	1945	1957	1967
21C102	34002	Salisbury	1945	-	1967
21C103	34003	Plymouth	1945	1957	1964
21C104	34004	Yeovil	1945	1958	1967
21C105	34005	Barnstaple	1945	1957	1966
21C106	34006	Bude	1945		1967
21C107	34007*	Wadebridge	1945		1965
21C108	34008	Padstow	1945		1967
21C109	34009	Lyme Regis	1945	1960	1966
21C110	34010*	Sidmouth	1945	1961	1965
21C111	34011	Tavistock	1945	1959	1963
21C112	34012	Launceston	1945		1966
21C113	34013	Okehampton	1945	1958	1967
21C114	34014	Budleigh Salterton	1945	1957	1967
21C115	34015	Exmouth	1945	1958	1965
21C116	34016*	Bodmin	1945		1967
21C117	34017	Ilfracombe	1945	1958	1964
21C118	34018	Axminster	1945	1957	1966
21C119	34019	Bideford	1945	1958	1967
21C120	34020	Seaton	1945		1964
21C121	34021	Dartmoor	1946	1958	1967
21C122	34022	Exmoor	1946	1957	1965
21C123	34023*	Blackmore Vale	1946		1967
21C124	34024	Tamar Valley	1946	1961	1967
21C125	34025	Whimple	1946	1957	1967
21C126	34026	Yes Tor	1946	1958	1966
21C127	34027*	Taw Valley	1946	1957	1964
21C128	34028*	Eddystone	1946	1958	1964
21C129	34029	Lundy	1946	1958	1964
21C130	34030	Watersmeet	1946		1964
21C131	34031	Torrington	1946	1958	1965
21C132	34032	Camelford	1946	1960	1966
21C133	34033	Chard	1946		1965
21C134	34034	Honiton	1946	1960	1967
21C135	34035	Shaftesbury	1946		1963
21C136	34036	Westward Ho	1946	1960	1967
21C137	34037	Clovelly	1946	1958	1967
21C138	34038	Lynton	1946		1966
21C139	34039*	Boscastle	1946	1959	1965
21C140	34040	Crewkerne	1946	1960	1967
21C141	34041	Wilton	1946	-	1966

SR No.	BR No.	Name	Built	Rebuilt	Withdrawn
21C142	34042	Dorchester	1946	1959	1965
21C143	34043	Combe Martin	1946	-	1963
21C144	34044	Woolacombe	1946	1960	1967
21C145	34045	Ottery St. Mary	1946	1958	1964
21C146	34046*	Braunton	1946	1959	1965
21C147	34047	Callington	1946	1958	1967
21C148	34048	Crediton	1946	1959	1966
21C149	34049	Anti-Aircraft Command	1946		1963
21C150	34050	Royal Observer Corps	1946	1958	1965
21C151	34051*	Winston Churchill	1946		1965
21C152	34052	Lord Dowding	1946	1958	1967
21C153	34053*	Sir Keith Park	1947	1958	1965
21C154	34054	Lord Beaverbrook	1947		1964
21C155	34055	Fighter Pilot	1947		1963
21C156	34056	Croydon	1947	1960	1967
21C157	34057	Biggin Hill	1947		1967
21C158	34058*	Sir Frederick Pile	1947	1960	1964
21C159	34059*	Sir Archibald Sinclair	1947	1960	1966
21C160	34060	25 Squadron	1947	1960	1967
21C161	34061	73 Squadron	1947		1964
21C162	34062	17 Squadron	1947	1959	1964
21C163	34063	229 Squadron	1947		1965
21C164	34064	Fighter Command	1947		1966
21C165	34065	Hurricane	1947		1964
21C166	34066	Spitfire	1947		1966
21C167	34067*	Tangmere	1947		1963
21C168	34068	Kenley	1947		1963
21C169	34069	Hawkinge	1947		1963
21C170	34070*	Manston	1947		1964
	34071	601 Squadron	1948	1960	1967
	34072*	257 Squadron	1948		1965
	34073*	249 Squadron	1948	1960	1966
	34074	46 Squadron	1948		1965
	34075	264 Squadron	1948	1960	1967
	34076	41 Squadron	1948		1963
	34077	603 Squadron	1948	1960	1967
	34078	222 Squadron	1948	1958	1967
	34079	141 Squadron	1948		1967
	34080	74 Squadron	1948	1959	1966
	34081*	92 Squadron	1948	1960	1964
	34082	615 Squadron	1948	-	1966

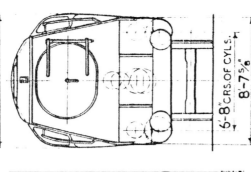

9'-0" 5'-8" CRS. OF CYLS. 8'-7⅝"

Class BB No.21C167 Tangmere as built (RH side).

All built at Brighton Works, except Nos 34095/7/9, 34101/2/4 completed at Eastleigh Works.
21C123/34023 Blackmoor Vale until 1950.
21C125 Rough Tor until 1948.
34071 615 Squadron until 8/1948.
34092 Wells until 1950.
34107 Blandford until 1952.
*Preserved.

SR No.	BR No.	Name	Built	Rebuilt	Withdrawn
	34083	605 Squadron	1948	-	1964
	34084	253 Squadron	1948	-	1965
	34085	501 Squadron	1948	1960	1965
	34086	219 Squadron	1948	-	1966
	34087	145 Squadron	1948	1960	1967
	34088	213 Squadron	1948	1960	1967
	34089	602 Squadron	1948	1960	1967
	34090	Sir Eustace Missenden Southern Railway	1948	1960	1967
	34091	Weymouth	1949	1960	1967
	34092*	City of Wells	1949	-	1964
	34093	Saunton	1949	1960	1964
	34094	Mortehoe	1949	-	1967
	34095	Brentor	1949	1961	1964
	34096	Trevone	1949	1961	1967
	34097	Holsworthy	1949	1961	1964
	34098	Templecombe	1949	1961	1966
	34099	Lynmouth	1949	-	1967
	34100	Appledore	1949	1960	1964
	34101*	Hartland	1949	1960	1966
	34102	Lapford	1950	-	1967
	34103	Calstock	1950	-	1965
	34104	Bere Alston	1950	1961	1967
	34105*	Swanage	1950	-	1964
	34106	Lydford	1950	-	1964
	34107	Blandford Forum	1950	-	1967
	34108	Wincanton	1950	1961	1964
	34109	Sir Trafford Leigh-Mallory	1950	1961	1967
	34110	66 Squadron	1951	-	1963

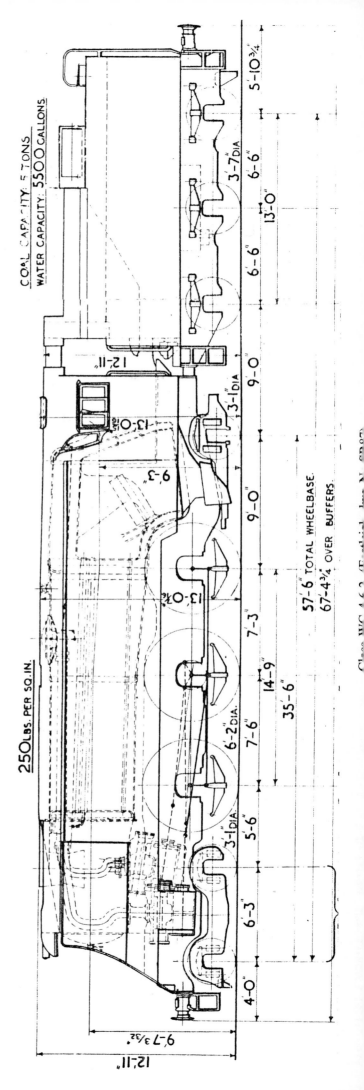

COAL CAPACITY: 5 TONS
WATER CAPACITY: 5500 GALLONS
250 LBS. PER SQ. IN.

57-6 TOTAL WHEELBASE.
67-4¾" OVER BUFFERS.

Class WC 4-6-2 (Tangmere). June N. SR007

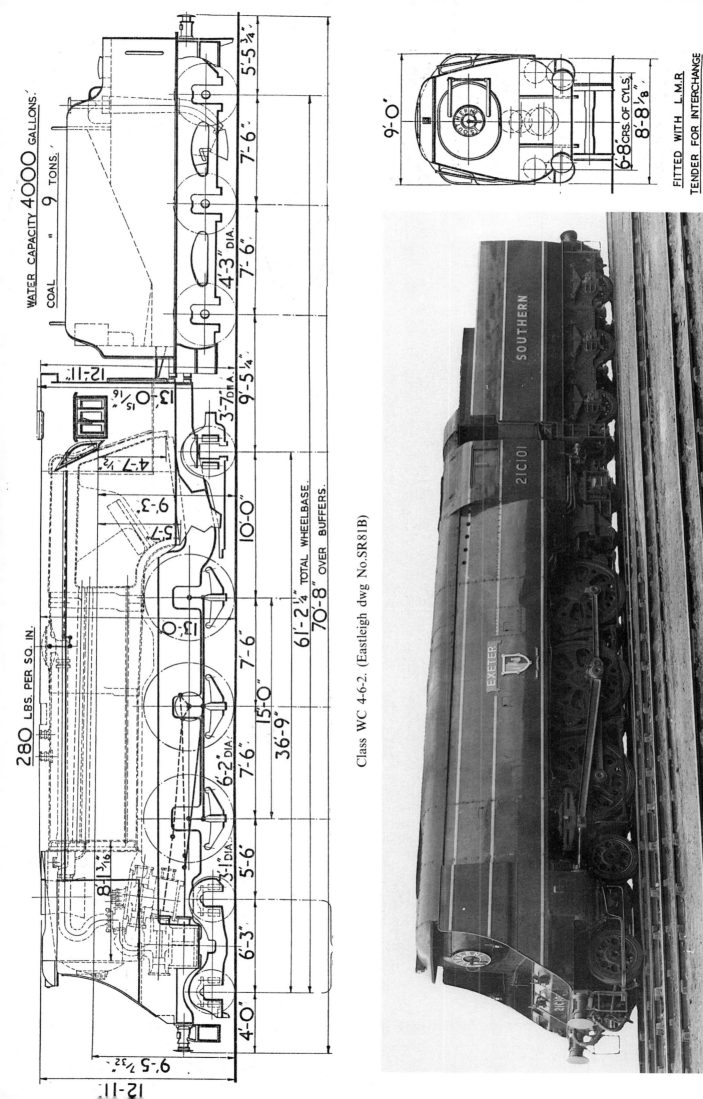

WATER CAPACITY 4000 GALLONS.

COAL " 9 TONS.

280 LBS. PER SQ. IN.

12'-11"

13'-0 15/16"

12'-11"

9'-5 7/32"

4'-3" DIA.

3'-7" DIA.

6'-2" DIA.

3'-1" DIA.

5-5 3/4"

7'-6"

7'-6"

9'-5 1/4"

5-7"

4'-7 1/2"

9'-3"

10'-0"

13'-0"

15'-0"

7'-6"

7'-6"

5'-6"

6'-3"

4'-0"

8'-3/16"

36'-9"

61'-2 1/4" TOTAL WHEELBASE.

70'-8" OVER BUFFERS.

Class WC 4-6-2. (Eastleigh dwg No.SR81B)

9'-0"

9'-0"

SOUTHERN

6'-8" CRS. OF CYLS.

8'-8 1/8"

FITTED WITH L.M.R

TENDER FOR INTERCHANGE

PAGE 327

SOUTHERN

EXETER

21C101

Class WC No.21C101 *Exeter* as built (LH side).

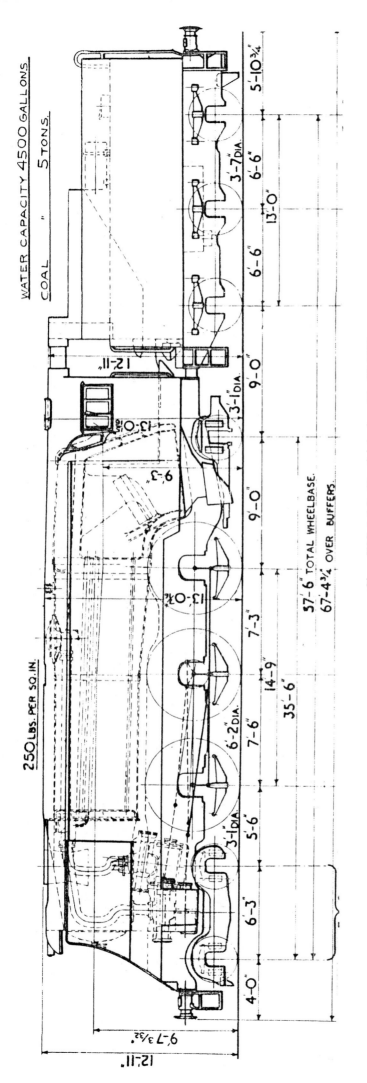

WATER CAPACITY 4500 GALLONS

COAL " 5 TONS.

250 LBS. PER SQ. IN.

5'-10¾"

3'-7" DIA. 6'-6"

13'-0"

6'-6"

12'-11"

9'-0"

3'-1" DIA.

13'-0"

9'-3"

13'-0½"

9'-0"

3'-1" DIA.

7'-3"

14'-9"

6'-2" DIA.

35'-6"

7'-6"

3'-1" DIA.

5'-6"

57'-6" TOTAL WHEELBASE.

67'-4¾" OVER BUFFERS.

6'-3"

4'-0"

9'-7 3/32"

12'-11"

Class WC 4-6-2. (Eastleigh dwg No. SR87B)

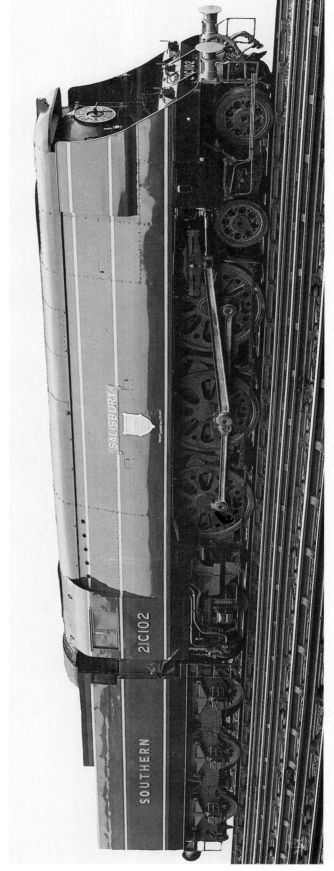

SOUTHERN   21C102   SALISBURY

Class WC No. 21C102 *Salisbury* ex-works (RH side)

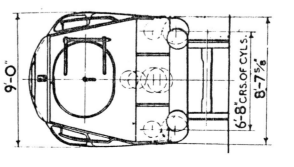

9'-0"

6'-8" CRS. OF CYLS.

8'-7⅝"

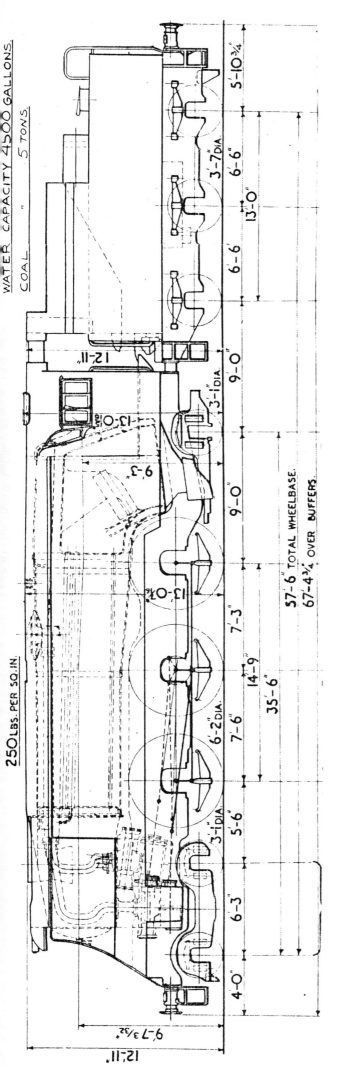

WATER CAPACITY 4500 GALLONS.

COAL   5 TONS.

250 LBS. PER SQ. IN.

12'-11"

9'-7 3/32"

4'-0" | 6'-3" | 5'-6" | 7'-6" | 14'-9" | 7'-3" | 9'-0" | 9'-0" | 6'-6" | 13'-0" | 6'-6" | 5'-10 3/4"

3"DIA. | 6'-2"DIA. | 3"DIA. | 35'-6" | 3"DIA. | 9'-3" | 3'-7"DIA.

13'-0 7/8" | 13'-0 7/8" | 12'-11"

57'-6" TOTAL WHEELBASE.

67'-4 3/4" OVER BUFFERS.

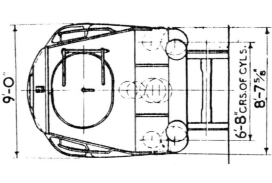

9'-0"

6'-8" CRS. OF CYLS.

8'-7 5/8"

Class WC 4-6-2.
(Eastleigh dwg
No.SR87C)

Class BB No.21C166
Spitfire.

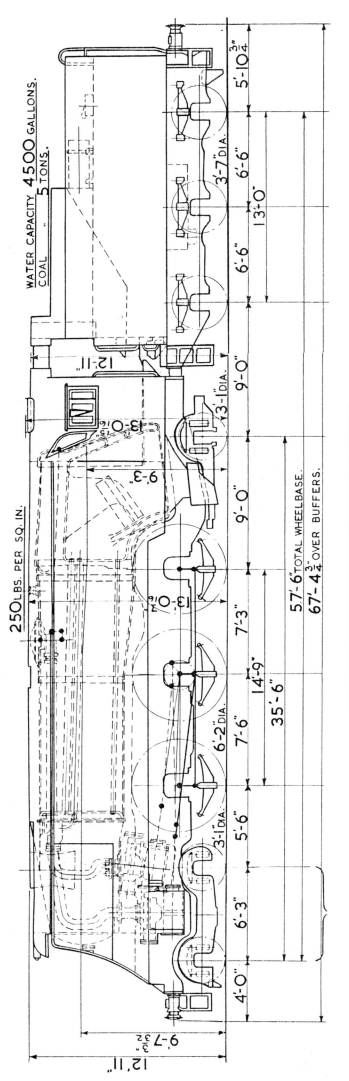

WATER CAPACITY 4500 GALLONS.
COAL " 5 TONS.

250 LBS. PER SQ. IN.

5'-10¼"
3'-7" DIA.
6'-6"
13'-0"
6'-6"
9'-0"
3'-1" DIA.
12'-11"
13'-0⅛"
9'-3"
9'-0"
13'-0⅛"
7'-3"
6'-2" DIA.
14'-9"
7'-6"
35'-6"
57'-6" TOTAL WHEELBASE.
67'-4¾" OVER BUFFERS.
5'-6"
3'-1" DIA.
6'-3"
4'-0"
9'-7³₃²"
12'-11"

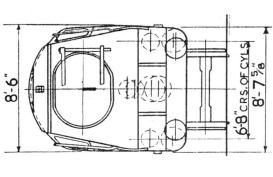

8'-6"
6'8" CRS. OF CYLS
8'-7⅝"

Class WC 4-6-2. (Eastleigh dwg
No.SR83A)

Class BB No.34074 *46 Squadron* on
the Golden Arrow.

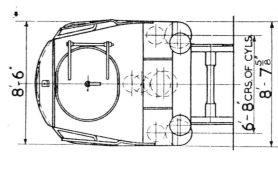

WATER CAPACITY: 4500 GALLONS.
COAL " : 5 TONS.

250 LBS. PER SQ. IN.

8'-6"

6'-8" CRS. OF CYLS
8'-7⅝"

4'-0"   6'-3"   5'-6"   7'-6"   7'-3"   9'-0"   9'-0"   6'-6"   6'-6"   5'-10¾"

3'-1" DIA   6'-2" DIA   3'-1" DIA   3'-1" DIA   3'-7" DIA

35'-6"
14'-9"
13'-0"

57'-6" TOTAL WHEELBASE
67'-4¾" OVER BUFFERS

12'-11"   12'-11"
9'-7³⁄₃₂"
13'-0"   13'-0⁷⁄₁₆"
9'-3"

Class WC 4-6-2. (Eastleigh dwg No.SR83C)

Class WC No.21C133 *Chard* at Brighton in June 1946.

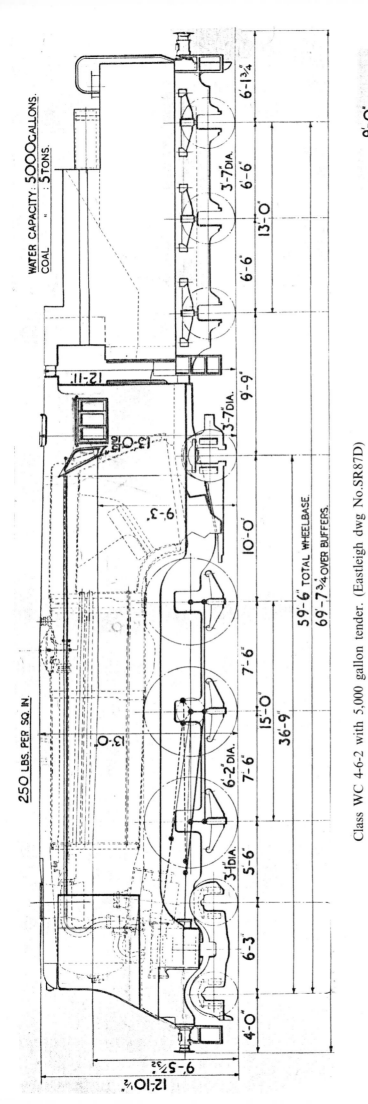

WATER CAPACITY: 5000 GALLONS.
COAL   : 5 TONS.

250 LBS. PER SQ. IN.

Class WC 4-6-2 with 5,000 gallon tender. (Eastleigh dwg No.SR87D)

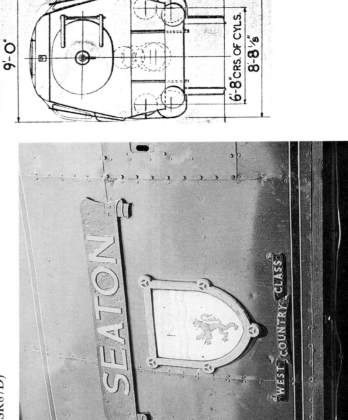

Class WC nameplate of No.34020 Seaton.

Class BB No.34067 Tangmere at Yeovil in 1963.

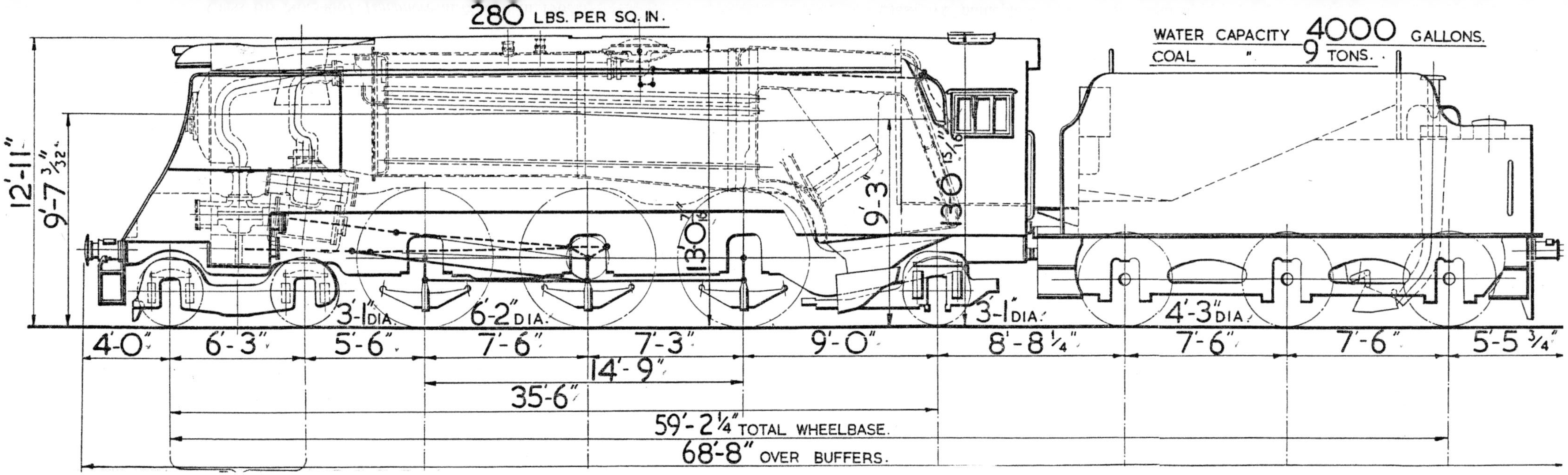

WATER CAPACITY **4000** GALLONS.

" COAL **9** TONS.

280 LBS. PER SQ. IN.

5-5¾

7-6

4-3 DIA.

7-6

8-8¼

3-1 DIA.

9-0

13'0 15/16"

9-3

13'0"

7-3

14-9

6-2 DIA.

7-6

35-6

3-1 DIA.

5-6

59-2¼ TOTAL WHEELBASE.

68-8 OVER BUFFERS.

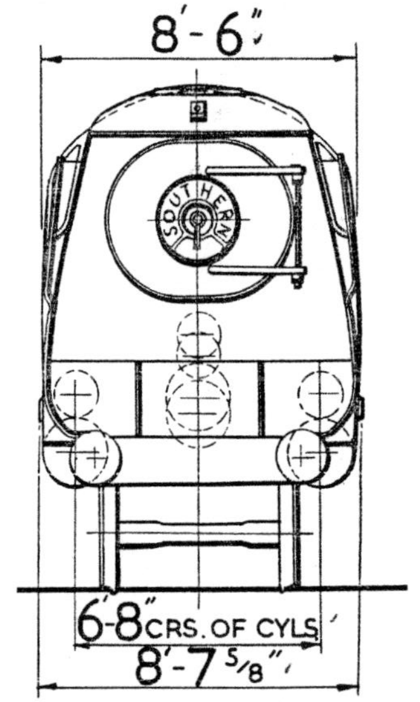

6-3

4-0

9-7 3/32"

12-11"

Class WC 4-6-2 with 4,000 gallon tender. (Eastleigh dwg No.SR83A)

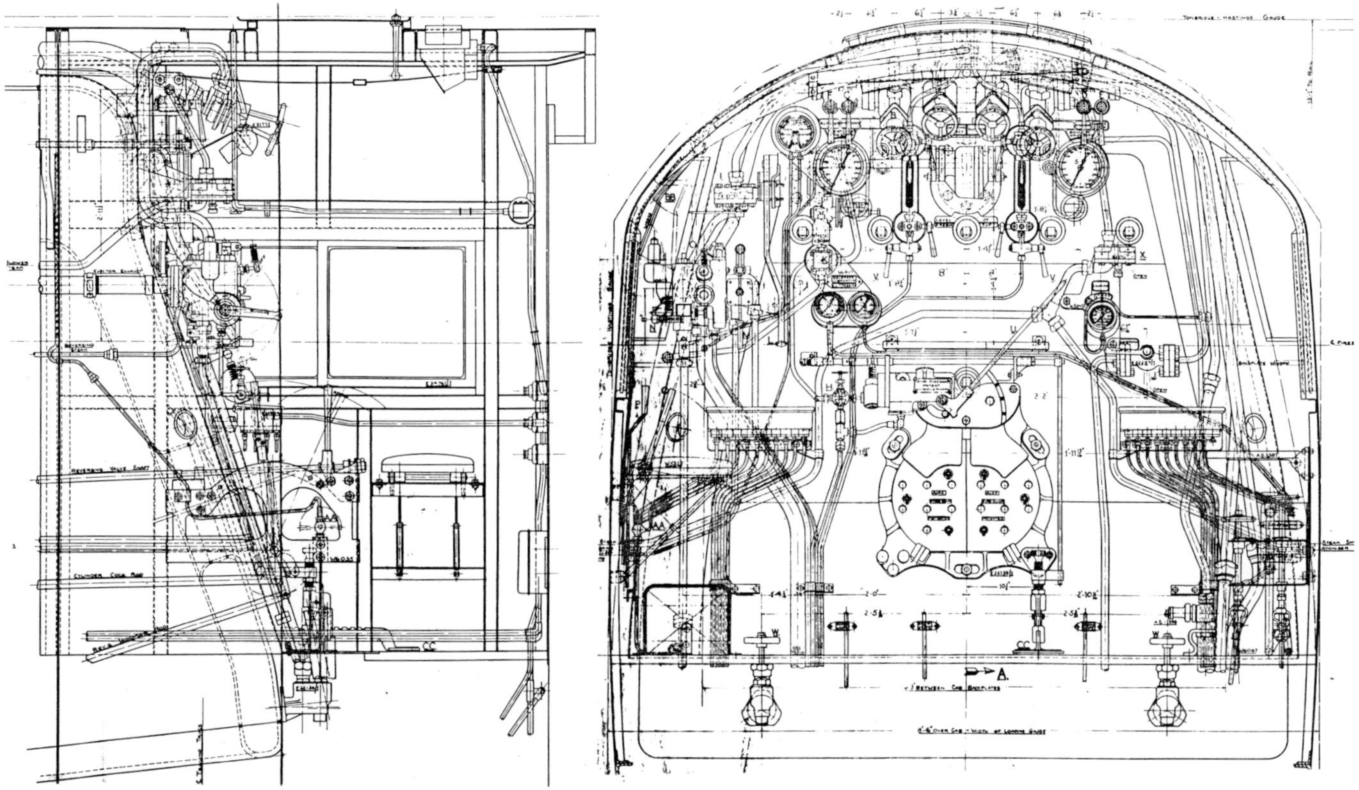

8-6"

SOUTHERN

6-8 CRS. OF CYLS.

8-7 5/8"

FITTED WITH L.M.R.
TENDER FOR INTERCHANGE
TRIALS.

Class WC 4-6-2 General
Arrangement of cab
controls.

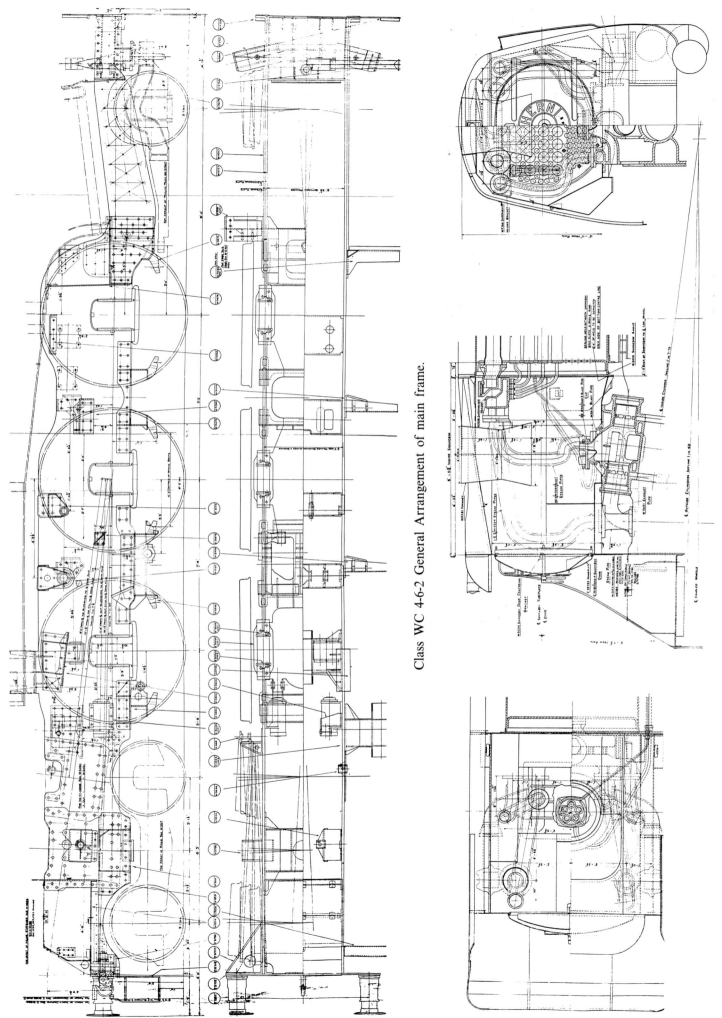

Class WC 4-6-2 General Arrangement of main frame.

Class WC 4-6-2 General Arrangement of smokebox.

Rebuilds of 'Merchant Navy' and 'West Country'/'Battle of Britain' class 4-6-2s

During 1955, BR decided to rebuild the Bulleid Pacifics, in an attempt to reduce fuel, water and oil consumption, and to make servicing of these engines easier on shed. It was quite a massive reconstruction, resulting in a new inside cylinder with inside admission, and with the steam chest off to the right-hand side. The outside cylinders had outside admission, and to retain these, a suspension rod had to be used, with a connecting link between the valve spindle and the radius rod; this obviated the need for valve spindle guides. The notorious oil bath enclosed inside motion was replaced by Walschaerts valve gear operating each of the three piston valves.

As the outer 'air smoothed' casing was removed, so a new smokebox of cylindrical shape resting on a saddle, which itself was part of the inside cylinder casing, was fitted. But perhaps surprisingly, the distinctive oval smokebox door was retained. To help with shed maintenance, a running plate was attached to the frames by brackets,

look. The Bulleid steam reverser was exchanged for a normal screw-type gear at the driver's hand. Cylinder and steam chest lubrication was effected by three mechanical lubricators, two on the left-hand running plate and one on the right, which had a large 10-feed oiler for the axle boxes, crossheads and slide-bars, etc. The boiler pressure was reduced to 250lbs, but this did not seem to affect performance, as seldom was the full 280lbs pressure maintained.

Where the cabs of the 'lightweights' were only 8ft 6in, the opportunity was taken upon rebuilding to push out the width to 9ft, as with the 'Merchant Navys'.

The first engine to be so reconstructed was No. 35018 *British India Line* in 1956, and after 15 others had been dealt with similarly, the first 'West Country', No. 34005 *Barnstaple*, appeared in 1957 as 'modified'. Altogether, 60 'lightweights' were rebuilt, and all 30 of the 'Merchant Navy' class. The summary under each class gives full details. (Personally, I thought they were magnificent locomotives when 'unfrocked'; and more than capable for any task allotted to them.)

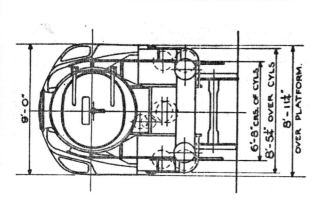

Class BB No.34051 *Winston Churchill*.

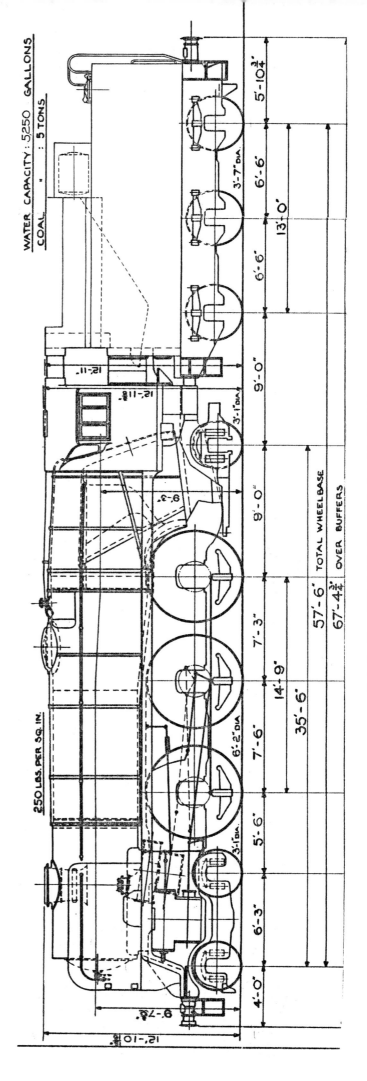

WATER CAPACITY: 5250 GALLONS

COAL " : 5 TONS

250 LBS. PER SQ. IN.

Rebuilt Class WC 4-6-2. (Eastleigh dwg No.SR93A)

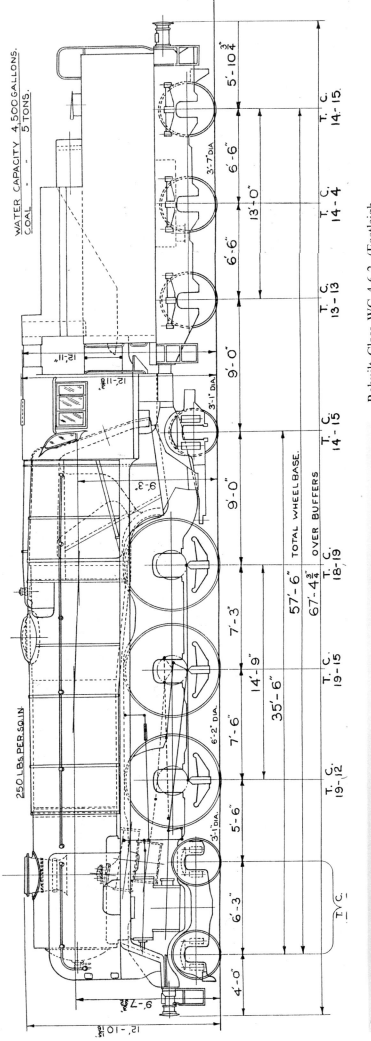

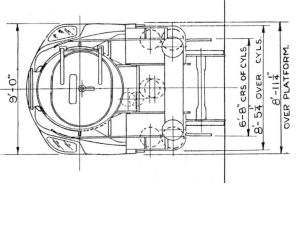

WATER CAPACITY 4,500 GALLONS.
COAL " " 5 TONS.

250 LBS. PER. SQ.IN.

5'-10¾"

3'-7" DIA.

6'-6"

6'-6"

13'-0"

9'-0"

12'-11"

3'-1" DIA.

9'-3"

3'-1" DIA.

6'-2" DIA.

9'-0"

57'-6" TOTAL WHEELBASE.

67'-4¾" OVER BUFFERS

7'-3"

14'-9"

35'-6"

7'-6"

5'-6"

6'-3"

4'-0"

9'-7"

12'-10"

T.C. 14-15

T.C. 14-4

T.C. 13-13

T.C. 14-15

T.C. 18-19

T.C. 19-15

T.C. 19-12

T.C.

9'-0"

6'-8" CRS. OF CYLS.
8'-5¼" OVER CYLS.
8'-11¼" OVER PLATFORM.

Rebuilt Class WC 4-6-2. (Eastleigh dwg No.SR94)

Class WC (Rebuilt) No.34005
Barnstaple at Dover, August 1957
(L.H. side)

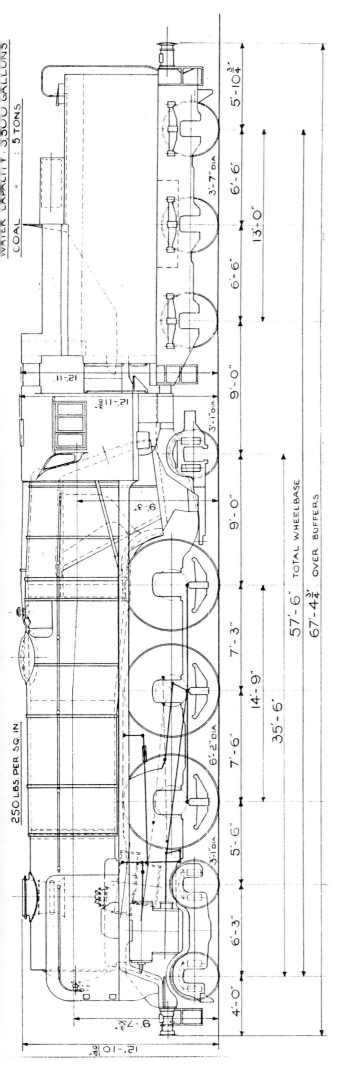

WATER CAPACITY: 5500 GALLONS

COAL " : 5 TONS

250 LBS. PER SQ. IN.

12'-10⅙"

9'-7¾"

4'-0" | 5'-6" | 7'-6" | 7'-3" | 9'-0"

14'-9"

35'-6"

57'-6" TOTAL WHEELBASE

67'-4¾" OVER BUFFERS

3'-1"DIA | 6'-2" DIA | 3'-1"DIA

9'-3"

12'-11"

12'-11⅝"

3'-1"DIA

9'-0" | 6'-6" | 6'-6"

13'-0"

3'-7" DIA

5'-10¾"

Rebuilt Class WC 4-6-2.

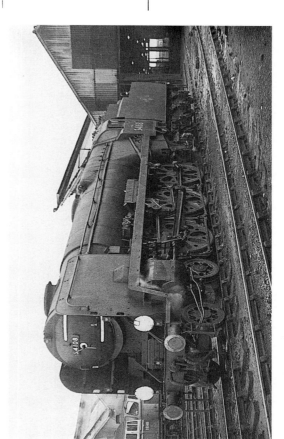

9'-0"

6'-8" CRS. OF CYLS

8'-5¼" OVER CYLS

8'-11¼" OVER PLATFORM

Class WC (Rebuilt) No.34108 *Wincanton* at Eastleigh.

Class BB (Rebuilt) No.34087 *145 Squadron* (RH side).

USA class 0-6-0T

At the end of the Second World War in 1945, the engines which were allotted to the Docks Department at Southampton, were in desperate need of major repairs and new boilers. The cost had escalated rapidly and the time factor for the rebuilding had stretched to approximately 18 months. With these stark facts in front of him, Bulleid had to look elsewhere for immediate replacements. They were eventually found at an American dump of war surplus items set within Newbury Race Course! It was in this unlikely place that Bulleid and his fitters located the 0-6-0 short wheelbase tank engines, which had been built in America by two locomotive firms, Messrs Porter and Messrs Vulcan Iron Works. These locomotives were in excellent condition, having done little or no work since being shipped to the UK. No. 4326 was taken in April of 1946 and put on trials around Southampton Docks. Successfully doing all that the B4s had done and more, so a further 13 were purchased at £2,500 each.

It was found that there were several structural differences between the Porter engines and the Vulcans, so in order to achieve a modicum of standardisation, Bulleid tried to obtain all 14 machines of one manufacturer, namely Vulcan. However, only 13 were available, which left the Southern Railway with one Porter and 13 Vulcans. To be sure of spares for the odd Porter, one extra engine built by Porter, was purchased but not taken into running stock, being kept for spares and was cannibalised.

These dock tanks were sturdy, compact little machines with the usual American bar frames, sandboxes sited on the top of the boiler, large roomy cabs and side tanks situated well clear of the motion, which was Walschaerts gear, working from the trailing driving wheels on to piston valves on top of the 16½in x 24in outside cylinders.

Several additions and modifications were necessary before these engines took over their rosters at the docks, such as sliding cab windows, lamp irons, vacuum ejectors, etc. Regulators were exchanged for English types, ventilators were put in the cab roofs, as with the firebox extending back into the cab, things became rather hot just moving slowly around the quays. The round, cab front and rear windows were changed to large rectangular style, three in front, and two at the rear, and the coal space was increased to carry 1½tons of coal, an extra 10cwt.

A few dimensions are as follows:

Six coupled wheels of 4ft 6in diameter on a wheelbase of 10ft. Boiler 4ft 4in x 9ft 4½in. Firebox 5ft 6in. Pressure 210lb. Water capacity 1,000 gallons. Total weight 46½ tons.

The USA tanks worked on at the docks until 1962, when they were ousted by the Ruston & Hornsby 275hp diesels. Some were withdrawn, while others went to various departmental depots. It was a nice gesture in 1963 to name two of the class after Southern engineers. Ex-No. 65, BR No. 30065, Dept.No. DS237, was painted malachite green and named *Maunsell*, whilst Ex-No. 70, BR No. 30070, Dept. No. DS238, was also given the green livery and named *Wainwright*.

SR No.	WD No.	Departmental No.	Builder & No.	Date built	Date to service	Withdrawn
61	1264	DS233	Porter 7420	1942	1947	1967
62	1277	DS234	Vulcan 4375	1942	1947	1967
63	1284	-	Vulcan 4382	1942	1947	1962
64*	1959	-	Vulcan 4432	1942	1947	1967
65*	1968	DS237	Vulcan 4441	1943	1947	1967
66	1279	DS235	Vulcan 4377	1942	1947	1965
67	1282	-	Vulcan 4380	1942	1947	1967
68	1971	-	Vulcan 4444	1943	1947	1964
69	1952	-	Vulcan 4425	1943	1947	1967
70*	1960	DS238	Vulcan 4433	1943	1947	1967
71	1966	-	Vulcan 4439	1943	1947	1967
72*	1973	-	Vulcan 4446	1943	1947	1967
73	1974	-	Vulcan 4447	1943	1947	1966
74 (A)	4326	DS236	Vulcan 4488	1943	1946	1965
- (B)	1261	-	Porter 7417	1942	-	-

No. 74 worked as No. 4326 from 18/5/46 until 16/10/48 when it entered Eastleigh Works for repair. It re-entered traffic as British Railways No. 30074 on 11th November 1948, therefore its Southern Railway number was never carried.

WD No. 1261 not taken into stock; dismantled for spares.

*Preserved

(A Yugoslavian-built example was imported for preservation on the Swanage Railway, 12/90.)

Class USA No 69 as bought and still numbered 1952. In Eastleigh Works, 1947

Class USA No 62 at Southampton Docks in 1947

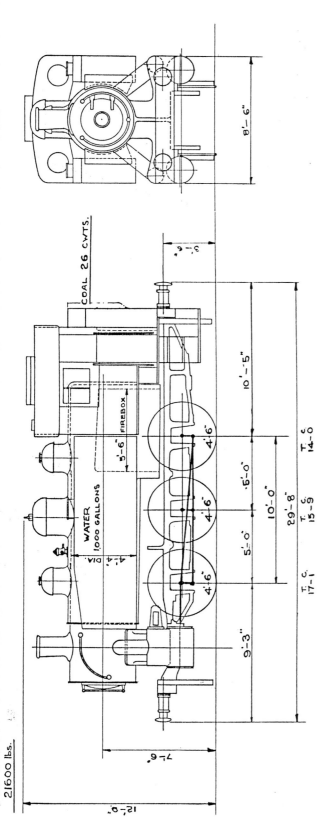

21600 lbs.

COAL 26 CWTS.

WATER
1,000 GALLONS

4'-1" DIA.

FIREBOX

5'-6"

9'-3"

4'-6"

5'-0"

10'-0"

29'-8"

4'-6"

4'-6"

10'-5"

5'-0"

4'-6"

T.C.
17-1

T.C.
15-9

T.C.
14-0

8'-6"

3'-6"

12'-0"

7'-6"

Class USA 0-6-0T. (Eastleigh dwg No. SR84)

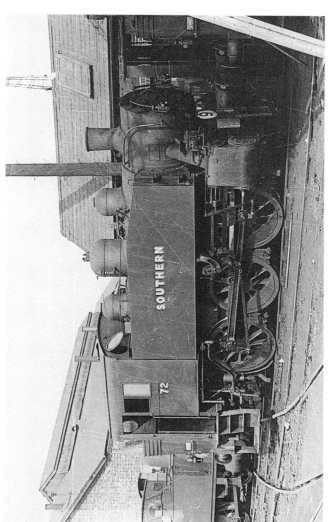

Class USA No.72, Southampton Docks, 1947.

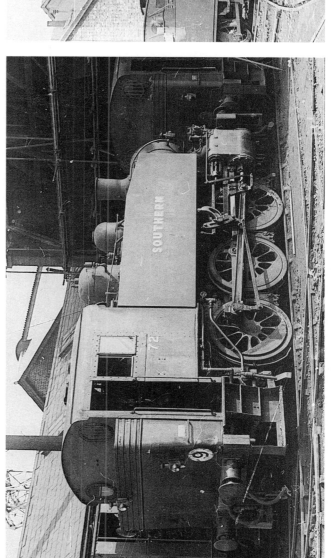

Class USA No.72, Southampton Docks, 1947 (RH side).

0-6-0 diesel-electric

As mentioned in the text for the Z class steam shunting engines, Maunsell decided in 1936 to experiment with internal-combustion locomotives for service in marshalling yards on the Southern system. He obtained sanction to purchase three six-wheel coupled units for trials in comparison with the Z class 0-8-0Ts.

However, at this time, no manufacturer could promise delivery before 1939, but the English Electric Co. Ltd. offered to supply just the power units only by July 1937, if the railway shops could provide and erect the body, cabs and framing, etc. themselves. This was carried out at Ashford, and the shells sent to the Preston works of English Electric for completion.

Delivery of the first two locomotives was in August of 1937 and the third followed in September. The trio were numbered in a special diesel-electric shunter list, becoming Nos 1, 2 and 3. The power unit consisted of two English Electric 6K assemblies, with six cylinders 10in x 12in. Coupled wheels were 4ft 6in diameter and the gearing was single reduction, output being 350bhp at 680 revs per minute.

Nos 1, 2 and 3 were engaged in shunting at Norwood, where they performed a continuous stint of 142 hours every week, as well as some trial runs on short distance London freight services. They must have proved their worth as Bulleid was ready to order eight more in 1939, but the outbreak of the war prevented this order going through. The first three did their war work on the Martin Mill Military Railway in the Dover area. All three entered BR stock at the Nationalisation and became Nos 15201, 15202 and 15203, the two latter engines spending a couple of years shunting at Old Oak Common on the Western Region. They were finally withdrawn in 1964.

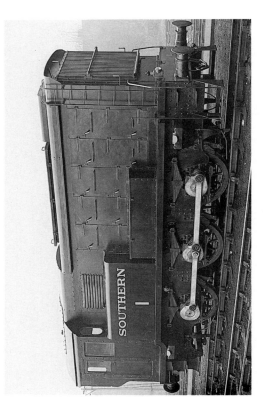

Class DE No.2 (RH side).

Class DE No.1 when new.

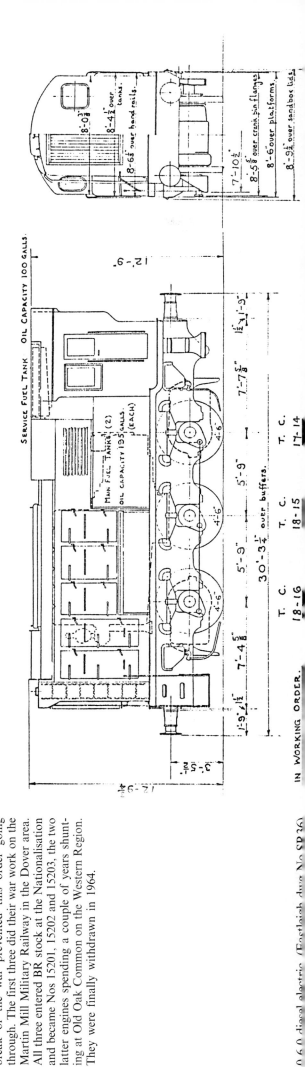

0-6-0 diesel-electric (Eastleigh dwg No SB 36).

Co-Co electric (BR Class 70)

As it is my intention to place on record as many types of Southern Railway locomotives as possible, mention must be made of the three large electric locomotives, designed jointly by Bulleid and the electrical engineer, Alfred Raworth. The need was for a long electric locomotive, which could spread over the third rail gaps which often occurred at the end of platforms. At the beginning of the war, only multiple-unit electric trains could span these gaps, so Bulleid and Raworth, not the most compatible of men, shelved their differences, and produced a 56ft 9in long box-like body mounted on two six-wheeled powered bogies (shades of the 'Leader'!).

Mr Raworth was responsible for the electrical side, which consisted of English Electric 245hp motors driving each axle through 65/17 gearing. These motors were supplied with current through a booster set, which was an electric motor of 600 volts coupled to a 600 volt generator. Between these two machines was a heavy flywheel which stored enough energy to carry the unit over the rail gaps. An emergency bank of batteries, and the control system, was supplied with electricity by another motor-generator slung below the under-

framing. An overhead pantograph was fitted centrally on the roof so that the engine could be used where the third rail was substituted for overhead wires. Bulleid's contribution was the body, frame, and running gear, the body having a cab at either end with duplicated control gear, and a central compartment which housed a boiler with electrical elements to supply steam for carriage heating, as well as other control equipment. The special six-wheeled bogies had no central pivot, this being replaced by four quadrants, two over the bogie frames and two over the outer axles. (This design was later used on the 'Leader' class). The bogie wheels were 3ft 6in diameter and of the BFB pattern as used on the Bulleid Pacifics.

When it is remembered that trials showed this locomotive could handle 1,000 ton freights and 750 ton passenger trains at speeds up to 75 mph and this in 1941, it can hardly be looked upon as a failure. Originally numbered CC1 in 1941, an improved version appeared in 1943 numbered CC2 and in 1948 a third, larger and more powerful machine appeared which took its BR number 20003. This is the 58ft 3in locomotive shown in the drawing. At the same time, Nos CC1 and CC2 were renumbered 20001 and 20002 respectively.

Electric locomotive No.CC2 at Eastleigh in 1948.

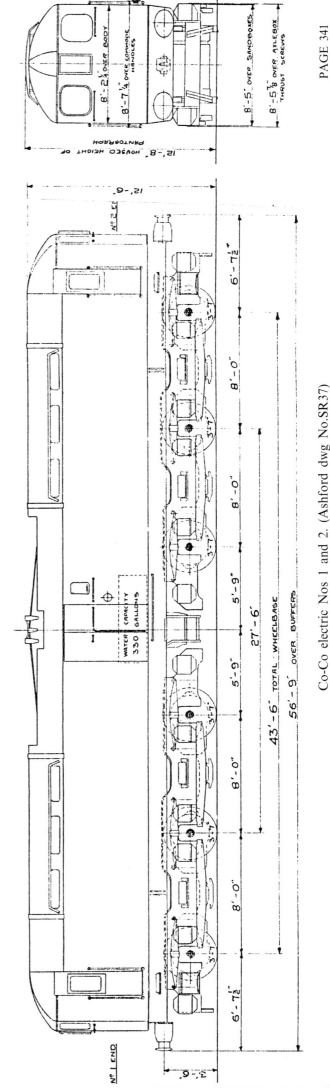

CLASS CC N⁰ˢ I & 2

SOUTHERN RAILWAY
Co.-Co. ELECTRIC LOCOMOTIVE

Co-Co electric Nos 1 and 2. (Ashford dwg No.SR37)

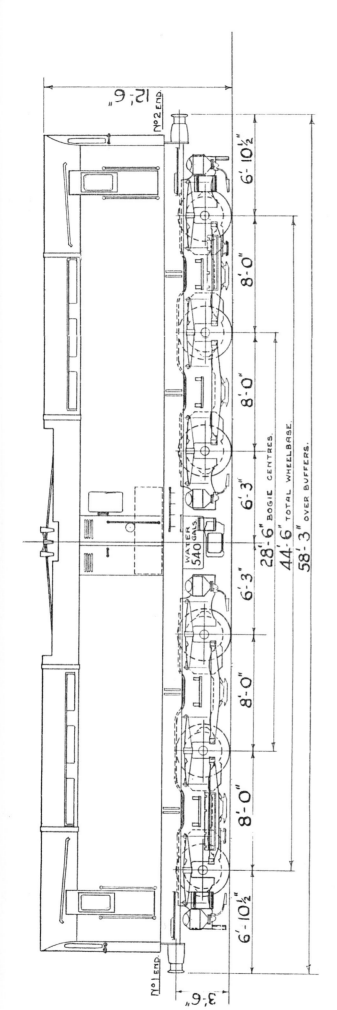

No 2 END.
No 1 END.

12'-6"
3'-6"

6'-10½" 8'-0" 8'-0" 6'-3" 6'-3" 8'-0" 8'-0" 6'-10½"

WATER
540 GALS.

28'-6" BOGIE CENTRES.

44'-6" TOTAL WHEELBASE.

58'-3" OVER BUFFERS.

Co-Co electric No.3.
(Ashford dwg
No.A9043)

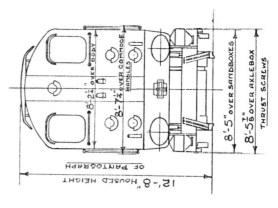

8'-2¼" OVER BODY
8'-7¾" OVER COMMODE HANDLES
8'-5" OVER SANDBOXES
8'-5⅛" OVER AXLEBOX THRUST SCREWS
12'-8" HOUSED HEIGHT
OF PANTOGRAPH

Electric locomotive
No.20003 at Newhaven
Harbour, July 1953

'Leader' class 0-6-6-0

In 1946 Bulleid addressed the Institution of Mechanical Engineers and declared that the ideal steam locomotive should have ten major requirements, and they are worth quoting:

1 To be able to run over the majority of the Company's lines.

2 To be capable of working all classes of trains up to 90 mph.

3 To have its whole weight available for braking and the highest possible percentage thereof for adhesion.

4 To be equally suitable for running in both directions without turning, with unobstructed lookout.

5 To be ready for service at short notice.

6 To be almost continuously available.

7 To be suitable for complete "common use".

8 To run not less than 100,000 miles between general overhauls with little or no attention at the running sheds.

9 To cause minimum wear and tear to the track.

10 To use substantially less fuel and water per drawbar horsepower developed.

He then calmly announced that such a new machine had already been designed for the Southern, and authorisation for the first five of a class of 35 had been given. This then was the first indication of the 'Leader' class, which was to be constructed, hopefully fulfilling all the above features. Breaking completely new ground, this locomotive was to be carried on two six-wheeled bogies, both of which were powered, being something akin to a 0-6-0 + 0-6-0 Garratt, which would fulfil items 3 and 9 above.

The middle axle of each bogie was to be driven by a double-acting 3-cylinder engine and the three axles of each bogie were coupled by rocker chains, all of which was totally enclosed in an oil bath; even the bogie springs were enclosed in a sort of oil tank. These two massive bogies, with their hollow side frames, did not have the usual central pivot, but were attached to the main frame by quadrant, similar to a military tank gun turret. The long main frame supported the usual Pacific style of smokebox, boiler and firebox, but all offset to the right-hand side of the engine, as was the firehole in the back plate. This enabled a corridor to run down the whole length of the engine, connecting each driving cab at the ends with the fireman's work space in the middle. The off-setting caused much trouble, as one side of the locomotive was ten tons heavier than the other, ballast weights were placed in the corridor to balance things, but imagine what this did for accessibility! Of course, Bulleid had always believed that oil firing would become the order of the day, and in the 'Leader', control of the oil jets from either of the end driving cabs would have eliminated the awful roasting the unlucky fireman of this engine had to endure. (Modellers should note that the fireman's door and window were only on the left-hand side of the machine).

The 3-cylinder engines mounted on each bogie, gave direct drive to the middle axles which were three-throw and solid forged. The cylinders were steam jacketed, and steam was supplied and exhausted by sleeve valves. This system had been tested in 1947 by Bulleid on No. 2039 *Hartland Point*, one of the ex-LBSCR Marsh Atlantics. It was never a resounding success, however, and eventually was the Achilles heel of the 'Leader' locomotive. It all sounds very simple in these few words, but in fact, it was a very complicated arrangement, good in theory, but subject to breakdowns in practice.

This 'swan song' of Bulleid was, without doubt, a brilliant design, but its chances of success were ruined by being rushed into production before Nationalisation, and by lack of enthusiasm of BR in denying the long-term trials to iron out the 'bugs'. I think it could have done all that its creator hoped for, given the chance.

Receiving the BR number of 36001 the 'Leader' started its trials in June 1949, but in November of the same year orders were issued to stop work on the other four machines, Nos 36002 to 36005, even though No. 36002 was only 48 hours from completion! Trials carried on with No. 36001 until November 1950, when it was abandoned at Eastleigh in the open air; Nos 36002 and 36003 were broken up at Brighton.

Some dimensions are as follows:

Overall length..67ft
Working weight.................................130 tons
Water capacity..........................2,500 gallons
Coal capacity.......................................3 tons
Boiler pressure..................280lbs per sq in
Wheels, 12 (six to each bogie)....5ft lin diameter
Cylinders, six (three to each bogie)......12¼in x 15in
Tractive effort 85%.........................26,300lb

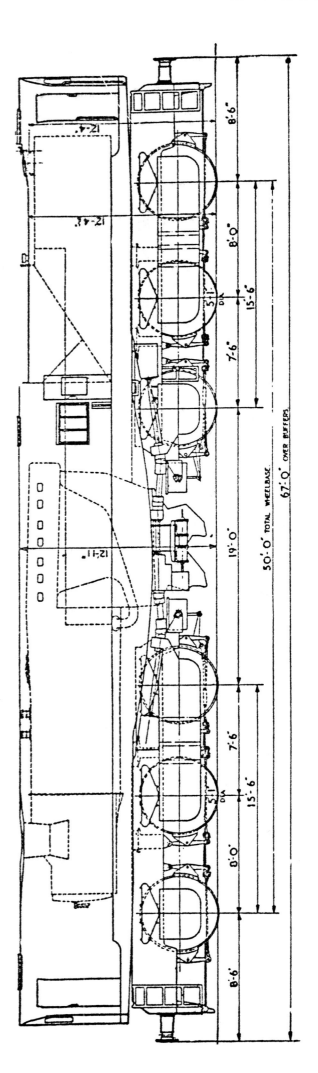

Class 'Leader'.

Class 'Leader' General Arrangement of frame and quadrants.

Class 'Leader' No.36001 on a test train at Eastleigh, August 1950.

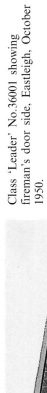

Class 'Leader' No.36001 showing fireman's door side, Eastleigh, October 1950.

Class 'Leader' No.36001, end view, Eastleigh, October 1950.

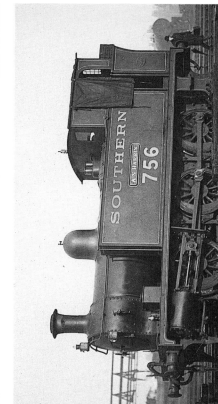

PDSWJ 0-6-2T and 0-6-0T

Three more locomotives taken over in 1923 by the Southern Railway, being the entire stock of the Plymouth, Devonport & South Western Junction Railway. This West country branch line had purchased these tank engines in 1907 from Hawthorn, Leslie & Co., two were 0-6-2Ts and one an 0-6-0T. The latter was named *A. S. Harris* and given the number 756 in 1922, the other two larger engines being named *Earl of Mount Edgcumbe* and *Lord St. Levan*, becoming LSWR/SR Nos 757 and 758 respectively, and being painted in SR livery in 1926/27. All three engines were painted in SR colours, and received the 'E' prefix until the 1931 renumbering, after which the 'E' was removed. All three were of Hawthorn, Leslie standard designs and dimensions are approximately as follows:

	Lord St. Levan and *Early of Mount Edgcumbe*	*A. S. Harris*
Coupled wheels	4ft dia	3ft 10in dia
Radial wheels	3ft dia	–
Cylinders	16in x 24in (Outside)	14in x 22in
Wheelbase	16ft 9in	10ft 6in
Pressure	170lbs	170lbs
Weight	49 tons 19 cwt	35 tons 5 cwt
Water	1,250 gallons	840 gallons
Coal	2 tons	1 ton 15 cwt
Length overall	31ft 5in	25ft 7in

No. until 1931	
E756	
E757	
E758	

Name	Withdrawn
A. S. Harris	1951
Earl of Mount Edgcumbe	1957
Lord St. Levan	1956

Right: PDSWJ No.756 *A. S. Harris* at Nine Elms in March 1934 (LH side).

Hawthorn, Leslie 0-6-0T No.756 *A.S. Harris*. (Eastleigh dwg No.SR66)

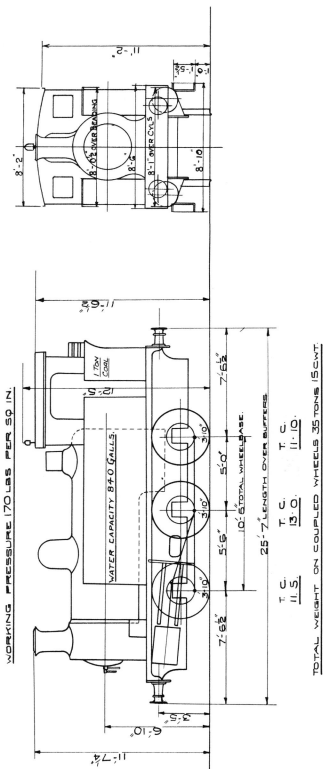

WORKING PRESSURE 170 LBS PER SQ IN.

WATER CAPACITY 840 GALLS.

1 TON COAL

TOTAL WEIGHT ON COUPLED WHEELS 35 TONS 15 CWT.

PDSWJ No. 758 *Lord St. Levan* at Plymouth Friary, August 1928 (LH side).

SOUTHERN 758

PDSWJ No. 758

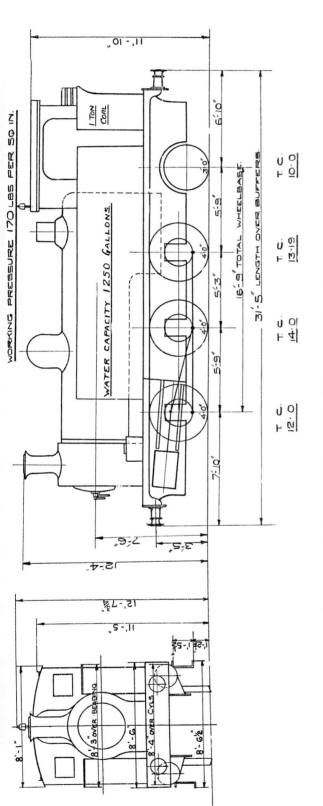

WORKING PRESSURE 170 LBS PER SQ IN.

1 TON COAL

WATER CAPACITY 1250 GALLONS.

11'-10"

12'-4"

7'-5"

3'-5"

7'-10"

5'-9"

4'-0"

5'-3"

4'-0"

5'-9"

4'-0"

3'-0"

6'-0"

16'-9" TOTAL WHEELBASE.

31'-5" LENGTH OVER BUFFERS.

T.C. 12·0	T.C. 14·0	T.C. 13·19	T.C. 10·0

12'-7¾"

11'-5"

2'-1½"

2'-1"

8'-1"

8'-3" OVER BEADING

8'-6"

8'-4" OVER CYLS.

8'-6½"

Hawthorn, Leslie 0-6-2T No.758 *Lord St. Levan.* (Eastleigh dwg No.SR67)

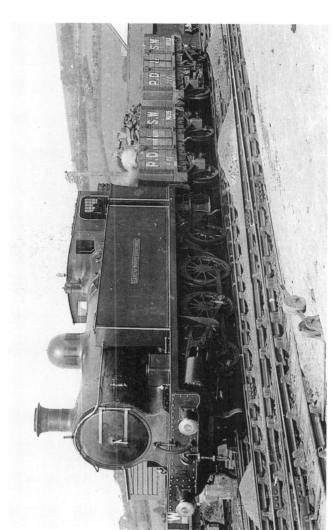

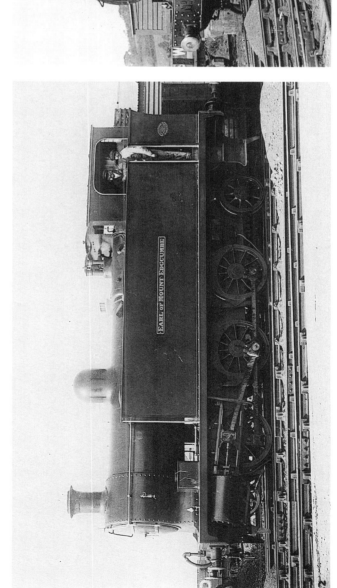

PDSWJ No.757 *Earl of Mount Edgcumbe.*

KES class 0-8-0T

Another Hawthorn, Leslie locomotive to come into Southern Railway ownership was the eight-coupled tank engine named *Hecate*. This all came about in 1932, when the Kent & East Sussex Light Railway, one of Col. Stephens' ventures, was placed in the hands of the receiver. A deal was struck between the KESLR and the Southern Railway who was the largest creditor, to the effect that the SR would take *Hecate* and three vintage six-wheeled carriages in exchange for a Beyer, Peacock saddle tank, No. E0335, one LSWR third class bogie carriage, and a LSWR brake-composite, together with some spares for the 0-6-0 saddle tank.

As the Kent & East Sussex could not use the big 0-8-0T on their system (she was originally bought for working goods traffic to Maidstone, which did not materialise) it seems that both sides were happy with the exchange. After a lengthy spell in Ashford Works, the engine was turned out painted black and lined out in 1933, and renumbered 949 but still retaining her cast nameplates on the side tanks.

She was dispatched to Nine Elms after running trials, and with one or two other duties continued there until 1939, when the firebox failed. Leaving

Eastleigh in December of 1939 with a new boiler, somewhat longer than the original, the engine was used at Clapham Junction as a pilot, and worked empty stock into Waterloo with a spell of shunting here and there during the war years. Later, in 1946 more repairs were carried out at Eastleigh, and in 1950, *Hecate* was in a mishap with a 'King Arthur' class on Nine Elms shed, which resulted in No. 949's frames being distorted badly, and Eastleigh withdrawing it from service, followed by breaking up on 26th March 1950.

No.949 *Hecate* in 1946 (RH side).

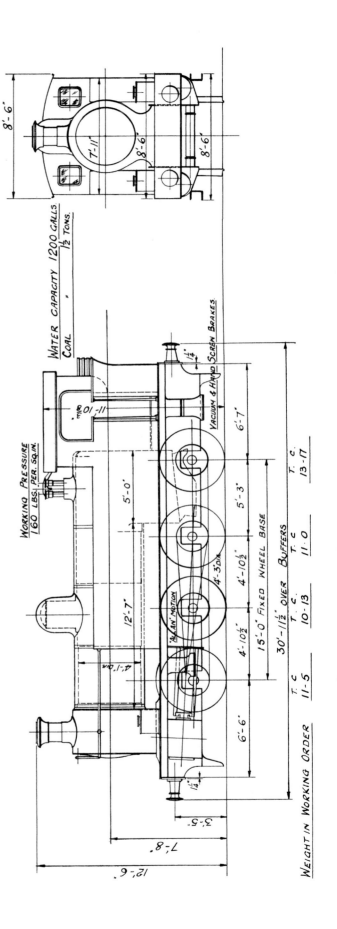

WATER CAPACITY 1200 GALLS.

COAL " ½ TONS.

WORKING PRESSURE 160 LBS. PER. SQ.IN.

VACUUM & HAND SCREW BRAKES.

15'-0" FIXED WHEEL BASE

30'-11½" OVER BUFFERS

4'-3" DIA.

4'-10½" 4'-10½" 4'-3"DIA. 4'-10½"

6'-7"   5'-3"

12'-7"   5'-0"

6'-6"

7'-8"

12'-6"

3'-5"

8'-6"   7'-11"   8'-6"   8'-6"

WEIGHT IN WORKING ORDER

T. C.	T. C.	T. C.	T. C.
11·5	10·13	11·0	13·17

Hawthorn, Leslie 0-8-0T. No. 949 *Hecate*. (Eastleigh dwg. No. SR70).

chased in 1868 and became *Ventnor*. The diagram shows the engines in the early days, as eventually cabs were fitted in place of the small weather-boards, and in 1896 they were all reboilered with a larger type having the dome placed on the middle ring.

In the year 1872, a fifth sister engine was acquired, which became *Wroxall*, and seven years later a larger version of the class arrived, to be named *Brading*. This latter locomotive had large water tanks capable of holding 1,000 gallons against the previous 820 gal. capacity, a bigger firebox was fitted, the cylinders increased to 16in x 24in, and the wheels were ½in larger than the previous engines.

Brading was followed in 1882 by a second-hand Manning, Wardle 0-6-0 saddle tank with 3ft coupled wheels and cylinders of 13in x 18in. This engine had been new to the contractor who built the Brading Harbour branch, and was taken over by the Isle of Wight Railway when the branch opened. This locomotive was named *Bembridge*, and was called up for war service in 1917, never to return to the Island.

The last engine built for the Company, was yet another 2-4-0 tank from Beyer, Peacock & Co., of the same type, but ever more powerful. Its cylinders were 17in x 24in, wheels the same as *Brading* but with a larger bunker capacity of 1¾ tons. This machine differed from the rest, by having the coal bunker outside the cab, and was fitted with a round-topped dome on the middle ring of the boiler, with Ramsbottom safety valves over the firebox. This then was *Bonchurch* built in 1883, which, on being shipped to the Island, had the misfortune to topple off the lighter into the sea off St Helens. (It was recovered several days later, presumably undamaged.)

Originally all these engines were painted a dark chocolatey red, but after 1910, the red became lighter until almost 'Midland' red. Modellers should note that the first five Beyer, Peacock tanks had three circular windows in the rear cab plate, whilst *Brading* and *Bonchurch* had two almost square ones. Also, the safety valve spring balances tended to be different on various engines, some side by side, parallel, and others at a 30° angle. All seven Beyer, Peacock 2-4-0Ts survived into Southern Railway ownership.

The next line to be opened on the Island was the Isle of Wight (Newport Jct) Railway, which ran from Sandown to Shide in 1875, and was extended to Pan Lane, Newport in 1879. Becoming bankrupt, the Official Receiver arranged for the line to connect up with other lines at Newport in 1880. At this time the IW(NJ)R owned one engine, a 2-2-2 inside-cylinder well tank, built by Messrs Hawthorns in 1861 for the Whitehaven Jct Railway and known as *Queen Mab*. Upon entering service on the IW(NJ)R tracks this engine became *Newport*, and in 1887, when taken into the IWCR she became their No. 6. It was scrapped in 1895. The only other engine worked by the IW(NJ)R was one of the Beattie 2-4-0 tanks, hired from the LSWR named *Comet* and numbered 36.

Part Five

Isle of Wight Section, Lynton & Barnstaple Railway and Sentinel Rail Bus

Isle of Wight Section (W)

This section is primarily concerned with the Southern Railway and its connections with the Isle of Wight, and in particular with the locomotives thereon, before and after the Grouping. I have found that researching into railway history on the Island, is rather like looking for Long John Silver's treasure – a few facts and a lot of hearsay. In the light of this, I have added a few paragraphs which, although out of context perhaps, might be of interest to other Isle of Wight enthusiasts.

The first company, the Cowes & Newport Railway, was incorporated in 1859, and opened in 1862, connecting the Island capital with the main port at that time. In 1870 the C&NR. built Medina Wharf near Cowes, which increased the coal and mineral traffic considerably.

The locomotive stock in those early days consisted of two outside-cylinder 2-2-2 tanks, built by Messrs Slaughter, Gruning & Co. of Bristol in 1861, and were named *Pioneer* and *Precursor*. They were painted light blue, lined out in red, had 13½ in x 16in cylinders, 5ft 3in diameter driving wheels, and carrying wheels 3ft 6in diameter. In 1870, the Company also bought a small 0-4-2 saddle tank from Messrs Black, Hawthorn & Co. of Gateshead, for shunting work at Medina Wharf. This little machine was originally painted olive green, and had outside cylinders 10in x 17in, with coupled wheels 3ft 3in diameter and trailing wheels of 2ft 4in. It became No. 3 of the Central Railway when the C&NR was absorbed in 1887, and was used as a relief to the IW(NJ)R Rail Motor, when hitched onto an old Midland Railway 12-wheeled carriage which had been acquired.

The second Island company opened in 1864, and ran from Ryde to Shanklin, and was given the title Isle of Wight Railway (originally termed the 'Isle of Wight Eastern Railway', this was changed to the simpler title, when a westward branch was proposed). After a tunnel ¾ mile long had been cut between Wroxall and Ventnor, the line actually reached the latter resort in 1866.

Three locomotives were bought from Beyer, Peacock & Co., inside-cylindered 2-4-0 side tanks, with 15in x 20in cylinders, 5ft diameter driving wheels, and leading wheels of 3ft 6in dia. They were all identical and were given the names *Ryde*, *Sandown* and *Shanklin* respectively. A fourth, identical locomotive was pur-

was built at Newport for this Ryde & Newport Railway to use, together with the old Cowes & Newport Railway. Eventually the three lines, Cowes & Newport, the Isle of Wight (Newport Jct) and the Ryde & Newport were amalgamated in 1887 to form the Isle of Wight Central Railway.

The Ryde & Newport purchased two locomotives for working their line, Beyer, Peacock 2-4-0 inside-cylinder tanks, similar to those on the Isle of Wight Railway, but slightly smaller. They had 14in x 20in cylinders, with coupled wheels 5ft in diameter, and leading wheels of 3ft 3in. The small side tanks had a capacity of 480 gallons only, and the inside bunkers held 15 cwt of coal. These two were named *Cowes* and *Osborne*, and when taken into the IWCR became Nos 4 and 5. At that time, the livery of the Ryde & Newport Railway was red, with polished brass domes, and copper-topped chimneys. One other engine should be mentioned. This was a 4-4-0 inside-cylindered side tank, built for the North London Railway in 1861 by Slaughter, Gruning. It was bought in 1880 by the Ryde-Cowes & Newport Joint Committee, and in 1887, as one of the IWCR machines, became their No. 7. It was cut up in 1906.

Following the forming of the IWCR, the company ordered a rather handsome outside-cylindered 4-4-0 side tank engine, from Black, Hawthorn in 1890, for heavy passenger work. This engine was numbered 6, taking over the old *Queen Mab's* number, the old 2-2-2T having been put on the duplicate list. Dimensions of the Black, Hawthorn engine were as follows. Cylinders (outside) 16in x 22in, coupled wheels 5ft 3in dia., water tanks held 700 gallons, and fuel in an outside bunker with a capacity of 45 cubic feet.

Yet another Beyer, Peacock, 2-4-0 side tank was ordered in 1898, which was a slightly bigger version of Nos 4 and 5. The wheels were 1in larger in diameter than the two earlier engines, and the water tanks held 520 gallons, with coal carried in an outside bunker. This then was No 8.

No. 9 purchased in 1899, was one of the ex-LBSCR Stroudley 'Terriers', built in 1872, it was originally No. 74 *Shadwell*. It was joined in 1900, by another 'Terrier', which had been built in 1874 as No. 69 *Peckham*, it became No. 10 of the IWCR, and two years later, old No. 40 *Brighton*, became No. 11 on the IWCR. Finally in 1903, a fourth 'Terrier', old No. 84 *Crowborough*, joined the other three, and took the number 12. When at work on the Island, these four engines had the coal bunkers enlarged, and the rear tool boxes removed. New boilers pressed for 50lbs were fitted and injectors replaced the old feed pumps. Westinghouse brake pumps were attached to the 'Terriers', in the angle formed by the rear of the right-hand side tank, and the cab side. Also, to their detriment, the handsome copper-topped chimneys were gradually replaced by other shapes.

In 1906, the IWCR purchased a steam rail motor from Hawthorn, Leslie & Co., one of the smallest units in the U.K. being only 61ft over buffers. The locomotive section was separate from the coach, being a small 0-4-0 side tank, although the front of the carriage pivoted on the rear of the engine. This unit, given the number 1, worked on the Ventnor West branch until late 1912, when it was divided, a bogie being placed under the leading end of the coach, and the locomotive being used as a small shunter until sold in 1918.

Dimensions of the little engine were: outside cylinders 9in x 14in, four coupled wheels 3ft 6in dia., water tanks 400 gallons, 12 cwt coal and weight in working order 15¼ tons.

The ex-North London Railway tank, IWCR No. 7, scrapped in 1906, was replaced in 1908 by yet another Beyer, Peacock, 2-4-0 side tank, this time, second-hand from the MSWJR. Built in 1882, this machine was larger and more powerful than Nos 4, 5 and 8, having 16in x 24in cylinders, with 5ft 6in coupled wheels, and 4ft dia. leading carrying wheels. One ton of coal could be accommodated, and the side tanks held 1,000 gallons. Numbered 6 on the MSWJR it was renumbered 7 on the IWCR.

The last engine to be acquired by the IWCR came from the Marquis of Londonderry Railway at Seaham, it was taken into the NER in 1900 as their No. 1712, and on the Island became No. 2 of the IWCR's stock. A 4-4-0 side tank, with 5ft 4½in coupled wheels, with a bogie having 3ft dia. wheels and a weight of nearly 46 tons, this engine proved too heavy, and was sold in 1917 to Messrs Armstrong, Whitworth. As built, this machine had long side tanks after the style of the North Eastern, but for service on the Island, these tanks were reduced drastically to hold a maximum of 600 gallons.

The livery of the Isle of Wight Central Railway prior to the Grouping was varied. In 1890 engines were painted dark red, in 1898 black, although in 1900/01 old *Pioneer*, *Precursor*, *Cowes* and *Osborne* were painted in red. No. 7 the ex-NLR tank was black until 1887. In 1906 engines were painted red-brown, 1914, engines painted black with white lining and I.W.C. on the tank sides. By 1922, the black livery now had red and white lining with gold letters and numbers.

Another unusual feature on the IWCR was the small destination boards fixed at the base of the chimney, or on the bunker rear, being painted red with the lettering in white. Some engines had their coupling rods painted red.

The next development on the Island, railwaywise, was the construction of a new ½ mile long pier out to sea at Ryde in 1880. The carried out by a joint committee of the LSWR and LBSCR. The inland end of the new pier railway, tunnelled under Ryde Esplanade to link up with St Johns Road station. The double track from Pier Head to St Johns Road, was staffed by the joint committee's employee, but the traffic was worked by the Island railways.

In 1882, another link in the Island network was completed, that of a branch from Ryde, along the north side of Brading Harbour, linking with a line from Bembridge via St Helens. This line became known as the Brading Harbour branch, and was opened in May 1882.

The railway connections to the west of the Island, finally came about in 1888/89 with the formation of the Freshwater, Yarmouth & Newport Railway. Opened for mineral traffic only in 1888, passengers were accepted in the next year, and from 1888 until 1913 the FYNR was operated by the IWCR, which meant through services from Freshwater to Ryde, one end of the island to the other, albeit a reversal of the trains at Newport being necessary! However, the directors of the FYNR could not agree to the rather high terms under which the line was being worked by the IWCR and so in 1913, decided to provide their own rolling stock and locomotives. This action irked the IWC Co, who promptly withdrew the facility of their Newport station, so forcing the FYNR to build their own independent station terminus just 100 yards away! Things settled down in 1920, when the FYNR trains were allowed to use the west platform at Newport Central.

The locomotives acquired by the little company were two, the first being one of the standard 0-6-0 saddle tanks built by Messrs Manning, Wardle in 1902, with inside cylinders 14in x 20in and coupled wheels 3ft 6in dia. Painted bright green with red coupling rods, it was lettered FYNR and numbered 1. The second engine was of course No. 2, and was yet another 'Terrier'. Built in 1876 by the LBSCR as No. 46 *Newington*, it was sold to the LSWR in 1903 for the Lyme Regis branch, and took the number 734, was reboilered and fitted with Drummond safety valves. On the Island, this engine ran for some years in LSWR livery, but eventually was repainted in the bright green of the FYNR with the red coupling rods.

Apart from these two steam locomotives, the only other motive power unit owned by the FYNR was a Drewry petrol railcar. This tiny, 4-wheeled 12-seater car had its place in Island history, as it was used for a fast service between Freshwater and Newport, calling only at Yarmouth, providing a sort of 'boat train' link with the Lymington-Yarmouth ferry. In fact this "express"(!) service between Yarmouth and Newport was limited to mainland travellers only.

The last branch line to be constructed on the Isle of Wight was the Newport, Godshill & St Lawrence Railway, aimed at eventually providing a direct link between Cowes, Newport and Ventnor. Opened in 1897, from Merstone on the Sandown-Newport line, to St Lawrence, it finally linked up with Ventnor Town station in 1900.

From 1897 until 1913 this branch, although a separate company as the NG&StLR, was worked by the IWCR, until once again, the Official Receiver decided the impoverished little concern should be absorbed into the Central Company.

Although there were many other schemes for extending the railway network on the Island, such as a branch from Newport to Wroxall, a line across the 'Back of the Wight' from Ventnor to Yarmouth, a proposed Shanklin-Chale Railway, an Ashey-Horringford branch, and even an ambitious plan to link the LSWR branch at Lymington on the mainland, with the FYNR via a tunnel under the Solent, surfacing somewhere between Freshwater and Yarmouth. There was also a proposal to extend the FYNR westwards to Totland – however, not one of these schemes materialised, and before the Grouping of 1923, the Island rail traffic was under the control of just the three Companies:

The Isle of Wight Railway

The Isle of Wight Central Railway

The Freshwater, Yarmouth and Newport Railway

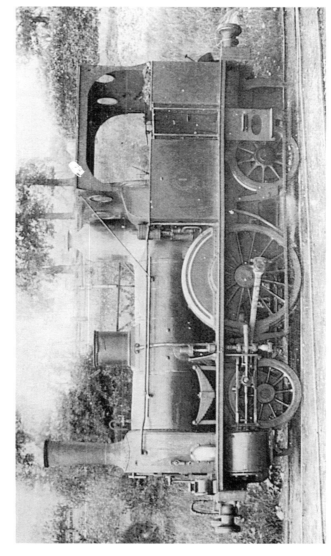

Railway map of the Isle of Wight circa 1920.

SCALE
0   1   2   3
MILES

— REFERENCE —
Formerly Isle of Wight Railway............
Isle of Wight Central Railway...............
Freshwater, Yarmouth & Newport Railway...
L.S.W.R. and L.B.&S.C.R Joint Lines......
London & South Western Railway............

Opening dates are as under:

1862 Cowes & Newport Rly
1865 Isle of Wight (Newport Jc) Rly } 1887 { Amalgamated to form The Isle of Wight Central Rly.
1875 Ryde & Newport Rly
1897 Newport, Godshill & St Lawrence Rly

1864 Isle of Wight (Eastern) Rly
1882 Brading Harbour Branch, absorbed to form the Isle of Wight Rly

1888 Freshwater, Yarmouth & Newport Rly. Always the FY&NR

1880 Ryde Pier Head–St Johns Road. LBSCR/LSWR Joint

All the above, including LSWR Yarmouth depot, went into the Southern Railway at the Grouping in 1923.

Pre-Grouping Isle of Wight Locomotives

Beyer, Peacock 2-4-0T, IWCR No.5 at Ventnor in June 1923.

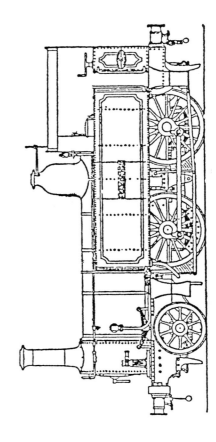

The first locomotive on the Isle of Wight, No.1 *Pioneer* of the Isle of Wight Central Railway.

IWR *Sandown* with the original boiler.

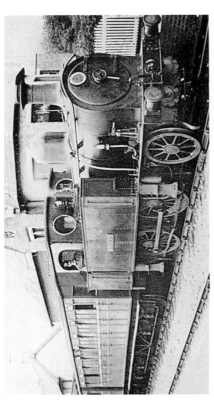

Beyer, Peacock 2-4-0T *Bonchurch* with train at Ventnor c1922.

Beyer, Peacock 2-4-0T (RH side) No.13 at Ryde in May 1933.

Beyer, Peacock 2-4-0T, IWCR No.5 at Sandown, June 1921.

Beyer, Peacock 2-4-0T *Shanklin* entering Shanklin station c1913.

A1x class (LH side) of IWCR No.9 at Ryde Pier Head in May 1920.

Beyer, Peacock 2-4-0T, old No.5 c1920.

A1x class (LH side) at Haven Street, 17th June 1990 as restored as IWCR No.11 on an OPC 'book launch' special.

Manning, Wardle 0-6-0ST FYNR No.1 at Newport, June 1921.

IWCR 4-4-0T (RH side) No.6 at Ryde in 1920.

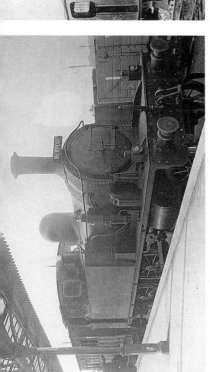

IWCR 4-4-0T No.6 at Newport June 1921.

Manning, Wardle 0-6-0ST, ex-FYNR, No.1 at Ryde shed in May 1933.

Manning, Wardle 0-6-0ST, ex-FYNR as SR No.W1 *Medina* (LH side) at Newport, June 1931.

Manning, Wardle 0-6-0ST No.W1 Medina (RH side) at Newport, June 1931.

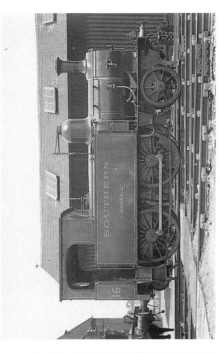

Beyer, Peacock 2-4-0T as SR No.W16 *Wroxall* at Newport, June 1931 (RH side).

Beyer, Peacock 2-4-0T, IWR *Wroxall* at Shanklin in June 1921.

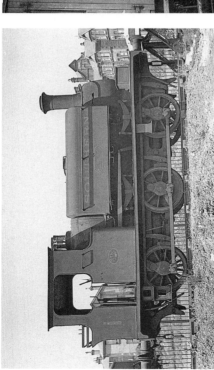

Manning, Wardle 0-6-0ST No.W1 (RH side) at Ryde shed in May 1933.

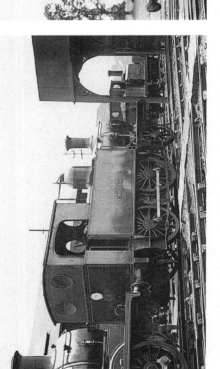

Beyer, Peacock 2-4-0T ex-IWR as SR No.W8 at Newport,

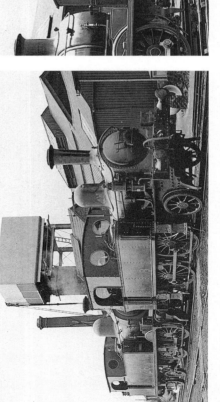

Beyer, Peacock 2-4-0T No.W16 *Wroxall* at Newport in

Beyer, Peacock 2-4-0T No.W8 at Newport in July 1928 with O2

Beyer, Peacock 2-4-0T No.W8 at Ryde in 1924 (LH side).

Beyer, Peacock 2-4-0T ex-IWR as SR No.18 *Bonchurch*, Newport, July 1928 (LH side).

Beyer, Peacock 2-4-0T No.W13 *Ryde* at Ryde shed in 1926 (LH side).

Beyer, Peacock 2-4-0T No.W8 at Ryde shed, 1928 (RH side).

Beyer, Peacock 2-4-0T IWCR No.4 at Sandown in June 1923.

Locomotives on the Isle of Wight after January 1923

Inheriting 18 various steam locomotives, each with 50 or more years of service, the newly constituted Southern Railway immediately set about implementing and improving the stock of Island engines.

In May of 1923, two of the ex-LSWR O2 class 0-4-4 Adams tanks, were shipped across to Ryde Pier Head station, and landed with the help of an Admiralty floating crane. These two were LSWR Nos 206 and 211. They had been refitted with the Westinghouse brake system for use on the Island, and were still painted in the LSWR livery. The arrival of the two O2s meant that the elderly Beyer, Peacock engine, *Sandown* of the old IWR could be dispatched to the mainland for scrapping, especially as it was found that this machine had a cracked frame.

The O2s were found to be very successful in service, and as this class was in surplus on the mainland, others were earmarked for transfer. Nos 205 and 215 were shipped in sections in June of 1924 to St Helens Wharf, and were re-erected there

The Southern Railway did not number either the native Island engines or those sent from the mainland into the 'A', 'B' and 'E' series, but instituted a separate group for the Isle of Wight with the prefix 'W'. The engines, which had belonged to the FYNR and the IWCR, retained their old numbers, with the prefix 'W' added, and the IWR locomotives which had previously only carried names, were included in the new listing, with numbers from W13 to W18, whilst retaining their old nameplates. Thus LSWR No. 206 became W19, and LSWR No. 211 was renumbered W20, and LSWR Nos 205 and 215 became W21 and W22 respectively.

In 1925 the Southern Railway acquired their own floating crane, and from then on all locomotives and rolling stock was off-loaded at Medina Wharf as St Helens had tidal difficulties. The first engine handled here was ex-LSWR No. 188, which was altered to W23, followed by 209/W24, 190/W25, and 186/W26 all landed in June of 1925. Nos 184/W27 and 186/W28 arrived in March 1926, 202/W29 and 219/W30 were shipped in April 1926, and May 1927 saw the arrival of LSWR No. 180/W31.

From 1923 until October 1928, all these O2s ran

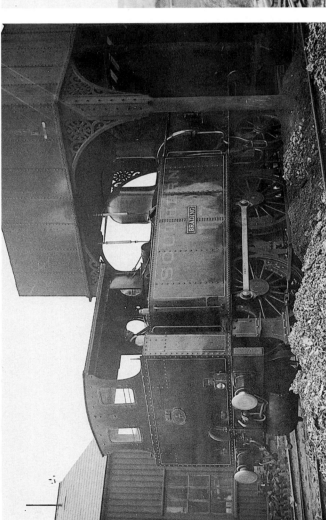

Beyer, Peacock 2-4-0T No.W17 *Brading* at Newport in July 1925.

Beyer, Peacock 2-4-0T SR No.W13 *Ryde* at Newport in 16th July 1925, when claimed to be the

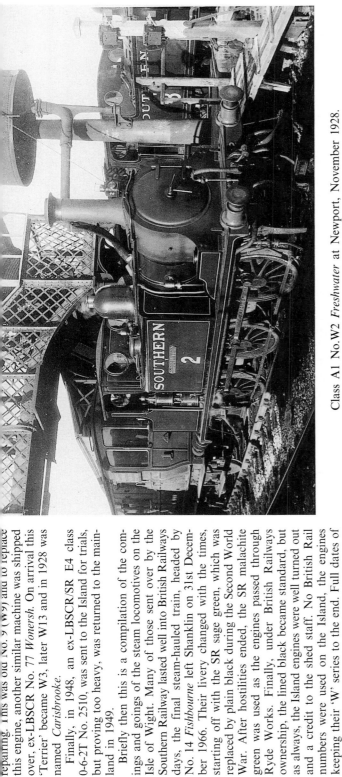

Class A1 No.W2 *Freshwater* at Newport, November 1928.

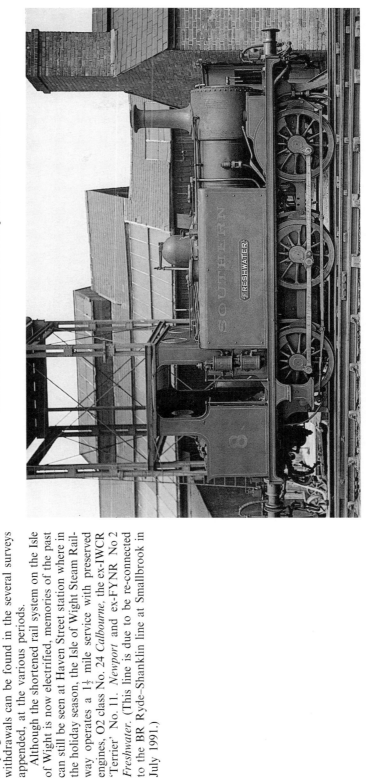

Class A1 No.8 *Freshwater* (RH side) at Newport, May 1933.

were provided with names of various Isle of Wight locations, many of which had been used on some of the original Island locomotives.

After the Amalgamation, the O2 class of 0-4-4 tanks worked the Island services alongside the old Beyer, Peacock 2-4-0Ts, the ex-LBSCR 'Terriers', and other odd machines, but as these old engines were gradually withdrawn, so more surplus O2s were supplied as set out hereunder.

LSWR No.	IoW No.	Shipped	Named
178	W14	May 1936	Fishbourne
195	W15	May 1936	Cowes
217	W16	May 1936	Ventnor
208	W17	May 1930	Seaview
220	W18	May 1930	Ningwood
206	W19	May 1923	Osborne
211	W20	May 1923	Shanklin
205	W21	June 1924	Sandown
215	W22	June 1924	Brading
188	W23	April 1925	Totland
209	W24	April 1925	Calbourne
190	W25	June 1925	Godshill
210	W26	June 1925	Whitwell
184	W27	March 1926	Merstone
186	W28	March 1926	Ashey
202	W29	April 1926	Alverstone
219	W30	April 1926	Shorwell
180	W31	May 1927	Chale
226	W32	May 1928	Bonchurch
218	W33	May 1936	Bembridge
201	W34	April 1947	Newport
181	W35	April 1949	Freshwater
198	W36	April 1949	Carisbrooke

Originally all the O2 class sent to the Island were fitted with Drummond boilers, but as these steamed badly on the hard schedules on the Wight network, and were also heavy on coal consumption, from 1932 onwards these engines were refitted with Adams boilers and enlarged bunkers.

In July of 1932, three of the ex-LBSCR E1 class 0-6-0Ts were transferred to the Isle of Wight, old No. 136 *Brindisi* was renumbered W1 and renamed *Medina*, replacing the old Manning, Wardle 0-6-0ST No. 1 of the ex-FYNR. LBSCR No. 152 *Hungary* became W2 *Yarmouth*, taking old W2's number, and LBSCR No. 154 *Madrid*, became W3 *Ryde*, replacing the old Beyer, Peacock *Ryde* of the IWR.

In June of 1933, a fourth E1 class was transferred. This was old LBSCR No. 131 *Gourney*, which became W4 *Wroxall*, taking the place of the old 1872 *Wroxall*, also ex-IWR.

In 1927, one of the 'Terriers' of the ex-IWCR was badly damaged, and found to be not worth repairing. This was old No. 9 (W9) and to replace this engine, another similar machine was shipped over, ex-LBSCR No. 77 *Wonersh*. On arrival this 'Terrier' became W3, later W13 and in 1928 was named *Carisbrooke*.

Finally, in 1948, an ex-LBSCR/SR E4 class 0-6-2T No. 2510, was sent to the Island for trials, but proving too heavy, was returned to the mainland in 1949.

Briefly then this is a compilation of the comings and goings of the steam locomotives on the Isle of Wight. Many of those sent over by the Southern Railway lasted well into British Railways days, the final steam-hauled train, headed by No. 14 *Fishbourne* left Shanklin on 31st December 1966. Their livery changed with the times, starting off with the SR sage green, which was replaced by plain black during the Second World War. After hostilities ended, the SR malachite green was used as the engines passed through Ryde Works. Finally, under British Railways ownership, the lined black became standard, but as always, the Island engines were well turned out and a credit to the shed staff. No British Rail numbers were used on the Island, the engines keeping their 'W' series to the end. Full dates of withdrawals can be found in the several surveys appended, at the various periods.

Although the shortened rail system on the Isle of Wight is now electrified, memories of the past can still be seen at Haven Street station where in the holiday season, the Isle of Wight Steam Railway operates a 1½ mile service with preserved engines, O2 class No. 24 *Calbourne*, the ex-IWCR 'Terrier' No.11. *Newport* and ex-FYNR No 2 *Freshwater*. (This line is due to be re-connected to the BR Ryde–Shanklin line at Smallbrook in July 1991.)

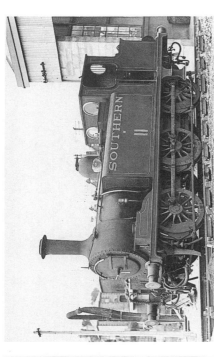

Class A1x No.W3 at Newport shed in July 1928.

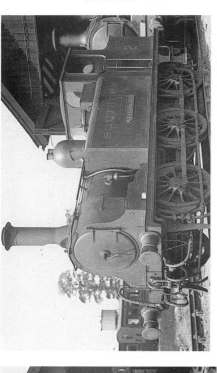

Class A1 No.W2 *Freshwater* (LH side) at Newport shed in June 1931.

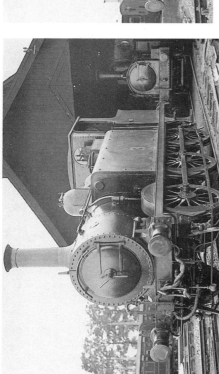

Class A1x No. W11 at Ryde shed, May 1930.

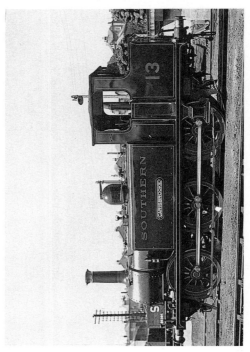

Class A1x No.W4 *Bembridge* (RH side) at Newport, May 1930.

Class A1x No.13 *Carisbrooke* at Ryde in May 1933.

Class A1x No.W12 *Ventnor* at Newport in May 1930.

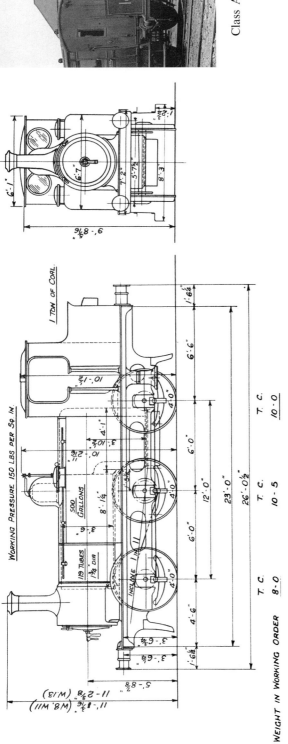

Class A1x No.W14 *Bembridge* at Newport in May 1933.

WORKING PRESSURE 150 LBS PER SQ. IN.

I TON OF COAL.

500 GALLONS

119 TUBES 1¾ DIA

INCLINE 1 IN 11

	T.C.	T.C.	T.C.
WEIGHT IN WORKING ORDER	8-0	10-5	10-0

Class A1x 0-6-0T for the Isle of Wight railways. (Eastleigh dwg)

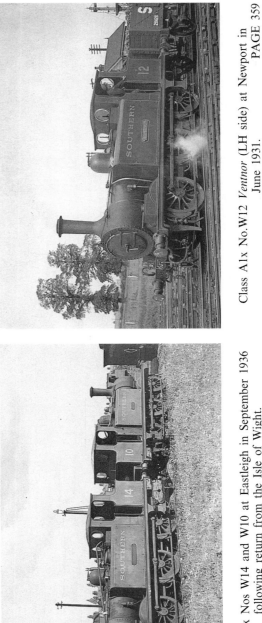

Class A1x No.W12 *Ventnor* (LH side) at Newport in June 1931.

Class A1x Nos W14 and W10 at Eastleigh in September 1936 following return from the Isle of Wight.

Class A1x No.W9 (LH side) at Newport in May 1930.

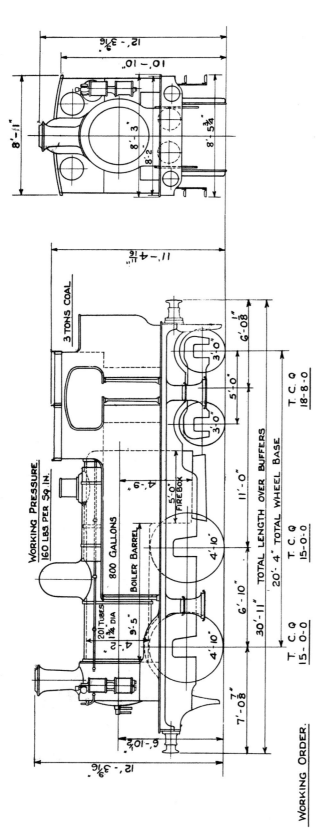

WORKING PRESSURE.
160 LBS PER SQ.IN.

3 TONS COAL

800 GALLONS

BOILER BARREL

201 TUBES 1¾ DIA

FIREBOX

WORKING ORDER.

Class O2 0-4-4T for the Isle of Wight railways. (Eastleigh dwg No.SR22A)

Class O2 No.23 *Totland* at Ryde in May 1933.

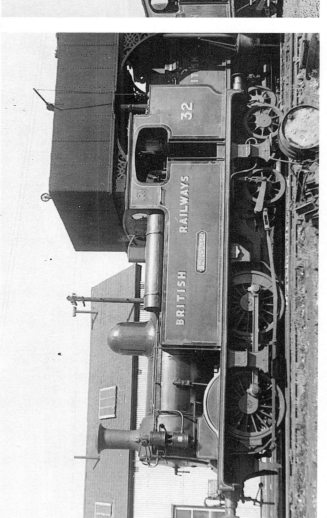

Class O2 No.32 *Bonchurch* (LH side) at Newport, September 1952.

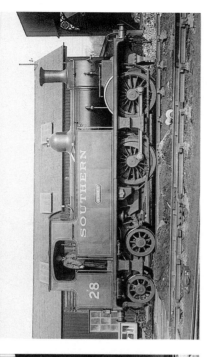

Class O2 No.W28 *Ashey* (RH side) at Newport in 1927.

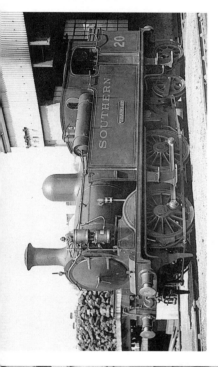

Class O2 No.20 *Shanklin* at Ryde shed, May 1933.

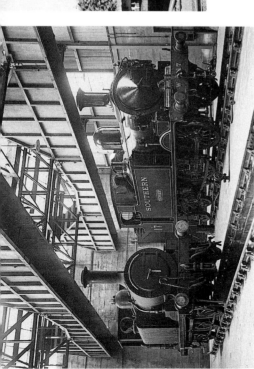

Class O2 No.W17 *Seaview* right, with Class A1x No.W11 left, in Ryde shed, May 1930.

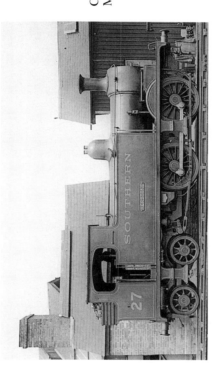

Class O2 No.27 *Merstone* (RH side) at Newport in May 1933.

Class E1 No.2 *Yarmouth* at Newport in 1933.

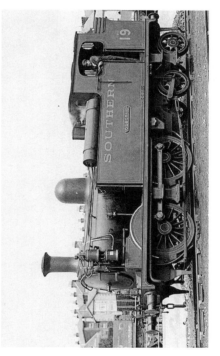

Class O2 No.W19 *Osborne* (LH side) at Ryde in June 1931.

Class O2 No. W19 at Newport in July 1928.

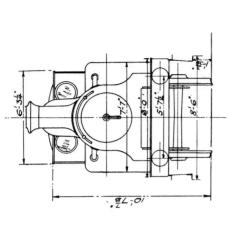

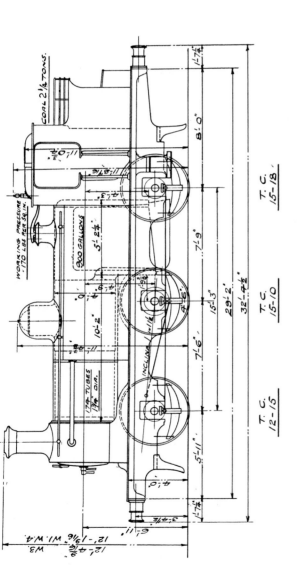

Class E1 0-6-0T for the Isle of Wight railways. (Brighton dwg No.29B)

Class E1 No.3 *Ryde* (RH side) at Newport in May 1933.

Class E1 No.1 *Medina* at Newport in May 1933.

Isle of Wight Locomotive Liveries

Isle of Wight Central Railway

The Isle of Wight Central Railway was the most important line on the island, running from Cowes to Ventnor and Cowes to Ryde, *via* Newport. It was formed in 1887 by the amalgamation of the Isle of Wight (Newport Junction) Railway (incorporated in 1868), the Cowes & Newport Railway (incorporated in 1859), and the Ryde & Newport Railway (incorporated in 1872). In 1913 the Newport, Godshill & St Lawrence Railway was acquired, thus bringing the total track mileage to 35.

The locomotive superintendent in 1913 was Mr Russell Willmott.

1890 Locomotives dark red.
1898 Locomotives black.
1900 Locomotives *Pioneer* and *Precursor* (ex-Cowes & Newport Railway) were repainted in the standard red of the Isle of Wight Central Railway, and their nameplates removed. They retained their brass domes and safety valve casings. Locomotive No. 3 was painted olive green and lined out in white.
1901 Locomotives Nos 4 and 5 (*Cowes* and *Osborne*) were painted the company's red, with copper-topped chimneys and brass domes. Locomotive No. 7 (ex-North London Railway) ran painted black until 1887, when the Newport & Ryde Railway was taken over by the Isle of Wight Central Railway.
1902 In addition to the standard locomotive livery the name of the company began to appear in gold block letters on the tank sides;

ISLE OF WIGHT CENTRAL RAILWAY

The ex-LBSCR engine *Peckham* was the first to so appear. Locomotive No. 1 (2-2-2T) had double brass beading round the driving wheel splashers, the outer bead being much wider than the inner one.

The engine number was painted inside a garter on the cab side sheets, which were double lined into a rectangular panel with rounded corners. A brass dome casing was fitted.
1906 Locomotives painted red-brown.
1907 Locomotive No. 9 (ex-LBSCR 'Terrier') had ISLE OF WIGHT – CENTRAL RAILWAY in two lines painted on the tanks in block letters, unshaded. The figure 9 also appeared in unshaded block on the bunker sides. The chimney was copper-capped, and there were brass beadings round the spectacle-plate windows. This engine ran for some time with the Stroudley type of buffer-beam panelling.
1914 Locomotives were black, with white lining and IWC on the tank sides. Some were lined out in vermilion.
1922 Locomotives were painted black with red and white lining with gold letters and numbers.

Isle of Wight Railway

Incorporated in July 1860 and opened in August 1864, this line was 15¼ miles long; running from Ventnor *via* Sandown and Brading to join the Isle of Wight Central Railway near St Johns Road station. There was also a branch line to Bembridge. The Company's

locomotive superintendent in 1918 was Mr H.D. Tahourdin.
1898 Locomotives painted crimson lake, with polished brass domes and copper-topped chimneys.
1910 Locomotives painted a much brighter red.
1914 Locomotives were a rich dark red, lined out in yellow and black; with brass name plates. No number plates were fitted, the seven engines constituting the total stock being named in lieu of numbers.
1922 Locomotives painted in a livery described as Midland red, and lined out in yellow and black.

Freshwater, Yarmouth & Newport Railway

This line was incorporated in 1880 and opened for passenger traffic in 1889, with a track length of twelve miles.
1898 Locomotives were painted a bright green with vermilion coupling rods.
1917 The saddle tank engine was green with red coupling rods. No. 1 (later W1) had F.Y.& N. in block letters on the tank sides.
1922 Locomotives were green with white and black lining.

Lynton & Barnstaple Railway Locomotives (1ft 11½in gauge)

The narrow gauge railway which ran from Barnstaple Town to Lynton in North Devon was opened in 1898, and became part of the Southern Railway in 1923. The Lynton & Barnstaple started operations with three locomotives, all 2-6-2 tank engines built by Manning, Wardle & Co. of Leeds. They were named after rivers in the area, *Exe*, *Yeo* and *Taw*. The directors realised that another locomotive was needed to deputise for any one of the original three, in the case of repairs, maintenance or mishap. Not being able to get quick delivery from English builders, they ordered a fourth machine from Baldwins in the USA and *Lyn* arrived on the scene in July 1898. This little engine was pure American, having bar frames, wooden cab, large side tanks, and was of 2-4-2T classification. Upon the SR acquiring the little company, it was decided to obtain yet another engine, and a sister Manning, Wardle 2-6-2T was bought and delivered in 1925. Named *Lew* it was slightly different from the original trio in that there was no rear coal bunker, the cab was smaller, as was the firebox and grate, which meant it was not so strong as the others. The little line only lasted another ten years, service ceasing at the end of 1935 *Yeo*, *Taw* and *Lyn*, were sold for scrap at £50 each and *Exe* for £34, whilst *Lew* fetched £52 and finally wound up in Brazil, its subsequent fate not known to this day, although recent thorough investigation may soon determine this. Dimensions etc. of the locomotives were as follows overleaf: PAGE 363

Class E1 No.3 *Ryde* at Newport in September 1952.

	Manning, Wardle	Baldwin
Gauge	1ft 11½in	1ft 11½in
Wheel arrangement	2-6-2T	2-4-2T
Coupled wheels	2ft 9in dia.	2ft 9in dia.
Pony wheels	2ft dia.	1ft 10in dia.
Total wheelbase	17ft 9in	17ft 7in
Boiler	9ft 1in long 3ft dia.	8ft 11in long 2ft 10in dia.
Firebox length	3ft 2¼in	3ft 1in
Pressure	160lbs	180lbs
Water	550 gallons	665 gallons
Coal	1 ton	15 cwt
Weight	22 tons 9½ cwt	22 tons 1 cwt

Name	SR No.	Builder	Date	Sold
Yeo	E759	Manning, Wardle & Co.	1897	1935
Exe	E760	Manning, Wardle & Co.	1897	1935
Taw	E761	Manning, Wardle & Co.,	1897	1935
Lyn	E762	Baldwin Locomotive Works	1898	1935
Lew	E188	Manning, Wardle & Co.	1925	1935

Manning, Wardle narrow gauge 2-6-2T for the Lynton & Barnstaple line, SR No.188 *Lew* at Barnstaple in May 1935.

Manning, Wardle (L&BR) 2-6-2T SR No.E188 *Lew* at Lynton in 1935.

Manning, Wardle (L&BR) 2-6-2T as SR No.759 *Yeo* at Lynton in May 1935.

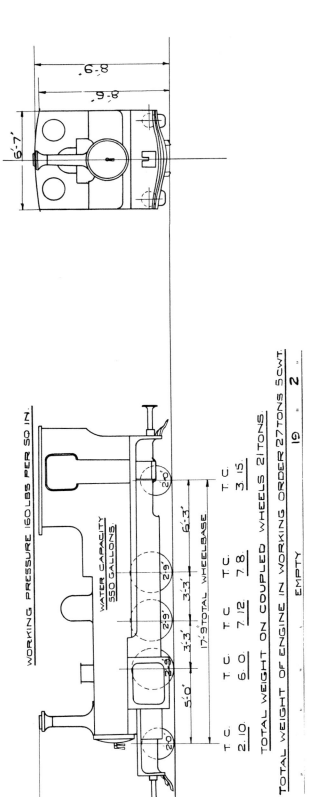

WORKING PRESSURE 160 LBS PER SQ IN.

WATER CAPACITY 550 GALLONS.

6'-8"

9'-8"

6'-7"

5'-0"   3'-3"   2'-9"   3'-3"   2'-9"   6'-3"

2'-0"   2'-0"

17'-9 TOTAL WHEELBASE

8'-11¾"

T.C.	T.C.	T.C.	T.C.	T.C.
2.10	6.0	7.12	7.8	3.15

TOTAL WEIGHT ON COUPLED WHEELS 21 TONS

TOTAL WEIGHT OF ENGINE IN WORKING ORDER 27 TONS 5 CWT.

EMPTY   19 "   2 "

Manning, Wardle 2-6-2T of the Lynton & Barnstaple Railway. (Eastleigh dwg No.E69)

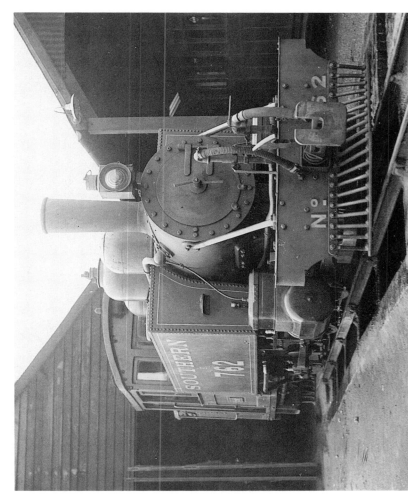

Right: L&BR, Baldwin 2-4-2T as SR No.E762 *Lyn* at Barnstaple in May 1935.

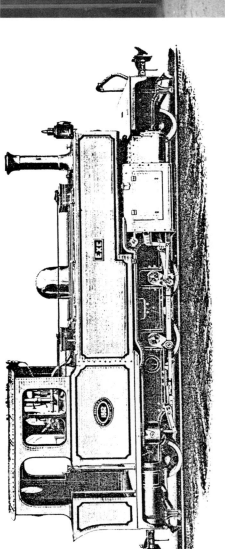

A sketch of Lynton & Barnstaple Railway locomotive from Manning, Wardle catalogue.

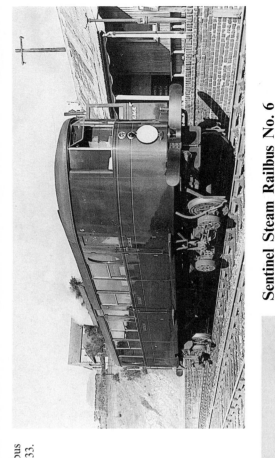

Sentinel steam railbus
No.6 at The Dyke in October 1933.

L&BR, Baldwin 2-4-2T as SR No.E762 *Lyn* in Pilton
shed, June 1926.

Sentinel steam railbus No.6
at The Dyke in October 1933.

Sentinel Steam Railbus No. 6

In 1927, main line electrification was in full swing, but the General Manager doubted the wisdom of electrifying small branch lines. He therefore ordered Maunsell to look into the feasibility of using petrol or steam railcars for these lightly loaded services. Later that year, a Drewry 4-wheel 50hp petrol railcar was ordered, and started operations on the Andover–Romsey service. From there it went to the Reading–Blackwater branch in 1928, and the following year saw it down on the Dungeness/New Romsey–Appledore line.

As the passenger capacity was only 22, the traffic outgrew the car, and it was sold to the Weston, Clevedon & Portishead Railway in 1934. However, the experience gained from this little vehicle encouraged Maunsell to try steam, and in 1933 an 8-wheel Sentinel steam railbus, seating 44 passengers, made the journey from Birmingham, under its own steam, all the way to Brighton for trials between Brighton and Worthing. The engine was a 97bhp 2-cylinder compound, totally enclosed, driving on one axle. The boiler was one of the standard vertical Sentinel type, pressed for 325lbs. The body was built on motorbus lines to save weight, and was 29ft 9in long, the whole contraption only scaling 17 tons, a disadvantage in high winds as it was later found!

This little machine started work in earnest on The Dyke branch on 1st May 1933. This branch, which climbed 400ft with grades of 1 in 40, was not easy on normal steam traction, but No. 6 made light work of it, so much so, that Maunsell suggested buying five more. However, the Traffic Department wanted something larger, and trials with various other forms of 2-car sets began, which were not conclusive. By 1936, the increase in passengers had become too much for No. 6, and the machine saw service on many of the Kentish branch lines before being tucked away at Ashford in 1938. Finally in 1940, stripped of its machinery and painted grey, it became a Home Guard and Firewatchers' cabin until broken up in 1946.

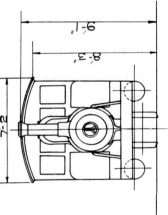

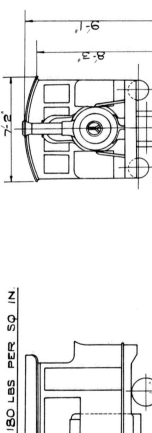

WORKING PRESSURE 180 LBS PER SQ IN.

WATER CAPACITY
800 GALLONS

TOTAL WEIGHT ON COUPLED WHEELS 16 TONS

Baldwin 2-4-2T No.E762 *Lyn*, of the Lynton & Barnstaple Railway. (Eastleigh dwg No.E70)

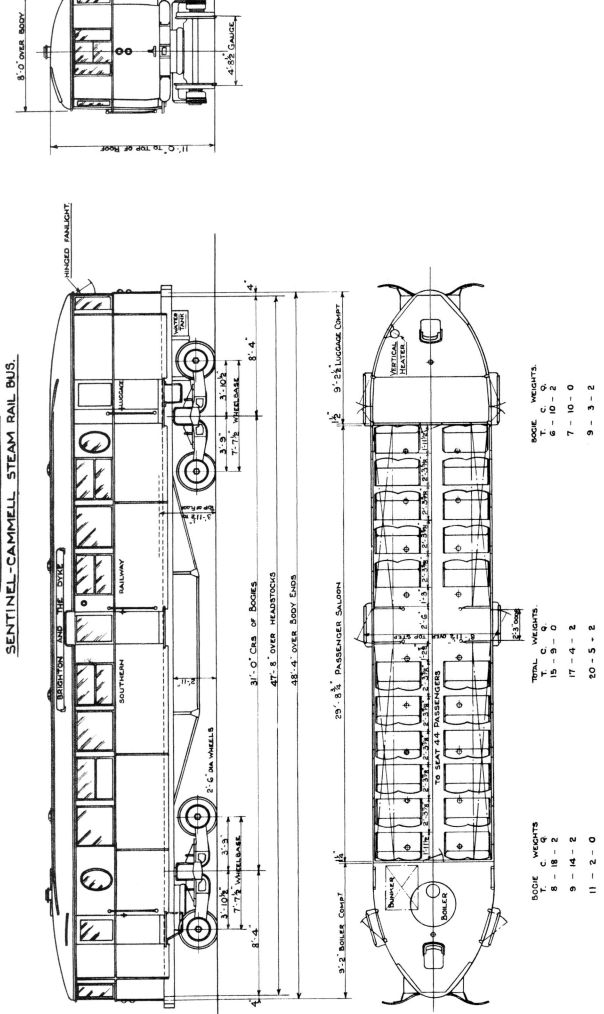

Sentinel-Cammell Steam Railbus. (Eastleigh dwg No.E71)

Part Six

Data and Appendices

Southern Railway Locomotive Liveries

1923-1939 At the Grouping the Southern Railway had inherited 2,254 locomotives from three major independent companies, each with their own individual livery. In July of 1924 the colour scheme for the Southern Railway engines was decided upon.

It was to be the old LSWR (Urie) olive green, with mid-chrome yellow lining for the passenger engines. Large numerals on tenders and side tanks were in gilt, with the word *SOUTHERN* above the number. The numbers also appeared on the buffer beams (which were red) and in the cabs. Goods locomotives were painted black with dark green lining. This particular lining was discontinued from 1935 onwards. (An exception to this livery was the B4 class 0-4-0 dock tanks, several of which had red lining from 1933-1936.)

To preserve the identities of the machines from the four sections, it was decided to let the engines retain the numbers given to them by their parent company, but to add the letters 'A' 'B' 'E' or 'W', above the number in each case, so as to be able to link any individual locomotive with the Eastern (A), Central (B), Western (E), and Isle of Wight (W) respectively. The 'A' being for Ashford, 'B' for Brighton, 'E' for Eastleigh and the 'W' for Ryde Works on the Isle of Wight.

Regarding the thorny question of the colour green used to paint the Southern engines, I seem to recall that the shade used by Eastleigh and Brighton was like that of a fresh fruit from an olive tree. It was slightly lighter in tone to that used at Ashford Works, their painting of the Eastern section engines always seeming to be a little 'bluer' than that of the other two factories.

This shade became known as 'Maunsell' green, and gradually, from 1926 onward, this darker green became standard, and eventually in the 1930s, was known as Brunswick green, the lining changing to black and white.

Named engines had brass plates with the polished letters standing out against the background of vermilion. The Goods engines in the mid-thirties were still painted black, but the lining was in pale green as opposed to the previous darker shade.

In 1931, the A, B and E letters were omitted, the LSWR or Western section engines keeping their numbers without any prefix; the ex-Ashford engines from the Eastern section were given 1000 to add to their numbers, the ex-Brighton locomotives of the Central section had an extra 2000, and eventually those on the duplicate list, previously prefixed with 'O', were placed in the 3000 list.

During 1938, a new colour scheme was introduced by Mr Bulleid, when a mock-up of a "streamlined" 'Schools' class, No. 935 *Sevenoaks* appeared in malachite green with broad yellow stripes longitudinally, starting from a sun motif on the smokebox right along each side through to the rear of the tender. A style similar to this was taken up for the first 'Merchant Navy' class 4-6-2 engine named *Channel Packet*, which had three yellow stripes on the malachite green sides. In August of 1938, six 'Schools' class engines were painted in the malachite green to match their trains on the Waterloo-Bournemouth express service, but with the outbreak of war in 1939 several locomotives were outshopped in the old olive green livery, without any lining. This livery was used at first on the 'Lord Nelson' series in 1940. In 1941 all SR engines were painted black as they passed through the works, with no lining, but with gold lettering shaded in malachite green. The advent of the 'West Country' light Pacifics in 1945, brought back the bright green with the yellow stripes, with everything below the running plate painted black, except the buffer beams which were always red. It must be mentioned however, that Eastleigh often painted the wheels green on both the WCs and the MNs.

1948 saw Nationalisation, and in May, June and December of that year seven light Pacifics were painted in an experimental apple green with cream bands, edged with red and grey, the lettering being in yellow with black edges. They were numbers 34011, 34056, 34064, 34065, 34086, 34087 and 34088.

1949 was the year for two 'Merchant Navys' to be painted dark blue, these being BR Nos 35024 and 35026 and they were lined out in red. These two were followed by Nos 35001 to 35030 from 1949 to 1951 in the blue livery but with black and white lining, except Nos 35011/14/23.

Finally all the MN Pacifics were repainted in the BR dark green livery with orange and black lining from 1951 to 1954. Similarly the WC Pacifics were all repainted in the dark green livery from late in 1949 to 1953.

Southern Railway – Eastern Section ('A')

Locomotives acquired at Grouping (1923) from the South Eastern & Chatham Railway. All numbers were prefixed with 'A' (for Ashford) from 1923 until 1931 when 1,000 was added to the original number of the then surviving locomotives. Those subsequently passing into British Railways stock then had 30,000 added to these numbers. See under individual class entries regarding rebuilding details undertaken after Grouping.

No.	Class	Date built	Built by	No.	Class	Date built	Built by	No.	Class	Date built	Built by	No.	Class	Date built	Built by
1	O	1878	SER	79	F1	1892	SER	159	E	1908	SECR	237	Q	1887	SER
2	F1	1886	"	80	O1	1897	"	160	E1	1907	"	238	O1	1893	"
3	O1	1896	"	81	Q1	1888	"	161	H	1909	"	239	H	1900	SECR
4	C	1901	SECR	82	Q	1889	"	162	H	1909	"	240	F1	1889	SER
5	H	1907	"	83	Q1	1888	"	163	E1	1909	"	241	F	1890	"
6	Q	1894	"	84	F1	1890	"	164	H	1909	"	242	C	1902	SECR
7	O1	1899	SER	85	Q1	1889	"	165	E1	1907	"	243	C	1902	"
8	O	1878	"	86	C	1900	"	166	E	1907	"	244	C	1902	"
9	F1	1893	"	87	F1	1897	"	167	O	1893	SER	245	C	1902	"
10	R1	1890	"	88	F1	1897	"	168	Q1	1895	"	246	D1	1902	"
11	F1	1895	"	89	F1	1895	"	169	Q	1893	"	247	D1	1903	Dubs
12	Q1	1887	"	90	C	1902	SECR	170	O	1893	"	248	O1	1896	SER
13	B	1898	"	91	F	1889	SER	171	O	1884	"	249	F1	1897	"
14	O1	1893	"	92	D	1903	Dubs	172	F	1893	"	250	F1	1897	"
15	O	1890	"	93	O1	1896	SER	173	Q	1888	"	251	O1	1896	"
16	H	1915	SECR	94	F1	1894	"	174	R1	1892	"	252	C	1902	SECR
17	B1	1899	SER	95	Q1	1894	"	175	E	1908	SECR	253	C	1902	"
18	C	1900	SECR	96	O	1896	"	176	E	1907	"	254	O	1898	"
19	E1	1908	"	97	F1	1893	"	177	H	1909	"	255	C	1900	"
21	B1	1898	SER	98	O	1899	"	178	P	1910	"	256	C	1900	"
22	F	1898	"	99	O	1899	"	179	E1	1908	"	257	C	1900	"
23	Q	1889	"	100	O	1899	"	182	H	1909	"	258	O1	1894	SER
24	F1	1894	"	101	B1	1898	"	183	F1	1884	SER	259	H	1905	SECR
25	F1	1894	"	102	C	1900	SECR	184	H	1915	SECR	260	C	1904	"
26	Q	1889	"	103	F1	1896	SER	185	F1	1898	SER	261	H	1905	"
27	P	1910	SECR	104	F	1885	"	186	B1	1899	"	262	C	1904	"
28	F1	1889	SER	105	F1	1896	"	187	F1	1893	"	263	H	1905	"
29	F1	1895	"	106	O1	1894	"	188	F1	1897	"	264	H	1905	"
30	F1	1898	"	107	R1	1898	"	189	B1	1899	"	265	H	1905	"
31	F1	1894	"	108	O1	1897	"	190	F1	1888	"	266	H	1905	"
32	F1	1886	"	109	O1	1896	"	191	C	1900	SECR	267	C	1904	"
33	C	1900	SECR	110	F1	1895	"	192	F1	1897	SER	268	C	1904	"
34	B	1899	"	111	O	1896	"	193	H	1909	SECR	269	H	1905	"
35	F1	1888	SER	112	C	1900	SECR	194	F	1889	SER	270	C	1904	"
36	E	1908	SECR	113	C	1902	"	195	F1	1897	"	271	C	1904	"
37	C	1901	"	114	F1	1886	SER	196	F1	1894	"	272	C	1904	"
38	C	1901	"	115	Q1	1891	"	197	F1	1890	"	273	E	1905	"
39	O1	1897	SER	116	F1	1884	"	198	F	1884	"	274	H	1905	"
40	Q	1887	"	117	F1	1895	"	199	F1	1885	"	275	E	1905	"
41	O1	1893	"	118	F1	1895	"	200	Q1	1887	"	276	H	1905	"
42	F1	1896	"	119	O1	1883	"	201	F1	1885	"	277	C	1904	"
43	F1	1885	"	123	O1	1896	"	202	F1	1886	"	278	H	1905	"
44	O1	1898	"	124	R	1892	"	203	F1	1885	"	279	H	1909	"
45	F	1896	"	125	R	1895	"	204	F1	1885	"	280	C	1908	"
46	O1	1894	"	126	R	1895	"	205	F1	1883	"	287	C	1908	"
47	R1	1895	"	127	R1	1895	"	206	F1	1885	"	291	C	1908	"
48	O1	1893	"	128	R1	1892	"	207	J	1913	SECR	293	C	1908	"
49	O	1898	"	129	J	1913	SECR	208	F1	1884	SER	294	C	1908	"
50	Q1	1894	"	130	F1	1891	SER	209	F1	1885	SECR	295	H	1909	"
51	O1	1898	"	132	B1	1899	"	210	F	1886	SER	297	C	1908	"
52	O	1896	"	133	F1	1892	"	211	F	1886	"	298	C	1908	"
53	F1	1897	"	134	Q1	1891	"	212	F1	1884	"	302	Crane Loco	1881	Neilson, Reid
54	C	1901	SECR	135	Q	1892	"	213	F1	1886	"	305	H	1906	SECR
56	F1	1888	SER	136	Q	1892	"	214	F1	1884	"	306	H	1906	"
57	D	1902	SECR	137	F1	1891	"	215	F1	1891	"	307	H	1906	"
58	Q1	1891	SER	138	Q1	1892	"	216	F1	1895	"	308	H	1906	"
59	C	1902	SECR	139	F	1891	"	217	B1	1898	"	309	H	1906	"
60	F1	1891	SER	140	F1	1891	"	218	C	1900	SECR	310	H	1906	"
61	C	1901	SECR	141	Q1	1888	"	219	C	1900	"	311	H	1907	"
62	F1	1897	SER	142	O	1896	"	220	Q	1889	SER	312	H	1906	"
63	C	1900	SECR	143	F1	1890	"	221	C	1901	SECR	313	Harbour shunter	1881	Manning, Wardle
64	O1	1896	SER	144	O	1890	"	222	F	1897	"	315	E	1909	SECR
65	O1	1896	"	145	D1	1903	Dubs	223	C	1901	"	316	O1	1882	SER
66	O1	1897	"	146	Q1	1891	SER	224	Q1	1891	SER	317	C	1908	SECR
67	E1	1908	SECR	147	R1	1890	"	225	C	1900	SECR	319	H	1909	"
68	C	1903	"	148	F1	1889	"	226	F1	1894	SER	320	H	1907	"
69	R1	1898	SER	149	F1	1890	"	227	C	1900	SECR	321	H	1906	"
70	R	1898	"	150	C	1902	SECR	228	F1	1897	SER	322	H	1909	"
71	C	1901	SECR	151	F1	1889	SER	229	C	1900	SECR	323	P	1910	"
72	Q	1887	SER	152	R	1892	"	230	F1	1897	SER	324	H	1907	"
73	Q	1891	"	153	R	1892	"	231	F1	1893	"	325	P	1910	"
74	F1	1890	"	154	R1	1892	"	232	F1	1892	"	326	H	1906	"
75	D	1903	Dubs	155	R	1898	"	233	F1	1898	"	327	H	1907	"
76	Q1	1895	SER	156	F1	1893	"	234	C	1901	SECR	328	H	1906	"
77	R	1890	"	157	E	1907	SECR	235	Q	1887	SER				
78	F1	1886	"	158	H	1909	"	236	F1	1889	"				

No.	Class	Date Built	Built by
329	H	1906	SECR
332	O	1886	SER
333	O	1887	,,
335	R1	1888	,,
336	R	1888	,,
337	R1	1888	,,
338	R	1888	,,
339	R1	1889	,,
340	R1	1889	,,
342	R	1889	,,
343	Q1	1889	Neilson, Reid
344	Q1	1889	,,
345	Q	1889	,,
346	Q	1889	,,
347	Q1	1889	,,
348	Q1	1889	,,
349	Q	1889	,,
350	Q1	1889	,,
351	Q1	1889	,,
352	Q	1889	,,
353	Yard shunter	1890	Manning, Wardle
354	Q1	1891	Neilson, Reid
355	Q1	1891	,,
356	Q	1891	,,
357	Q1	1891	,,
358	Q	1891	,,
359	Q1	1891	,,
360	Q	1891	,,
361	Q1	1891	,,
362	Q1	1891	,,
363	Q1	1891	,,
364	Q1	1891	,,
365	Q1	1891	,,
366	Q1	1891	,,
367	Q1	1891	,,
368	Q	1891	,,
369	O1	1891	Sharp, Stewart
370	O1	1891	,,
371	O1	1891	,,
372	O	1891	,,
373	O1	1891	,,
374	O1	1891	,,
375	O	1891	,,
376	O	1891	,,
377	O1	1891	,,
378	O1	1891	,,
379	O1	1893	,,
380	O1	1893	,,
381	O1	1893	,,
382	O	1893	,,
383	O1	1893	,,
384	O1	1893	,,
385	O1	1893	,,
386	O1	1893	,,
387	O	1893	,,
388	O1	1893	,,
389	O1	1893	,,
390	O1	1893	,,
391	O1	1893	,,
392	O	1893	,,
393	O1	1893	,,
394	O	1893	,,
395	O1	1893	,,
396	O1	1893	,,
397	O1	1893	,,
398	O1	1893	,,
399	Q	1893	,,
400	Q1	1893	,,
401	Q	1893	,,
402	Q1	1894	,,
403	Q1	1894	,,
404	Q1	1894	,,
405	Q	1893	,,
406	Q1	1894	,,
408	Q1	1914	,,
409	Crane Loco	1896	Neilson, Reid
410	Q	1897	SER
411	Q1	1897	,,
412	Q1	1897	,,
413	Q1	1897	,,
414	Q	1897	Neilson, Reid
415	Q1	1897	,,
416	Q1	1897	,,
417	Q	1897	,,
418	Q	1897	,,
419	Q1	1897	,,
420	Q1	1897	,,
421	Q	1897	,,
422	Q	1897	,,
423	Q1	1897	,,
424	Q	1897	,,
425	O1	1897	Sharp, Stewart
426	O1	1897	,,
427	O	1897	,,
428	O1	1897	,,
429	O1	1897	,,
430	O1	1897	,,
431	O	1897	,,
432	O1	1897	,,
433	O	1897	,,
434	O1	1897	,,
435	O	1897	,,
436	O	1897	,,
437	O1	1897	,,
438	O1	1897	,,
439	O1	1897	,,
440	B1	1898	Neilson, Reid
441	B1	1898	,,
442	B1	1898	,,
443	B1	1898	,,
444	B1	1898	,,
445	B1	1898	,,
446	B1	1898	,,
447	B1	1898	,,
448	B1	1898	,,
449	B1	1898	,,
450	B1	1898	,,
451	B1	1898	,,
452	B1	1898	,,
453	B1	1898	,,
454	B1	1898	,,
455	B1	1898	,,
456	B1	1898	,,
457	B1	1898	,,
458	B	1898	,,
459	B1	1898	,,
460	C	1902	SECR
461	C	1902	,,
462	M3	1897	,,
463	M3	1899	,,
464	M3	1897	,,
465	M3	1898	,,
466	M3	1898	,,
467	M3	1899	,,
468	M3	1901	,,
469	M3	1901	,,
470	D	1906	,,
471	M3	1895	,,
472	M3	1896	,,
473	M3	1892	,,
474	M3	1895	,,
475	M3	1893	,,
476	M3	1894	,,
477	D	1907	,,
478	M3	1897	,,
479	M3	1894	,,
480	C	1904	,,
481	C	1904	,,
482	M3	1896	,,
483	M3	1898	,,
484	M3	1892	,,
485	M3	1900	,,
486	C	1903	,,
487	D1	1902	,,
488	D	1902	,,
489	D1	1903	Dubs
490	D	1902	SECR
491	E	1907	,,
492	D	1903	Dubs
493	D	1903	,,
494	D1	1903	,,
495	C	1904	SECR
496	D	1907	SECR
497	E1	1907	,,
498	C	1904	,,
499	C	1904	,,
500	H	1905	,,
501	D	1903	Dubs
502	D1	1903	,,
503	H	1905	SECR
504	E1	1905	,,
505	D	1907	,,
506	E1	1905	,,
507	E1	1908	,,
508	C	1904	,,
509	D	1906	,,
510	C	1904	,,
511	E1	1905	,,
512	H	1909	,,
513	C	1908	,,
514	E	1907	,,
515	E	1907	,,
516	E	1908	,,
517	H	1909	,,
518	H	1909	,,
519	H	1909	,,
520	H	1909	,,
521	H	1909	,,
522	H	1909	,,
523	H	1909	,,
524	A	1875	Vulcan
525	A	1875	,,
526	A	1875	,,
527	A	1875	,,
528	A	1875	,,
529	A	1875	,,
530	H	1905	SECR
531	H	1905	,,
532	H	1905	,,
533	H	1905	,,
534	A2	1883	Stephenson
535	A2	1883	,,
536	A2	1883	,,
537	A2	1883	,,
538	A2	1884	,,
539	A2	1884	,,
540	H	1904	SECR
541	H	1904	,,
542	H	1904	,,
543	H	1909	,,
544	H	1904	,,
545	D1	1906	,,
546	H	1904	,,
547	E	1908	,,
548	H	1904	,,
549	D	1906	,,
550	H	1904	,,
551	H	1904	,,
552	H	1905	,,
553	H	1905	,,
554	H	1909	,,
555	P	1910	,,
558	P	1910	,,
560	A	1875	Neilson
561	A	1875	,,
562	A	1875	,,
563	A	1875	,,
564	A	1875	,,
565	A	1875	,,
566	A	1875	,,
567	A	1875	,,
568	A	1875	,,
569	A	1875	Vulcan
571	A	1875	,,
572	C	1903	SECR
573	C	1903	,,
574	D	1907	,,
575	C	1903	,,
576	C	1903	,,
577	D	1906	,,
578	C	1903	,,
579	C	1903	,,
580	C	1903	,,
581	C	1903	,,
582	C	1903	,,
583	C	1903	,,
584	C	1903	,,
585	C	1903	SECR
586	D	1907	,,
587	E	1907	,,
588	C	1908	,,
589	C	1908	,,
590	C	1908	,,
591	D	1907	,,
592	C	1902	,,
593	C	1902	,,
597	J	1913	,,
600	T	1879	LCDR
601	T	1879	,,
602	T	1893	,,
603	T	1893	,,
604	T	1891	,,
605	T	1890	,,
606	T	1891	,,
607	T	1890	,,
608	T	1889	,,
609	T	1891	,,
611	J	1913	SECR
614	J	1913	,,
622	A1	1880	Kitson
623	A1	1880	,,
624	A1	1880	,,
625	A1	1880	,,
626	A1	1880	,,
627	A1	1880	,,
628	A1	1880	,,
629	A1	1880	,,
630	A1	1880	,,
631	A1	1880	,,
632	A1	1880	,,
633	A1	1880	,,
641	M2	1884	Dubs
646	M3	1891	Vulcan
647	M3	1891	,,
648	M3	1891	,,
649	M3	1891	,,
650	M3	1891	,,
651	M3	1891	,,
652	B2	1891	,,
653	B2	1891	,,
654	B2	1891	,,
655	B2	1891	,,
656	B2	1891	,,
657	B2	1891	,,
658	R	1891	Sharp, Stewart
659	R	1891	,,
660	R	1891	,,
661	R	1891	,,
662	R	1891	,,
663	R	1891	,,
664	R	1891	,,
665	R	1891	,,
666	R	1891	,,
667	R	1891	,,
668	R	1891	,,
669	R	1891	,,
670	R	1891	,,
671	R	1891	,,
672	R	1891	,,
673	R	1891	,,
674	R	1891	,,
675	R	1891	,,
676	G	1899	Neilson, Reid
677	G	1899	,,
678	G	1899	,,
679	G	1899	,,
680	G	1899	,,
681	C	1900	,,
682	C	1900	,,
683	C	1900	,,
684	C	1900	,,
685	S	1900	,,
686	C	1900	,,
687	C	1900	,,
688	C	1900	,,
689	C	1900	,,
690	C	1900	,,
691	C	1900	,,
692	C	1900	,,
693	C	1900	,,

No.	Class	Date Built	Built by
694	C	1900	Neilson, Reid
695	C	1900	,,
696	R1	1900	Sharp, Stewart
697	R1	1900	,,
698	R1	1900	,,
699	R1	1900	,,
700	R1	1900	,,
701	R1	1900	,,
702	R1	1900	,,
703	R1	1900	,,
704	R1	1900	,,
705	R1	1900	,,
706	R1	1900	,,
707	R1	1900	,,
708	R1	1900	,,
709	R1	1900	,,
710	R1	1900	,,
711	C	1901	,,
712	C	1901	,,
713	C	1901	,,
714	C	1901	,,
715	C	1901	,,
716	C	1901	,,
717	C	1901	,,
718	C	1901	Sharp, Stewart
719	C	1901	,,
720	C	1901	,,
721	C	1901	,,
722	C	1901	,,
723	C	1901	,,
724	C	1901	,,
725	C	1901	,,
726	D	1901	,,
727	D1	1901	,,
728	D	1901	,,
729	D	1901	,,
730	D	1901	,,
731	D	1901	,,
732	D	1901	,,
733	D	1901	,,
734	D	1901	,,
735	D1	1901	,,
736	D	1901	SECR
737	D	1901	,,
738	D	1901	,,
739	D1	1901	,,
740	D	1901	,,
741	D	1903	Stephenson
742	D	1903	,,
743	D	1903	Stephenson
744	D	1903	,,
745	D	1903	,,
746	D	1903	Vulcan
747	D1	1903	,,
748	D	1903	,,
749	D1	1903	,,
750	D	1903	,,
751	A1	1875	LBSCR
752	Harbour shunter	1879	Manning, Wardle
753	P	1909	SECR
754	P	1909	,,
760	L	1914	Beyer, Peacock
761	L	1914	,,
762	L	1914	,,
763	L	1914	,,
764	L	1914	,,
765	L	1914	,,
766	L	1914	,,
767	L	1914	,,
768	L	1914	,,
769	L	1914	,,
770	L	1914	,,
771	L	1914	,,
772	L	1914	Borsig
773	L	1914	,,
774	L	1914	,,
775	L	1914	,,
776	L	1914	,,
777	L	1914	,,
778	L	1914	,,
779	L	1914	,,
780	L	1914	,,
781	L	1914	,,
790	K	1917	SECR
	U Rbt	1928	SR
810	N	1917	SECR
811	N	1920	,,
812	N	1920	,,
813	N	1920	,,
814	N	1920	,,
815	N	1920	,,
816	N	1922	,,
817	N	1922	,,
818	N	1922	,,
819	N	1922	,,
820	N	1922	,,
821	N	1922	,,
822	N1	1922	,,
823	N	1923	SR
824	N	1923	,,

Locomotives built after Grouping

Renumbered in 1000 Series from 1931, 30,000 from 1948.

No.	Class	Date built	Built by
A610	U	1928	SR
A611	U	1928	,,
A612	U	1928	,,
A613	U	1928	,,
A614	U	1928	,,
A615	U	1928	,,
A616	U	1928	,,
A617	U	1928	,,
A618	U	1928	,,
A619	U	1928	,,
A620	U	1928	,,
A621	U	1928	,,
A622	U	1929	,,
A623	U	1929	,,
A624	U	1929	,,
A625	U	1929	,,
A626	U	1929	,,
A627	U	1929	,,
A628	U	1929	,,
A629	U	1929	,,
A630	U	1931	,,
A631	U	1931	,,
A632	U	1931	,,
A633	U	1931	,,
A634	U	1931	,,
A635	U	1931	,,
A636	U	1931	,,
A637	U	1931	,,
A638	U	1931	,,
A639	U	1931	,,
A753	L1	1926	NBL Co.
A754	L1	1926	,,
A755	L1	1926	,,
A756	L1	1926	,,
A757	L1	1926	,,
A758	L1	1926	,,
A759	L1	1926	,,
A782	L1	1926	,,
A783	L1	1926	,,
A784	L1	1926	,,
A785	L1	1926	,,
A786	L1	1926	,,
A787	L1	1926	,,
A788	L1	1926	,,
A789	L1	1926	,,
A791	K	1925	A.W.
	U Rbt	1928	SR
A792	K	1925	A.W.
	U Rbt	1928	SR
A793	K	1925	A.W.
	U Rbt	1928	SR
A794	K	1925	A.W.
	U Rbt	1928	SR
A795	K	1925	A.W.
	U Rbt	1928	SR
A796	K	1925	A.W.
	U Rbt	1928	SR
A797	K	1925	A.W.
	U Rbt	1928	SR
A798	K	1925	A.W.
	U Rbt	1928	SR
A799	K	1925	A.W.
	U Rbt	1928	SR
A800	K	1926	,,
	U Rbt	1928	,,
A801	K	1926	,,
	U Rbt	1928	,,
A802	K	1926	,,
	U Rbt	1928	,,
A803	K	1926	,,
	U Rbt	1928	,,
A804	K	1926	,,
	U Rbt	1928	,,
A805	K	1926	,,
	U Rbt	1928	,,
A806	K	1926	,,
	U Rbt	1928	,,
A807	K	1926	,,
	U Rbt	1928	,,
A808	K	1926	,,
	U Rbt	1928	,,
A809	K	1926	,,
	U Rbt	1928	,,
A825	N	1928	,,
A826	N	1924	R.A. Woolwich
A827	N	1924	,,
A828	N	1924	,,
A829	N	1924	,,
A830	N	1924	,,
A831	N	1924	,,
A832	N	1924	,,
A833	N	1924	,,
A834	N	1924	,,
A835	N	1924	,,
A836	N	1924	,,
A837	N	1924	,,
A838	N	1924	,,
A839	N	1924	R.A. Woolwich
A840	N	1924	,,
A841	N	1924	,,
A842	N	1924	,,
A843	N	1924	,,
A844	N	1924	,,
A845	N	1924	,,
A846	N	1925	,,
A847	N	1925	,,
A848	N	1925	,,
A849	N	1925	,,
A850	N	1925	,,
A851	N	1925	,,
A852	N	1925	,,
A853	N	1925	,,
A854	N	1925	,,
A855	N	1925	,,
A856	N	1925	,,
A857	N	1925	,,
A858	N	1925	,,
A859	N	1925	,,
A860	N	1925	,,
A861	N	1925	,,
A862	N	1925	,,
A863	N	1925	,,
A864	N	1925	,,
A865	N	1925	,,
A866	N	1925	,,
A867	N	1925	,,
A868	N	1925	,,
A869	N	1925	,,
A870	N	1925	,,
A871	N	1925	,,
A872	N	1925	,,
A873	N	1925	,,
A874	N	1925	,,
A875	N	1925	,,
A876	N1	1930	SR
A877	N1	1930	,,
A878	N1	1930	,,
A879	N1	1930	,,
A880	N1	1930	,,
A890	K1	1925	,,
	U1 Rbt	1928	,,
A891	U1	1931	,,
A892	U1	1931	,,
A893	U1	1931	,,
A894	U1	1931	,,
A895	U1	1931	SR
A896	U1	1931	,,
A897	U1	1931	,,
A898	U1	1931	,,
A899	U1	1931	,,
A900	U1	1931	,,
1400	N	1932	,,
1401	N	1932	,,
1402	N	1932	,,
1403	N	1932	,,
1404	N	1932	,,
1405	N	1932	,,
1406	N	1933	,,
1407	N	1933	,,
1408	N	1933	,,
1409	N	1933	,,
1410	N	1933	,,
1411	N	1933	,,
1412	N	1933	,,
1413	N	1934	,,
1414	N	1934	,,
1901	U1	1931	,,
1902	U1	1931	,,
1903	U1	1931	,,
1904	U1	1931	,,
1905	U1	1931	,,
1906	U1	1931	,,
1907	U1	1931	,,
1908	U1	1931	,,
1909	U1	1931	,,
1910	U1	1931	,,
1911	W	1931	,,
1912	W	1932	,,
1913	W	1932	,,
1914	W	1932	,,
1915	W	1932	,,
1916	W	1935	,,
1917	W	1935	,,
1918	W	1935	,,
1919	W	1935	,,
1920	W	1935	,,
1921	W	1935	,,
1922	W	1935	,,
1923	W	1936	,,
1924	W	1936	,,
1925	W	1936	,,

Southern Railway – Central Section ('B')

Locomotives acquired at Grouping (1932) from the London, Brighton & South Coast Railway. All numbers were prefixed with 'B' (for Brighton) from 1923 until 1931 when 2000 was added to the original number of the then surviving locomotives. Those subsequently passing into British Railways stock and then had 30,000 added to these numbers. See under individual class entries regarding rebuilding details undertaken after Grouping.

No.	Class	Date built	Built by
1	I1	1907	LBSCR
2	I1	1907	,,
3	I1	1907	,,
4	I1	1907	,,
5	I1	1907	,,
6	I1	1907	,,
7	I1	1907	,,
8	I1	1907	,,
9	I1	1907	,,
10	I1	1907	,,
11	I2	1907	,,
12	I2	1907	,,
13	I2	1907	,,
14	I2	1907	,,
15	I2	1908	,,
16	I2	1908	,,
17	I2	1908	,,
18	I2	1908	,,
19	I2	1908	,,
20	I2	1908	,,
21	I3	1907	,,
22	I3	1907	,,
23	I3	1908	,,
24	I3	1909	,,
25	I3	1909	,,
26	I3	1909	,,
27	I3	1909	,,
28	I3	1909	,,
29	I3	1909	,,
30	I3	1909	,,
31	I4	1908	,,
32	I4	1908	,,
33	I4	1908	,,
34	I4	1908	,,
35	I4	1908	,,
37	H1	1905	Kitson
38	H1	1905	,,
39	H1	1906	,,
40	H1	1906	,,
41	H1	1906	,,
42	B4	1902	LBSCR
43	B4	1902	,,
44	B4	1902	,,
45	B4	1902	,,
46	B4	1902	,,
47	B4	1901	Sharp, Stewart
48	B4	1901	,,
49	B4	1901	,,
50	B4	1901	,,
51	B4	1901	,,
52	B4	1899	LBSCR
53	B4	1900	,,
54	B4	1900	,,
55	B4x	1901	Sharp, Stewart
56	B4	1901	,,
57	B4	1901	,,
58	B4	1901	,,
59	B4	1901	,,
60	B4x	1901	,,
61	B4	1901	,,
62	B4	1901	,,
63	B4	1901	,,
64	B4	1901	,,
65	B4	1901	,,
66	B4	1901	,,
67	B4	1901	,,
68	B4	1901	,,
69	B4	1901	,,
70	B4	1901	,,
71	B4	1901	,,
72	B4	1901	,,
73	B4	1901	,,
74	B4	1901	,,
75	I3	1909	LBSCR
76	I3	1909	,,
77	I3	1909	LBSCR
78	I3	1910	,,
79	I3	1910	,,
80	I3	1910	,,
81	I3	1910	,,
82	I3	1912	,,
83	I3	1912	,,
84	I3	1912	,,
85	I3	1912	,,
86	I3	1912	,,
87	I3	1912	,,
88	I3	1913	,,
89	I3	1913	,,
90	I3	1913	,,
91	I3	1913	,,
92	E1	1883	,,
94	E1/R	1883	,,
95	E1	1883	,,
96	E1/R	1883	,,
97	E1	1874	,,
100	E2	1913	,,
101	E2	1913	,,
102	E2	1912	,,
103	E2	1913	,,
104	E2	1914	,,
105	E2	1915	,,
106	E2	1915	,,
107	E2	1916	,,
108	E2	1916	,,
109	E2	1916	,,
110	E1	1877	,,
112	E1	1877	,,
113	E1	1877	,,
116	E1	1877	,,
120	E1	1877	,,
122	E1	1877	,,
123	E1	1877	,,
124	E1/R	1877	,,
125	E1	1878	,,
126	E1	1878	,,
127	E1	1878	,,
128	E1	1878	,,
129	E1	1878	,,
131	E1	1878	,,
132	E1	1878	,,
133	E1	1878	,,
135	E1/R	1878	,,
136	E1	1878	,,
137	E1	1878	,,
138	E1	1878	,,
139	E1	1879	,,
140	E1	1879	,,
141	E1	1879	,,
142	E1	1879	,,
143	E1	1879	,,
144	E1	1879	,,
145	E1	1880	,,
147	E1	1880	,,
150	E1	1880	,,
151	E1	1880	,,
152	E1	1880	,,
153	E1	1881	,,
154	E1	1881	,,
156	E1	1881	,,
158	E3	1891	,,
159	E1	1891	,,
160	E1	1891	,,
161	E1	1891	,,
162	E1	1891	,,
163	E1	1891	,,
164	E1	1891	,,
165	E3	1894	,,
166	E3	1894	,,
167	E3	1894	,,
168	E3	1894	,,
169	E3	1894	,,
170	E3	1894	,,
171	B2x	1910	LBSCR
172	B1	1891	,,
173	B1	1891	,,
174	B1	1890	,,
175	B1	1890	,,
176	B1	1890	,,
177	B1	1890	,,
179	B1	1890	,,
180	B1	1890	,,
181	B1	1890	,,
183	B1	1890	,,
184	B1	1890	,,
185	B1	1890	,,
187	B1	1890	,,
188	B1	1890	,,
190	B1	1888	,,
191	B1	1888	,,
192	B1	1888	,,
193	B1	1888	,,
194	B1	1888	,,
197	B1	1888	,,
198	B1	1888	,,
199	B1	1888	,,
200	B1	1888	,,
201	B2x	1897	,,
202	B2x	1897	,,
203	B2x	1897	,,
204	B2x	1897	,,
205	B2x	1897	,,
206	B2x	1897	,,
207	B2x	1897	,,
208	B2x	1897	,,
209	B2x	1897	,,
210	B2x	1897	,,
211	B2x	1897	,,
212	B2x	1897	,,
213	B2x	1897	,,
214	D1/M	1874	,,
215	D1/M	1875	,,
216	D1x	1875	,,
217	D1/M	1876	,,
218	D1	1886	,,
219	D1/M	1885	,,
220	D1/M	1885	,,
221	D1/M	1885	,,
222	D1	1885	,,
223	D1	1885	,,
224	D1/M	1885	,,
225	D1	1885	,,
226	D1/M	1885	LBSCR
227	D1/M	1884	,,
228	D1/M	1884	,,
229	D1/M	1888	,,
230	D1	1884	,,
231	D1/M	1884	,,
232	D1/M	1884	,,
233	D1/M	1883	Neilson
234	D1/M	1881	,,
235	D1/M	1881	,,
236	D1	1881	,,
237	D1/M	1881	,,
238	D1/M	1881	,,
239	D1/M	1881	,,
240	D1	1881	,,
241	D1/M	1881	,,
242	D1	1881	,,
243	D1	1881	,,
244	D1/M	1881	,,
245	D1/M	1881	,,
246	D1/M	1881	,,
247	D1/M	1881	,,
248	D1	1881	,,
249	D1/M	1881	,,
250	D1/M	1881	,,
251	D1/M	1881	,,
252	D1/M	1881	,,
253	D1/M	1882	,,
254	D1/M	1882	,,
255	D1	1882	,,
256	D1/M	1882	,,
257	D1/M	1882	,,
258	D1/M	1882	,,
259	D1/M	1882	,,
260	D1/M	1882	,,
261	D1/M	1882	,,
262	D1/M	1882	,,
263	D1/M	1882	,,
264	D1/M	1882	,,
265	D1/M	1882	,,
266	D1/M	1882	,,
267	D1/M	1882	,,
268	D1/M	1880	LBSCR
269	D1/M	1880	,,
270	D1/M	1880	,,
271	D1/M	1880	,,
272	D1/M	1880	,,
273	D1/M	1880	,,
274	D1/M	1879	,,

Class B4 No.2068 at Eastleigh, 15th October 1938.

No.	Class	Date built	Built by	No.	Class	Date built	Built by	No.	Class	Date built	Built by	No.	Class	Date built	Built by
275	D1/M	1879	LBSCR	360	D1	1886	LBSCR	452	C2	1894	Vulcan	537	C2x	1900	Vulcan
276	D1	1879	,,	361	D1/M	1886	,,	453	E3	1895	LBSCR	538	C2x	1900	,,
277	D1	1879	,,	362	D1	1887	,,	454	E3	1895	,,	539	C2x	1900	,,
278	D1	1879	,,	363	D3	1892	,,	455	E3	1895	,,	540	C2x	1900	,,
279	D1	1879	,,	364	D3	1892	,,	456	E3	1895	,,	541	C2x	1901	,,
280	D1	1879	,,	365	D3	1892	,,	457	E3	1895	,,	542	C2	1901	,,
281	D1	1879	,,	366	D3	1892	,,	458	E3	1895	,,	543	C2x	1901	,,
282	D1/M	1879	,,	367	D3	1892	,,	459	E3	1895	,,	544	C2x	1901	,,
283	D1/M	1879	,,	368	D3	1892	,,	460	E3	1895	,,	545	C2x	1901	,,
284	D1/M	1879	,,	369	D3	1892	,,	461	E3	1895	,,	546	C2x	1902	,,
285	D1/M	1879	,,	370	D3	1892	,,	462	E3	1895	,,	547	C2x	1902	,,
286	D1	1879	,,	371	D3	1892	,,	463	E4	1897	,,	548	C2x	1902	,,
287	D1	1879	,,	372	D3	1892	,,	464	E4	1897	,,	549	C2x	1902	,,
288	D1/M	1879	,,	373	D3	1892	,,	465	E4	1898	,,	550	C2x	1902	,,
289	D1/M	1879	,,	374	D3	1892	,,	466	E4x	1898	,,	551	C2x	1902	,,
290	D1/M	1879	,,	375	D3	1893	,,	467	E4	1898	,,	552	C2	1902	,,
291	D1/M	1879	,,	376	D3	1893	,,	468	E4	1898	,,	553	C2x	1902	,,
292	D1/M	1877	,,	377	D3	1893	,,	469	E4	1898	,,	554	C2x	1902	,,
293	D1/M	1877	,,	378	D3	1893	,,	470	E4	1898	,,	555	C2	1902	,,
294	D1/M	1877	,,	379	D3	1893	,,	471	E4	1898	,,	556	E4	1901	LBSCR
295	D1/M	1877	,,	380	D3	1893	,,	472	E4	1898	,,	557	E4	1901	,,
296	D1/M	1877	,,	381	D3	1893	,,	473	E4	1898	,,	558	E4	1901	,,
297	D1/M	1877	,,	382	D3	1893	,,	474	E4	1898	,,	559	E4	1901	,,
298	D1/M	1873	,,	383	D3	1893	,,	475	E4	1898	,,	560	E4	1901	,,
299	D1/M	1873	,,	384	D3	1893	,,	476	E4	1898	,,	561	E4	1901	,,
300	C3	1906	,,	385	D3	1893	,,	477	E4x	1898	,,	562	E4	1901	,,
301	C3	1906	,,	386	D3	1893	,,	478	E4x	1898	,,	563	E4	1901	,,
302	C3	1906	,,	387	D3	1894	,,	479	E4	1898	,,	564	E4	1901	,,
303	C3	1906	,,	388	D3	1894	,,	480	E4	1898	,,	565	E4	1902	,,
304	C3	1906	,,	389	D3	1894	,,	481	E4	1898	,,	566	E4	1902	,,
305	C3	1906	,,	390	D3	1894	,,	482	E4	1898	,,	567	E5	1902	,,
306	C3	1906	,,	391	D3	1896	,,	483	E4	1899	,,	568	E5	1902	,,
307	C3	1906	,,	392	D3	1896	,,	484	E4	1899	,,	569	E5	1902	,,
308	C3	1906	,,	393	D3	1896	,,	485	E4	1899	,,	570	E5x	1902	,,
309	C3	1906	,,	394	D3	1896	,,	486	E4	1899	,,	571	E5	1902	,,
314	B2x	1895	,,	395	D3	1896	,,	487	E4	1899	,,	572	E5	1902	,,
315	B2x	1895	,,	396	D3x	1896	,,	488	E4	1899	,,	573	E5	1903	,,
316	B2x	1895	,,	397	D3x	1896	,,	489	E4x	1899	,,	574	E5	1903	,,
317	B2x	1896	,,	398	D3	1896	,,	490	E4	1899	,,	575	E5	1903	,,
318	B2x	1896	,,	399	E5	1904	,,	491	E4	1899	,,	576	E5x	1903	,,
319	B2x	1896	,,	400	E5	1904	,,	492	E4	1899	,,	577	E4	1903	,,
320	B2x	1896	,,	401	E5x	1904	,,	493	E4	1899	,,	578	E4	1903	,,
321	B2x	1896	,,	402	E5	1904	,,	494	E4	1899	,,	579	E4	1903	,,
322	B2x	1896	,,	403	E5	1904	,,	495	E4	1899	,,	580	E4	1903	,,
323	B2x	1896	,,	404	E5	1904	,,	496	E4	1900	,,	581	E4	1903	,,
324	B2x	1896	,,	405	E5	1904	,,	497	E4	1900	,,	582	E4	1903	,,
325	J1	1910	,,	406	E5	1904	,,	498	E4	1900	,,	583	E5	1903	,,
326	J2	1912	,,	407	E6x	1904	,,	499	E4	1900	,,	584	E5	1903	,,
327	L	1914	,,	408	E6	1904	,,	500	E4	1900	,,	585	E5	1903	,,
2327	N15x Rbt	1935	SR	409	E6	1904	,,	501	E4	1900	,,	586	E5x	1903	,,
328	L	1914	LBSCR	410	E6	1904	,,	502	E4	1900	,,	587	E5	1903	,,
2328	N15x Rbt	1936	SR	411	E6x	1905	,,	503	E4	1900	,,	588	E5	1903	,,
329	L	1921	LBSER	412	E6	1905	,,	504	E4	1900	,,	589	E5	1904	,,
2329	N15x Rbt	1934	SR	413	E6	1905	,,	505	E4	1900	,,	590	E5	1904	,,
330	L	1921	LBSCR	414	E6	1905	,,	506	E4	1900	,,	591	E5	1904	,,
2330	N15x Rbt	1935	SR	415	E6	1905	,,	507	E4	1900	,,	592	E5	1904	,,
331	L	1921	LBSCR	416	E6	1905	,,	508	E4	1900	,,	593	E5	1904	,,
2331	N15x Rbt	1936	SR	417	E6	1905	,,	509	E4	1900	,,	594	E5	1904	,,
332	L	1922	LBSCR	418	E6	1905	,,	510	E4	1900	,,	595	I1x	1906	,,
2332	N15x Rbt	1935	SR	421	H2	1910	,,	511	E4	1901	,,	596	I1	1906	,,
233	L	1922	LBSCR	422	H2	1910	,,	512	E4	1901	,,	597	I1	1906	,,
2333	N15x Rbt	1935	SR	423	H2	1910	,,	513	E4	1901	,,	598	I1	1907	,,
337	K	1913	LBSCR	424	H2	1910	,,	514	E4	1901	,,	599	I1	1907	,,
338	K	1913	,,	425	H2	1911	,,	515	E4	1901	,,	600	I1	1907	,,
339	K	1914	,,	426	H2	1911	,,	516	E4	1901	,,	601	I1	1907	,,
340	K	1914	,,	430	C1	1887	,,	517	E4	1901	,,	602	I1	1907	,,
341	K	1914	,,	433	C2	1893	Vulcan	518	E4	1901	,,	603	I1	1907	,,
342	K	1916	,,	434	C2x	1893	,,	519	E4	1901	,,	604	I1	1907	,,
343	K	1916	,,	435	C2	1893	,,	520	E4	1901	,,	605	D1/M	1873	,,
344	K	1916	,,	436	C2	1893	,,	521	C2x	1900	Vulcan	606	E1	1876	,,
345	K	1916	,,	437	C2x	1893	,,	522	C2x	1900	,,	607	E1	1876	,,
346	K	1916	,,	438	C2	1893	,,	523	C2x	1900	,,	608	E1/R	1876	,,
347	K	1920	,,	439	C2	1893	,,	524	C2x	1900	,,	609	E1	1877	,,
348	K	1920	,,	440	C2x	1893	,,	525	C2x	1900	,,	610	E1/R	1874	,,
349	K	1920	,,	441	C2x	1893	,,	526	C2	1900	,,	611	E1	1877	,,
350	K	1920	,,	442	C2x	1893	,,	527	C2	1900	,,	612	D1	1874	,,
351	K	1921	,,	443	C2	1893	,,	528	C2x	1900	,,	614	D1	1874	,,
352	K	1921	,,	444	C2x	1893	,,	529	C2x	1900	,,	615	D1/M	1874	,,
353	K	1921	,,	445	C2x	1894	,,	530	C2	1900	,,	616	D1/M	1875	,,
354	D1	1886	,,	446	C2x	1894	,,	531	C2	1900	,,	617	D1	1875	,,
355	D1/M	1886	,,	447	C2x	1894	,,	532	C2x	1900	,,	623	D1/M	1875	,,
356	D1/M	1886	,,	448	C2x	1894	,,	533	C2	1900	LBSCR	624	D1	1875	,,
357	D1/M	1886	,,	449	C2x	1894	,,	534	C2x	1900	,,	625	D1/M	1876	,,
358	D1/M	1886	,,	450	C2x	1894	,,	535	C2x	1900	,,	626	D1/M	1876	,,
359	D1	1886	,,	451	C2	1894	,,	536	C2x	1900	,,	627	D1/M	1876	,,

No.	Class	Date built	Built by	No.	Class	Date built	Built by	No.	Class	Date built	Built by	No.	Class	Date built	Built by
629	D1	1876	LBSCR	647	A1x	1876	LBSCR	678	A1x	1880	LBSCR	692	E1	1875	LBSCR
631	D1/M	1876	"	650	A1x	1876	"	680	A1x	1880	"	693	E1	1875	"
633	D1	1876	"	653	A1x	1875	"	682	A1x	1880	"	694	E1	1875	"
634	D1	1878	"	655	A1x	1875	"	685	E1	1883	"	695	E1/R	1876	"
635	A1x	1878	"	659	A1x	1875	"	686	E1	1883	"	696	E1/R	1876	"
636	A1x	1872	"	661	A1x	1875	"	687	E1	1883	"	697	E1/R	1876	"
642	A1	1877	"	662	A1x	1875	"	689	E1	1883	"	698	D1/M	1876	"
643	A1x	1877	"	663	A1x	1875	"	690	E1	1883	"	699	D1/M	1876	"
644	A1x	1877	"	677	A1x	1880	"	691	E1	1883	"				

Southern Railway – Western Section ('E')

Locomotives acquired at Grouping (1923) from the London & South Western Railway. All numbers were prefixed with 'E' (for Eastleigh) from 1923 until 1931 when the then surviving locomotives reverted to their original numbers. Those subsequently passing into British Railways stock then had 30,000 added to these numbers. * Transferred to the Isle of Wight and renumbered.

No.	Class	Date Built	Built by	No.	Class	Date Built	Built by	No.	Class	Date Built	Built by	No.	Class	Date Built	Built by
1	T1	1894	LSWR	63	T1	1888	LSWR	125	M7	1911	LSWR	187	O2	1890	LSWR
2	T1	1894	"	64	T1	1888	"	126	M7	1911	"	188	O2 *	1890	"
3	T1	1894	"	65	T1	1888	"	127	M7	1911	"	189	O2	1890	"
4	T1	1894	"	66	T1	1888	"	128	M7	1911	"	190	O2 *	1890	"
5	T1	1894	"	67	T1	1888	"	129	M7	1911	"	191	O2	1890	"
6	T1	1894	"	68	T1	1889	"	130	M7	1903	"	192	O2	1890	"
7	T1	1894	"	69	T1	1889	"	131	M7	1911	"	193	O2	1890	"
8	T1	1894	"	70	T1	1889	"	132	M7	1903	"	194	O2	1890	"
9	T1	1894	"	71	T1	1889	"	133	M7	1903	"	195	O2 *	1890	"
10	T1	1894	"	72	T1	1889	"	134	L11	1904	"	196	O2	1891	"
11	T1	1895	"	73	T1	1889	"	135	K10	1902	"	197	O2	1891	"
12	T1	1895	"	74	T1	1889	"	136	K10	1902	"	198	O2	1891	"
13	T1	1895	"	75	T1	1889	"	137	K10	1902	"	199	O2	1891	"
14	T1	1895	"	76	T1	1890	"	138	K10	1902	"	200	O2	1891	"
15	T1	1895	"	77	T1	1890	"	139	K10	1902	"	201	O2 *	1891	"
16	T1	1895	"	78	T1	1890	"	140	K10	1902	"	202	O2 *	1891	"
17	T1	1895	"	79	T1	1890	"	141	K10	1902	"	203	O2	1891	"
18	T1	1895	"	80	T1	1890	"	142	K10	1902	"	204	O2	1891	"
19	T1	1895	"	81	B4	1893	"	143	K10	1902	"	205	O2 *	1891	"
20	T1	1895	"	82	B4	1908	"	144	K10	1902	"	206	O2 *	1891	"
21	M7	1904	"	83	B4	1908	"	145	K10	1902	"	207	O2	1891	"
22	M7	1899	"	84	B4	1908	"	146	K10	1902	"	208	O2 *	1891	"
23	M7	1899	"	85	B4	1891	"	147	B4	1902	"	209	O2	1891	"
24	M7	1899	"	86	B4	1891	"	148	L11	1902	"	210	O2 *	1891	"
25	M7	1899	"	87	B4	1891	"	149	K10	1902	"	211	O2 *	1892	"
26	M7	1899	"	88	B4	1892	"	150	K10	1902	"	212	O2	1892	"
27	M7	1904	"	89	B4	1892	"	151	K10	1902	"	213	O2	1892	"
28	M7	1904	"	90	B4	1892	"	152	K10	1902	"	214	O2	1892	"
29	M7	1904	"	91	B4	1892	"	153	K10	1902	"	215	O2 *	1892	"
30	M7	1904	"	92	B4	1892	"	154	L11	1903	"	216	O2	1892	"
31	M7	1898	"	93	B4	1892	"	155	L11	1903	"	217	O2 *	1892	"
32	M7	1898	"	94	B4	1892	"	156	L11	1903	"	218	O2 *	1892	"
33	M7	1898	"	95	B4	1893	"	157	L11	1903	"	219	O2 *	1892	"
34	M7	1898	"	96	B4	1893	"	158	L11	1903	"	220	O2 *	1892	"
35	M7	1898	"	97	B4	1893	"	159	L11	1903	"	221	O2	1892	"
36	M7	1898	"	98	B4	1893	"	160	G6	1900	"	222	O2	1892	"
37	M7	1898	"	99	B4	1893	"	161	L11	1903	"	223	O2	1892	"
38	M7	1898	"	100	B4	1893	"	162	G6	1900	"	224	O2	1892	"
39	M7	1898	"	101	B4	1908	"	163	L11	1903	"	225	O2	1892	"
40	M7	1898	"	102	B4	1893	"	164	L11	1903	"	226	O2 *	1892	"
41	M7	1899	"	103	B4	1893	"	165	L11	1903	"	227	O2	1894	"
42	M7	1899	"	104	M7	1905	"	166	L11	1904	"	228	O2	1894	"
43	M7	1899	"	105	M7	1905	"	167	L11	1904	"	229	O2	1894	"
44	M7	1899	"	106	M7	1905	"	168	L11	1904	"	230	O2	1894	"
45	M7	1905	"	107	M7	1905	"	169	L11	1904	"	231	O2	1894	"
46	M7	1905	"	108	M7	1904	"	170	L11	1904	"	232	O2	1894	"
47	M7	1905	"	109	M7	1904	"	171	L11	1904	"	233	O2	1895	"
48	M7	1905	"	110	M7	1904	"	172	L11	1904	"	234	O2	1895	"
49	M7	1905	"	111	M7	1904	"	173	L11	1904	"	235	O2	1895	"
50	M7	1905	"	112	M7	1904	"	174	L11	1906	"	236	O2	1895	"
51	M7	1905	"	113	T9	1899	"	175	L11	1906	"	237	G6	1898	"
52	M7	1905	"	114	T9	1899	"	176	B4	1893	"	238	G6	1898	"
53	M7	1905	"	115	T9	1899	"	177	O2	1889	"	239	G6	1898	"
54	M7	1905	"	116	T9	1899	"	178	O2 *	1889	"	240	G6	1898	"
55	M7	1905	"	117	T9	1899	"	179	O2	1890	"	241	M7	1899	"
56	M7	1906	"	118	T9	1899	"	180	O2 *	1890	"	242	M7	1897	"
57	M7	1906	"	119	T9	1899	"	181	O2	1890	"	243	M7	1897	"
58	M7	1906	"	120	T9	1899	"	182	O2	1890	"	244	M7	1897	"
59	M7	1906	"	121	T9	1899	"	183	O2	1890	"	245	M7	1897	"
60	M7	1906	"	122	T9	1899	"	184	O2 *	1890	"	246	M7	1897	"
61	T1	1888	"	123	M7	1903	"	185	O2	1890	"	247	M7	1897	"
62	T1	1888	"	124	M7	1903	"	186	O2 *	1890	"	248	M7	1897	"

No.	Class	Date Built	Built by
249	M7	1897	LSWR
250	M7	1897	,,
251	M7	1897	,,
252	M7	1897	,,
253	M7	1897	,,
254	M7	1897	,,
255	M7	1897	,,
256	M7	1897	,,
257	G6	1894	,,
258	G6	1894	,,
259	G6	1894	,,
260	G6	1894	,,
261	G6	1894	,,
262	G6	1894	,,
263	G6	1894	,,
264	G6	1894	,,
265	G6	1894	,,
266	G6	1894	,,
267	G6	1894	,,
268	G6	1896	,,
269	G6	1896	,,
270	G6	1896	,,
271	G6	1897	,,
272	G6	1898	,,
273	G6	1898	,,
274	G6	1898	,,
275	G6	1898	,,
276	G6	1900	,,
277	G6	1900	,,
278	G6	1900	,,
279	G6	1898	,,
280	T9	1899	,,
281	T9	1899	,,
282	T9	1899	,,
283	T9	1899	,,
284	T9	1899	,,
285	T9	1900	,,
286	T9	1900	,,
287	T9	1900	,,
288	T9	1900	,,
289	T9	1900	,,
290	C8	1898	,,
291	C8	1898	,,
292	C8	1898	,,
293	C8	1898	,,
294	C8	1898	,,
295	C8	1898	,,
296	C8	1898	,,
297	C8	1898	,,
298	C8	1898	,,
299	C8	1898	,,
300	T9	1900	,,
301	T9	1900	,,
302	T9	1900	,,
303	T9	1901	,,
304	T9	1901	,,
305	T9	1901	,,
306	700	1897	,,
307	T9	1901	,,
308	700	1897	,,
309	700	1897	,,
310	T9	1901	,,
311	T9	1901	,,
312	T9	1901	,,
313	T9	1901	,,
314	T9	1901	,,
315	700	1897	,,
316	700	1897	,,
317	700	1897	,,
318	M7	1900	,,
319	M7	1900	,,
320	M7	1900	,,
321	M7	1900	,,
322	M7	1900	,,
323	M7	1900	,,
324	M7	1900	,,
325	700	1897	,,
326	700	1897	,,
327	700	1897	,,
328	M7	1911	LSWR
329	K10	1901	LSWR
330	F13	1905	,,
331	F13	1905	,,
332	F13	1905	,,
333	F13	1905	,,
334	F13	1905	LSWR
335	H15	1914	,,
336	T9	1901	,,
337	T9	1901	,,
338	T9	1901	,,
339	700	1897	,,
340	K10	1901	,,
341	K10	1901	,,
342	K10	1901	,,
343	K10	1901	,,
344	K10	1901	,,
345	K10	1902	,,
346	700	1897	,,
347	K10	1902	,,
348	G6	1900	,,
349	G6	1900	,,
350	700	1897	,,
351	G6	1900	,,
352	700	1897	,,
353	G6	1900	,,
354	G6	1900	,,
355	700	1897	,,
356	M7	1900	,,
357	M7	1900	,,
358	T1	1896	,,
359	T1	1896	,,
360	T1	1896	,,
361	T1	1896	,,
362	T1	1896	,,
363	T1	1896	,,
364	T1	1896	,,
365	T1	1896	,,
366	T1	1896	,,
367	T1	1896	,,
368	700	1897	,,
369	E10	1901	,,
370	E10	1901	,,
371	E10	1901	,,
372	E10	1901	,,
373	E10	1901	,,
374	M7	1903	,,
375	M7	1903	,,
376	M7	1903	,,
377	M7	1903	,,
378	M7	1903	,,
379	M7	1904	,,
380	K10	1902	,,
381	K10	1902	,,
382	K10	1902	,,
383	K10	1902	,,
384	K10	1902	,,
385	K10	1902	,,
386	K10	1902	,,
387	K10	1902	,,
388	K10	1902	,,
389	K10	1902	,,
390	K10	1902	,,
391	K10	1902	,,
392	K10	1902	,,
393	K10	1902	,,
394	K10	1902	,,
395	S11	1903	,,
396	S11	1903	,,
397	S11	1903	,,
398	S11	1903	,,
399	S11	1903	,,
400	S11	1903	,,
401	S11	1903	,,
402	S11	1903	,,
403	S11	1903	,,
404	S11	1903	,,
405	L11	1906	,,
406	L11	1906	,,
407	L11	1906	,,
408	L11	1906	,,
409	L11	1906	,,
410	L11	1906	,,
411	L11	1906	,,
412	L11	1906	,,
413	L11	1906	,,
414	L11	1906	LSWR
415	L12	1904	,,
416	L12	1904	,,
417	L12	1904	,,
418	L12	1904	,,
419	L12	1904	LSWR
420	L12	1904	,,
421	L12	1904	,,
422	L12	1904	,,
423	L12	1904	,,
424	L12	1904	,,
425	L12	1904	,,
426	L12	1904	,,
427	L12	1904	,,
428	L12	1905	,,
429	L12	1905	,,
430	L12	1905	,,
431	L12	1905	,,
432	L12	1905	,,
433	L12	1905	,,
434	L12	1905	,,
435	L11	1906	,,
436	L11	1906	,,
437	L11	1906	,,
438	L11	1907	,,
439	L11	1907	,,
440	L11	1907	,,
441	L11	1907	,,
442	L11	1907	,,
443	T14	1911	,,
444	T14	1911	,,
445	T14	1911	,,
446	T14	1911	,,
447	T14	1911	,,
448	P14	1910	,,
449	P14	1910	,,
450	P14	1910	,,
451	P14	1910	,,
452	P14	1910	,,
453	G14	1908	,,
454	G14	1908	,,
455	G14	1908	,,
456	G14	1908	,,
457	G14	1908	,,
458	T14	1911	,,
459	T14	1912	,,
460	T14	1912	,,
461	T14	1912	,,
462	T14	1912	,,
463	D15	1912	,,
464	D15	1912	,,
465	D15	1912	,,
466	D15	1912	,,
467	D15	1912	,,
468	D15	1912	,,
469	D15	1912	,,
470	D15	1912	,,
471	D15	1912	,,
472	D15	1912	,,
473	460	1884	Stephenson
474	460	1884	,,
475	460	1884	,,
476	460	1884	,,
477	460	1884	,,
478	460	1884	,,
479	M7	1911	LSWR
480	M7	1911	,,
481	M7	1911	,,
482	H15	1914	,,
483	H15	1914	,,
484	H15	1914	,,
485	H15	1914	,,
486	H15	1913	,,
487	H15	1914	,,
488	H15	1914	,,
489	H15	1914	,,
490	H15	1914	,,
491	H15	1914	,,
492	G16	1921	,,
493	G16	1921	,,
494	G16	1921	,,
495	G16	1921	,,
496	S15	1921	,,
497	S15	1920	,,
498	S15	1920	,,
499	S15	1920	,,
500	S15	1920	,,
501	S15	1920	,,
502	S15	1920	,,
503	S15	1920	,,
504	S15	1920	LSWR
505	S15	1920	,,
506	S15	1920	,,
507	S15	1920	,,
508	S15	1920	,,
509	S15	1920	,,
510	S15	1921	,,
511	S15	1921	,,
512	S15	1921	,,
513	S15	1921	,,
514	S15	1921	,,
515	S15	1921	,,
516	H16	1921	,,
517	H16	1921	,,
518	H16	1922	,,
519	H16	1922	,,
520	H16	1922	,,
526	460	1887	,,
527	A12	1887	,,
528	A12	1887	,,
529	A12	1887	,,
530	A12	1887	,,
531	A12	1887	,,
532	A12	1887	,,
533	A12	1887	,,
534	A12	1887	,,
535	A12	1887	,,
536	A12	1887	,,
537	A12	1888	,,
538	A12	1888	,,
539	A12	1888	,,
540	A12	1888	,,
541	A12	1888	,,
542	A12	1888	,,
543	A12	1888	,,
544	A12	1888	,,
545	A12	1888	,,
546	A12	1888	,,
547	A12	1888	,,
548	A12	1888	,,
549	A12	1888	,,
550	A12	1889	,,
551	A12	1889	,,
552	A12	1889	,,
553	A12	1889	,,
554	A12	1889	,,
555	A12	1889	,,
556	A12	1889	,,
557	T3	1892	,,
558	T3	1892	,,
559	T3	1892	,,
560	T3	1892	,,
561	T3	1892	,,
562	T3	1892	,,
563	T3	1892	,,
564	T3	1892	,,
565	T3	1892	,,
566	T3	1892	,,
567	T3	1892	,,
568	T3	1892	,,
569	T3	1892	,,
570	T3	1892	,,
571	T3	1892	,,
572	T3	1892	,,
573	T3	1892	,,
574	T3	1892	,,
575	T3	1892	,,
576	T3	1892	,,
577	X2	1890	,,
578	X2	1890	,,
579	X2	1890	,,
580	X2	1890	,,
581	X2	1890	,,
582	X2	1890	,,
583	X2	1891	,,
584	X2	1891	,,
585	X2	1891	,,
586	X2	1891	,,
587	X2	1891	,,
588	X2	1891	,,
589	X2	1891	,,
590	X2	1891	,,
591	X2	1891	,,
592	X2	1892	,,
593	X2	1892	,,

No.	Class	Date Built	Built by
594	X2	1892	LSWR
595	X2	1892	,,
596	X2	1892	,,
597	O4	1893	,,
598	O4	1893	,,
599	O4	1893	,,
600	O4	1893	,,
601	O4	1894	,,
602	O4	1894	,,
603	O4	1894	,,
604	O4	1894	,,
605	O4	1894	,,
606	O4	1894	,,
607	O4	1892	Neilson
608	O4	1892	,,
609	O4	1892	,,
610	O4	1892	,,
611	O4	1892	,,
612	O4	1892	,,
613	O4	1892	,,
614	O4	1892	,,
615	O4	1892	,,
616	O4	1892	,,
617	O4	1892	,,
618	O4	1892	,,
619	O4	1892	,,
620	O4	1892	,,
621	O4	1892	,,
622	O4	1893	,,
623	O4	1892	,,
624	O4	1893	,,
625	O4	1893	,,
626	O4	1893	,,
627	O4	1893	,,
628	O4	1893	,,
629	O4	1893	,,
630	O4	1893	,,
631	O4	1893	,,
632	O4	1893	,,
633	O4	1893	,,
634	O4	1893	,,
635	O4	1893	Neilson
636	O4	1893	,,
637	O4	1893	,,
638	O4	1893	,,
639	O4	1893	,,
640	O4	1893	,,
641	O4	1893	,,
642	O4	1893	,,
643	O4	1893	,,
644	O4	1893	,,
645	O4	1893	,,
646	O4	1893	,,
647	O4	1894	LSWR
648	O4	1894	,,
649	O4	1894	,,
650	O4	1895	,,
651	O4	1895	,,
652	O4	1895	,,
653	O4	1895	,,
654	O4	1895	,,
655	O4	1895	,,
656	O4	1895	,,
657	X6	1895	,,
658	X6	1895	,,
659	X6	1895	,,
660	X6	1895	,,
661	X6	1895	,,
662	X6	1895	,,
663	X6	1896	,,
664	X6	1896	,,
665	X6	1896	,,
666	X6	1896	,,
667	M7	1897	,,
668	M7	1897	,,
669	M7	1897	,,
670	M7	1897	,,
671	M7	1897	,,
672	M7	1897	,,
673	M7	1897	,,
674	M7	1897	,,
675	M7	1897	LSWR
676	M7	1897	,,
677	T6	1895	,,
678	T6	1895	,,
679	T6	1895	,,
680	T6	1895	,,
681	T6	1895	,,
682	T6	1895	,,
683	T6	1896	,,
684	T6	1896	,,
685	T6	1896	,,
686	T6	1896	,,
687	700	1897	Dubs
688	700	1897	,,
689	700	1897	,,
690	700	1897	,,
691	700	1897	,,
692	700	1897	,,
693	700	1897	,,
694	700	1897	,,
695	700	1897	,,
696	700	1897	,,
697	700	1897	,,
698	700	1897	,,
699	700	1897	,,
700	700	1897	,,
701	700	1897	,,
702	T9	1899	,,
703	T9	1897	,,
704	T9	1897	,,
705	T9	1897	,,
706	T9	1897	,,
707	T9	1897	,,
708	T9	1897	,,
709	T9	1897	,,
710	T9	1897	,,
711	T9	1897	,,
712	T9	1897	,,
713	T9	1897	,,
714	T9	1897	,,
715	T9	1897	Dubs
716	T9	1897	,,
717	T9	1897	,,
718	T9	1897	,,
719	T9	1897	,,
720	T7	1897	LSWR
721	T9	1899	Dubs
722	T9	1899	,,
723	T9	1899	,,
724	T9	1899	,,
725	T9	1899	,,
726	T9	1899	,,
727	T9	1899	,,
728	T9	1900	,,
729	T9	1900	,,
730	T9	1900	,,
731	T9	1900	,,
732	T9	1900	,,
733	T9	1899	LSWR
734	458	1890	Hawthorn Leslie
735	735	1874	LBSCR
736	N15	1918	LSWR
737	N15	1918	,,
738	N15	1918	,,
739	N15	1919	,,
740	N15	1919	,,
741	N15	1919	,,
742	N15	1919	,,
743	N15	1919	,,
744	N15	1919	,,
745	N15	1919	,,
746	N15	1922	,,
747	N15	1922	,,
748	N15	1922	,,
749	N15	1922	,,
750	N15	1922	,,
751	N15	1922	,,
752	N15	1922	,,
773	T9	1900	,,

Southern Railway – Western Section

Duplicate List. Locomotives were renumbered in the 3,000 series in 1931.

Dupl. No.	Class	Date built	Built by	BR No.
029	0395	1885	Neilson	30564
045	0415	1883	Stephenson	—
046	046	1879	Beyer, Peacock	—
047	0415	1883	Stephenson	—
048	0415	1883	,,	—
050	0415	1883	,,	—
051	0415	1883	,,	—
052	0415	1883	,,	—
053	0415	1883	,,	—
054	0415	1883	,,	—
055	0415	1883	,,	—
057	0415	1883	,,	—
058	0415	1885	,,	—
059	0415	1885	,,	—
083	0395	1885	Neilson	30565
0101	0395	1885	,,	30566
0106	0415	1885	Stephenson	—
0111	0111	1878	Vulcan	—
0123	046	1879	Beyer, Peacock	—
0125	0415	1885	Stephenson	30582
0126	0415	1885	,,	—
0127	0330	1882	Beyer, Peacock	—
0128	0330	1882	,,	—
0129	0415	1885	Stephenson	—
0130	046	1879	Beyer, Peacock	—
0131	0330	1882	,,	—
0132	046	1879	Beyer, Peacock	—
0147	0460	1884	Stephenson	—
0149	0330	1882	Beyer, Peacock	—
0150	0330	1882	,,	—
0151	0302	1878	,,	—
0152	0302	1878	Beyer, Peacock	—
0153	0395	1883	Neilson	—
0154	0395	1883	,,	30567
0155	0395	1883	,,	30568
0160	0380	1879	Beyer, Peacock	—
160A	0302	1878	,,	—
0161	0330	1882	,,	—
0162	0380	1879	,,	—
162A	0302	1878	,,	—
0163	0395	1883	Neilson	30569
0167	0395	1883	,,	30570
0169	0415	1884	Dubs	—
0170	0415	1884	,,	—
0173	0415	1884	,,	—
0229	0278	1872	Beyer, Peacock	—
229A	0302	1878	,,	—
273A	0278	1878	,,	—
0277	0380	1879	,,	—
277A	0278	1872	,,	—
278A	0278	1872	,,	—
286A	0278	1873	,,	—
0288	0380	1879	,,	—
288A	0278	1873	,,	—
0298	0298	1874	,,	30587
0307	0135	1880	,,	—
0310	0135	1880	,,	—
0311	0302	1874	,,	—
0312	0135	1880	,,	—
0314	0298	1874	,,	30585
0316	0330	1877	,,	—
0328	0330	1877	,,	—

Dupl. No.	Class	Date built	Built by	BR No.	Dupl. No.	Class	Date built	Built by	BR No.
0329	0298	1875	Beyer, Peacock	30586	0446	0445	1883	Stephenson	—
0330	0330	1876	"	—	0447	0455	1883	"	—
0331	0330	1876	"	—	0448	0445	1883	"	—
0332	0330	1876	"	—	0449	0445	1883	"	—
0333	0330	1876	"	—	0450	0445	1883	"	—
0334	0330	1876	"	—	0451	0445	1883	"	—
0335	0330	1876	"	—	0452	0445	1883	"	—
0337	0380	1879	"	—	0453	0445	1883	"	—
337A	0302	1876	"	—	0454	0445	1883	"	—
0338	0302	1876	"	—	0455	0445	1883	"	—
0341	0302	1876	"	—	0456	0445	1883	"	—
0342	0302	1876	"	—	0458	0458	1890	Hawthorn, Leslie	—
0343	0302	1876	"	—	0460	0460	1884	Neilson	—
0345	0302	1876	"	—	0461	0460	1884	"	—
0347	0302	1876	"	—	0462	0460	1884	"	—
0369	0302	1878	"	—	0463	0460	1884	"	—
370A	0302	1878	"	—	0465	0460	1884	"	—
0374	046	1879	"	—	0466	0460	1884	"	—
0375	046	1879	"	—	0467	0460	1884	"	—
0377	046	1879	"	—	0468	0460	1884	"	—
0378	046	1879	"	—	0469	0460	1884	"	—
0379	046	1879	"	—	0470	0460	1884	"	—
0380	0380	1879	"	—	0471	0460	1884	"	—
0381	0380	1879	"	—	0472	0460	1884	"	—
0382	0380	1879	"	—	0473	0460	1884	"	—
0384	0380	1879	"	—	0474	0460	1884	"	—
0385	0380	1879	"	—	0475	0460	1884	"	—
0386	0380	1879	"	—	0476	0460	1884	"	—
0388	0380	1879	"	—	0477	0460	1884	"	—
0390	0380	1879	"	—	0478	0460	1884	"	—
0397	0395	1881	Neilson	30571	0480	0415	1883	"	—
0400	0395	1882	"	30572	0481	0415	1883	"	—
0408	0111	1878	Vulcan	—	0482	0415	1883	"	—
0409	0330	1882	Beyer, Peacock	—	0483	0415	1885	"	—
0410	0330	1882	"	—	0485	0415	1885	"	—
0411	0330	1882	"	—	0486	0415	1885	"	—
0412	0330	1882	"	—	0487	0415	1885	"	—
0413	0330	1882	"	—	0490	0415	1884	Dubs	—
0414	0330	1882	"	—	0493	0415	1884	"	—
0416	0415	1882	"	—	0496	0395	1885	Neilson	30579
0417	0415	1882	"	—	0506	0395	1885	"	30580
0419	0415	1882	"	—	0509	0395	1885	"	30581
0420	0415	1882	"	—	0515	0395	1886	"	—
0422	0415	1882	"	—	0516	0415	1885	Dubs	—
0426	0415	1882	"	—	0517	0415	1885	"	—
0427	0415	1883	Stephenson	—	0518	0415	1885	"	—
0428	0415	1883	"	—	0519	0415	1885	"	—
0429	0415	1883	"	—	0520	0415	1885	"	30584
0430	0415	1883	"	—	0521	0415	1885	"	—
0431	0415	1883	"	—	0522	0415	1885	"	—
0433	0395	1883	Neilson	30573	0523	0415	1885	"	—
0436	0395	1883	"	30574	0524	0415	1885	"	—
0439	0395	1883	"	30575	0525	0415	1885	"	—
0440	0395	1883	"	30576	0741	C14	1906	LSWR	30588
0441	0395	1883	"	30577	0744	C14	1907	"	30589
0442	0395	1883	"	30578	0745	C14	1907	"	77S
0445	0445	1883	Stephenson	—	3488	0415	1885	Neilson	30583

Locomotives Acquired from Other Companies

Kent & East Sussex Light Railway

SR No.	Date built	Built by
949	1904	Hawthorn, Leslie

Plymouth, Devonport & South Western Junction Railway

SR No.	Date built	Built by
756	1907	Hawthorn, Leslie
757	1907	"
758	1907	"

Lynton & Barnstaple Railway (1ft 11½in gauge)

SR No.	Date built	Built by
E759	1897	Manning, Wardle
E760	1897	"
E761	1897	"
E762	1897	Baldwin

Southern Railway and British Railways (SR)

Locomotives taken into Southern Railway Stock after Grouping, including those built after Nationalisation in 1948. 30,000 was added to these numbers following Nationalisation.

No.	Class	Date Built	Built by
61	USA	1942	Porter
62	USA	1942	Vulcan Iron Works
63	USA	1942	,,
64	USA	1943	,,
65	USA	1943	,,
66	USA	1942	,,
67	USA	1942	,,
68	USA	1943	,,
69	USA	1943	,,
70	USA	1943	,,
71	USA	1943	,,
72	USA	1943	,,
73	USA	1943	,,
74	USA	1942	,,
E188	'L&B'	1925	Manning, Wardle
330	H15	1924	SR
331	H15	1924	,,
332	H15	1924	,,
333	H15	1924	,,
334	H15	1925	,,
448	N15	1925	,,
449	N15	1925	,,
450	N15	1925	,,
451	N15	1925	,,
452	N15	1925	,,
453	N15	1925	,,
454	N15	1925	,,
455	N15	1925	,,
456	N15	1925	,,
457	N15	1925	,,
473	H15	1924	,,
474	H15	1924	,,
475	H15	1924	,,
476	H15	1924	,,
477	H15	1924	,,
478	H15	1924	,,
521	H15	1924	,,
522	H15	1924	,,
523	H15	1924	,,
524	H15	1924	,,
530	Q	1938	,,
531	Q	1938	,,
532	Q	1938	,,
533	Q	1938	,,
534	Q	1938	,,
535	Q	1938	,,
536	Q	1938	,,
537	Q	1938	,,
538	Q	1938	,,
539	Q	1938	,,
540	Q	1938	,,
541	Q	1939	,,
542	Q	1939	,,
543	Q	1939	,,
544	Q	1939	,,
545	Q	1939	,,
546	Q	1939	,,
547	Q	1939	,,
548	Q	1939	,,
549	Q	1939	,,
753	N15	1923	,,
754	N15	1923	,,
755	N15	1923	,,
763	N15	1925	,,
764	N15	1925	,,
765	N15	1925	,,
766	N15	1925	,,
767	N15	1925	,,
768	N15	1925	,,
769	N15	1925	,,
770	N15	1925	,,
771	N15	1925	,,
772	N15	1925	,,
773	N15	1925	,,
774	N15	1925	,,
775	N15	1925	,,
776	N15	1925	,,
777	N15	1925	SR
778	N15	1925	,,
779	N15	1925	,,
780	N15	1925	,,
781	N15	1925	,,
782	N15	1925	,,
783	N15	1925	,,
784	N15	1925	,,
785	N15	1925	,,
786	N15	1925	,,
787	N15	1925	,,
788	N15	1925	,,
789	N15	1925	,,
790	N15	1925	,,
791	N15	1925	,,
792	N15	1925	,,
793	N15	1926	,,
794	N15	1926	,,
795	N15	1926	,,
796	N15	1926	,,
797	N15	1926	,,
798	N15	1926	,,
799	N15	1926	,,
800	N15	1926	,,
801	N15	1926	,,
802	N15	1926	,,
803	N15	1926	,,
804	N15	1926	,,
805	N15	1927	,,
806	N15	1927	,,
823	S15	1927	,,
824	S15	1927	,,
825	S15	1927	,,
826	S15	1927	,,
827	S15	1927	,,
828	S15	1927	,,
829	S15	1927	,,
830	S15	1927	,,
831	S15	1927	,,
832	S15	1927	,,
833	S15	1927	,,
834	S15	1927	,,
835	S15	1927	,,
836	S15	1927	,,
837	S15	1928	,,
838	S15	1936	,,
839	S15	1936	,,
840	S15	1936	,,
841	S15	1936	,,
842	S15	1936	,,
843	S15	1936	,,
844	S15	1936	,,
845	S15	1936	,,
846	S15	1936	,,
847	S15	1936	,,
850	LN	1926	,,
851	LN	1928	,,
852	LN	1928	,,
853	LN	1928	,,
854	LN	1928	,,
855	LN	1928	,,
856	LN	1928	,,
857	LN	1928	,,
858	LN	1929	,,
859	LN	1929	,,
860	LN	1929	,,
861	LN	1929	,,
862	LN	1929	,,
863	LN	1929	,,
864	LN	1929	,,
865	LN	1929	,,
900	V	1930	,,
901	V	1930	,,
902	V	1930	,,
903	V	1930	,,
904	V	1930	,,
905	V	1930	,,
906	V	1930	,,
907	V	1930	,,
908	V	1930	,,
909	V	1930	SR
910	V	1932	,,
911	V	1932	,,
912	V	1932	,,
913	V	1932	,,
914	V	1932	,,
915	V	1933	,,
916	V	1933	,,
917	V	1933	,,
918	V	1933	,,
919	V	1933	,,
920	V	1933	,,
921	V	1933	,,
922	V	1933	,,
923	V	1933	,,
924	V	1933	,,
925	V	1934	,,
926	V	1934	,,
927	V	1934	,,
928	V	1934	,,
929	V	1934	SR
930	V	1934	,,
931	V	1934	,,
932	V	1935	,,
933	V	1935	,,
934	V	1935	,,
935	V	1935	,,
936	V	1935	,,
937	V	1935	,,
938	V	1935	,,
939	V	1935	,,
950	Z	1929	,,
951	Z	1929	,,
952	Z	1929	,,
953	Z	1929	,,
954	Z	1929	,,
955	Z	1929	,,
956	Z	1929	,,
957	Z	1929	,,

Locomotives designed by O.V.S. Bulleid.

C1–C40 renumbered 33001–33040. 21C1–21C21 and 21C101–21C170 renumbered 35001–35012 and 34001–34070 respectively by British Railways.

No.	Class	Date built	Built by
C1	Q1	1942	SR Brighton
C2	Q1	1942	,,
C3	Q1	1942	,,
C4	Q1	1942	,,
C5	Q1	1942	,,
C6	Q1	1942	,,
C7	Q1	1942	,,
C8	Q1	1942	,,
C9	Q1	1942	,,
C10	Q1	1942	,,
C11	Q1	1942	,,
C12	Q1	1942	,,
C13	Q1	1942	,,
C14	Q1	1942	,,
C15	Q1	1942	,,
C16	Q1	1942	,,
C17	Q1	1942	SR Ashford
C18	Q1	1942	,,
C19	Q1	1942	,,
C20	Q1	1942	,,
C21	Q1	1942	,,
C22	Q1	1942	,,
C23	Q1	1942	,,
C24	Q1	1942	,,
C25	Q1	1942	,,
C26	Q1	1942	,,
C27	Q1	1942	,,
C28	Q1	1942	,,
C29	Q1	1942	,,
C30	Q1	1942	,,
C31	Q1	1942	,,
C32	Q1	1942	,,
C33	Q1	1942	,,
C34	Q1	1942	,,
C35	Q1	1942	,,
C36	Q1	1942	,,
C37	Q1	1942	SR Brighton
C38	Q1	1942	,,
C39	Q1	1942	,,
C40	Q1	1942	,,

No.	Class	Date built	Built by	Rebuilt	No.	Class	Date built	Built by	Rebuilt
21C1	MN	1941	SR Eastleigh	1959	21C126	WC	1946	SR Brighton	1958
21C2	MN	1941	,,	1958	21C127	WC	1946	,,	1957
21C3	MN	1941	,,	1959	21C128	WC	1946	,,	1958
21C4	MN	1941	,,	1958	21C129	WC	1946	,,	1958
21C5	MN	1941	,,	1959	21C130	WC	1946	,,	—
21C6	MN	1941	,,	1959	21C131	WC	1946	,,	1958
21C7	MN	1942	,,	1958	21C132	WC	1946	,,	1960
21C8	MN	1942	,,	1957	21C133	WC	1946	,,	—
21C9	MN	1942	,,	1957	21C134	WC	1946	,,	1960
21C10	MN	1942	,,	1957	21C135	WC	1946	,,	—
21C11	MN	1944	,,	1959	21C136	WC	1946	,,	1960
21C12	MN	1944	,,	1957	21C137	WC	1946	,,	1958
21C13	MN	1945	,,	1956	21C138	WC	1946	,,	—
21C14	MN	1945	,,	1956	21C139	WC	1946	,,	1959
21C15	MN	1945	,,	1958	21C140	WC	1946	,,	1960
21C16	MN	1945	,,	1957	21C141	WC	1946	,,	—
21C17	MN	1945	,,	1957	21C142	WC	1946	,,	1959
21C18	MN	1945	,,	1956	21C143	WC	1946	,,	—
21C19	MN	1945	,,	1959	21C144	WC	1946	,,	1960
21C20	MN	1945	,,	1956	21C145	WC	1946	,,	1958
21C21	MN	1948	,,	1959	21C146	WC	1946	,,	1959
21C101	WC	1945	SR Brighton	1957	21C147	WC	1946	,,	1958
21C102	WC	1945	,,	—	21C148	WC	1946	,,	1959
21C103	WC	1945	,,	1957	21C149	BB	1946	,,	—
21C104	WC	1945	,,	1958	21C150	BB	1946	,,	1958
21C105	WC	1945	,,	1957	21C151	BB	1946	,,	—
21C106	WC	1945	,,	—	21C152	BB	1946	,,	1958
21C107	WC	1945	,,	—	21C153	BB	1947	,,	1958
21C108	WC	1945	,,	1960	21C154	BB	1947	,,	—
21C109	WC	1945	,,	1961	21C155	BB	1947	,,	—
21C110	WC	1945	,,	1959	21C156	BB	1947	,,	1960
21C111	WC	1945	,,	—	21C157	BB	1947	,,	—
21C112	WC	1945	,,	1958	21C158	BB	1947	,,	1960
21C113	WC	1945	,,	1957	21C159	BB	1947	,,	1960
21C114	WC	1945	,,	1958	21C160	BB	1947	,,	1960
21C115	WC	1945	,,	—	21C161	BB	1947	,,	—
21C116	WC	1945	,,	1958	21C162	BB	1947	,,	1959
21C117	WC	1945	,,	1957	21C163	BB	1947	,,	—
21C118	WC	1945	,,	1958	21C164	BB	1947	,,	—
21C119	WC	1945	,,	—	21C165	BB	1947	,,	—
21C120	WC	1945	,,	—	21C166	BB	1947	,,	—
21C121	WC	1946	,,	1958	21C167	BB	1947	,,	—
21C122	WC	1946	,,	1957	21C168	BB	1947	,,	—
21C123	WC	1946	,,	—	21C169	BB	1947	,,	—
21C124	WC	1946	,,	1961	21C170	BB	1947	,,	—
21C125	WC	1946	,,	1957					

Locomotives built by British Railways (Southern Region)

No.	Class	Date built	Built by BR	Rebuilt
34071	BB	1948	Brighton	1960
34072	BB	1948	,,	—
34073	BB	1948	,,	—
34074	BB	1948	,,	—
34075	BB	1948	,,	—
34076	BB	1948	,,	—
34077	BB	1948	,,	1960
34078	BB	1948	,,	—
34079	BB	1948	,,	—
34080	BB	1948	,,	—
34081	BB	1948	,,	—
34082	BB	1948	,,	1960
34083	BB	1948	,,	—
34084	BB	1948	,,	—
34085	BB	1948	,,	1960
34086	BB	1948	,,	—
34087	BB	1948	,,	1960
34088	BB	1948	,,	1960
34089	BB	1948	,,	1960
34090	BB	1949	,,	1960
34091	WC	1949	,,	—
34092	WC	1949	,,	—
34093	WC	1949	,,	1960
34094	WC	1949	,,	—
34095	WC	1949	Eastleigh	1961
34096	WC	1949	Brighton	1961
34097	WC	1949	Eastleigh	1961
34098	WC	1949	Brighton	1961
34099	WC	1949	Eastleigh	—
34100	WC	1949	Brighton	1960
34101	WC	1950	Eastleigh	1960
34102	WC	1950	,,	—
34103	WC	1950	Brighton	—
34104	WC	1950	Eastleigh	1961
34105	WC	1950	Brighton	—
34106	WC	1950	,,	—
34107	WC	1950	,,	—
34108	WC	1950	,,	1961
34109	BB	1950	,,	1961
34110	BB	1951	,,	—
35022	MN	1948	Eastleigh	1956
35023	MN	1948	,,	1957
35024	MN	1948	,,	1959
35025	MN	1948	,,	1956
35026	MN	1948	,,	1957
35027	MN	1948	,,	1957
35028	MN	1948	,,	1959
35029	MN	1949	,,	1959
35030	MN	1949	,,	1958
36001	Leader	1949	Brighton	—
36002	Leader	1949	,,	—
36003	Leader	1949	,,	—

Summary of Southern Railway and British Railways (Southern) Locomotives Added to Stock 1940–1951

Class	Type	1940	1941	1942	1943	1944	1945	1946	1947	1948	1949	1950	1951	Total
MN	4–6–2		6	4		1	12			5	2			30
Q1	0–6–0			40										40
WC	4–6–2						20	28			11	8		67
BB	4–6–2							4	18	19		1	1	43
CC1	Electric		1			1				1				3
Leader	0–6–6–0							1†						1
USA	0–6–0T							14‡						14
	Total	0	7	44	1	1	32	47	18	25	13	9	1	198

†Five ordered; two only part built; two cancelled.
‡Purchased from War Department.

Locomotive Stock on the Isle of Wight
Summary Pre-Grouping

Isle of Wight Locomotives

Date	Railway	Type	Name	No. on IWCR	Built	Builder	Old Rly No.	Origin and Notes	Became SR No.	Disposal	Withdrawn
1862	C&NR	2-2-2WT	Pioneer	1	1861	Slaughter, Gruning	—	Isle of Wight Central Railway 1887	—		1904
1862	"	2-2-2WT	Precursor	2	1861	"	—		—		1904
1870	"	0-4-2ST		3	1870	Black, Hawthorn	—		—	Sold	1918
1876	NR	2-4-0T	Cowes	4	1876	Beyer, Peacock	—	New	W4		1925
1876	"	2-4-0T	Osborne	5	1876	"	—	"	W5		1926
1875	IWNJct	2-2-2WT	Newport	6	1861	Hawthorn	36	*Queen Mab* Duplicated 1890	—		1895
1872	"	2-4-0T	Comet		1872	LSWR (Beattie)	35	On hire, returned to mainland 1875	—		1894
1880	RC&NJc	4-4-0T		7	1861	Slaughter, Gruning	—	Ex-NLR	W6		1906
1890	IWCR	4-4-0T		6	1890	Black, Hawthorn	—	New (Replaced old No. 6)	W6		1926
1898	"	2-4-0T		8	1898	Beyer, Peacock	—	"	W8		1932
1899	"	0-6-0T	Carisbrooke	9	1872	LBSCR	75	(Replaced by LBSCR No. 77 in 1929 W3)	W9		1926
1900	"	0-6-0T	Cowes	10	1874	"	69		W10		1936
1902	"	0-6-0T	Newport	11	1878	"	40		W11	Preserved	1963
1903	"	0-6-0T	Ventnor	12	1880	"	84		W12		1936
1906	"	S.R.M.		1	1906	Hawthorn, Leslie	—	Replacing *Pioneer*	—	Sold	1918
1908	"	2-4-0T		7	1882	Beyer, Peacock	—	Ex-MSWJR (Replaced old No. 7)	W7	Sold	1926
1909	"	0-4-4T		2	1895	NER	21	& 1712 (Replacing *Precursor*)	—	Sold	1917
1864	IWR	2-4-0T	Ryde		1864	Beyer, Peacock	—	New	W13		1932
1864	"	2-4-0T	Sandown		1864	"	—	"	—		1923
1864	"	2-4-0T	Shanklin		1864	"	—	"	W14		1927
1868	"	2-4-0T	Ventnor		1868	"	—	"	W15		1925
1872	"	2-4-0T	Wroxall		1872	"	—	"	W16		1933
1879	"	2-4-0T	Brading		1879	"	—	"	W17		1926
1882	"	0-6-0ST	Bembridge		1875	Manning, Wardle	—	Purchased from contractor of B.H.Branch	—	To W.D.	1917
1883	"	2-4-0T	Bonchurch		1883	Beyer, Peacock	—	New	W18		1928
1913	FYN	0-6-0ST	Medina	1	1902	Manning, Wardle	—	Previously on construction GW/GC JT	W1		1932
1913	"	0-6-0T	Freshwater	2	1876	LBSCR	46	Ex-LSWR 1903–1913 their No. 734. (W8 1932)	W2		1932
1913	"	4 wheeled Railcar		—	1913	Drewry & Co.	—	Drewry petrol engined	—		1920? (Sold 1934)

S.R.M. – Steam Rail Motor

Summary – at Grouping 1923

Name or No.	Company	Type	Became SR No.	Builder	Built	Scrapped
1	FYNR	0-6-0ST	W1	Manning, Wardle	1902	1932
2	"	0-6-0T	W2	LBSCR	1876	1925
4	IWCR	2-4-0T	W4	Beyer, Peacock	1876	1926
5	"	2-4-0T	W5	"	1876	1926
6	"	4-4-0T	W6	Black, Hawthorn	1890	1926
7	"	2-4-0T	W7	Beyer, Peacock	1882	1926
8	"	2-4-0T	W8	"	1898	1932
9	"	0-6-0T	W9	LBSCR	1872	1926
10	"	0-6-0T	W10	"	1874	1936
11	"	0-6-0T	W11	"	1878	1963 (Preserved)
12	"	0-6-0T	W12	"	1880	1936
Ryde	IWR	2-4-0T	W13	Beyer, Peacock	1864	1932
Shanklin	"	2-4-0T	W14	"	1864	1927 (Sold)
Ventnor	"	2-4-0T	W15	"	1868	1925
Wroxall	"	2-4-0T	W16	"	1872	1933
Brading	"	2-4-0T	W17	"	1879	1926
Bonchurch	"	2-4-0T	W18	"	1883	1928
Sandown	"	2-4-0T	—	"	1864	1923

Locomotives passed to Southern Railway at 1st January 1923:

Freshwater, Yarmouth & Newport Railway	2
Isle of Wight Central Railway	9
Isle of Wight Railway	7
Total	18

Summary – Post Grouping 1930

No.	Name	Type	Builder	Old No.	To Island	Withdrawn	Replaced by	Class	Type	Date	Notes
W1	Medina	0-6-0OST	Manning, Wardle	1	1913	1932	W1 Medina	E1	0-6-0T	1932	
W2 (Later W8)	Freshwater	0-6-0T	LBSCR	2	1913	1949	W2 Yarmouth	E1	0-6-0T	1932	
W3 („ W13)	Carisbrooke	0-6-0T	„	677	1927	1949	W3 Ryde	E1	0-6-0T	1932	
W4 („ W14)	Bembridge	0-6-0T	„	678	1929	1936	W4 Wroxall	E1	0-6-0T	1933	
W9	Fishbourne	0-6-0T	„	650	1930	1936	W14 Fishbourne	O2	0-4-4T	1936	Old LSWR No. 178
W10	Cowes	0-6-0T	„	69	1900	1936	W15 Cowes	O2	0-4-4T	1936	„ „ 195
W11	Newport	0-6-0T	„	40	1902	1963	—	—	—	—	Preserved at Havenstreet
W12	Ventnor	0-6-0T	„	84	1903	1936	W16 Ventnor	O2	0-4-4T	1936	Old LSWR No. 217
W13	Ryde	2-4-0T	Beyer, Peacock	—	1864	1932	(W13) Carisbrooke	A1x	0-6-0T	1932	LBSCR No. 677
W16	Wroxall	2-4-0T	„	—	1872	1930					
W18	Bonchurch	2-4-0T	„		1883	1930	W18 Ningwood	O2	0-4-4T	1930	Old LSWR No. 220
W17	Seaview	0-4-4T	LSWR	208	1930	1967					Replacing old No. W14 – Sold 1927
W19	Osborne	0-4-4T	„	206	1923	1955					Replacing Sandown, scrapped 1923
W20	Shanklin	0-4-4T	„	211	1923	1967					Replacing No. W17, scrapped 1926
W21	Sandown	0-4-4T	„	205	1924	1966					
W22	Brading	0-4-4T	„	215	1924	1967					
W23	Totland	0-4-4T	„	188	1925	1955					
W24	Calbourne	0-4-4T	„	209	1925	1967					Preserved at Havenstreet
W25	Godshill	0-4-4T	„	190	1925	1962					
W26	Whitwell	0-4-4T	„	210	1925	1966					
W27	Merstone	0-4-4T	„	184	1926	1967					
W28	Ashey	0-4-4T	„	186	1926	1967					
W29	Alverstone	0-4-4T	„	202	1926	1966					
W30	Shorwell	0-4-4T	„	219	1926	1965					
W31	Chale	0-4-4T	„	180	1927	1967					
W32	Bonchurch	0-4-4T	„	226	1928	1964					Replacing old No. W18, scrapped 1930

Southern Railway Locomotives added to Isle of Wight Stock 1932–1948

No.	Name	Old No.	To Island	Class	Builder	Type	Withdrawn
W1	Medina	136	1932	E1	LBSCR	0-6-0T	1957
W2	Yarmouth	152	1932	E1	„	„	1956
W3	Ryde	154	1932	E1	„	„	1959
W4	Wroxall	131	1933	E1	„	„	1960
W33	Bembridge	218	1936	O2	LSWR	0-4-4T	1967
W34	Newport	201	1947	O2	„	„	1955
W35	Freshwater	181	1949	O2	„	„	1966
W36	Carisbrooke	198	1949	O2	„	„	1964
2510	—	510	1948	E4	LBSCR	0-6-2T	Returned to mainland

Appendix 1
Principal Dimensions of Locomotives
Designed by Urie, LSWR, as Built 1913–1922

Class	Type	No.	Cylinders Dia. × Stroke (× in)	Coupled Wheel Dia. ft in	Boiler Pressure, lb per sq in	Tubes	Firebox	Super	Total	Grate Area sq ft	T.E. at 85% B.P. in lb	Weight in working order Engine, Tons	Weight in working order Eng. & Tender Tons	Adhesion Ratio
N15	4-6-0 Passenger Tender	2	22 × 28	6 7	180	1716	162	308	2186	30	26200	77.85	134.9	4.78
H15	4-6-0 Mixed Traffic Tender	2	21 × 28	6 0	180	1759	167	360	2286	30	26200	79.1	136.6	5.01
						1716	167	333	2216					
S15	4-6-0 Freight Tender	2	21 × 28	5 7	180	2025 / 1716	162	— / 308	2192 / 2186	30	28200	77.4	135.05	4.44
G16	4-8-0 Freight Tank	2	22 × 28	5 1	180	1267	139	231	1637	27	34000	95.1	—	4.4 *
H16	4-6-2 Freight Tank	2	21 × 28	5 7	180	1267	139	231	1637	27	28200	96.4	—	4.32*

Designed by Billinton, LBSCR, as Built 1912–1922

Class	Type	No.	Cylinders Dia. × Stroke (× in)	Coupled Wheel Dia. ft in	Boiler Pressure, lb per sq in	Tubes	Firebox	Super	Total	Grate Area sq ft	T.E. at 85% B.P. in lb	Weight in working order Engine, Tons	Weight in working order Eng. & Tender Tons	Adhesion Ratio
L†	4-6-4 Passenger Tank	2	22 × 28	6 9	170	1535	152	383	2070	26.7	24200	98.5	—	4.75*
K	2-6-0 Freight Tender	2	21 × 26	5 6	170	1155	139	279	1573	24.8	25100	63.75	105.25	4.93
E2	0-6-0 Freight Tank (Shunter)	2	17½ × 26	4 6	170	983	97	—	1080	17.35	21300	52.75	—	5.15*

Designed by Maunsell, SECR, as Built 1913–1922

Class	Type	No.	Cylinders Dia. × Stroke (× in)	Coupled Wheel Dia. ft in	Boiler Pressure, lb per sq in	Tubes	Firebox	Super	Total	Grate Area sq ft	T.E. at 85% B.P. in lb	Weight in working order Engine, Tons	Weight in working order Eng. & Tender Tons	Adhesion Ratio
K	2-6-4 Passenger Tank	2	19 × 28	6 0	200	1390.6	135	203	1728.6	25	23870	82.6	—	4.5 *
N	2-6-0 Freight Tender	2	19 × 28	5 6	200	1390.6	135	203	1728.6	25	26040	59.4	98.65	4.37
N1	2-6-0 Freight Tender	3	16 × 28	5 6	190	1390.6	135	203	1728.6	25	26310	64.25	103.5	4.57

* With tanks and bunker half-full

† Converted to 4-6-0 passenger tender engine 1934-6

Appendix 2

South Eastern & Chatham Railway 1914–1923
Southern Railway 1923–1938

New Designs and Construction Carried out by R. E. L. Maunsell

Class	Type	1st Batch	2nd Batch	3rd Batch	4th Batch	5th Batch	Remarks
K	2–6–4T	1 in 1917	19 in 1925–6	—	—	—	Rebuilt as 2–6–0. See U class.
K1	2–6–4T (3 cyl.)	1 in 1925	—	—	—	—	Rebuilt as 2–6–0. See U1 class.
N	2–6–0	1 in 1917	5 in 1920	9 in 1922–23	50 in 1924–5	15 in 1932–4	Last 15 have 4,000 gallon tenders.
N1	2–6–0 (3 cyl.)	1 in 1922	5 in 1930	—	—	—	Last 5 have 4,000 gallon tenders.
N15	4–6–0	10 ex. E'leigh / 30 ex. N.B.L.	14 in 1926–27	—	—	—	Last 14 have 3,500 gallon tenders. (Note: 15 engines ordered from Eastleigh, 14 N15 and the LN)
S15	4–6–0	15 in 1927–8	10 in 1936	—	—	—	'King Arthur' design with 5ft 7in wheels. Some have 6-wheel tenders for Central Section working.
Lord Nelson	4–6–0 (4 cyl.)	1 in 1926	10 in 1928–9	5 in 1929	—	—	First 15 engines have cranks set at 135°; last engine has cranks at 180°.
Z	0–8–0T (3 cyl.)	8 in 1929	—	—	—	—	Central Section boiler; cylinders as N1 class.
V	4–4–0 (3 cyl.)	10 in 1930	30 in 1932–5	—	—	—	Design incorporates many 'Lord Nelson' details; boiler based on 'King Arthur' type.
U	2–6–0	1 (as K Cl.) 1917	19 (as K Cl.) 1925–6	20 in 1928–9	10 in 1931	—	See K class above.
U1	2–6–0 (3 cyl.)	1 (as K1 Cl.) 1925	20 in 1931	—	—	—	See K1 class above.
W	2–6–4T (3 cyl.)	5 in 1931–2	10 in 1935–6	—	—	—	Utilising tanks and bogies discarded in rebuilding K class to U class.
Q	0–6–0	20 in 1938–39	—	—	—	—	Outside admission piston valves; design incorporates many N class details.
L1	4–4–0	15 in 1926	—	—	—	—	Modification of Wainwright's L class.
Diesel	0–6–0	3 in 1937	—	—	—	—	Built at Ashford works in collaboration with English Electric Co.
Electric	Co-Co	—	—	—	—	—	Designed in collaboration with Chief Electrical Engineer; 2 locomotives ultimately constructed at Ashford works in 1941 and 1945 respectively.

Appendix 3

Principal Dimensions of New Locomotives Added to Stock 1923–1939

Class	Type	Total	Cylinders No.	Dia × Stroke (× in)	Coupled Wheel dia (ft in)	Boiler Pressure (lb per sq in)	Tubes	Firebox	Super.	Total	Grate Area (sq ft)	TE at 85% BP (lb)	Engine (Tons)	Engine & Tender (Tons)	Adhesion Ratio
N15	4–6–0 Passenger Tender (Urie)	3	2	22 × 28	6 7	180	1716	162	308	2186	30	26200	77.85	134.9	4.78
N15	4–6–0 Passenger Tender (Maunsell)	54	2	20½ × 28	6 7	200	1716	162	337	2215	30	25320	80.95	138.5	5.31
LN	4–6–0 Passenger Tender	16	4	16½ × 26	6 7	220	1795	194	376	2365	33	33500	83.5	140.2	4.14
L1	4–4–0 Passenger Tender	15	2	19¼ × 26	6 8	180	1252.5	154.5	235	1642	22.5	18910	57.8	98.3	4.45
V	4–4–0 Passenger Tender	40	3	16½ × 26	6 7	220	1604	162	283	2049	28.3	25130	67.1	109.5	3.74
K	2–6–4 Passenger Tank	19	2	19 × 28	6 0	200	1390.6	135	285	1810.6	25	23870	84	—	4.6
K1	2–6–4 Passenger Tank	1	3	16 × 28	6 0	200	1390.6	135	285	1810.6	25	25390	88.75	—	4.6
H15	4–6–0 Mixed Traffic Tender	10	2	21 × 28	6 0	180	1716	162	308	2186	30	26200	79.95	137.5	5.03
U	2–6–0 Mixed Traffic Tender	30	2	19 × 28	6 0	200	1390.6	135	285	1810.6	25	23870	62.3	102.8	5.02
U1	2–6–0 Mixed Traffic Tender	20	3	16 × 28	6 0	200	1390.6	135	285	1810.6	25	25390	65.3	107.7	4.83
S15	4–6–0 Freight Tender	25	2	20½ × 28	5 7	200	1716	162	337	2215	28	29860	80.7	137.1	4.5
N	2–6–0 Freight Tender	68	2	19 × 28	5 6	200	1390.6	135	203	1728.6	25	26040	59.4	98.65	4.38
N1	2–6–0 Freight Tender	5	3	16 × 28	5 6	200	1390.6	135	285	1810.6	25	27700	64.25	106.65	4.35
Q	0–6–0 Freight Tender	20	2	19 × 26	5 1	200	1125	122	185	1432	21.9	26160	49.5	90	4.24
Z	0–8–0 Freight Tender (Shunter)	8	3	16 × 28	4 8	180	1173	106	—	1279	18.6	29380	71.6	—	5.1
W	2–6–4 Freight Tank	15	3	16½ × 28	5 6	200	1390.6	135	285	1810.6	25	29450	90.7	—	4.0
		340													

Appendix 4

Locomotive Alterations, Rebuilding and Acquisitions Under R. E. L. Maunsell
South Eastern & Chatham Railway 1914–1923. Southern Railway 1923–1938

Class	Type	*Previous Work Done, etc.*	*Work done under R. E. L. Maunsell*
Central Section			
B4x	4-4-0	R. Billinton B4 class rebuilt by L. Billinton.	Completion of programme.
C2x	0-6-0	R. Billinton C2 class reboilered by Marsh.	Reboilering continued as C2 boilers wore out.
E1R	0-6-2T	Stroudley E1 class 0-6-0T.	N class pony truck added, frame extended and enlarged bunker. Vacuum brake fitted.
H1 H2	4-4-2	Marsh Atlantics.	Alterations to conform to composite loading gauge. H1 superheated.
I1x	4-4-2T	Marsh I1 class.	20 engines rebuilt with B4 boilers released upon rebuilding B4 to B4x and B4 boilers released by further superheating of I3 class with new boilers. Cab similar to that of Eastern K class.
I3	4-4-2T	Marsh's I3 class having saturated B4 class boilers replaced by superheater boilers.	Completion of superheating of class; engines brought in to composite loading gauge.
J1 J2	4-6-2T		Brought in to composite loading gauge; new cabs similar to those of Eastern K class.
N15	4-6-0	L. Billinton L class, 4-6-4T.	Rebuilt as tender engines with Urie bogie tenders; cylinders lined up to 21in. Boiler pressure raised to 180lbs per sq in. LN type cabs.
Eastern Section			
B1	4-4-0	Stirling B class reboilered by Wainwright.	Further reboilering as domeless boilers wore out. 21 Wainwright D class rebuilt with new cylinders having long travel piston valves and larger Belpaire fireboxes.
E1	4-4-0		11 Wainwright E class rebuilt with new cylinders having long travel piston valves and larger Belpaire fireboxes.
F1	4-4-0	Stirling F class reboilered by Wainwright.	Further reboilering as domeless boilers wore out.
H	0-4-4T	Wainwright design.	2 engines outstanding from uncompleted order were built at Ashford in 1915.
K, K1	2-6-4T	Maunsell design.	Converted to 2-6-0 tender engines.
L	4-4-0	Wainwright uncompleted design.	Design completed incorporating some Great Southern & Western Railway of Ireland features; 22 engines built.
O1	0-6-0	Stirling O class reboilered by Wainwright.	Further reboilering as domeless boilers wore out; some old horizontal steam reversers replaced by standard vertical type; new cab. Some given LCDR tenders of scrapped engines.
R, R1	0-4-4T	Kirtley (LCDR) design.	All given H class boilers.
Q1	0-4-4T	Stirling Q class reboilered by Wainwright with H class boiler.	Remainder reboilered. (This class scrapped with opening of electrification.)
R1	0-6-0T	Stirling R class reboilered by Wainwright and new cab.	Some further reboilering done.
Western Section			
H15	4-6-0	330–335 series. Drummond 4-cylinder. Rebuilt by Urie as 2-cylinder.	Outstanding work completed.
H15	4-6-0	Original Urie design.	One fitted with N15 boiler to create spare boiler for class.
H15	4-6-0	R16 series. Urie design.	Ten engines built with N15 class boiler.
L12	4-4-0	Drummond design superheated by Urie.	Some brought into composite loading gauge and given 6-wheel tenders for Eastern Section working.
N15	4-6-0	Engines to Urie's original design.	Some engines fitted with double-exhaust ported valves. Cylinders lined up to 21in.
O2	0-4-4T	Adams design.	Some engines with enlarged bunkers and Westinghouse brake for IoW.
T9	4-4-0	Drummond design superheated by Urie.	Completion of work; some given 6-wheel tenders for Eastern Section working.
T14	4-6-0	Drummond 4-cylinder superheated by Urie.	Removal of 'paddleboxes'; improvement to smokebox. Mechanical lubrication for axleboxes.
700	0-6-0	Drummond design superheated by Urie.	Completion of work.
Miscellaneous			
KES	0-8-0T	Hawthorn, Leslie construction.	Taken over from Kent & East Sussex Light Railway; too large for their requirements.
L&B	2-6-2T	Manning, Wardle construction. 1ft 11½in gauge for Lynton & Barnstaple line.	One new engine with modifications to Maunsell's requirements.
Rail bus	1-A+1-1	Sentinel-Cammell construction of steam rail motor car.	One purchased for trial.
Petrol cars	4-wheel	Ryde pierhead railway.	Obsolete electric cars replaced by petrol driven cars and trailers.